Wireless, Inc.

Using Mobile Devices and Wireless
Applications to Connect With Customers,
Reduce Costs, and Maximize Profits

CRAIG SETTLES

AMACOM

American Management Association

New York • Atlanta • Brussels • Buenos Aires • Chicago • London • Mexico City
San Francisco • Shanghai • Tokyo • Toronto • Washington, D.C.

This publication is designed to provide accurate and authoritative information in regard to the subject matter covered. It is sold with the understanding that the publisher is not engaged in rendering legal, accounting, or other professional service. If legal advice or other expert assistance is required, the services of a competent professional person should be sought.

Library of Congress Cataloging-in-Publication Data

Settles, Craig.
    Wireless, Inc. : using mobile devices and wireless applications to connect with customers, reduce costs, and maximize profits / Craig Settles.
        p.   cm.
Includes bibliographical references and index.
    ISBN 0-8144-0725-0
    1. Wireless communication systems.   2. Business communication.
I. Title.
    HF5541.T4 S48   2002
    658.8'4—dc21   2002000966

Printing number

10 9 8 7 6 5 4 3 2 1

Dedicated to my mom, who sometimes doesn't understand exactly what it is I do, but won't hesitate to tell you that I do it better than anyone else. Moms are great that way.

Contents

Just the FAQs, Ma'am—
An Introduction for the Wireless Age xi

Part I: Focus 1

CHAPTER 1
The Big Picture View of Wireless Strategy and Tactics 3

Proper Planning Puts You on the Road to Success 4

A Methodology for Developing an Effective Wireless Business
Plan 4

Those Who Forget Technology History Are Doomed to Repeat
It 6

You Have to Start the Planning Process with the Right Focus ... 7

You Need Effective Strategies 8

You Need Effective Tactics 10

Perceptions and Misconceptions That Can Hinder Wireless
Implementations 12

Wireless Technology Isn't as "New" as You Might Think It Is ... 13

Wireless Benefits More Than Large Corporations 14

The World's a Wireless Stage, Every Country Has a Role 15

Even with the Right Technology, Consumer Applications in the
United States Will Be Different 16

The Misconception of the Wireless Mobile Net 18

The Myth of M-Commerce 19

You Don't Have To Do It All, All at Once 19

Don't Get Caught on the Downside of Long-Term ROI 20

A Few Helpful Wireless Terms to Know 21

Demographics of Mobile Device Users 28

CHAPTER 2
Three Focus Points Keep You on the Right Wireless Path.... 30

Communication Is Where the Pot of Gold Lies 30

Understand the Fundamentals to Successful Implementation .. 34

Executive Participation Is Not an Option, It's Mandatory 42

Part II: Strategic Options **45**

CHAPTER 3
Communicating with Existing Customers 49

Determine if This Is the Right Strategic Dimension for You....... 49

Know Your Customers.. 52

Calculate the Financial Impact of Communicating Effectively
with Customers 53

Increasing Revenue per Customer 57

Increasing Customer Referrals 59

Main Strategic Objectives 61

Waiting for an Epiphany? 68

Food for Thought 72

CHAPTER 4
Provide More Effective Service and Support 73

What Is Service, What Is Support? 73

Determine if This Is the Right Strategic Dimension for You....... 74

Calculate the Financial Impact of Providing More Effective
Service and Support 79

Main Strategic Objectives 82

Wireless Early Warning Systems Make Sense—and Dollars 89

Turn Service Contacts into Sales Opportunities........................ 92

Food for Thought 97

CHAPTER 5
Communicating with Prospective Customers 99

Determine if This Is the Right Strategic Dimension for You....... 99

Calculate the Financial Impact of Communicating Effectively
with Prospects.. 104

Main Strategic Objectives 110

Food for Thought 122

CHAPTER 6
Reduce Costs and Improve Efficiency of Internal Business
Operations 124

Determine if This Is the Right Strategic Dimension for You....... 124

Calculate the Financial Impact of More Effective Internal
Communication 135

Main Strategic Objectives 138

Shifting to Tactics 146

Food for Thought 147

Part III: Tactics **149**

CHAPTER 7
Building Brand Awareness and Loyalty 153

What Is a Brand Anyway?.. 154

When Your Logo Goes Wireless 156

The Wireless Medium Can Be the Brand Message 157

Communicating Your Brand Message Wirelessly...................... 162

The Brand Experience—You Only Get One Chance to Make a
First Impression 171

The Wireless Branding Campaign... 173

Help Employees and Business Partners Present Consistent
Brand Messages 176

Food for Thought 178

CHAPTER 8
Generating Immediate Responses from Your Audiences 180
Use Direct Response to Motivate External Audiences 181
Direct Response Tactics Specifically for Prospects 189
Direct Response Tactics Can Improve Service and Support 191
Use Direct Response Within Your Organization 193
Exploring Other Direct Response Tactical Options 197
Food for Thought 205

CHAPTER 9
Educating Your Markets and Various Business Audiences 207
What Does Education Mean in a Wireless World? 207
Wireless Lessons from the Hallowed Halls of Academia 208
Educating Outside Audiences—To Know You Is to Do Business
    with You 213
Internal Education Tactics 225
Food for Thought 231

CHAPTER 10
Demonstrating Your Products and Services 232
What Kind of Organizations Can Use "Try It Before You Buy It"
    Tactics? 233
Three Ways to Make Your Products Come Alive Online 236
Product Demonstrations in the Marketing Mix 247
General Do's and Don'ts 248
Food for Thought 249

CHAPTER 11
Reducing Costs and Enhancing the Value of Your Research 251
Secondary Research Tactics 252
Primary Research Tactics 259
In-Person Data Tracking—a Major Burden Made Lighter 264
Food for Thought 271

CHAPTER 12
Taking Your Press Relations Effectiveness to New Heights .. 273
Walk a Mile in Journalists' Shoes—the First Step to Successful
  Online PR 274
Building the Foundation for a Winning Online PR Effort—the
  Online Press Center 282
Executives, Managers, and Staff Hold the Key for Online PR
  Success 290

CHAPTER 13
Public Relations Roundtable: The Impact of Wireless on the
Public Relations Profession 297
Seize the Moment 306
Food for Thought 309

CHAPTER 14
Inside These Castle Walls: Operational Tactics to Facilitate
Successful Wireless Implementation 311
Facilitating the Nuts and Bolts of Internal Communications 312
Starting at the Top—the Executive Challenge 313
Show Me the Money—Determining ROI 322
Budget Management Issues 329

CHAPTER 15
More Operational Tactics to Facilitate Successful Wireless
Implementation 335
Vendor Selection Recommendations 335
The Interface That Launched a Thousand Ships—the Value of
  Good UI Design 342
Tips and Recommendations on UI Design 343

Part IV: The Plan **355**

CHAPTER 16
Delivering the Written Word—the Wireless Strategy and
Tactics Plan 357

Create a Winning Combination of Strategic Options 358

Brainstorming for Tactics 362

Direct Response Communication 364

The Written Tactical Plan 367

The Wrap-Up 372

Gazing into the Future 373

Index 379

Just the FAQs, Ma'am— An Introduction for the Wireless Age

If you want to use wireless applications and mobile devices to reduce costs, increase revenue, and operate a more efficient organization, you're at the right place.

This guide will answer the question, "What are the best wireless strategies and tactics for my organization's specific needs, resources, market, and industry?" Each chapter contributes to your blueprint for a successful wireless implementation, and a web supplement keeps you abreast of new business and technology developments that can influence your ongoing efforts.

Internet discussion groups and quite a few company Web sites post frequently asked questions (FAQs) to introduce people to the group and the benefits of participating in the discussion or buying the product.

If you're thinking about buying this book, you probably have some questions. To help you with your decision, let's look at the FAQs.

What Is *Wireless, Inc.* About?

This book helps you to make informed decisions about the best way to use wireless technology. Whether your organization has implemented wireless technology and you want to know how to increase its value, or you're still trying to determine if it makes financial sense to implement wireless applications, this book will help.

Wireless, Inc. shows you how to create new communication channels to reach customers, sales prospects, employees, and others with whom you do business. It also shows you how to increase business operating efficiency and wireless-enable physical assets such as vehicles, equipment, and inventory so you can better track, manage, and protect them. Regardless of the size of your organization or what industry you're in, you will get valuable information you can put to work immediately.

The focus here is not on generating sales transactions through mobile devices, but using wireless to reduce the costs and increase the efficiency of doing business with your various audiences. You will learn how effective wireless communication can save you tens of thousands of dollars while becoming an important vehicle for increasing customer retention, improving customer service, generating referral leads, and enhancing employee productivity.

Wireless, Inc. presents lessons through real-life examples and will ignite your creativity, and at the same time give you an overview of some of the detail work that you have to manage. An online supplement to the book (at www.wirelessinconline.com) will give you additional lessons, plus access to a valuable network of other individuals who are working in the trenches and bringing good wireless ideas to life.

Who Can Benefit from Reading *Wireless, Inc.*?

This book is for top executives, managers, entrepreneurs, and web teams in organizations of all sizes and in all industries.

If you are responsible for ensuring that your budget is used wisely, this book is for you. Millions of dollars were wasted on poorly conceived Internet initiatives in the early days of the Web, largely because people could not separate the hype from the real value. You face the same dilemma today with wireless technology. This book will help you make the right decisions.

If you want to communicate more effectively with customers, prospects, and others in your industries, open new markets, improve employee productivity, and increase your business growth, you will definitely benefit from this book. Throughout *Wireless, Inc.,* I examine how wireless technologies can impact various business functions—marketing, service and support, human resources, manufacturing, and shipping—to name a few.

This is a great handbook for those who will shoulder direct responsibility for making wireless implementations work, including advertising, public relations agencies, and other consulting firms that can play an important role in executing wireless tactics.

Wireless, Inc. gives you a good overview of a wide spectrum of wireless data communication options so you can see the potential benefits and pitfalls of this exciting medium. To help you make wise decisions, this book also provides insights and advice from others who are already implementing applications and executing tactics.

Will This Book Help Me if My Organization Is in the Government or Nonprofit Sector?

Definitely. Executives in education, government, and nonprofit organizations share stories about their use of wireless Net applications. Plus, there are many lessons from commercial operations that can be modified and applied to the government and commercial sectors.

How Will Wireless Technology Benefit My Organization?

Wireless, Inc. cuts through the hype, hope, and hysteria surrounding various wireless technologies to give you a clear picture of the opportunities these tools offer. This book shows you how to analyze your conventional communication and business operating costs and determine if wireless applications can eliminate or significantly reduce these costs.

One of the values of wireless as a business communication tool is that it can reach large numbers of people frequently and at relatively little cost. It can enable your staff or external audiences to access business operations data, product information, and customer support tools from locations where access to the Internet and your computer networks is impossible or impractical. Wireless enables you to push this data and business capabilities out to people wirelessly at a fraction of current costs.

Wireless can become a valuable extension to your website, intranet, extranet, or back-office software applications that reduces the cost of sales and customer support and improves the efficiency of your sales team, support staff, resellers, and others. You can even embed wireless devices into physical assets such as vehicles, inventory, and computer networks, further increasing operating efficiency and eliminating business losses.

While this book helps you understand basic wireless technology, it doesn't go into great detail about how the technology works. From a management perspective, the intricacies of how wireless technologies work are not as important as understanding how the technology impacts your organization and improves the way you do business. Your IT staff can deal with many of the technical details of selecting and implementing specific applications.

What Will I Learn by Reading *Wireless, Inc.*?

This book presents a methodology for developing and writing a plan to implement wireless applications that are suited to your specific business needs. It shows you step-by-step how to determine the appropriate wireless strategy and produce effective tactics, as well as providing many examples of organizations that are implementing these tactics.

Starting with a general overview of the key wireless technologies that can impact your organization, you will learn how various types of internal and external audiences can benefit through two-way wireless data communication. Through specific stories you will get a sense of how people in commercial, government, and nonprofit organizations are using mobile devices to improve personal and business productivity. By first understanding the main capabilities of wireless and how people can and cannot use this technology, you will better determine what type of applications make sense for your organization.

Wireless, Inc. presents four strategic options for wireless implementations and shows you how each one can impact your bottom line in measurable financial terms. By applying wireless technologies to your company you can:

1. Reduce the cost and increase the effectiveness of communicating with existing customers.

2. Provide faster, better, and less expensive customer service and support.

3. Reduce costs of communicating with prospective customers and shorten your sales cycles.

4. Improve internal communications so that employees are more productive, business operations are more efficient, and greater value is derived from your physical assets.

Wireless, Inc. will also also help you brainstorm for specific tactics that will enable you to implement your strategies. There are seven key tactical options:

1. Increase awareness of your product and your organization's image (brand) which, in turn, increases customer loyalty.

2. Create "direct response" activities that motivate people to take immediate action.

3. Implement market education activities that build your position as an industry leader.

4. Demonstrate products and services so prospects can "try it before they buy it."

5. Enhance research and data collection.

6. Increase press relations effectiveness (including investor relations and crisis management).

7. Develop activities to win executive and employee support for wireless applications and facilitate wireless application implementations.

Wireless, Inc. concludes with a chapter that presents tips for incorporating the strategies and tactics that you develop into a written plan. These lessons on strategies and tactics are reinforced by executives and managers who reflect on a variety of wireless applications. These wireless pioneers describe how they developed initial plans and pilot projects, addressed management and budget issues, and most importantly, determined the return on investment (ROI) for these activities.

At first glance this may seem like a challenging process that will require a major business overhaul in order to implement. In fact, just the opposite is true. The stories about organizations' wireless implementations reinforce the lesson that technology and tactics should be adjusted to fit your particular business operations, not the other way around.

Will I Make a Quick Fortune if I Read Your Book?

Probably not. *Wireless, Inc.* is not a book for "get rich quick" schemers and scam artists. It's a discussion for smart businesspeople who want to cost-effectively enhance their organization's communication and operating efficiency, as well as build strong business relationships. It's for people who know that they have to put some serious effort into achieving these goals.

Similar to the Internet, wireless is a new communication and business tool. Because wireless offers a unique way of doing business, it requires that you commit time to learn how to use this medium properly. *Wireless, Inc.* gets you moving in the right direction. If your organization is already communicating through wireless channels, this book will help you get more mileage from your current efforts.

A lot of the hype about wireless implies that companies will make billions of dollars from people ordering products with mobile devices. *Wireless, Inc.* reinforces the point that wireless is a great tool for facilitating the shopping process, meaning the research that goes on before someone makes the final decision to buy. It shows you how to motivate people to call, fax, or e-mail an order, and how to help your sales people and retailers to answer questions and sell your products more effectively.

While there are situations in which people will use mobile devices to order products, it's important that you have a realistic picture of what can be accomplished wirelessly in the area of sales and facilitating the sales of your products or services. The greater sales potential will come from existing customers who use their mobile devices to order additional products or services, and this book shows you how to do this effectively.

How Is *Wireless, Inc.* Different from Other Books About Wireless?

Wireless, Inc. is not preoccupied with promoting the hype about wireless technologies and m-commerce. Instead it focuses on the impact that wireless technologies can have on your entire organization. Here you will find practical information that helps you to devise a wireless strategy for your unique needs and tactical ideas that you can use now. There are no "one size fits all" solutions in this book.

Instead, I present a process for reviewing your business needs and developing strategies that advance these needs. I give you a framework for brainstorming for tactical ideas, I present case stories of organizations that are actually using wireless applications, and I conclude with guidelines for writing your wireless business plan.

Are the Strategies and Tactics Based on Real-World Implementations?

This book is based on careful research of organizations that are successfully using wireless technology. I interviewed executives in organizations that use wireless applications, vendors who sell them, and others in the wireless industry.

These people are implementing proven tactics and continually creating new tactics to address new situations. Some of these people have been using wireless technology for years. And they're not just in U.S. organizations; I also tapped into sources and stories from Europe and Asia as well.

No, *Wireless, Inc.,* isn't about theory. It's about going out there and getting the job done right.

What If I Have More Questions After I Finish the Book?

I plan for this book to become the basis of a two-way discussion between you and me. There is an online supplement for this book (www.wirelessincon line.com) where you can correspond with me in discussion rooms to ask questions, offer suggestions for adding related online content, or present your own success stories. I also hope to host monthly live chat sessions so you can ask me questions directly, as well as exchange ideas in real time with others.

The supplement will have links to the companies I interviewed so you can get more details about the applications and wireless devices that are at the heart of the strategies and tactics I present in *Wireless, Inc.* Some of these companies will develop special online documents that expand on some of my points, plus provide information on new products and services that may help your wireless plans.

There will also be links to articles, websites, and other resources that will give you ongoing updates to developments in wireless business strategies. I believe that building an online community of readers will help you and others derive significant long-term value from your investment in this book. That is the ultimate goal of the online book supplement and wireless communication activities I will implement in the upcoming months as an extension to the supplement.

Do I Need to Have a Technical Background to Understand This Book?

Absolutely not. The methodology I present here is written in easy-to-understand, low-tech terms, flexible enough to be used by organizations in various industries, but detailed enough so that you can do extensive planning. This methodology is not tied to any specific technology, so it will still be useful even as wireless technologies advance. These factors ensure the long-term value of this book.

Why Is It Important for Business Executives to Have a Wireless Plan? A Lot of Them Didn't Have a Plan for the Web

Over the years I have found that the lack of a written plan, usually resulting from a lack of any business direction at all for the Web, is a major contributing factor to organizations' dismal result online. If it is not written, you do not have a plan. All you have are a lot of good ideas. If you do not have a written plan, it is difficult to lead because there is nothing concrete for people to follow.

Without clear direction in the early days of the Web, businesspeople threw out the rules for planning and testing new technologies before they were deployed. As the rush to get online increased, Web sites became digital Taj Mahals, monuments to outrageous spending and corporate egos run amok. It seemed that every week brought new technologies that promised to be the killer application, the standard of standards. There were animated gifs, Java, streaming video, streaming audio, and streaming money chasing every outlandish technological scheme. And just when we thought the Web world couldn't get any crazier, here came dot-com mania and the "New Economy." Executives, VCs, retirees, even the bastion of fiscal conservativism, Wall Street, lost all sense of economic reality, and chased after anything with a pulse and a PowerPoint presentation, throwing away billions to fund shaky ideas and shakier business plans

Businesses ran on the philosophy of (literally!) "We'll build it for $100, sell it for $85, throw in free shipping, and through the powers vested in us by the gods of the New Economy, we shall have greater valuation than IBM." For two years or so, the dollars flowed, the technology overflowed with money-is-no-object feature sets, whatever business discipline was left went south, and ROI stood for Running On Insanity.

Unless you want to wander down this sorry path again with wireless technology, you need a clear sense of direction and a well-crafted plan, which is what this book gives you.

What Should I Do Next?

I think now is probably a good time to walk over to the cashier, buy this book, head to your favorite reading spot, grab your favorite beverage on the way, and read about this new era of wireless technology.

PART I

Focus

This section lays the foundation for the eventual strategies and tactics that you will develop. You will get a brief overview of my complete methodology for making the most effective use of wireless technology, some misconceptions about wireless that you should avoid, and an overview of key wireless technologies. You will also get some guidelines on developing the proper focus for your wireless efforts so you maximize your personnel and financial resources when implementing wireless tactics.

CHAPTER 1

The Big Picture View of Wireless Strategy and Tactics

Credo che la tecnologia sia spesso come una croce sulla quale vengono crocefissi il buon senso e le buone valutazioni. Translation: I believe that technology is often a cross upon which common sense and good judgment are crucified. This opening to a presentation I delivered in Italy In 2001 explains why organizations overspent and underachieved so much with Internet technology, and what you don't want to do with wireless.

Because there is so much hype about what wireless technology can do, plus a myriad of possible wireless applications to choose from, it's easy to become confused about what are the best options for your organization. Faced with an abundance of hype and options, but a scarcity of clear guidelines, some executives and managers make decisions based on the appeal of new technology rather than the best interest of their organizations. This leads to costly mistakes and unmet expectations.

I will help you create a plan to make wireless applications and data communication valuable assets that benefit your organization rather than collectively become a cross to bear. I will give you focus points so you spend resources wisely, strategic options for using wireless to increase your profitability, and tactics that enable you to reach these strategic objectives.

This chapter presents an overview of a methodology to help you plan more effectively, some of the perceptions and misconceptions that can hinder successful execution of your plan, and a few general technology terms that are helpful to know. With this big picture view you will be well prepared to tackle the meaty details that follow.

Proper Planning Puts You on the Road to Success

As you ponder wireless technology and wonder what it can do for your organization, it will help to have a planning guide that maps out how to use wireless as a business tool. You see a steady parade of stories about m-commerce, broadband wireless, location-based services and Bluetooth in connection with wireless. Along with these new terms, are also confusing uses of terms we already know: the wireless Web, the mobile Internet, wireless branding, and other buzzwords.

Recently I heard someone say, "Wireless is going to be so important that anyone who isn't using it will soon be out of business." People said the same thing in 1996, which led to panic website development. Executives would proclaim, "We have to be on the Web because our competitors are there!" They'd throw truckloads of money at a website, turn control of it over to a bunch of outsiders who didn't know business strategy from a Ouija board, then retreat to the boardroom in blissful ignorance of what was happening with that investment.

It was a ridiculous approach to the Web, and it is a ridiculous way to proceed with wireless technology. Unless you want to pursue a strategy of "panic" wireless implementations, I propose a more methodical and effective approach.

A Methodology for Developing an Effective Wireless Business Plan

The purpose of the methodology presented in this book is to give you a procedure to follow that helps you create a wireless business plan that is best for your organization whether it is in the commercial, government, or nonprofit sector. There are three main phases to follow in this methodology.

First, you must have the right focus. Organizations that are successfully using wireless technology have a clear understanding and realistic expectations of what it can and cannot do. They worry less about throwing money at the "next big thing" and implement applications that address business needs today.

Second, you need to identify and evaluate strategies for using wireless to enhance how your marketing, service and support, manufacturing, human resources, and other departments operate and communicate with customers, prospects, business partners, and each other. This strategic thinking will enable you to determine potential ROI, establish quantifiable objectives, and define benchmarks for measuring the progress and eventual success of your wireless efforts.

Once you have your strategic objectives, the final step of your wireless plan is to create the tactical activities such as wireless customer training and branding campaigns that will enable you to reach these objectives. Generally this final step is the easiest after learning about the capabilities of wireless technologies and doing a thorough job of strategy development. Without a sound strategy, your tactics will amount to undirected and uncoordinated efforts—just random stuff thrown against the wall to see what sticks.

Here are the specific elements of the methodology.

Three Focus Points to Keep You on the Right Path

1. Communication is where the pot of gold lies.

2. Understand the fundamentals of successful wireless implementation.

3. Executive participation is not an option, it's mandatory.

Four Strategic Options That Reduce Costs, Increase Revenue, and Enhance Business Operations Wireless Success

1. Communicate more effectively to customers.

2. Provide more effective service and support.

3. Communicate more effectively with prospective customers.

4. Improve and enhance internal communication.

Seven-Point Tactical Framework That Creates the Means for Reaching Your Strategic Objectives

1. Build brand awareness and loyalty.

2. Create direct response communication.

3. Educate your various markets and business audiences.

4. Demonstrate products or services.

5. Conduct research to keep wireless fingers on the pulse.

6. Enhance your PR effectiveness.

7. Create operational tactics to facilitate successful wireless implementation.

Before reviewing these elements in detail, it's helpful to take a quick peek at some recent history because there are lessons to learn that will ensure you greater success with planning your wireless projects.

Those Who Forget Technology History Are Doomed to Repeat It

In the early days of the Web, the hype machines waxed poetic about the Internet as the Information Superhighway that would lead us to all things that are good for society. Communication would be changed, learning would be elevated to great new heights, cultures would be bridged, peace would guide the planets, and love would steer the stars. This was the dawning of the Age of the Internet.

We made the Internet a place and called it cyberspace, a mystical land where the laws of physics and human interaction would somehow be suspended. People would meet in cyberspace and interact with new levels of sincerity and openness that would break down all the barriers to the advancement of brotherhood and sisterhood. It was kind of a cross between a 24-hour street fair and Xanadu.

Someone wrote a book called *How to Make a Million Dollars on the Net* that sold a bazillion copies and suddenly everyone was in a mad dash to stake out a claim on this new frontier. People spent millions of dollars to build websites, but without any business plan or a strategic clue about what they hoped to achieve on the Net in terms of quantifiable business objectives.

Dot-com mania and the "new economy" overtook the land, but mercifully this Internet bubble collapsed in 2000 and calmer executives started reclaiming the asylum back from the inmates. However, just as people began to see the Net for what it is—a tool that adds a new dimension to communication—a new drumbeat sounded in the distance. It signaled the dawning of wireless, the next big thing.

M-commerce began to take the place of e-commerce in the hype machine. The "wireless Web" is becoming the cyberspace of the new millennium—a place that really isn't a place, and research groups are talking about the billions of dollars that will soon be made from people buying products through cell phones and Palm Pilots.

New technology threatens to enable retail businesses to zap ads to the mobile devices of random people walking by cafés and copy centers. They call it location-based services. We read about a brave new 3G wireless world that has awesome capabilities: movies that beam through a cell phone, video conferencing from PDAs (personal digital assistants), and more.

Wait a minute. Enough! Let's get a grip, take a deep breath, and allow common sense and good judgment take over before we go any further. Let's get some focus on wireless technologies.

You Have to Start the Planning Process with the Right Focus

There are some important "rules" to consider when crafting your focus regarding wireless technologies. If you keep these in mind and check your ideas against them, you will be well on your way to crafting a wireless plan that will effectively support your business goals.

It's About Communication, Not Sales

In terms of focus, let's cut to the chase. Your first focus should be on communication. It will be quite a while before sales through mobile devices (i.e., m-commerce) are the primary business benefits of using wireless technology. Most of the sales that initially come through wireless devices will be from people who have previously purchased products from you. For many, particularly government and nonprofit organizations, product sales through mobile devices may never happen.

The real benefits of wireless result from improved data communication and data access that reduce costs, increase personal and organizational efficiency, and build closer relationships with customers, prospects, and others with whom you do business. Wireless also offers the benefit of being a great tool to facilitate the process of generating revenue, but the actual sales transaction might not come through a wireless device.

If you let your organization get distracted by all of those pie-in-the-sky promises of untold billions of dollars to be made, it is likely that mistakes will be made, money will be wasted, and opportunities will be lost. Instead, be smart and focus on the real return on investment (ROI) potential of wireless technology as a communication tool.

Adhere to the Fundamentals of Implementing Wireless Applications

The second focus should be on fundamental issues regarding how you select and deploy wireless applications that are dictated by the inherent shortcomings of the technology. As Dirty Harry (Clint Eastwood) once said after he blew away one of the bad guys, "A man's gotta know his limitations." Well, before you blow away a lot of money, your organization's gotta know the limitations of wireless and develop your strategies and tactics accordingly so you reap the many rewards that wireless offers.

For the next year or two, most mobile devices will have small screens (about 3×3 inches or smaller) and slow, expensive access speeds to the Net. Wireless coverage will not be everywhere and many people will not have "always on" Net access. What's more, some wireless technologies cannot stand alone as business tools, but act as a conduit into the Internet, intranets, and software applications.

As a result, keep your implementations fairly simple in terms of user interface (UI) design (what's seen on mobile device screens), the amount of data you make available, and the number of business needs each application addresses. Most of your wireless applications should enable people to get online, access and input information quickly, then move on rather than try to replicate the desktop web-browsing experience. Also make sure they integrate well with your business processes and existing technology and that there is some flexibility to work with future technologies.

In this book you will read about a lot of organizations that are generating significant benefits from their wireless implementations. But in every case, they focused on the things you can do well with wireless technology now, and they didn't get burned trying to do the impossible or the impractical. Often their applications are simple but the benefits are huge.

Executive Responsibility Is Critical to Success
A third area of focus should be on your top executives. It's surprising how many people I've spoken with who said they were suddenly given responsibility for their organization's web strategy, but they were given little direction from upper management. However, every truly successful wireless initiative has one common denominator—executive involvement and support. This is apparent in many of wireless implementations in the following chapters.

When you need to fight for budget, resources, and political support to buy and use wireless technology applications effectively, it can be a serious uphill battle without executive support. In order to get maximum long-term, company-wide benefits from your wireless implementations, the top dogs have to be onboard pulling the same sled in the same direction. In Chapter 14, I devote an entire section to tactics you can use to get executive buy-in, but you should start giving thought to this issue as you read the chapters that come before it.

You Need Effective Strategies
Once you get your head in the right place by focusing correctly on wireless technology, you need to determine the business strategy for using it. There are

several major areas of your organization's business operation in which you can use wireless technology to help save money, increase revenues, and enhance business efficiency right now. Consider the following four strategic options within the context of your own organization and see how they can work for you.

   1. *Communicate to existing customers.* Because they already have relationships with you, it is easier to measure and subsequently reduce the cost of communicating with customers using wireless technology. If they have a good relationship with you, customers are a good force to mobilize into proactive marketing efforts, and you can do so with fast results thanks to the convenience of wireless communication.

   You can use wireless technology to increase customer retention and also provide a sales channel that boosts upselling and reduces the costs of processing repeat orders. Remember that customers are more than the people who buy your products. They also include resellers, journalists, investors, and others with whom you have ongoing business relationships.

   2. *Enhance customer service and support.* Service and support have become major operating costs, as well as key contributors to organizations' competitive advantage in the marketplace. Service and support are expensive activities, and wireless technology can help significantly reduce these costs.

   Wireless also can significantly increase the response time and efficiency of providing good service. When implemented properly, this technology can convert some basic self-help transactions by customers into potential sales opportunities for you.

   3. *Communicate to prospective customers.* Given the limitations of wireless technology and devices, online sales to people who are not already customers will work best when the average person knows who you are (e.g., Hertz, the American Red Cross, McDonald's), your products or services are easy to understand, and the price is relatively small. Otherwise, the main goal of wireless data communication to prospects' mobile devices is to facilitate prospects' shopping and decision-making, help reduce the cost of sales, and be an important bridge to closing sales.

   Wireless technology can play an important role in enabling sales staff, resellers, and even inanimate objects such as wireless kiosks to be more effective at presenting and selling your products and services. Wireless tactics also can help "close" prospective employees, business partners, investors, and journalists who are finding out about your organization for the first time and are looking for compelling reasons to do business with you.

4. *Communicate internally.* The big value of the wireless technology within an organization is in its ability to lower costs and increase productivity. It can also give employees greater flexibility to carry out their jobs, which may or may not have direct measurable financial results, but can have indirect financial benefits such as increased employee retention. Since business partners such as outsourced customer support, subcontractors, and consultants can be so intricately woven into the operation that they function the same as internal staff, wireless communication with these groups is part of this strategic option.

Organizations are learning that they can imbed wireless technology into physical assets such as vehicles and office equipment, products coming off assembly lines, and software applications in order to prevent problems and facilitate operations. Once they establish wireless communication between assets and mobile workers, the results can be a complete change in the way an organization does business that redefines its position in the marketplace.

You Need Effective Tactics

The seven-point framework for developing tactics is a great brainstorming tool once you establish your strategic objectives. When you get a group together and lay out all of the strategic possibilities, ideas start to pop up left and right. Thinking through these tactical options systematically as a group will help filter, organize, and prioritize ideas before moving them into your written plan.

1. *Brand Awareness and Loyalty.* Discussions about brand (image) building as a wireless activity are frequently amusing because traditional brand-marketing folks get so stressed about how they can reproduce the company logo in its full color and splendor on a monochrome screen the size of a matchbook. Or they worry about how they will ever be able to recreate banner ads and generate click-throughs or video ads on PDAs.

Well, the truth of the matter is, brand building in the wireless world is a multidimensional exercise, but one that may not include any of the aforementioned stress points. These tactics introduce people to your product or organization, shape the image that they have of both, and engage people in two-way communication that increases the number of times they do business with you, and refer your organization to others.

2. *Direct Response Activities.* These tactics will find their finest moments in the age of wireless communication. The idea of getting a beep and an ad on my PDA as I walk past a Starbucks is offensive and will ultimately prove to be useless, but there are creative ways to get people to take immediate action in response to the right wireless tactics.

You need to consider using conventional communications that motivate direct response through wireless devices, as well as implementing wireless tactics that trigger quick reactions through conventional activities such as telephone calls and store visits.

3. *Education of Your Audiences.* Educating your different audiences about the various aspects of your business operations and products is a valuable business practice that can be significantly enhanced through wireless technologies. Traditional educational institutions from kindergarten through adult education and professional development organizations can use wireless tactics to significantly alter the face of academic learning.

You get the impression from so many articles that stock quotes, news, sports, and weather are the only things that people want to learn about through mobile devices. In reality there are a lot that people need and want to know, and wireless is a great way to facilitate that knowledge gathering, either by providing access to content and learning tools or through structured training courses.

4. *Product or Service Demonstration.* This tactical option will face the toughest challenge in the wireless world, primarily because of the size, bandwidth, and computing power limitations of most mobile devices. However, those who sell services, digital content (e.g., music, text, or one day maybe video), and simple-to-use products will still be able to let prospects try it before they buy it even if it's only a virtual test drive.

5. *Research.* This is the natural complement to educating your various audiences because it capitalizes on the ability of the Net and wireless to facilitate two-way dialogue and swift, real-time communication. Wireless access to web-based surveys, instant messaging, and, eventually, wireless chat rooms will enable you to quickly gather and respond to vital external feedback.

While wireless research tactics do not lend themselves to the traditional button-down process of quantitative research, they do stimulate all kinds of qualitative feedback that keeps you in tune with the needs and interests of those with whom you do business. They also make traditional data collection for activities such medical research, census taking, transit rider studies, and "man-in-the-street" interviews much easier and less expensive.

6. *Press Relations.* I am amazed by how many organizations fail to use the Web to reach even 50 percent of its potential to develop and strengthen relationships with journalists and generate more media coverage. As I peer into the well of wireless applications that some organizations are developing, I don't foresee the situation improving with this newest technology.

However, there are a few organizations that eagerly use wireless technology not only for PR but also for investor relations, but as a key component of their crisis management plans. I have a strong case to make for those visionary souls who can seize the opportunity to capitalize on the anywhere, anytime communication capabilities of wireless to deliver press documents, facilitate web access, and coordinate mobile executives.

7. Operational Tactics to Facilitate Successful Wireless Implementation. Many organizations develop grand plans for automating aspects of their internal operations. But the best-laid plans often fall short because people fail to adequately address the main components to implementing new technology: motivating the executives and employees who have to use it, budgeting resources, selecting vendors, and getting the technology to fit the business.

There are many potential pitfalls to implementing wireless applications and opening wireless communication channels with your different audiences. If you are going to effectively avoid these, your tactical planning has to address issues such as office politics, technophobia, technology standards, data security, vendors going out of business, and other issues.

So there you have the general overview of my methodology. Call it the 3-4-7 for Maximizing Your Wireless Business Plan. Don't worry about how your final plan should look. This book concludes with a chapter that gives you some guidance in organizing and writing your plan. Before we get into the nitty gritty details of developing your strategy and tactics, let's look at some perceptions and misconceptions that can cloud your view of what wireless can offer your organization.

Perceptions and Misconceptions That Can Hinder Wireless Implementations

There are a number of perceptions that people have that can distort the reality of what is and isn't possible with using wireless as a business tool. There are also quite a few misconceptions floating around about wireless technology that need to be stamped out early and often.

Some of these come from basic misunderstandings about the technology and also the people who use it. Other perceptions and misconceptions stem from the overzealous evangelism of engineering-driven telecommunication and wireless vendors who understand the depth of their technology, but fail to grasp the realities affecting its implementation. Then there are those myths such as the "wireless Web" that come out of left field inspired by a catchy slogan that gets picked up by the pundits and industry insiders, then develops a life of its own.

In these next few pages I will provide some clarity to the more common perceptions of wireless technologies and try to put to rest some misconceptions that could possibly stand in the way of generating wireless benefits sooner rather than later.

Wireless Technology Isn't as "New" as You Might Think It Is

Quite a few headlines on press releases from companies in the wireless industry tout wireless data communication as "new," "leading edge technology," and "the next big thing." Not that there's anything wrong with this per se. But when you combine "new" with "technology," you scare a lot of people into avoiding the technology until it becomes older, less scary, and more predictable in terms of performance and ROI. That reluctance to act only delays the benefits organizations could be receiving today.

If you look around, you will find that a number of midsize and large manufacturers have been using wireless technology for a decade. Tom Turner, senior vice president of marketing and business development at WhereNet (www.wherenet.com), a company that provides wireless technology that helps companies track their assets states, "At first there were wireless local area networks (LANs) for in-store applications and large manufacturing facilities. Distribution companies such as FedEx started using wireless to support scanners and other hand held devices that came into play around 1992–1993."

Turner continues, "In the early 1990s the use of wireless was application specific. For example, a company would make a decision to implement wireless to solve an inventory management or a shipping and receiving problem. Now you see large organizations making commitments to technology such as wireless LANs throughout the physical offices and treating that investment in wireless infrastructure the same as installing ethernet networks or heating and plumbing in buildings. It's a resource they expect to put into facilities to connect with mobile workers and physical assets." In essence, wireless isn't a new technology, but rather, it's a technology that people are finding new uses for.

Many of the organizations I will talk about in this book started using wireless technologies to produce measurable ROI in 1996, even government groups and companies with fewer than 20 employees. So it's time to get over this "new" thing. Wireless has been beneficial for quite a while.

Wireless Benefits More Than Large Corporations

Many of the early articles about organizations using wireless technology highlight the big conglomerates such as Office Depot and Citibank, so smaller organizations might think that wireless doesn't offer any benefits for them at the moment. However, there are many relatively small companies that have successfully deployed wireless technologies in their businesses. For example, there is Mann Consulting, a company that has seven people using wireless modems. This implementation is delivering value that far outweighs the investment the company made in the modems.

Legacy Chiller Systems is a 12-person manufacturer that reduced its customer support costs and beat competitors in more bids since they now embed wireless technology into their products. Borba Farms is a 180-employee business that uses wireless services to save between $20,000 and $50,000 a year in overhead costs. The list of small organizations goes on.

Ladies and gentlemen, in the world of wireless and who can benefit from wireless applications, size doesn't matter.

A strong case can be made for government and nonprofit groups to use wireless technology as well. Tom Nogles, vice president of strategic services for wireless applications vendor ThinAirApps (www.thinairapps.com) sees opportunities for acceptance of wireless by government organizations.

Nogles says, "Initially they will concentrate on improving the effectiveness of internal operations. People in government are looking for wireless technologies that will enhance existing computer network applications and continue to work without having to replace the wireless applications, even as these networks get upgraded. I think their focus on shaping community perception (brand building) will come further on down the road."

Telephia (www.telephia.com), which offers research-based business solutions to the wireless industry, performs a biannual, in-depth study of the habits, attitudes, and perceptions of people who use wireless technology. John Dee Fair, their vice president of research and development, comments that "nonprofit organizations may need to look at less robust infrastructure because their back-end systems may not be as complex as many businesses, but there is still value for them [in using wireless technologies]. I know someone who's a social worker, and wireless is a good technology that could make him more efficient, help him process paperwork faster, and ultimately enable him to provide better services to clients."

Hans Wynholds, founder and CEO of ServiceHub (www.service hub.com), a wireless application service provider, sums it up this way. "Government or nonprofits might look more at cost savings than revenue generation as commercial businesses do, but ultimately it's the same mission for all three groups and that is to [positively] impact the financial aspects of the organization. At their root, three things come into play for all organizations: their wireless applications' impact on customers, the applications' impact on human resources, and what are the benefits that must accrue for the organization."

Throughout the book, I will present some of the issues and opportunities that government and nonprofit organizations can and should address regarding wireless.

The World's a Wireless Stage,
Every Country Has a Role

It seems that every other news article about wireless mentions how much the United States lags behind Europe and Asia in terms of wireless technology. In some ways this is true, such as the lack of certain technology standards among wireless carriers. But for the most part, it's not so much a question of who's ahead. It's just that there are differences in how wireless technology is used in different countries.

In many European and Asian countries, cell phone use is significantly higher than PC use, even by businesspeople. In the United States, it is the opposite; PC use surpasses cell phone use. While people in the United States spent the past seven years surfing (and getting addicted to) the Web on desktop computers, many European and Asian consumers' exposure to the Net has come primarily through text messaging and limited surfing with cell phones. The result?

In Europe, you can't even date if you do not have a cell phone. Everyone from age 4 to 104 uses them to communicate with each other for business and personal use. And they type literally billions of text messages each month using those tiny phone keypads!

Enable cell phones to play downloadable audio files or colorful animated graphics, or buy soda from vending machines, and European and Asian markets quickly adopt these features. People get instant messaging (IM) and chat room capabilities as they become available for cell phones. In countries like Sweden it's practically a law to max out the use of your cell phone. And there are telecom companies such as Japan's NTT DoCoMo that can add millions of subscribers within months to its new mobile phone services.

For example, a group of Japanese businessmen stopped a conversation and circled around a colleague with a cell phone. The way they were speaking at 90 words a second and gesturing wildly you would have thought their company just closed the deal of the century. It turns out that the colleague was playing a fly-tackle fishing game (during the conversation, no less) and had just hooked a big digital fish.

The sex appeal and potential profits of these leading consumer applications get U.S. telecom companies and the media salivating, and so they start saying the United States has to catch up. But whereas European and Asian consumers are pushing the wireless technology envelope with interesting and entertaining applications, it is the U.S. business community that is on the leading edge of wireless applications.

In the United States, with its "work till you drop" mindset, businesses are taking their addiction to web access from PCs and extending this addiction to mobile devices (primarily PDAs) with wireless access. That, together with the fact that companies have spent so much time and money building web-based application infrastructures, means the United States leads the world in wireless business-to-business applications. But alas, these applications are not nearly as sexy as consumer applications and the financial impact to telecom companies may not be as great, so business applications have been slow to get the kind of press that counters the United States' laggard image.

So don't make the mistake, if you're operating in the United States, of not pursuing wireless applications until the United States "catches up." Let's get past that. As you will read in the upcoming chapters, there are many things that you can do right now in the U.S. market with wireless to impact your bottom line.

Even with the Right Technology, Consumer Applications in the United States Will Be Different

There are articles that imply that if the United States gets 3G (third-generation fast speed) wireless networks, Americans will be able to do all the cool things that consumers do using cell phones elsewhere. Or when all the wireless carriers use the same standards, businesses will be able to engage consumers in data dialogues via their cell phones.

This creates the perception that the right technologies will lead to a change in how American consumers will use cell phones, a perception I believe is off base. After many years of ingrained behavior using PCs and full-sized keyboards to access e-mail and surf the Web, I doubt that huge numbers of consumers will suddenly shift to using cell phones to exchange files, chat, and send messages to each other. At least not anytime soon, and not with the same intensity or for the same applications that are driving consumer wireless usage in other countries.

Even if all of the right technology is in place, one of two things has to happen (though probably both) before we see the average U.S. consumer using wireless applications the same way that consumers around the world do. Either PDA use has to skyrocket or teenagers have to be mobilized (okay, bad pun) to change the cultural fabric.

Why PDAs more so than cell phones? Because PDAs resemble the desktop in design and functionality much more than cell phones do. Some Americans never leave home without a cell phone, and you can't pry them from some people's ears, but their addiction is to the voice communication not data. People might be okay with scrolling through short text messages on a phone, yet when they have to type detailed messages or navigate web content, the device that comes closest to the PC-type keyboard will be the device of choice. And that, my friends, is the PDA.

If you still have any doubt about people learning to use cell phones as serious data input and web surfing tools, consider the fact that the United States is a country where people can own a VCR for ten years and the clock display never stops blinking "12:00." A speaker at a recent technology forum said, "My wife and I bought new cell phones the other day, and if I didn't have anything else to do for about three weeks, I might be able to learn how to program the thing."

On the teen front, Apple Computer in the 1970s offered a valuable lesson. Apple understood that a good way to become popular in broad consumer and business markets is to get technology into the hands of students and watch it blossom from there as students get older. Apple gave thousands of computers to students in first grade up to college, and as those students entered jobs and started families, they promoted the use of Macintoshes everywhere they went. If you want to some day have wireless be a major communication channel from your organization to general consumers, create if you can a plan to win over the under-20 crowd and ride that wave.

It's hard to predict if today's teens will grow up using PDAs or cell phones more for data communication, but you should cover all of your bets so you're better prepared for future developments. Assuming you market to general consumers, research how teens today are using all types of mobile devices to determine if (for example) in three or four years they will use cell phones to buy your products from vending machines. To be safe, plan to develop content that is accessible by phones and PDAs, a task that will be made easy by software tools that automatically format content for different mobile devices.

There is one more important fact to keep in mind, probably THE most important fact. Regardless of whether cell phones or PDAs become the predominant mobile device among consumers, without compelling, easy-to-use content or useful applications, businesses will not be able to build relationships with consumers using wireless communication.

PDA sales did not skyrocket until Palm made it much easier than previous PDA companies for the average person to use the device and provided one or two uncomplicated but compelling applications (phone book, scheduler). America Online (AOL) continually reigns supreme among consumers as an Internet service provider because they make it incredibly easy to access the Net and because AOL delivers applications such as chat and instant messaging that consumers love. There will be a lot of floundering around and money wasted until organizations learn how to replicate the successes of companies such as Palm and AOL.

The Misconception of the Wireless Mobile Net

The Internet is not wireless, period. It is very much wired. Nor is the Net mobile. You have wireless access to it and to software applications running on regular servers. But when you pack up your Palms, BlackBerries, and iPAQs, you are not taking the Net with you. These phrases "wireless Net" and "mobile Net" are the by-products of some creative minds, and they do a disservice to organizations that have to use wireless technology.

These phrases can suggest to some people that the experience they have when surfing the Web from PCs will be the same experience when they access web content from mobile devices. Not only that, it gives people the idea that they have access to all of the information on the Internet from their wireless devices.

Well, it doesn't work that way. Web page, intranet, and Web-accessible business software applications have to be modified significantly for content to be viewed easily from PDAs and cell phones, while graphic elements and multimedia files often have to be dropped completely to enable wireless access by some devices. Trying to type in URLs, or navigate typical web pages from these devices is a real pain, plus wireless connections to the Internet are slow and expensive.

When there are unrealistic expectations and these expectations subsequently are not fulfilled, many people will walk away from the technology, not to return soon. If the executives who pay for your organization's wireless applications think that they can buy the ability to pop the Net into everyone's back pocket, they will be disappointed.

You owe it to yourselves and your organization to put the myth of the "wireless mobile Net" out of people's collective minds.

The Myth of M-Commerce

There are the breathless articles and promotional materials about the potential of sales through mobile devices (m-commerce), and how this will be a driving force that determines what applications organizations will deploy. Hmm, I think not.

"I contend that selling is going to be a second- or third-generation wireless application rather than be widely popular now because of the limitations of the devices and the user interfaces," comments Telephia's John Dee Fair. "It's true that people are trading stocks on wireless devices, but the stress levels worrying about being disconnected are higher than when they call someone on the same device. Wireless networks are improving, but the experience can be inconsistent depending on where you are, time of day, etc. If you're selling or buying, you are more demanding about a consistent wireless experience. Today wireless communication is about getting specific info and getting on with life."

Don Pohly, Business Manager for Airport IS at FMC Technologies, a wireless applications company that helps companies track physical assets, says "It's apparent to us in the trenches that the sales aspects of wireless are popular in the news. But in our market where we tend to get new technological developments later than other industries, a lot of the promise of great sales volumes through wireless devices has lost its sheen. However the real money comes in when you use the technology to improve your core business operations."

You will see quite a few examples of this in the upcoming chapters, but Chapters 3 and 5 put the topic of m-commerce into proper perspective.

You Don't Have To Do It All, All at Once

Some people have the misconception that they must implement every (or most) wireless application they're going to need all at once. If you take this approach, you may be bogged down for months in countless meetings, evaluations and re-evaluations, requests for proposals (RFP), and purchase procedures before you even begin the implementation. This results in missed opportunities to generate benefits in the short term.

The best way to get involved with wireless is to start with a pilot project. You can take advantage of benefits today that do not require you to bet your entire technology budget on one deal. Consider, for example, SARCOM, a systems integration company that gave 100 executives mobile devices in 1999 before wireless was on most people's radar screens. They sized up the need, estimated the productivity increases, and moved forward with what turned out to be a good pilot project.

SARCOM used the results from this pilot project to map out the rest of their wireless strategy that was implemented in stages. Every stage was to pay for itself in money saved or increased productivity. By easing in with a pilot program, you don't spend a fortune to build a full-blown online presence without a clear idea of what you're going to achieve, you spend moderate amounts of money to test small implementations now, then expand on what succeeds. Continually move towards long-term strategic goals.

Don't Get Caught on the Downside of Long-Term ROI

"I avoid worrying about this by making sure my ROI is reached quickly. Don't do something that will pay off in years, but implement an application that produces immediate results. Otherwise you're dependent on trends and waves in technology development." Thus spoke Harrold Mann of Mann Consulting.

While I advocate a long-term strategy based on forecasting financial results, I agree with Mr. Mann that you need to have some short-term ROI objectives. Why? First, you can make the longer-term objectives more realistic based on results in the early days of implementation. Second, you don't throw away major dollars heading down the wrong path. Third, you're able to fund or at least cost-justify money to expand your efforts based on your initial successes.

In the early days of Federal Express's web presence, they had a fairly anemic website for an international powerhouse. In fact, some companies with a dozen people had bigger sites. But the FedEx site had a feature that let customers check online to see where their packages were, which saved the company about $20 each time someone found out where his or her package was online rather than from a Fedex customer service representative. At one point, 200,000 people per month used the website rather than called a rep. With $4 million a month in cost savings, FedEx could probably afford to expand their Internet technology projects rather well, thank you very much.

So there you have it—some of the more common perceptions and misconceptions that you shouldn't let become anchors on your efforts to move forward with wireless strategies and tactics. To conclude this chapter, I think it will be good to have a big picture view of some of the main wireless technologies that are discussed in the upcoming chapters.

A Few Helpful Wireless Terms to Know

Before you can begin to put together your strategy about wireless technology, you need to understand some basic wireless terms and issues. The following are general definitions of some of the key technologies that will help you understand the wireless implementation stories presented later in the book. You will also get a brief overview of some of the business issues associated with using these technologies that I will expand upon throughout the book.

There is a book by Ron Schneiderman for nontechnical executives and managers called *The Mobile Technology Question and Answer Book*. It answers nearly 100 questions regarding wireless technologies. I highly recommend that you pick this up as a companion to my book if you want to know more in-depth details about wireless technology. There will be a glossary of technical terms in the online supplement that accompanies *Wireless, Inc.*

Wireless

First, let's be clear on the term wireless. There are many people who think wireless technology is only voice communication over cell phones and voice messages and text data over pagers. Others might add wireless PDAs such as Palm Pilots and Compaq iPAQs to the list.

But in reality, and within this book, wireless means any technology that enables digitized data (text, audio, video, graphics, or voice) to be sent from one point to another without wires or cables. The term wireless data means everything EXCEPT voice communication when one person calls another. Data can also include a recording of someone's voice that has been converted into a computer digital file. Wireless communication does not always involve access to the Net.

Wireless data communication can involve data sent person-to-person, from inanimate objects to other objects, from objects to people, and from people to objects. For example, you can embed wireless devices into a refrigeration system at a brewery that monitor the system to make sure the temperature stays constant. If the temperature drops because of a power outage in the plant, a message will be sent wirelessly to a device that turns on a backup generator. The same device in the refrigeration system can also send a wireless alert to a repair team that will either show up and fix the cause of the outage, or use laptops with wireless modems to take charge of the power network and fix the problem remotely.

Wireless communication between people tends to receive more press than machines talking to machines, but it's very important that you remember the full definition of wireless when developing your strategy. It would be unfortunate to overlook some benefits your organization may be able to receive from these less publicized technologies.

Wireless Networks

To make wireless communication work, you have to have a way to transport data between mobile devices (e.g., cell phone, PDA, wireless modem) and your computer networks, individual computers, the Internet, and other mobile users. That transportation system is referred to as wireless networks, of which there are several types.

■ *Cellular Networks.* Cellular networks are those towers planted from sea to shining sea that enable people on cell phones to talk to people on both cell and regular phones. The cellular networks also are used to communicate digital data, and many are being upgraded so they can send this data through at faster speeds.

Cellular and pager networks (described in the following paragraphs) are the most prevalent of the wireless networks since they cover the entire country. Cellular networks were not originally built to support data traffic and as a result, data speeds over cellular are slow—19,000 bits per second (bps) modem speed on a good day, with 56K bps speeds only recently available. However, the companies that run these networks (wireless carriers) are working frantically to enhance their networks to run data faster.

As you probably know, cellular coverage can be spotty when moving from place to place and you can be dropped in the middle of a call. Slow speeds and incomplete coverage make communicating complex data problematic, and this is something you have to account for in your planning. Also, the current cellular networks force you to dial up to make an Internet connection every time you want to access the Web, which is time consuming especially if you have to make several tries before you actually connect.

The next chapter specifically talks about how your wireless applications need to address this shortcoming. For now, keep in mind that your optimal applications are those which allow people to get data, download or upload it, then sign off the network to work with the data on their mobile devices. There are software tools being developed to help organizations overcome these limitations, and as they become available evaluate how they may be able to enhance your specific applications.

■ **Wireless Pager Networks.** Wireless pager networks are comprised of thousands of towers similar to the cellular network towers that are deployed nationwide to enable people to send numeric, alphanumeric, and voice messages from phones and computers to individuals with pagers.

The data transfer speeds of pager networks are even slower than cellular networks. As a result, the most popular business application for these networks are those that involve e-mail communication because these messages (not including attachments) are usually short in terms of data size. You can access websites and back office applications, but the wait between each function you perform can be frustrating.

Pager networks compensate for slow speed by being "always on," meaning that once you log in to the network you stay connected, but without racking up per-minute fees as you do on cellular networks since you pay only a monthly access fee. One of the big values of always-on capability is that you can constantly have e-mail delivered to you without having to go through the ritual of getting connected, so important messages get to you as soon as possible. When there is a crisis back at the office, or a big deal that needs your sign off is hanging in the balance, immediate notification is crucial.

The BlackBerry communication device and service from Research in Motion (RIM) and the Motorola Personal Communicators are two popular mobile devices that use the pager networks. While devices that use pager networks capitalize on e-mail capabilities, businesses are starting to see a greater potential value, which is that you can "push" (automatically send) data to workers. Even if the data files are large, the always-on feature means recipients don't have to dial up, sit, and wait for the download to finish as they do with cellular networks. Downloading happens while people are doing other things.

■ **Radio Frequency (RF) Networks.** RF networks are made up of a number of radio transmitters that relay data from point to point using a particular radio frequency that the Federal Communication Commission (FCC) allocates for commercial, government, or emergency use. These networks can be deployed within the parameters of an organization's physical premises or throughout a city or larger geographic region.

For now, RF networks communicate faster than everything else that's available. You can put an RF modem on a laptop and a mobile user within the network coverage area will get the same computing capabilities accessing web and network data that he or she gets sitting at his or her desk directly linked to the network. However, RF coverage options have limits.

One option is to pay for access to a RF network that is owned by a service provider such as Motorola, Ricochet Networks, or Wayport (www.wayport.

com). But then your mobile access is limited to where that provider operates their RF networks, which can be problematic for business needs. Motorola networks, which are used by many of municipal emergency response organizations, typically cover entire cities while Wayport puts its systems into airports and hotel properties. Giving your sales force Wayport access means they will only be able to communicate wirelessly if they can run into a nearby hotel lobby, assuming the hotel actually supports the service. I see Ricochet becoming the best of the RF networks for meeting business needs.

After being raised up by Aerie Networks from the ashes of Ricochet's (www.ricochet.com) former owner Metricom, this service promises to be a major business wireless tool if deployed right. With a Ricochet modem users get ISDN speeds on their laptops or PDAs such as the iPAQ that support the card. Many of the strategies and tactics in this book that address sales force automation, internal communication, and field service automation can best be implemented with Ricochet. The network is deployed (though not activated) in seventeen major cities, and more likely will come online.

You can build your own RF network, which can be expensive if you use high-end transmitters and base stations, but you should be able to recover your investment within six to twelve months. Organizations such as manufacturers and shipping companies build their own RF networks on their physical locations for tracking assets such as parts, shipping containers, vehicles, and other items that move around acres of property. RF networks are also an alternative to wired LANs.

■ *Wireless Local Area Networks (LANs).* Wireless LANs, often referred to as just 802.11a and 802.11b networks, also work using radio frequency transmissions. However, these LANs are best suited for indoor use. They require that you have special RF modem cards in laptops, PDAs, and even desktops, and a relay station (called an access point) that has hardwire cabling into a computer network. Whenever devices with RF modems are within range of an access point (within 80 to 150 feet) in the same conference room, office complex, or other location where you want to provide wireless access, users can have a connection to your computer network and through this get to the Internet. You can also configure a wireless LAN to provide access only to the Net.

Wireless LANs are popular with organizations because they are less expensive to build and use than other RF networks (a few thousand dollars versus several hundred thousand dollars). They don't require that you install cabling, just strategically place relay stations throughout your facilities so laptop users can be in coverage areas at the most important places within your locations. Many laptop manufacturers are building their products with wireless LAN cards already included that support these networks, so that saves you more money.

Wireless LANs are not without their downsides, however. They have security weaknesses, and the quality of the network connections can break down if you have dozens of people in one location (e.g., classrooms or auditoriums) trying to get access one station at the same time.

■ *Bluetooth.* Another RF option is Bluetooth, which is more suited to people wirelessly accessing computer devices within 11 to 110 yards rather than communicating through the Net or accessing productivity and collaboration software. A typical use would be to have a Bluetooth-enabled card in a PDA. If you're in a room with a printer with similar capability, you could print out a document without a physical connection between the PDA and the printer. Don't make any short-term plans for Bluetooth because it's not cheap, widely deployed, or bug-free enough to take off anytime soon.

■ *3G Networks.* The 3G networks, described in simple terms, are networks that will enable mobile devices to wirelessly access the Net through an "always on" connection at speeds of up to two megabytes per second versus the 19,000 bytes per second of cellular networks. In essence, you could broadcast a live sales presentation, deliver video press releases, or quickly download software programs or music CDs to mobile devices through an always-on connection. Great in theory, but questionable in terms of eventual reality.

For one thing, the availability in the United States of radio spectrum needed to make 3G networks work is very limited, so there's not enough to go around to the number of wireless carriers that would like to buy the spectrum. And since there is a scarcity, what spectrum does become available will be extremely expensive, so fewer carriers will be able to afford it. If you can get past the issue of few companies building out a 3G network, current mobile device users will have to upgrade their units or buy new devices. It's not clear to me that a lot of people will be compelled to invest that expense.

I recommend that you plan strategy and tactics around the limitations of slower-speed mobile devices and be prepared to enhance your tactics as you're able to send more data (i.e., larger files, more graphics, etc.) at higher speeds. Also, keep an eye on the changes that wireless carriers are making to existing cellular networks to increase the speeds at which they send data. You may see these referred to as 2.5G or GRPS (General Packet Radio Systems) networks. As you will read in the following chapters, it will be a great feature to have, but you don't always need to send huge files and do video conferencing on mobile devices to implement profitable wireless strategies.

■ *Infrared Technology.* Infrared technology enables data to be sent from point to point using an infrared beam, though the devices using infrared have to be in the "line of sight" of each other in order to work. Besides PDAs, many laptops, desktops, printers, and other computing-related equipment are built with this technology already included, though for some reason manufacturers don't seem to heavily publicize this feature. With it, for example, two laptop users sitting in an airport can exchange data without have a cable connection between them.

Infrared capability facilitates limited personal communication, what some computer magazines call personal access networks, compared to the wireless networks that let you reach greater numbers of people in larger geographic areas. One infrared source has to be within a certain range as well as be in the line of sight of another infrared source to communicate with it. These distances can be anywhere from a couple of feet to a few yards.

Despite the range limitations, there are wireless applications that you can create using infrared when you are sure that the people you need to communicate with are within this relatively short range. You can transmit a large amount of data, including graphics, without the problem of bandwidth constraints or spotty network coverage. A large number of PDA owners don't have Internet access, so infrared gives you a way to pass information to them by first distributing it to those PDA owners with Net access who will pass it on to their friends and colleagues.

Some of the wireless tactics in *Wireless, Inc.* depend on the ability to deliver content wirelessly or otherwise to a base station with infrared capability in a store or other location where people can access the content. Other tactics involve delivering information to people with wireless Net access, then having them pass this information on to others who just have infrared capability.

■ *Global Positioning System (GPS).* The GPS network is a set of particular space satellites that transmit precise positioning data to receivers on the earth's surface. The most common applications that you may read about for GPS involve using the technology to track moving objects and people, such as vehicles or executives, and plot their locations on a map. Once the position of an object or person has been determined, the data is sent to a cellular network, which in turn sends it to the Net for display on a website.

One important note about using GPS. If you use it to track your assets, a major limitation is that whatever devices you use will not be able to receive a signal from satellites if the asset goes into a garage or other enclosed space. If you're tracking a fleet car that has been stolen, once it gets into the chop shop, you're out of luck.

In the future, you may see the GPS network used to pinpoint locations of delivery vehicles, trucks carrying freight and field service staff, and then linking this data with a customer data base (for example) to access details about specific customers in the area. Based on the needs of the customer, wireless messages can be manually or automatically sent to the individuals in these vehicles with special instructions to fill product orders, repair equipment, or maybe even just pay a courtesy call.

Wireless Mobile Devices

I define wireless mobile devices as PDAs with or without Internet- and computer network-access capability, data cell phones, wireless modems that enable laptops to access the Net, and any handheld computing hardware that can communicate without wires. This even includes walkie-talkies, though you may not have too many business applications for these.

I will address mobile device issues in more detail in Chapter 15, but let me point out here the three main types of PDAs, and my general feeling about the roll of cell phones in your wireless strategy. PDAs run on an operating system (OS) that comes from either Palm (which is the market leader in terms of numbers of devices running this OS) Microsoft, or RIM. Palm Pilots and Handspring Visors are two PDAs that run the Palm OS; Compaq's iPAQ and the HP Jornada are two PDAs using the Microsoft PocketPC OS; and RIM's proprietary OS runs only on that company's BlackBerry communicator.

There are distinct differences among these PDAs that can affect the type of applications that you can implement, such as always-on capability, color screens, or ability to use Microsoft Word documents. But within a year or two, buying a PDA is going to be similar to buying laptops in that their major capabilities and features will be similar. If you get a Dell or an IBM laptop, you're still able to run all of your applications, so it's price, bells and whistles, quality of customer service, and similar issues that determine which one you buy.

The main point is to focus on the business objectives you want to reach and the device needs of individuals. Don't get held up in major discussions about what type of mobile device to use. Some of the specific applications that I present in the upcoming chapters may run only on a Palm OS PDA or a PocketPC device, but similar types of applications often can be created using the other OS devices. Chapter 15 presents several companies that sell products to enable your applications to automatically detect the type of device that is accessing the applications and modify themselves to run on the respective device's OS.

In general, data cell phones with Internet access are not the tools I would distribute to executives and employees as the main mobile device to use with wireless applications unless there is limited typing and data entry required to use the applications effectively. If you can reduce applications to a simple set of drop-down menus with multiple choice options and three-to-six word entries, data cell phones can make sense, particularly if a lot of your employees already have them.

The exceptions are "smartphones"—cell phones that have PDA capabilities, including a larger display screen and typewriter-style keyboard that pops up on the screen. These are better suited for writing a lot of messages or heavy data input, and people can still make voice calls. The Kyocera Smartphone, which uses the Palm OS, is one of the more popular in this category. The recently released Motorola Accompli has all of the typical smartphone features. Though it has the look of a tiny PC, it also allows you to access cellular networks both in the United States and other countries just by adding a chip.

Handspring (www.handspring.com) has a device called the Treo that reflects an end-user focus you should look for from vendors that are combining cell phone and PDA functions into one device. The Treo (which runs the Palm OS) uses a typical PDA design, but you flip up the fold-out lid to use the cell phone features as you would a regular cell phone, or you can use a phone headset to talk.

You access U.S., European, and Asian cell phone networks with the same chip, removing the hassle of changing chips. You can send SMS messages (similar to AOL or Yahoo instant messaging) to mobile phone users on these three continents, which expands the type of individual and business needs you can meet. And as faster GRPS networks come into play, you only have to download software to the TREO to enable the phone to access the new networks rather than have to buy a new device.

The danger of combining the features of distinctly different tech gadgets into one device is that vendors often end up with products that are a major hassle for the average person to use. The upcoming chapters help you define business goals that will influence your mobile device choices. But equally important in choosing devices are the needs and comfort of the people using them, and the devices' abilities to keep pace with quickly changing technology. Keep these facts in mind as you evaluate smartphones.

Demographics of Mobile Device Users

If you are planning on developing tactics to communicate with prospective customers, it will help to know some of the general demographics of users of mobile devices with wireless Net access. According to figures released by Telephia in 2001, 43 percent of data cell phone users and 36 percent of PDA users are twenty-five to thirty-six-years-old. Thirty-seven percent of data phone users and about 41 percent of PDA users fall into the thirty-seven to fifty-five-year-old bracket.

Men comprise 55 percent of data phone users and 70 percent of PDA users. In terms of annual income, 43 percent of PDA users earn between $50,000 and $100,000, and another 13 percent earn between $100,000 and $150,000. Among data phone users, 38 percent earn between $50,000 and $100,000 and a significant 23 percent earn between $100,000 and $150,000.

There are other demographics you may want to consider, such as occupation, education, and geographic location, but the overall market of mobile device users is constantly shifting as prices of devices and services drop and economic conditions gyrate. You will have to do some analysis of mobile device users within your specific target markets to determine the suitability of using wireless to reach those markets.

One thing to keep in mind, though, is that ownership and web surfing are not the same thing. Telephia surveyed a nationwide sample of 1,130 data phone users in 2000 and found that only 29 percent used their phones to access the Net. If you plan to pursue prospects with data phones, make sure they are will even be on the Web to find you. A website you might want to bookmark is www.commnow.com. This portal from The Strategis Group, a telecommunications industry research company, provides various wireless industry reports and e-mail-delivered newsletters. They intend to do a detailed survey of PDA users in 2002 that could be useful for your tactical planning.

Well, now that you have a bird's eye view of wireless strategy and tactics, as well as some of the general business and technology issues that can influence your wireless implementations, let's dig into the details beginning with getting the right focus.

CHAPTER 2

Three Focus Points Keep You on the Right Wireless Path

"Readiness is all." This is a maxim of Spenser, the private detective in Robert Parker's novels, as he prepares to deal with events whose outcomes he can't predict with total certainty. Similarly, many executives find themselves in Spenser's position when they implement wireless applications.

Despite all the hype about wireless, there are quite a few definite benefits. But plan as you may, uncertainties will always cloud the future of your implementations. What you need to do to properly prepare for the uncertainties and increase your levels of success, even before you write your wireless business plan, is to have the right focus on the mission at hand.

If you approach wireless technology with the wrong focus, you will set yourself and your organization up for disappointment, failure, or missed business opportunities. For example, if you focus on wireless only as a marketing tool rather than technology that potentially can impact several other departments, you may miss opportunities to add tens of thousands of dollars to the bottom line.

To be ready to take maximum advantage of all that wireless has to offer and dodge some of the many pitfalls that threaten your success, you have to focus on three things: 1) the communication potential of wireless technology; 2) the fundamentals of good technology implementation; and 3) the roles of your top executives. That's what this chapter will help you do.

Communication Is Where the Pot of Gold Lies

This section could be subtitled "Avoid the pitfalls that plagued the early days of the Web." During those rough and tumble days organizations built websites for the wrong reasons, while overlooking some incredible benefits the Net offered even when access for most people was only 14,000 bps. The most common mistake was focusing on sales as the primary reason for building a website. Some people are making this same mistake with wireless.

When an organization makes sales generation its primary objective for wireless, it creates expectations that can increase the likelihood of failure, which in turn results in upper management's withdrawal of support for the project. Usually, the expectation is that sales are going to start pouring in from people with PDAs and cell phones. Here's how this scenario often plays out: Driven by that expectation, a wireless team often tries to jam a lot of product or service information through a small device with relatively slow bandwidth, resulting in a painful experience for the person holding the device. Then the team waits impatiently for a percentage of the billions of m-commerce dollars that research analysts have predicted (but which may not happen for a couple of years). The result is a painful experience for the person who holds wireless responsibility.

After spending a truckload of money and energy to win sales that don't materialize, senior management then reenacts the Battle of the Little Big Horn and the wireless team has its last stand—a painful experience for everyone. In the meantime, the company misses several opportunities to implement wireless applications that could reduce its support costs by 30 or 40 percent.

Other organizations that view wireless as only a sales channel won't consider using the technology because they believe people are not going to use a wireless device to buy their products or services. In essence these organizations shut themselves off from any other potential and much more exciting benefits that wireless offers. Government and nonprofit organizations in particular risk falling into this category, along with companies that sell expensive, complex, or specialized products and services.

Wireless technology is not about sales; it's about communication. Let me say this one more time. Wireless technology is not about sales. It is new technology that allows you to communicate in a different way with those people most important to your organization's success including your customers, employees, and business partners. It even allows your physical assets to communicate important operations and location data so you can better manage these assets.

Since there will be a lot of advertising, research reports, and articles that will try to convince you of the value of sales through mobile devices, I think it is important that you understand some of the reasons why this won't be a reality for several years.

Barriers to Sales to First-Time Customers

Entities such as financial services companies, some retail outlets, sports teams, and pizza palaces should do well in the short-term with wireless-based sales, but there are a few hurdles to the promise of m-commerce for many companies.

Reaching people wirelessly who have never done business with you before can cost you more than any sales benefits you might produce. Federico Aloisi, vice president of marketing and business development for neXui (www.nexui.com), an Italian wireless applications company, feels that "Wireless may not be right for communicating with prospective customers because you're wasting so many resources to reach the ones who will buy. The cost of communicating the amount of information required to close a sale is high."

Mr. Aloisi doesn't see wireless as great for basic advertising that communicates a smaller amount of data "because you have to hit such a large number of potential customers. The cost of the time online and for each bit of data is very high, especially when you have to send this data to so many people who will never be your customers. When you communicate with someone you know, you are more efficient and you know exactly what to say."

First, the predominant mobile device by number is the cell phone. But until a lot more people have cell phones with large screens and PDA features built into them, such as the Kyocera Smartphone that has Palm Pilot capabilities, few consumers will be interested in surfing web pages to read about your products. Even some companies in Europe (where cell phone use for text messaging is high) question the viability of generating sales from wireless devices of people who don't know your company.

Another hurdle to the growth of m-commerce is that, while PDAs give people a larger screen to view data and keyboards that are adequate for typing messages, there is a relatively small number of them. Estimates predict that between 11 and 14 million PDAs will be in use in the United States by 2003. But not all of these PDAs will have wireless access to the Net. Fourteen million units in a population of 250 million people makes for a small universe of potential customers to fight over for sales. The penetration of PDAs in countries outside the United States is even smaller.

A third hurdle to the growth of m-commerce is that even if half the population buys PDAs next year and everyone has cell phones on steroids with bigger screens and real keyboards, you're still constrained by bandwidth. If and when 3G is in wide use, m-commerce will be a much more viable application for wireless technologies. However, it looks like high-speed access through 3G probably won't be widely available until the end of 2002 or early 2003 in the United States. Then you must factor in time for companies to work the bugs out of the software that drives the yet-to-be mass-produced mobile devices that enable people to use 3G efficiently.

A fourth hurdle to the growth of m-commerce is that many companies design such poor shopping carts, order forms, and navigation tools through the transaction process on websites, that people often stop the process before they get to the final "submit" button. If organizations are doing such a poor job of designing systems for prospects with full desktop computer screens, I shudder to think about what they will design for people with mobile devices.

Sales to Existing Customers Make Sense

There is one type of m-commerce that can work in the short-term: sales to existing customers. If someone already has a relationship with you, he or she understands your product or service features and capabilities. So if you create a simple interface for the mobile device, you can generate a lot of repeat sales. You don't have to be concerned as much with the total universe of prospects when you work with existing customers. You just focus on the universe you can control.

Even in this case, you must understand that you can't just set up a page of product information and a shopping cart, then expect customers to fall all over themselves to buy additional products from you.

Kate Everett-Thorp, CEO of interactive ad agency Lot21, observes that, "In order to sell something through a wireless device, [the device] has to improve the buying experience in some way. A lot of companies offer a wireless purchase capability just to give users an additional way to buy, or they see this as a way to have a competitive advantage. But companies have to make the wireless experience for the customer worthwhile in order for people to take advantage of the capability."

In essence, you have to use wireless technology and conventional communication to create an ongoing dialog with customers that results in multiple sales over time. Then the wireless sales transaction process, or wireless experience, has to be convenient and easier to use than alternative ways of buying your products. While using a mobile device to place an order, people might need more information, or have a question and want to talk to a sales rep immediately, so the transaction process has to accommodate these communication needs.

The Benefits of Wireless Technology as a Communication Tool

Focus on wireless for communication and you will reduce business costs, speed up the process by which people actually shop for and buy your products or services, and run a more efficient, productive, and competitive organization. For example, instead of mailing pamphlets to customers announcing new products (a process which can cost a small fortune) send wireless alerts (after getting permission from customers) for mere pennies per person. Or arrange for your retail outlets to have kiosks that use infrared (IR) ports to beam materials to prospects' PDAs so they have enough data to make a purchase immediately rather than taking two or three weeks to decide.

Wireless technology enables you to communicate faster, in more places, and at more times than any other medium, including the Web. As a result, you can reduce business costs in various ways. You can enable your employees to complete tasks faster and more efficiently by giving them wireless access to business software, your intranet, and web-based business information resources while they're in meetings or in other locations where regular modem or network access isn't possible.

Shorten your sales cycles by giving field salespeople access to crucial data so they can provide more details, resolve problems, and complete other tasks while they are with customers, rather than having them lose time going back to the office to send materials. Mobile devices enable salespeople to process paperwork, initiate order fulfillment and billing, and track orders, which speeds up product delivery and cash flow.

Use software to monitor information from the Internet, news services, customers, and prospects (addressed in detail in Chapter 11), then deliver this data wirelessly to mobile executives, salespeople, and others to capitalize on new business opportunities. Quickly spot and respond to shifting market trends by wirelessly coordinating changes in your ad campaigns that increase sales leads. Collect customer data that shows an interest in features your new products offer, then deliver the data and new sales materials wirelessly to retailers so they can immediately change their in-store sales presentations.

Embed wireless devices into your physical assets so they can immediately communicate their locations, performance efficiency, changes within their environment, and other data that improve your business operations. Likewise, workers with mobile devices can communicate with your assets to remotely control their functions, respond to problems, and upgrade their performance, which saves travel time and enables you address these issues faster.

The upcoming chapters will give you a myriad of examples of how organizations are reaping significant rewards through a wide range of wireless implementations. But what you will find is the common message that runs through all of these stories is that, if you focus on the new communication opportunities that wireless offers, you will produce measurable financial benefits.

Understand the Fundamentals to Successful Implementation

We've established that focusing building new communication channels through your wireless efforts can significantly impact your organization by reducing costs, contributing to your revenue flow, and/or improving your operating efficiency. Now you need to have a solid foundation of guidelines to keep your strategic thinking and tactical implementation on the right track. These are the fundamentals to successful implementation.

To build a solid foundation for your wireless efforts, you must a) keep things simple, b) minimize the time you keep people wirelessly connected, c) avoid desktop thinking, and d) put wireless in context of the big picture. These are the fundamentals in implementing successful wireless projects.

Keep It Simple

If you want to develop wireless applications and communication activities that are used by the greatest number of people to produce the most useful benefits to them and you, simplicity must be the watchword.

Many organizations spent a ton of money to build complex websites because some designer pumped up the corporate ego by saying, "As an industry leader, you have to have the latest and greatest, flashiest, most technology-burdened site on the planet." But for visitors to these sites, the experience was often horrendous. Pages took forever to download, the flashy designs were distracting, and whatever important information might have been on the sites was buried in mindless meandering text. Don't make the same mistake with wireless.

Some organizations have spent as little as $100 to $200 per month for wireless implementations that produce tens of thousands of dollars in benefits, such as reducing the cost of communicating with their truck drivers, farm hands, and other mobile workers. Of course, there are also organizations that have implemented projects costing six- figures for applications as simple as giving mobile executives and managers wireless e-mail access. In spite of their simplicity, these applications produce a payback in increased efficiency and productivity that is enormous.

Steve Cox, vice president of marketing at OpenGrid (www.opengrid. com), a company that markets wireless applications for the conference and hospitality industries, relates a story from his days working at SkyTel. "When we met with customers we discovered that people don't want services like stock quotes and other third party content. A Bank of America executive told us what he wanted was to have key data from a specific web page sent to everyone's pagers as the data was updated. This was a very simple application, but it was vitally important to him."

So rather than trying to solve complex business problems with a single application, Cox worked with customers to develop simple implementations that enabled executives to access specific software and Internet data with paging devices. These applications were easy to implement, the benefits more than paid for the costs, and customers were able to easily understand and promote their use within the organizations.

One of OpenGrid's products, mobilePlanIt, typifies this focus on meeting simple needs. This product helps people who run conferences provide a valuable service to exhibitors and attendees by enabling them to store schedules of the seminars and keynote addresses, survey software, and data about the exhibitors in infrared stations. Attendees of the conference access all of this data with their PDAs to plan their schedule of sessions to attend, wirelessly network with other attendees, participate in interactive polls conducted by session speakers, and coordinate meetings with exhibitors.

mobilePlanIt is relatively easy for the conference organizers to use since they have the data already on their computers, and the benefits to both the attendees and exhibitors are significant enough to encourage participation in future conferences. For attendees and exhibitors the application is easy to comprehend and use, yet it reduces many of the hassles of tracking down the right people, navigating exhibitor guides and confusing schedules, and building business relationships.

Research in Motion or RIM (www.rim.net) developed the BlackBerry, a wireless communication device that is the embodiment of simplicity, whose initial primary function was to provide always-on e-mail access. Duncan Bradley, RIM's manager of market knowledge, surveyed their customers about the return on investment on an application as simple as improving e-mail management by mobile workers.

Bradley found that the average user receives sixty e-mails a day and 35 percent of these users require a response within an hour. Sometimes the value of these important messages can be $10 per e-mail. So if 21 e-mails a day are important, that's about $210 saved for every full day that a person can use a BlackBerry or other PDA to answer key messages that otherwise would not be responded to quickly. Perhaps if you did a similar survey within your organization, you may find the same potential benefits.

BlackBerry users also find that they experience an increase of fifty minutes per day in productive time by being able to communicate while in cabs, airports, subways, waiting in between meetings, etc. Telephone, network, and user-support costs that are normally incurred when mobile workers with laptops dial into remote-access servers can be reduced by 66 percent per person.

Simplicity applies not only to the type of wireless applications you select, but also to the software user interface (UI) on those applications. A simple interface to access complex data such as sales figures, equipment repair directions, or vehicle locations guarantees high participation rates by people both inside and outside of your organization. Some companies have spent hundreds of thousands of dollars to build or buy sales force automation (SFA) software to improve the effectiveness of their sales people, but the software's UIs were often so difficult to learn that people refuse to use them. Those who have successful wireless projects have focused on applications with easy-to-use development tools, simple user interfaces, and content that is easy to comprehend.

It is okay for wireless applications to give people access to complex data on intranets or multifeatured software, but having them wade through a lot of functions on the mobile devices and the applications that run on the devices is a recipe for disaster. Focus on a few needs of many people. When people are comfortable, responsive, and productive using your first wireless application, add another simple layer of functionality.

If you want your wireless applications to meet simple needs and also be easy to use, design their functions and capabilities for users, not engineers. Engineers are smarter at software and hardware design than many of us will ever be in twenty lifetimes, but they aren't the ones in the field tracking customer orders, fixing broken equipment, or trying to approve a press release. Chapter 15 goes into detail about effective UI design, but the important point here is that your executives and managers have to constantly enforce this concept of simplicity. Do not take the people who have to use your applications too far out of that comfort zone or you're asking for rejection.

A final thought on simplicity comes from Ray DePaul, RIM's director of product planning. "The KISS (keep it simple stupid) approach is the one that's resonating with companies that are launching wireless projects. We've become indulgent in the web world and have gotten used to creating massive applications and complex graphical interfaces running on computers with gigabytes of storage space. But a whole PC industry was launched on 64K memory and 5 megabytes of disk storage. I think we may have reached a point of diminishing returns with our overloading on graphics and huge software programs. There is room for creativity, but the UI window dressing won't make the user more productive."

Minimize the Time People Need to Stay Connected

Keep in mind that wireless does not have to mean wirelessly connected all the time. Let people quickly get what information they need, sign off, and go on with the rest of their lives. Eventually, 2.5 and 3G networks will enable people to have always-on, high-speed access, but this will take some time to become a nationwide reality.

Be proactive with content delivery whenever possible. Anticipate what people need and have it in the queue ready to go so they don't have to search for it. Sometimes the concern isn't about bandwidth, but the fact that when most people are mobile, they only have a few minutes before the next meeting or flight to read and respond to content. Don't chew up that precious time by causing people to hunt for information.

If customers have ten questions that they always ask whenever they buy one of your products, include short answers to those questions when you send them an alert that the newest version of your product is available. If your salespeople are always calling back to the office asking for the latest stock quotes for the prospects they will see that day, make the stock quotes available every time a sales person logs onto your server.

And, of course, try to make the navigation through wireless content a speedy process. The rule for web design is to give people many options for surfing content so they can search in a way that makes them most comfortable. Considering the limitations of mobile devices, you should give people fewer navigation options rather than more, as long as the greater majority of people still use the content.

AvantGo (www.avantgo.com) markets software and services that enable organizations to create wireless content and ad delivery applications. They also have a network of over 4 million registered users who can access a plethora of content categorized by dozens of topics from business news and foreign language lessons to personal finance and auto repair. A big contributor to AvantGo's success, and something that you should emulate, is that each topic category, called a channel, is specially configured for quick access and easy use by PDAs so people can log on, "git it, and git."

Individuals and organizations can use AvantGo to create channels for personal use and for communicating with employees, customers prospects, and others. AvantGo further facilitates the "git it and git" philosophy by enabling organizations to automatically deliver, or push, content to mobile device users who subscribe to their channels, but only data that has changed since the person last received content.

A start up named Aramira (www.aramira.com) takes this one step further. Its technology called Jumping Beans allows organizations to wirelessly deliver a full-functioning application to a PDA, shut down the connection, and, when the person finishes using it, the application automatically deletes from the PDA. This not only eliminates the need to stay connected while using a particular application, such as a time and billing, or expense reporting programs, but it also saves on what precious little storage space PDAs have.

Avoid Desktop Thinking

Get past desktop thinking, which is the tendency to develop content the same way for wireless devices that you do for websites that are accessed through a desktop.

In the early days of the Web, many organizations designed content like they were laying out a print brochure. They could not grasp that the Web gave them new opportunities to communicate in a different and better way. People did this because it was easier doing what they were comfortable with rather than taking the time to learn the nuances of the new medium. Now that they are comfortable with the Web, some organizations are just trying to shrink web pages down to fit a PDA and cell phone screen, rather than learning the nuances of this newest medium. This is not good. Not good at all.

I cringed when I first read about wireless access protocol (WAP), a set of specifications and protocols to use to modify web content for access by mobile devices. The basic premise was that an organization could use WAP to create a site that is primarily a text replication of their existing website (until wireless advances allow you to include graphics). However, just as people do not use a website the same way they use a printed brochure, people do not use a mobile device the same way they use a PC, even when they are accessing websites.

AvantGo's CEO Richard Owen believes that "If you're developing the same content for mobile devices as what you'd use on desktop, you're not thinking it through well enough. You have to put your mobile user hat on. The desktop is a fire hydrant—we can get an infinite amount of information from it. If I query a site to learn something about African cooking, the Web brings back a ton of material.

On a mobile device, people are looking for small, relevant amounts of data, such as a form to complete or directions to a restaurant. What small percentage of the total amount of data will tide me over from desktop to desktop? Also, data that has no value on the desktop might be very valuable on mobile devices. For example, you may ignore many of the e-mail notifications you get when you're in your office, but getting an alert in the middle of a meeting about e-mail with data you need to close a sale is vitally important. People assume the current approach to developing web applications apply to wireless technology, and this is what gave us WAP."

This assumption not only gave us WAP but also a number of other web development tools that replicate existing websites for wireless access, thus leaving organizations with the idea that this alone will result in effective wireless communication. You have to do two things to get out of desktop thinking mode. First, you have to ask why did people buy the device they're using? Second, you have to take into account what people are doing at the time you are communicating with them or when they are accessing your information.

If someone has a cell phone in the United States, they most likely bought it primarily for voice communication. Those who bought phones with Internet access capabilities possibly use it for exchanging text messages, but maybe not for surfing. Some people may buy PDAs for general web surfing or to access an intranet, but it's more likely that they buy the devices to run personal productivity applications such as general e-mail and personal information managers (PIMs).

Whatever the case, you have to build applications that conform to people's vision of what they want to do with the device they bought, not your assumptions. Steve Cox of OpenGrid believes that your application has to fit into what people expect to do in their daily lives. "If a person is not convinced that he or she wants to pay your bills through a website, then he or she is not going to do it on a wireless device. You have to make an extra effort these days to determine what is appropriate because wireless users are a small segmented market and the technology is in its beginning stages."

To fully divorce yourself from desktop thinking you also have to seriously consider how people are using the devices at the time you communicate with them. Sergeant Ed Koler, who develops wireless applications for the Pough-keepsie Police Department, spends days with the officers who use the applications in the field to understand what they're doing and thinking at the time data is being collected or delivered to them.

For example, Koler's department might use an application that was designed for people to record and track crime scene evidence while sitting at desktops when they have all the time they need and access written crime reports. But officers in the field may have to enter data wirelessly on a PDA while walking around the crime scene. Their demands are different because they are using a PDA, and only have a few minutes to enter data because they need to race off to another call. Because this work environment is more frantic, officers are distracted and they have fewer resources to work with, the wireless application will have to operate differently from the desktop software, even though the information has to feed into the same database.

The staff at Lot21 is excited about the potential of location-based services that deliver wireless content to people that is specifically for the recipients' physical location (i.e., in front of an auto dealer, at the public library, at a rock concert). But even though you know where people are and their general demographic data, "you still have to focus on mindset of the people at the time you communicate with them," states Lot21 CEO Kate Everett-Thorp. "Is the thirty-year-old mother of a baby accessing the Net with her PDA to read about teething or about financial services? Was the person we pinged with a message when he or she passed a billboard walking or driving? Don't become fixated on a mobile device for the device's sake, but look at how people are using them."

This issue of the recipient's frame of mind is important. It is probably the most vexing challenge of delivering wireless content to general consumers since you know less about their behavior than the people who work for you. The Carolina Hurricane hockey team used a location-based based service to select people within a certain geographic area to send ads to, but also factored in what websites people were browsing to further determine if it was the appropriate timing to send the ads. You will have to put some thought into how (or if) your organization will try to meet this challenge.

Look at the Big Technology Picture

Finally, you have to continually view wireless technology within the bigger picture of all of the technology that your organization uses for the various business processes you are trying to enhance or replace. Despite what you might read, wireless is usually not a technology that solves problems by itself, but one that integrates with other technologies. What other products at your offices or at your customers' locations have to work with your wireless applications (e.g., web servers, desktop computers, intranets, business software, etc.)?

Sometimes a department will buy a technology product with a myopic intent to solve a single problem, such as a wireless field service tracking program, without realizing that it may not integrate with other technology within the organization. Once the tracking program is bought, installed, and running, someone discovers that the data it collects won't work with the accounting software that has to bill customers for the service provided. As improbable as such a scenario may seem, it happens more times than you would expect.

If you want to maximize your investment for wireless implementations, you need to consider not only the other technologies that are in place throughout your organization, but also what technologies might become prevalent in the upcoming year or two. For example, will you be able to take the data generated by applications that you put in place now and migrate it to CRM applications that might be next year's market leader? This type of assessment and forward thinking is time consuming, but vital to your success.

Executive Participation Is Not an Option, It's Mandatory

Many web initiatives fell short of their potential benefits to the organizations, and continue to fall short, because of the lack of top executive vision and direction. If you do not have the enthusiastic buy-in of the senior executive team for wireless implementation, particularly the president and the person who signs the checks, your successes will be limited. You will not reap the full potential that wireless technologies offer.

I have watched this scenario unfold up close and personal. A manager or maybe even a worker with initiative approaches senior management with some great ideas for wireless. This person either gets shot down outright and the plan never sees the light of day, or the person gets a passive approval and the top execs don't think about it any more.

That lack of top-level interest prevents widespread acceptance and cooperation from line managers as well as rank-and-file employees. This in turn prevents the necessary resources from being committed. It also results in a lack of political support, which is the kiss of death when the inevitable roadblocks to progress pop up. Then there is the problem of people underachieving because they have a narrow view of the organization's needs, and none of the senior execs are available to broaden that view. Subsequently, the application isn't used to solve as many problems as it could because the employee doesn't see the big picture.

Conversely, many of the organizations that are producing impressive results with wireless applications are doing so because they have that top-level support. There are a number of ways of getting this vital support, and I will explore some of them in Chapter 14. However you decide to tackle the issue, you have to get the executives front and center cheerleading for the wireless cause. And if you're the top kahuna of which I speak, step willingly and aggressively into the breach.

Management participation does not stop at the executive suite, though. The department and business unit managers hold key positions in any major wireless initiative that you will undertake. They must have vision and provide the direction for how wireless can enhance their departments' respective operations. These managers must also coordinate cross-departmental efforts.

Later, when I discuss tactics, keep in mind that hierarchical and compartmentalized business organizational structures are evolving to flattened, interdepartmental, cooperative operations. Internet and wireless technologies collectively will speed this transformation, and the line managers are responsible for ensuring that the troops maximize the opportunities resulting from these changes.

If you are successful at engaging the necessary support and participation from senior executives and line managers, the employees will execute the tactical plans more effectively, which benefits everyone in the organization. They will have clear direction and (hopefully) the confidence that comes from knowing that those at the top care about what the workers are doing.

At this point, you should have a clearer focus on the communication value of wireless and what you need to do to implement effective wireless strategies and tactics. Let's look at the specifics of developing a plan best suited to your organization's needs. Readiness is all.

PART II

Strategic Options

Pull out the calculators and prepare to begin some hard-core calculating because these next chapters on strategy development will enable you to take the first steps in defining the ROI possibilities that wireless technology holds for your organization.

You may remember this IBM e-commerce ad from a few years ago. A guy walks in to see his manager and the manager asks the guy to explain the value of their Internet effort—and in terms that management can understand. There's a pause that stops your breathing while you watch the guy get a look of serious consternation. Then he relaxes and says simply, "For every dollar we put into the Internet we get two dollars back."

The camera shifts to the manager's face, on which there is a look of satisfaction and salvation because he has everything he needs to face the rest of management. In my ideal world, you should be able to state just as simply and just as powerfully your organization's purpose for using wireless technology after you finish reading this book.

At the very least, when you finish reading about the four strategic dimensions of this powerful methodology and begin applying them to your organization, you should be able to answer these questions:

- Where are we going with this wireless technology?
- Why are we going there?
- How will we know when we get there?

Then you can tackle the remaining chapters and begin developing specific tactics that will help you successfully reach your objectives.

Each of the strategic dimensions relates to a key aspect of your business operations and shows how wireless communication can impact your bottom line. They are:

1. Communicating with existing customers

2. Providing more effective service and support

3. Communicating with prospective customers

4. Developing more effective internal communication

By applying wireless technology to these business functions, you should be able to significantly reduce costs, improve your cash flow, and increase your organization's productivity and operating efficiency. Each strategic dimension will provide you with guidelines for developing a strategy that meets your business needs, as well as a way to establish milestones by which you can measure six or twelve months later the financial impact of your wireless activities.

Your organization may not have a need for all four dimensions, or you may find that it is better to give each one a different priority and timeline for implementation so you don't overwhelm your resources. And it is possible you may decide that now isn't the time to implement any wireless capabilities. But you should examine and weigh each dimension so you have a complete picture of your options and opportunities.

Strategic Dimensions Defined

Each strategic dimension addresses an aspect of your operation that can have a significant measurable and positive impact on your organization.

1. *Communicating with Existing Customers.* Customers are the most valuable assets you have. If you can increase your customer retention, the benefits go straight to the bottom line. It's easier and less expensive to reach customers to sell them something else than to close a sale with a prospect who has never done business with you before. Also, existing customers are the most effective source of referral leads, and they can unleash the most incredible word of mouth campaigns that are hard to match even with expensive communication efforts.

Wireless communication to customers has the added value of being a cheaper and faster way to communicate than other methods you have available to you. You can justify some wireless expenditure in this area just by the amount of money you save over conventional communication costs. I know of one distributor of building materials who could save about $7,000 per customer by having contractors in the field order products using wireless devices rather than faxing and phoning in orders. Faxes are often illegible so the wrong items are sometimes shipped, or the distributor's staff has to call repeatedly before they can reach contractors to clarify or confirm orders.

It is important to realize that "customers" are more than the consumers and business people who buy and use your products. Your customers can be journalists, investors, retailers, donors, and business partners who have already "bought" your product, but you need to frequently sell them on what's new at your organization. There is a cost for communicating with these customers conventionally, and wireless technology can reduce these costs.

2. Providing More Effective Service and Support. Though service and support is often directed to customers, it has become such an important business tool to help organizations differentiate themselves from competitors that it deserves to stand alone as a strategic option. Also, service is a key factor in turning prospects into customers, as well as creating opportunities to generate referral leads.

If your organization is in the governmental or nonprofit sector, service is most likely the primary purpose for which it exists, so this can easily become the most compelling reason to implement wireless applications.

Delivering service and support also can be quite expensive, so tools such as wireless technology that reduce these costs without lowering the quality are quite valuable. However, with the limitations of mobile devices, you will more likely provide support for routine, simple service problems rather than for those requiring extensive help.

3. Communicating with Prospects. Communicating to prospective customers is really about lowering the costs and speeding up the time of your sales cycles by helping prospects shop more effectively for your products or services. You really don't care if people buy from you through a cell phone, from a sales clerk holding a PDA, or by sending their orders via smoke signals. Wireless communication is also about expanding your reach, even when budgets are tight.

In these early days of wireless, there is little proactive wireless searching by prospects for information. So using wireless to reach this audience will have to be part of a larger communication campaign. Combine conventional and web-based communication to introduce yourself to prospects, then employ wireless to maintain an active long-term dialogue until the prospects actually buy.

While it would be nice to get prospects to buy from you through a mobile device, the main focus of this strategic dimension is to determine how to guide people down a path, then give them every option (including wireless) to make the actual transaction. As with existing customers, "prospects" include journalists, retailers, and others interested in doing business with you for the first time, including prospective new employees.

4. *Developing More Effective Internal Communication.* Internal communication is important because your employees are as valuable as your customers, and it's not cheap to maintain the proper care and feeding of these people (metaphorically speaking). The Internet and intranets have done a lot to reduce communication costs and make employees more efficient. Wireless promises to take communication and efficiency to even greater new heights, not only for making people more productive, but to enable you to better manage your physical assets.

Wireless technology can significantly reduce the time it takes for a variety of executives and employees (both mobile and those located on the premises) to complete tasks, and it often increases the quality of their work. Mobile workers potentially will have anytime, anywhere access to greater amounts of information. You can also increase the speed with which your organization resolves problems, responds to customer needs, and capitalizes on new business opportunities.

Internal communication often goes to more than just employees. There are contractors and even vendors who become so important to your operations that they're a vital element of your business structure. Subsequently, it may be valuable for your wireless strategy for employees to include these important business partners. Your strategy also could include embedding wireless devices in physical assets such as vehicles, equipment, and products coming off the assembly line, even the business software running on your servers.

As I go through each one of these strategic options in detail in the upcoming chapters, I will show you how to estimate the potential financial impact each can have on your organization and establish benchmarks for assessing the progress of your wireless efforts. It's important to look at all four options so you can see all of the possibilities for applying wireless technology in your company, then prioritize them in order of value that they potentially can deliver to you.

If you're not working in a large organization, you should still review these options because even the smallest organization can benefit at some level from one or two of these strategic dimensions. I will provide examples and scenarios to show how strategic implementations might differ depending the size of your organization or whether you are in the commercial, government, or nonprofit sector.

Once you have a clear picture of which strategic options make the most sense, you can better determine which tactics will best help you reach your objectives. Let's take an in-depth look at how you can communicate more effectively and profitably with your current customers.

CHAPTER 3

Communicating with Existing Customers

Although we're talking about wireless technology, much of the content that customers will access through mobile devices will come from Internet or intranet sites. It is therefore helpful to discuss the three collectively. For many organizations, if they can improve certain aspects of their websites, it can only help their wireless efforts.

Determine if This Is the Right Strategic Dimension for You

Whether or not you should pursue this strategic option depends on determining if you have the right type of customers. Ask yourself the following questions about your customers:

- Do my customers travel a lot?
- Are my customers away from their desks (or at least desktop computers) for significant periods of time even when they're at their place of work?
- Are my customers the kind of people who need to have information immediately and at all times?
- Do my customers lead a social lifestyle in which they're always on the move?
- Are my customers part of a professional or social crowd that considers it hip to have a mobile phone or PDA?
- Do my customers have web-accessible mobile devices?

A "yes" answer to any of these questions is good impetus to consider developing wireless communication strategies to reach this audience, particularly for the first two questions. The more questions that you answer in the affirmative, the stronger the case that can be made for wireless, as you will see in the upcoming pages.

These questions stem from a point I presented in the last chapter: You have to focus on what it is that people are doing when you expect or want to communicate with them wirelessly. Executives and managers who travel a lot, or workers who spend a lot of time away from their desks, are the type of people who need access to information immediately and are in situations in which wireless is the best way to get that access. Let's look at some other factors that make wireless a viable strategy.

Location and Context

Location and context are important factors in assessing the value of wireless strategies. When customers are most in need of your add-on products or services, are mobile devices the best or only way for them to reach you? If so, and these are customers who will buy from you several times a year or month, give them mobile devices if they don't already have them. If you sell clothing, entertainment, and other general consumer products, customers who have a mobile, social lifestyle often might be doing activities which put them in a receptive mind-set to receive messages about movie tickets, new shoes, or a special vacation packages.

Gathering Knowledge in a Hurry

While doing their jobs, are customers frequently acquiring knowledge in a hurry (industry trends, competitive data, etc.)? If so, then subscribe to Avant-Go's service that lets you set up and automatically deliver the wireless equivalent of a cable TV channel that you can program with whatever you want. For example, you can create a free channel with content related to customers' professions, such as updates on tax laws if they are accountants. Customers will subscribe to the channel if they can derive value from the content, and you can intersperse ads for your organization within the content to create a fairly inexpensive customer retention tool (less than $6 per year per person).

Type of Business or Industry

You should also consider the type of business or industry that your organization is in, or the category of customer (e.g., resellers, journalists, or investors) you want to reach to determine whether you should pursue this particular wireless strategy. Here are some business and industry categories for which wireless offers value:

■ *Financial Services Companies.* Some of these companies often offer free PDAs if people sign up for their services. They know that the demographics of their likely customers (college-educated executives, managers, and professionals who are frequently mobile) are such that PDAs will be a good draw. They also know that there are many times when people want to do a stock trade or start a loan application process (such as sitting in the airport, waiting for a meeting to start, or riding the commuter train), but no other communication option is available or practical.

■ *Manufacturers and Distributors of Construction Products.* Companies in the construction industry also like the wireless option because contractors work all day on sites locations without access to fax lines or the Net. This holds true for any business that regularly supplies repair people, drivers, consultants, and people in other professions who are frequently on the move.

■ *Federal or State Government Agencies.* Government agencies do not sell products, but if the constituents for whom you provide services are city agencies whose employees are constantly mobile (such as building or food inspectors), wireless is a good way to deliver the data they need. Wireless access to state building codes, federal meat inspection guidelines, and other data that is too voluminous to carry or changes regularly can save money and make field workers' jobs easier.

■ *Nonprofit Organizations.* This business segment is often ignored by technology providers. But the customers, patrons, and donors of nonprofit organizations are often mobile executives and professionals who may be receptive to wireless messages about concerts, new art exhibits, or fundraising drives. Some nonprofits such as the American Red Cross, in addition to providing services directly to people who need it, also provide services through emergency personnel, health care officials, volunteers, and other individuals who are mobile. For them, and organizations like them, wireless is a good strategy to increase efficiency and reduce costs.

■ *Retailers.* If retailers comprise one of your categories of customers, you know that their employees are often only mobile within the aisles of their stores. Nevertheless, retailers still can justify an investment in wireless communication. Most personnel in retail rarely have Net access and almost never have enough time to learn as much about your product as you would like them to. Delivering wireless content at the time their customers have a question can help retail clerks close more sales.

■ *Journalists.* Journalists on deadline when writing about your company are not in the mood for playing telephone tag. Journalists using wireless devices with instant messaging capabilities can close the information loop quickly, get the facts they want from you, and as a result, your organization can come out looking good.

Know Your Customers

It will help you evaluate the viability of using wireless applications and promotional or other activities to communicate with customers if you understand the demographics of PDA adoption and usage within your customer base.

The easiest way to do this is to survey your customers. If many of your customers are not using wireless devices, then you have to determine if it is worth the effort to distribute these devices or spend time and money to convince customers to use the devices for communicating with you. Some of the calculations that are recommended in the following pages will help you do this.

Another way to get a handle on how, or if, your customers are using wireless devices is to retain industry research firms such as the IDC, Gartner, and Jupiter Media Metrix that track this type of data. For fees that range from a few thousand dollars to tens of thousands of dollars, you can buy prepared reports (the low end of the fee spectrum) or have these firms do custom research of your customer base and/or the markets your customers represent. Telephia is an exclusively wireless market research firm that does detailed surveys of wireless users every six months. Given the speed at which things change in this industry, you want a firm like this that keeps frequent tabs on real users of technology, a task that many companies don't do nearly enough.

It is also good to observe what other organizations in your industry are doing so you can pick up valuable lessons from people who have been through the ups and downs of implementing wireless applications. That applies when considering all strategic options.

Many of the stories I will present can be modified and enhanced for larger or smaller organizations, as well as for organizations in different industries As you review each story look for ideas that expand your strategic thinking and the creativity of the people around you. Also observe how some organizations determine their ROI for their wireless efforts. Some results rely on cut-and-dried financial numbers, other results are less tangible but still very compelling.

Customer characteristics and categories are important criteria to help you determine if this is a strategic dimension that you want to pursue since they give you an idea if customers might be receptive to wireless communication. However, those of you who live by the phrase "show me the money" may want to get down into the nitty-gritty of evaluating the specific financial impact that this and the other strategic dimensions can have on your organization. Let's look at some of the potential financial benefits.

Calculate the Financial Impact of Communicating Effectively with Customers

How much is it worth to your organization to implement wireless solutions? For each strategic dimension I will provide you with some parameters for calculating the possible financial impact of wireless technology. It's not a complex process, but it may require a lot of brainwork by you and department or business unit managers involved in the project. During this exercise you may think of other calculations to add. Go for it! The idea here is that the calculation process should conform to the specific needs of your organization.

When you finish, you will have an idea of the potential financial benefits each strategic dimension offers your business. These figures also will help you create milestones so that six or twelve months after you implement your wireless plan you can measure your level of success. The numbers that you come up with here will help you determine how much you will actually want to spend on your wireless applications. When you are calculating the financial impact of a wireless project, you must consider all customer groups that would be affected by the project including regular customers, resellers, journalists, investors, and business partners.

I use generic estimates for these calculations and those in the upcoming chapters, but there will be a calculator in the online supplement in which you can input your own data to generate financial estimates specific to your organization.

Regular Customers (Those Who Buy Your Products)

Let's start with your regular paying customers and determine how much you are currently spending per year on conventional communications activities targeted primarily to customers to build and maintain loyalty and generate add-on sales. Then we'll explore how wireless may be able to reduce some of these costs. Costs for activities aimed primarily to prospective customers, even though some existing customers may view the same material, will be addressed in Chapter 5.

What are your annual costs for each of these activities? (Write down the amounts.)

- Print materials (brochures, newsletters, etc.)
- Direct mail (postage, materials, creative) and special promotions such as contests and discount sales
- Telemarketing, including staff and phone costs
- Hosted seminars/conferences
- Advertising specifically for customers (placement, creative, copywriting)
- Administrative costs such as support personnel and project management

These costs collectively represent your total annual customer communication costs. What is the total amount you are spending annually for customer communications?

Next you want to determine approximately how many customers you have that do business with you on a regular basis (at least once or twice a year). For business-to-business companies, you may sell to a department or an entire organization that has 500 employees, but each department or business collectively represents one customer. For government and nonprofit groups substitute constituents, clients, or patrons for "customers."

Finally, divide the total annual customer communication costs by the number of customers and you will see how much you are spending per customer to maintain communication with them. Can you eliminate or significantly reduce the total cost per customer for conventional communication if you can beam the same information to customers wirelessly? For example, if you're spending $1,000 per year per customer to reach them through direct mail, telemarketing, and special promotions, maybe you can eliminate $200 in direct mail and telemarketing costs, and lower special promotions costs by $100.

If many customers have PDAs or other mobile devices, it's easier to make a straightforward case for using wireless communication. But if they don't have mobile devices, consider giving these customers a PDA should you find that you can reduce per-person costs by $200 (the current cost of some PDAs with Internet access) or more. It's possible that, even after adding costs for developing and delivering wireless content, the overall investment will pay for itself within a year or two. If giving away PDAs gives your CFO heart palpitations, do some research to determine how many of your customers own PDAs, will soon own them, or can be motivated to buy PDAs.

Are there other areas in which wireless can reduce the costs of doing business with your customers? For one thing, you have the costs of transacting the sales of additional products. In many industries, the costs of dealing with customers who call to place orders, faxed orders that require call backs to decipher illegible writing, and a myriad of other factors, drove companies to build websites and intranets. This online effort can save as much as thousands of dollars per customer each year, and wireless-enabling this content can further increase savings.

Once you establish these numbers, calculate how much it will cost to use activities such as direct mail or promotional inserts in invoices to motivate customers to do business with you wirelessly, and also the costs for delivering wireless content. You may have to finish reading the chapters on tactics before you can determine that last cost.

You may have to do a lot of estimating for these costs since we're going into mostly uncharted waters, and there will be a lot of trial and error. However, it is better to have some reasonable estimates that you can refine each month rather than to go into this without due consideration. And since a lot of what happens interactively can be measured almost immediately, you won't get too far into a wireless project before you'll have feedback that can help you adjust your estimates.

If, after you finish doing all of calculations and estimate cost savings, the numbers favor moving in the wireless direction, you should have a set of statements to place in your wireless business plan that read much like following statements:

- We have 2,500 customers. Each year we spend $875,000 total dollars for conventional communication such as direct mail, telephone calls, and customer-specific vertical market advertising, plus the staff time to implement these activities. These costs average $350 per customer.
- Our marketing team determined that we can reduce the communication cost per customer to $150 if we deliver the same information wirelessly for a maximum saving of $500,000 in total communication costs if we get all of our customers on wireless devices. The $150 amount includes the cost of developing and delivering wireless content.
- Based on our marketing team's assessment, we plan to spend $10,000 on a direct mail and telemarketing campaign to get 20 percent of our customers using wireless devices so we can communicate with them and save $100,000 per year. This investment in wireless will pay for itself within two months. In addition, we plan to distribute PDAs to an additional 500 customers. This investment will pay for itself in one year, and begin saving us $100,000 per year thereafter.

Now that you've calculated the savings you can achieve by communicating wirelessly with your regular customers, you need to use these same calculations to determine the value of wireless to reach your other types of customers.

Resellers

How much are you currently spending per year on conventional communications with resellers (distributors, retailers) to keep them informed about your company, convince them to stock new products, and to build and maintain their loyalty? When you calculate these costs, do not include expenditures for tactics that support the effort of resellers to sell and support your products (i.e., in-store promo materials, training). These should be addressed with the strategic option regarding providing effective service and support.

The list of expenditures may differ from company to company, but the most common include print materials, direct mail, and telemarketing to explain why they should carry your new product lines. You may have special promotions to get dealers to buy more products per order, multimedia presentations about new markets you plan to open, tradeshow meetings to renew contacts, and administrative costs.

Using the same exercise outlined for regular customers, calculate your total annual communication costs, the average cost per reseller, the estimated amount you can save per reseller if you use wireless, and the cost of moving resellers to wireless communication. You should come up with statements similar to the following to place in your wireless business plan.

- We have 400 resellers and each year we spend $92,000 total dollars for conventional communication, or $230 per reseller. We have identified $3,000 per reseller in additional expenses such as processing orders and tracking shipments.
- It is possible to reduce the communication cost per reseller to $130 by delivering materials wirelessly rather than through direct mailings and printed materials such as newsletters. We will do this by spending $1,000 per resellers, or $400,000, to give all of our resellers infrared stations so we can push content to the stations that the personnel can then access with PDAs. Though it will take quite a few years to recover the investment in terms of cost savings, with the stations we can afford to communicate with resellers three or four times a week rather than just once a month.
- We will build and wireless enable an intranet to facilitate product ordering and reduce other transaction costs, which will save us $2,600 per reseller each year. Our investment in this wireless implementation will pay for itself in six to eight months.

Journalists

Communication with journalists also has overhead costs that may be reduced through the use of wireless technology. Get together with your PR people to work through the same series of calculations to determine how much you are currently spending on conventional communications with journalists and industry analysts with whom you already have relationships. This amount varies by company and industry.

It may turn out that you only work with a dozen or so journalists, or you only contact them two or three times a year, and these numbers do not merit developing separate wireless content just for them. But when you build applications such as an AvantGo channel for reaching other customers, maybe you should alert your media contacts about how to access this material if they have mobile devices.

In any case, here are some of the customary PR expenses that you may be able to reduce or eliminate through wireless communication. Print materials such as press kits and briefing papers can easily be sent wirelessly to journalists who agree to this mode of delivery, saving materials, mailing, and faxing costs. When wireless technology advances, wireless video conferencing or chat room capabilities could reduce the number of press tours and the related costs for travel, executives' time (assign monetary value to hours spent traveling, in meetings, etc.), and presentation materials production.

Investors and Business Partners

Investors and business partners are two other customer groups that you may be able to communicate with using wireless technology in such a way that it reduces some of your other communication costs. If you follow the same procedure of breaking down all of your conventional communication costs, determine if you can deliver some portion of that information wirelessly.

Increasing Revenue per Customer

Some of you will find that, for various reasons, there isn't a lot to be gained in terms of cost reductions by communicating wirelessly with customers. Perhaps your customer base is not that large, or maybe you have already cut a lot of costs by communicating with them through your website rather than with conventional means. In that case, consider how much you can improve your bottom line by increasing customer retention and customer referrals.

Let's look at the financial implications of wireless communication as a customer retention tool. Around 1998, customer relationship management

(CRM) started to become a popular term in business circles because companies realized that if they spent more effort keeping customers around longer, profits would increase. You have (or should have) good customer contact information. Subsequently, existing customers should be easier and less expensive to reach than potential customers. They are already familiar with you and hopefully like your company and product, so they will be more likely than first-time customers to communicate with you and buy additional products or services using technology such as wireless.

The first step in calculating the value of customer retention, since you have already calculated how many customers you have, is to estimate how much each one is worth to you annually in terms of additional products and services they buy from you. In some cases, people don't necessarily buy a new product every year, such as cars, refrigerators, and other big-ticket items but they may buy accessories and services. A faster printer to go with a computer or more powerful speakers to complement a car stereo system, for example.

Next, estimate the average amount of time that a customer hangs in there as your customer. Is it several months, a year, 3.25 years? Finally, calculate what would the bottom-line impact on your business be if these customers relationships lasted twice or three times as long. This little exercise is simple but potent. For example, if you find that the average customer relationship lasts only two years and customers spend $3,000 per year, increasing customer retention by 50 percent (one year) adds $3,000 per customer to your balance sheet. Assuming you close 2,500 customers this year, increasing customer retention by 50 percent equals $7.5 million of additional income after three years.

Using wireless communication may not be the sole contributor to increasing customer retention, or the contribution that wireless makes may be much less than 50 percent, 5 percent or 10 percent perhaps. Every organization is going to produce different numbers when they estimate income and predict potential increases in customer retention. However, because you can track income as well as the results that your wireless activities generate, you can establish quantifiable customer retention goals and measure how effectively wireless helps you reach these goals.

You may add a sentence to the "Objectives" section of your wireless business plan that is similar to the following statement: We have 2,500 customers and, after their initial purchase, each one spends an average of $3,000 every year with us for an average of two years. Our goal is to execute a long-term campaign to deliver wireless promotional coupons that increase our customer retention by 25 percent, resulting in $1,500 of additional revenue per customer or $3.75 million.

Now, let's look at another element of the retention issue, getting customers to buy more while they're staying with you longer.

Knowing your customer better than you know your own family and understanding your products or services as well as your most cherished personal possessions, how much more can you sell to your customers if you leverage the power of wireless anywhere, anytime communication with your customers? For example, research may show that customers' average monthly spending for your home improvement tools, supplies, and so forth is $250. So you set up a "Tips for Home Improvement" channel on AvantGo that includes coupons for various products associated with these tips, and as a result increase monthly spending to $312.50 (a 25 percent increase).

By increasing the amount of time that customers stay with you, and also increasing how much they spend with you on a monthly or annual basis, you can establish some significant potential revenue increases. Until you implement a wireless communication campaign, the costs and the impact of wireless on these numbers may be purely speculative. But again, this is fine because it is better to have some general estimates when launching a wireless effort than having little or no clue as to what you should expect. A pilot program is a good way to test the waters for a limited amount of investment, analyze results, and then adjust your expectations accordingly.

Doing these calculations to determine how much wireless technology can impact customer retention and spending per customer can benefit some nonprofits such as museums, symphonies, and educational institutions. These organizations are identical to commercial entities in that they have paying customers, plus they have donors, patrons, and others who live (and die) to give them money. Explore wireless as a way to increase retention and the amount of spending from these customer groups.

By the way, some factors can reduce your ability to retain customers for which wireless cannot compensate, such as people moving away of your region or out of the demographic (e.g., age, income, etc.) that defines your market. These can affect your calculations. Also, many financial considerations go into deciding the value of retaining customers, such as the cost and profit margins of products that customers buy after their initial purchase. But the calculations that I've recommended here are a foundation to get you started. Add or alter them as necessary to meet your specific needs.

Increasing Customer Referrals

Increasing customer retention and spending produces a revenue and profitability increase, but equal attention should be given to increasing the number of sales leads that customers refer. While you have to spend more time to close sales to referral leads than existing customers, it will require less effort than closing sales with prospects who have never spoken with any of your customers.

I worked for Metricom, the company that sold the Ricochet wireless Internet access service, and one of the most phenomenal aspects of the company was that existing customers referred 50 percent of new customers. And this happened for a long time with little effort by Metricom to actively promote referrals. These referrals were "slam dunk" sales—just answer the phones and take the orders.

Your organization likely has the potential to generate a similar level of success if you put some attention to converting customers into your "in the trenches" sales force. I will discuss the mechanics of doing this wirelessly when I discuss communicating to prospective customers, but to determine the potential financial impact of referral generation, consider the following equation. Of course, the real value to these referrals is not how many you generate but how many of them that actually close, which is information that your marketing should have available.

To determine the potential financial impact of using wireless to increase customer referrals, start by calculating how may referrals you are currently generating per customer. For the benefit of this discussion, let's say that each of your 2,500 customers will refer an average of five leads during the two years that the customer has a relationship with you, and two of these leads (40 percent) usually become customers. Since we've already determined in the previous calculations that customers spend an average of $6,000 for two years, closing two referral leads represents $12,000 in addition to the revenue from their initial product purchase.

After reviewing these numbers, you may decide that you want to wirelessly deliver special incentive promotions that triple the number of referral leads from 5 to 15 per customer, and also double the close rate to 80 percent, producing 12 new customers. When you do the math and determine how much additional income your specific organization can produce by increasing the number of referrals per customer, this should help you decide if you want to use wireless communication for this purpose.

As with the previous calculations, when you finish you should be able to state the financial impact you expect your wireless efforts to product, and also use these same figures to establish the benchmarks for measuring your success. For example, your statement might read something like this: We have budgeted $50,000 for a wireless communication campaign to increase our customer referral leads from 5 to 15 by year two of the campaign. If our customer referrals increase to ten per customer by the end of the campaign's first year, we will be successful at that point. If customer referrals reach or exceed 15 per customers by the end of the second year, the campaign will be a success.

This financial exercise is applicable to government organizations and non-profit organizations as much as commercial ones, even though customers may not necessarily have a direct income value. A government health program may determine that wireless communication is a success if it reduces the costs of distributing information to users of the service from $200 per year to $125 per year. A nonprofit may similarly feel its campaign is successful if wireless promotions to donors result in donors referring 50 percent more people who volunteer their time to the organization.

Once you finish gauging the potential financial benefits of wireless for communicating with customers, and if this proves to be a viable opportunity for you, establish the strategic objectives that will drive your tactical planning. Since there may be several financial goals worth pursuing, you should narrow these down to the two or three that are most practical given your resources and make them your primary strategic objectives. The next section presents three that might make your final list.

Main Strategic Objectives

There are three objectives I recommend pursuing with wireless technology if you decide this strategic dimension is important:

1. Reduce the cost of communicating with customers

2. Increase referrals of new customers

3. Increase customer retention

These objectives give you simple goals that you can reach quickly to prove the long-term viability of wireless on a broader scale. You can add more or substitute objectives for ones for the ones listed, but these three will jump-start the planning process.

Cost Reduction

The value of wireless as a cost reduction tool can be summed up simply—it is more times than not cheaper to send information wirelessly than it is to use print, faxes, telephones, radio, television, and other forms of conventional communication. At one level, web-delivered content may be cheaper than content delivered wirelessly, but customers are often in places where Internet access is difficult or impossible. Wireless fills that void.

Some of the cost savings of wireless come from being able to communicate more frequently with the same budget you are using for conventional methods, and not having to wait for days or weeks to get messages to customers and receive product orders from them.

When you read through the chapters on tactics, keep your list of customer communication expenses handy. As you cover key points and get ideas from the stories about other organizations' wireless implementations, see how they can work to reduce or eliminate expenses. The following story describes how one company tackled one of those universal burdens on the budget.

Meetings—The Challenge

One of the more costly aspects of communication with customers is the meeting. Whether you sell products or services, whether you're a government agency with constituents across town or across the country, meetings can be the expensive bane of your existence.

Depending on how often you have them and how many people you have to send to them, the costs can rise. If you can't use wireless technology to eliminate meetings, at least you can use the technology to help them run more efficiently.

Analysts International is a technology consulting firm that has meetings, a lot of them. Collaboration and fast-paced decision making with clients are a way of life. In those meetings it's often necessary to access databases which, before getting wireless technology, required the staff and managers to use laptop PCs to dial into the firm's network. But since remote dial up was inconvenient and distracting, the staff would conduct the meetings without having the data access they needed. Decisions requiring database information were postponed and information collected from meetings had to be input back at the home office.

By replacing employees' laptops with Palm mobile devices, an improvement in meeting efficiency and eliminating redundant work paid for the devices within a few weeks. After that, PDA use represented pure cost savings. In addition, it made a great impression on clients to see Analysts' staff (who used to show up with piles of paper, calculators and so forth) come in with only a Palm. At the end of meetings the staff just synchronized the devices through a wireless connection with the home office databases to upload information from the meeting.

During meetings the staff can link to Analysts' Lotus Notes for CRM, PIM, e-mail, and other applications. The user interface for the applications are set up so the staff can use checklists and menus to quickly capture critical data during meetings, and then make that data available to the entire Analysts International organization.

For this company, the decision was a fairly easy one to make. They identified a problem and could quantify enough of the costs of postponed decisions and cost redundancy so that determining ROI wasn't difficult. They also could show that giving mobile staff $1,000 desktops and $300 Palms saved $1,700 over the $3,000 laptops that the company had previously issued. The Palms are all the staff needs in the field, and they can synchronize the devices with the desktop when they get back to the office so individuals can complete the more complex computing tasks.

Developing and deploying wireless integration with Notes and other applications was done in-house in less than 30 days, and that cost was easy to amortize across the entire mobile workforce. Analysts' IT group was able to train each staff person in an hour and there was no resistance by the staff toward the mobile devices.

If customer meetings are a way of life for a lot of people in your organization, here is one area where wireless can knock down some of the cost. With a network like Ricochet in place that will enable the data speeds necessary to do video conferencing, you have the potential to eliminate a number of face-to-face meetings altogether.

Additional Ways to Reduce Costs

Sometimes organizations don't pursue certain communication activities or eliminate other activities as a way to reduce costs. Wireless can allow you to change the way you reach out to customers so you maintain communication but save money. For example, keeping customers informed about new developments, particularly if there is an air of urgency to these developments. If you sell artificial limbs to doctors, you probably want to alert them as soon as possible if you discover a defect that causes these limbs to suddenly rotate at the joints without reason or warning. Wireless lets you communicate with the doctors quickly without having to worry about the communication costs.

Sometimes the value of wireless is not that you can update customers with news about your organization, but that you can alert them about something vitally important because you know their interests or professions. For example, if you're the San Francisco Symphony's PR director and 10,000 of your patrons use PDAs and mobile phones, you can alert them to an art gallery auction that you just found out about, or remind them about a PBS special on Beethoven that's on television tonight. With wireless messages, you can add these kinds of communication activities without adding to your budget.

Gathering valuable feedback from customers so you can provide better products, services, and marketing to them should be a mainstay at every organization, but often this is not the case because of the high expense of conventional research. If you know your customers have mobile devices, use wireless technology to deliver quick (three or four questions) surveys that they can complete and zip right back to you. By combining your website and wireless content, you can create a system that enables you to solicit AND respond to feedback within hours for just pennies per contact.

Generate and Increase Customer Referrals

There is no better sales opportunity than the person referred to your organization by a happy customer. You know from personal experience that you're more likely to buy a product that a friend or colleague recommends than one that is pitched to you by a complete stranger who calls you at dinnertime. And there is no greater (or less expensive) sales force than a band of rabid customers singing your praises. Subsequently, using wireless to increase referrals should be one of your primary objectives. Not only are referral leads well-qualified and motivated to buy, you can start seeing results from a good referral campaign within a few weeks.

Have you ever listened to teenagers talking on mobile phones? Or watched people at conferences or business meetings walk up to other people and point their PDAs at each other like *Star Trek* crew members taking tricorder readings (they're exchanging business cards through infrared ports)? These are a couple of market segments that live and die to communicate through these devices, which makes them natural vehicles for referral campaigns.

The first step of a good wireless referral campaign is to deliver messages to your customers that give them an incentive to refer you to their friends, family, or business colleagues. Even though this is a technology-based campaign, you often have to rely on the usual conventional incentives to get them to take action—free products, discounts, or bonus points redeemable for gifts, to name a few. But that's okay if the value of the qualified sales lead exceeds the cost of the incentives. These incentives can be promoted through coupons attached to product announcements and updates you may send customers wirelessly, ads delivered on AvantGo channels, or ads in your website content that customer access with mobile devices.

The second step is to get people to use their mobile devices to pass on the promo messages and generate the referral leads. Some of the businesses in countries (such as Japan) that are most successful are those that create support for their products among the teenagers who are trendsetters at their schools. The trendsetters, who are heavy users of voice and text messages on cell phones, promote the products to other teens and eventually to adults. Teens in the United States who use cell phones and voice or e-mail pagers can likewise be motivated to generate referral leads.

Adults can use their PDAs as part of the referral campaign by beaming your product messages to other PDA users through the infrared ports on the devices. Whether your customers receive your incentive messages when they synch the devices with their PCs, when they wirelessly connect to your content, or you beam it to them, be sure to include a promotional message that customers can pass on. There are websites that pop up a screen that says "Send this to a friend" and has a space for you to add an e-mail address. Once you add the address and hit "submit," a precomposed message is sent automatically. Consider adding a similar feature to your wireless content.

Increase Customer Retention

As part of the customer retention goal, you want to create a frequently used communication channel between you and your customers. If you and your customers start communicating once, twice, or more times a month, they aren't likely to leave you. Or if they do leave, it will be with enough warning that you should at least be able to make a good attempt to save the relationship.

To retain customers, you will need to deliver information or create a dialogue that builds loyalty. That means valuable information, even if it's not directly related to your company or product. While the wireless world at this moment doesn't allow you to build customer communities the same way as you can with chat rooms on the Net, you want to encourage customers to talk to other people they know using their mobile devices.

Customer Retention from Cradle to Grave

The following two stories illustrate the potential of embedding wireless devices inside of products to maintain an inexpensive communication link with customers to increase customer retention.

A Little Pot for Grandma

Japan's Zojirushi Corp. (www.mimamori.net) markets the i-pot, which is an Internet-enabled hot pot that dispenses boiling water for tea, to elderly people whose children live too far away to check in them regularly. Hot pots are common, everyday items in Japanese homes. But besides being a tea maker, i-pots send usage statistics to a website that tracks users' tea-drinking patterns. Apparently sudden changes in drinking patterns of people at this age can be a sign of a medical problem.

When the customer fills the i-pot with water, it sends a signal (using NTT DoCoMo's DoPa packet data communication service) to servers that create a report and post it to a website. The only customer data reported is the time the person turns on the machine, when he or she adds water, and how long the pot remains on, keeping the water warm. The person's children can either receive e-mail twice a day or check the website to see if there are any breaks in the pattern.

What lessons can we learn here? First, if you can incorporate a wireless application that requires little or no human intervention, which the i-pot does, you are well on your way to getting a lot of customers to use it. Second, if you track a minimal amount of data and only data related to using the product, you further increase the rate of use of the application. The higher the usage rate, the more profitable the investment will be for you.

Third, assuming you can be successful at the first two tasks, creating the ability to track how your product is used, or the condition of it as it gets older, can allow you to provide information that increases customer loyalty. For example, if you saw that an i-pot user went from one pint of tea to two quarts every Tuesday at 4:00 p.m., maybe the person isn't sick, just entertaining friends for a weekly tea party. You can then send the customer a short message to a small display screen on the i-pot asking if he or she wants to buy a lovely set of teacups and saucers.

If this seems a little too Orwellian for you, consider what the folks at Whirlpool have done, which is less intrusive.

Will It Go 'Round in Circles?

Whirlpool's commercial laundry products can interact with Palm handhelds to make it easier for owners and operators of laundromats to manage the machines. With this capability the owner can determine how frequently their machines are being used, or make changes such as increasing the cost for using hot water because of energy shortages and high overhead.

All an owner has to do is indicate what changes he or she wants to make using a custom PC software program he or she gets with the machines, synchronize the changes to the Palm handheld, then beam the information from the Palm's infrared port to the machine's electronic panel. Immediately, any cost changes are implemented and usage data is beamed back to the Palm handheld for later analysis.

In both of these products, the manufacturers are giving customers the ability to get more value from their product in fairly simple ways, but important enough to the customers (I am only guessing about the i-pot) to keep them using the products.

Give 'Em the Means

Previously I mentioned that one approach you may want to consider for strengthening the communication ties with customers is to give them mobile devices. Here are a couple of companies that are doing just that.

A Safeway in the U.K., Okay

Safeway supermarkets located in the United Kingdom gave 200 of their customers PDAs with little magnets on the back so they can attach the devices to refrigerators when the customers aren't using them outside of their homes. As people devour various items in the fridge, they can check these items on a list on the PDA to wirelessly order more food. Actually, software was designed for the PDAs that lists 20,000 products, so customers can create electronic lists of anything they want that Safeway carries.

This may seem like a risky venture by Safeway, but I think not. The convenience keeps customers loyal. Safeway can increase the amount of sales by sending special coupons based on previous buying patterns, or recipes that include not only items that people check, but also other ingredients that customers may not already have. And since customers still have to go to the store to pick up the orders, Safeway still gets all those impulse purchases that stores thrive on.

Some other benefits that Safeway gets from this effort is that they can stock products more effectively based on real-time information and advanced orders coming in from customers. Safeway can also generate referral customers by using special promotions ("Bring a friend, get a dozen free buffalo wings from the deli") and savings coupons that can be passed on to relatives and friends. These devices can provide a regular feedback channel by distributing regular surveys.

A Customer's Pledge to Fidelity

During that IPO madness of the 1990s, Fidelity Investments allowed their best customers to participate in IPOs as they were coming out. To adhere to all of the strict Securities and Exchange Commission regulations regarding trades, their investment representatives had to participate in about six phone calls back and forth to answer customers' questions.

To reduce some of that time overhead cost, customers were required to have a pager. Some of these IPO deals were priced after normal business hours, so the pagers made it was easy for customers to respond from wherever they happened to be when they got a message. If customers wanted in on a particular deal, they could send a request instantly and in a way that met all of the regulatory requirements for the communication with the customer.

Fidelity did well on three fronts with this activity. First, the company reduced the amount of time that their reps had to spend with each customer, which lowered overhead and increased revenues by enabling reps to deal with more customers in less time. Second, they provided a convenience for customers that enabled them to participate in more deals, earning Fidelity additional revenue.

Third, the convenience increased customer loyalty and increased the chances that customers would buy other Fidelity services. One word of caution, though, if you're thinking about implementing wireless along similar lines. Be sure that you provide ample guarantees of privacy because there will be some concerns about organizations using these devices to track customers' wireless activities.

Waiting for an Epiphany?

One of the major buzzwords (or buzz acronyms) these days is CRM (customer relationship management). It's as if people woke up in the new century and realized that keeping the customer satisfied was the most important thing in the world short of breathing. Not that it isn't important, but customer relationship management has been important since the beginning of time.

Part of your evaluation of wireless technology's potential to impact customer relationships should include a look at all of the ways in which you communicate with this audience. I believe the current popular phrase is "touch points." What are all of the touch points or instances where you contact customers or they contact your organization: incoming phone calls from customers, advertising, trade shows, contacts through resellers?

A leading vendor of products and services that help organizations monitor, manage, and maneuver in response to activities at the various customer touch points is Epiphany (www.epiphany.com). Along with professional services, they market a set of data mining, data warehouse, and other software tools that analyze customer profiles, transactions, and behaviors at many touch points: website, retail outlet, direct marketing campaigns, and in-bound calls, to name a few.

These applications create a profile of customers en masse or on an individual basis. They can analyze the data in terms of one event compared to many others, such as how many customers bought accessories after an e-mail offer compared to customer responses from all other marketing activities. Or they can analyze the results of the same marketing activity that occurred at different times of the year.

While data analysis is important, it's how the software responds to the analysis and the role that wireless can play in this response that help an organization define its wireless strategy. As customers communicate through the various touch points, Epiphany's software can use business rules and past data to determine what type of content or offer to send a customer, then tell the server that stores the offers and content to deliver "x," "y," or "z" information. The software could also determine that wireless is the best way to deliver the special offer because past data shows that the faster this customer receives an offer, the more likely she is to buy.

Another software feature can use computer telephony integration (CTI) to determine a response based on the value of the customer to the company. Based on software stored in its database, the software could place calls from heavy-spending customers higher in the queue or transfer these people to a specific agent who also receives a wireless alert with the customers' data, or the system can send information wirelessly to a retail salesperson (in response to a customer's wireless inquiry) telling them what action to take for a specific type of customer.

Whether you use Epiphany, their competitors' software, or build your own, it is important that you find a way to tie all of your conventional, web, AND wireless communication together in what engineers might describe as an "infinite DO loop." This means customer communication comes into the organization, is routed to appropriate departments and/or software applications that analyze the communication, and the results of the analysis trigger communication back out to the customers. This loop continues ad infinitum. For maximum impact, you need to automate as much of this process as possible.

Let's see what happens when an organization puts this kind of process into motion.

Nissan—Driven to Excel at CRM

Ted Ross is the vice president of CRM solutions at i-loft (www.i-loft. com), a consulting firm that provides technology and services to help clients maximize the value of CRM without losing their shirts or their minds. In a prior life, Mr. Ross was the corporate manager, CRM for Nissan Motors, where he totally revamped how the automaker managed its customer relationships.

"We bought Epiphany's analytic module to do research and customer profiling," recalls Ross. "Before that, Nissan only did focus groups, yet they never really knew who their customers were. They had assumptions about customer behavior that were often right. But say your assumptions were right for 15 percent of the total number of customers. What about the remaining customers? Details about the remaining 85 percent could be so different that you miss a lot of sales opportunities."

With the analytical tools in place, Nissan determined that first-time visitors to the website do preliminary research 90 days before their actual purchase. Based on certain actions they take on the site, you can tell if visitors are likely to come back, but this isn't the time to do the hard sell. Maybe you just give the person 10 tips to better car shopping.

But a return visitor who participates in a campaign that that includes agreeing to be contacted by a dealer—this is a person ready for a real-time offer. Once he or she completes an online form, the system evaluates this data along with past activities in the data warehouse, then guides the customer through processes such as selecting a car, completing a loan form, and indicating how soon he or she plans to buy.

When customer clicks the submit button, the system tabulates a score. If it's high enough, this information, along with details on the customer's previous actions with Nissan (phone calls, site visits, etc) and anything the customer volunteers, goes to a dealer's wireless device. The device has built-in templates to guide the dealer's actions and the ability to send the customer an original message.

After the system was put in place and started gathering feedback from dealers to add to the data it already had, Nissan discovered changes they needed to make to the website. They became selective about which incentives to give to customers. Because Nissan had a better idea about how customers would respond, they didn't have to waste the offer on thousands of people who may never buy anything.

And what about dollars and cents ROI?

Ross reports that "The early ROI of the wireless CRM deployed for Nissan North America's Infiniti channel dealerships was significant. Within 60 days, 1,500 new sales leads were created within the website and delivered to the dealers. Approximately 18 percent, or 270 customers purchased vehicles. Assuming a conservative gross profit of $2,500 on each vehicle sale—the process returned $675,000 in the first 60 days. Nissan's invested approximately $1.5 million in its new "lead management" system—so the annualized ROI on the deployment was roughly 2.7 to one." Not too bad for two months. As I will mention several times in this book, think long-term, but shoot for quick ROI that refines your long-term vision.

Don't Forget that CRM Is a Team Effort

Reading the Nissan story you might get the impression that the only human beings involved in their wireless implementation were the dealers taking the orders. In reality, there are many people within an organization who are directly or indirectly touch points for a CRM campaign.

Brad Wilson, Epiphany's vice president of product marketing, states that "Wireless technology is best for targeted communication in the context of relationships that customers have with your organization. This includes salespeople, marketing staff, and customer service. When customers access web content wirelessly for self-selling, you want them to be able to send a notification that will get immediate response, so customers need to have the option to receive some sort of real-time response from a person. Maybe your wireless service product portal can look up information based on a customer's ID number and ask the customer if he or she wants a sales rep to contact them."

Your internal sales force needs to have access to leads, information about sales opportunities coming in from various sources, customer data about the status of orders, demographics, and so forth. Service managers need wireless access to alerts about problems with orders, or special promotional events that they are tracking, and these alerts need to follow the managers when they are away from their desks. The retail floor service people in a place like Nordstrom can use a wireless device to help customers find what they need, or get information on customers' accounts.

Marketing people need wireless access to monitor campaigns when marketing activities reach response thresholds, such as when 200 leads an hour start coming in from a *Wall Street Journal* ad, and 50 leads an hour start coming in from a *Los Angeles Times* ad. Your employee population in general may need wireless access to report on things such as developments with the website, software applications, or supply chain activities.

"The key here is to think about how you can create the same kind of rich experience for a customer on a wireless page that you can on a wired page," Wilson says. "The wireless Web is in a billboard phase right now, meaning that most wireless web pages are text-only and allow little interactivity. But the richness of that wireless environment is rapidly developing and any business that doesn't adopt this technology will be left in the dust of their competitors that do. Customers will buy from companies that are most responsive to their needs."

This may seem to be going down that path I mentioned in Chapter 1 where people created websites just because their competitors did. However, Wilson's point makes a subtle but important difference. His recommendation is to respond to customers' needs and desires, not make knee-jerk reactionary decisions based on the actions of other organizations.

Food for Thought

At the end of these chapters there will be a short set of questions (such as those listed below) for you that help you reflect and put each strategic and tactical option into focus before you move on. The online supplement (www.wirelessinconline.com) will have additional materials, links, and updates for each chapter so you can further benefit from the key points in this book.

1. Given what it costs you to close a new customer, does it make sense to invest in wireless activities to help increase customer retention?

2. Does the value of each customer justify creating wireless content specifically for them?

3. What specific steps will you take (conventional, web, or wireless) to motivate your customers to do business with you wirelessly?

4. What information (e.g., documents, customer records, etc.) will you wireless-enable to encourage repeated use by customers?

5. Will it be easy to modify your back end customer databases and CRM applications for wireless access?

6. Do you feel comfortable collecting payments online (if your customers are comfortable with this too), or do you prefer to prime them for resellers?

7. As the technology evolves, are you willing to create interactive wireless features for your customer section (i.e., message boards, chat rooms, instant messaging)?

8. What executives or managers will communicate with customers wirelessly?

9. Should you give away products or services through wireless promotions to further increase customer loyalty?

With that, let's look at the next wireless strategic option—providing more effective service and support.

CHAPTER 4

Provide More Effective Service and Support

The second strategic dimension is using wireless technology and communication to help you provide more effective service and support. This is important because, for many organizations, the quality of customer service often makes the difference between success and failure, profit and loss, budget increase, or budget reduction. The level of service you provide for customers and prospects, possibly more than the quality of your products, may be all that separates your organization from competitors. For some organizations, service is their product.

Wireless technology is quickly shaping up to be an important tool in the effort to provide more service faster and with greater efficiency. This chapter presents wireless communication as a vehicle for delivering service and support, and a tool for improving the efficiency of those who provide service in the field. Sometimes wireless is the service itself. Many benefits await you with the successful implementation of this strategic option.

For purposes of this discussion, I first want to define a couple of terms to make the discussion that follows clear.

What Is Service, What Is Support?

Some people use the terms service and support as if they are interchangeable. It is true that to a large degree they are similar. For example, in the technology industry, if your computer is broken or your software won't run, your call goes to customer support. But if your car breaks, you take it to the car dealer's service department. So is there a difference? Well, in this book, yes.

Service will apply to all of those tasks associated with helping customers AND prospects resolve a range of issues and questions about anything having to do with your company and products. "Why is your stock price at bargain basement level?" "When will your newest widget ship?" "I ordered your purple shirt but I received black jeans." Service also includes adding value to the business relationship that people have with you. For example, service from some car rental companies includes not just solving problems, but also providing local maps so you can find your destinations easily without getting lost or picking you up at your home or office to take you to pick up your rental.

I isolate support to all of the tasks you do to help customers use the product, fix products when they're broken, and upgrade the functionality of the product. These include issues such as, "My widget stopped working, what's wrong with it?" or "I'm assembling your toy and Part A won't connect to Part C."

In a wireless implementation, typical service applications could be those that enable people to find out when your newest prenuptial agreement software ships, issue alerts about changes in flight arrival times, or locate the best restaurants near their hotels. People can learn how a recent law that passed will affect their property value, or how to get the local food bank to make a pickup at their homes.

A support application would be one that beams a message from a refrigeration unit that tells you that you need to replace a gasket that just broke or you will lose $10,000 worth of meat. Or it might beam you repair notes for fixing a piece of heavy machinery at a construction site where land telephone lines are not available to the site crew.

Wireless service and support goes beyond giving customers and prospects the ability to communicate with you when they need help. It includes giving wireless capabilities to your employees who are out in the field providing service or support and embedding wireless devices into equipment and other physical assets so they "talk" to people before or after they have a problem.

Determine if This Is the Right Strategic Dimension for You

If your service and support department deals with many people asking the same (and often simple) questions, one of the benefits of wireless is that you can create content with answers to these questions that thousands of people can access with mobile devices. This will remove a heavy burden from your service staff so they can deal with situations that require detailed personal attention.

To determine if resolving the mundane small questions offers benefits large enough to merit a wireless implementation, divide service and support calls into categories of "easy to resolve" and "difficult to resolve." If you find that a lot of time is spent dealing with the easy problems, both by your staff people and the people calling into your organization, wireless makes sense if you can develop a good process for wirelessly handling issues. Your staff will save time and customers will be happy to have a faster alternative for getting answers then sitting on hold for an hour.

On the flip side, though, all of the potential benefits you could derive from providing wireless support for simple problems could go straight out the window if you cannot respond to the inquires that your wireless application generates. If people access the answers to frequently asked questions (FAQs) and don't contact you by e-mail or phone call with additional questions, you will be okay. But if your wireless support content results in a flood of more inquiries than your staff can handle, you need to respond to e-mail within 24 to 48 hours or people will become very unhappy with you. You don't want to overlook this potential downside.

Wireless is also a great tool if your service and support staff are mobile and work at customer locations where it is difficult or impossible to access all the data they need to solve problems. The times when a field rep needs a modem line or network access the most are usually the times when it's impossible to find either.

Even though there may be times when it's difficult to reach a person wirelessly because he or she is deep inside some massive concrete and steel structure, you likely will have more situations in which wireless is a lifesaver. If your field reps can access customer data wirelessly while in route to a customer's location, this is a major benefit because once data is on the mobile device, the support person can access it at the customer site whether or not they are connected, or regardless of the quality of the wireless connection.

This ability for mobile support staff to wirelessly access your intranet and the rest of your computer network, both when traveling to customer locations and at customer sites, can pay for itself by speeding up the time for resolving each problem so reps can visit more customers per day. If you provide the kind of service that customers pay for each time you visit them, the ability to send data back from the field allows you to bill faster and more accurately, which can be a major boost to your cash flow.

When you review your business operation, you may find that there are several significant benefits to using wireless to proactively resolve issues before they become expensive problems. If a customer buys a product that you know diminishes in performance after three years, you or the product can automatically send a wireless reminder to them to buy an upgrade before it malfunctions, thus saving the customer a lot of aggravation. Consider this and similar applications "heroware."

Organizations in a service industry such as financial planners can use wireless applications to alert mobile clients about late-afternoon news announcements that could impact clients' portfolios negatively in the upcoming days. Agencies such as the National Weather Service can offer a service that people can sign up for to get wireless notifications before they leave on trips about places where they might be stranded by sudden bad weather conditions. Local nonprofits could warn their key patrons about pending legislative actions that threaten to adversely impact the nonprofits' operations.

Heroware makes sense for many organizations and it often pays for itself quickly. When you solve problems before customers know that they have one, customer retention increases because they recognize the value of doing business with a proactive organization. There are direct savings to your support department because every problem you solve ahead of time is one less phone call you have to take or one less stop a field support person has to make. Another benefit is that, by getting to customers before a product wears out, you get the opportunity to sell them a new product before they can think about shopping around and maybe buying a competitor's product.

Proactively delivering warning messages has a fourth, less obvious benefit. Because people with mobile devices might be in an area where there is no wireless coverage, an alert that is sent only after a problem occurs may be delayed in getting to the right people. Even if delivery of a proactive alert is delayed by a few hours, it will likely still be received before anything bad happens.

When you combine wireless alerts with wired intranet content, you have an effective one-two-three punch. You deliver the essential message immediately, you give customers the option to go to the intranet and find more information if they want, and you can have an intranet feature that alerts your support staff who can provide rapid follow up if necessary.

Another element of your support operation that may benefit from wireless technology is customer training. To determine if wireless training applications are appropriate for your organization, a lot depends on the complexity of your products. If you sell software or medical equipment that requires two weeks of instructor-student interactive lessons for eight hours a day, web and wireless technology could facilitate training and reduce costs such as travel expenses and some materials production. However, it's unlikely that you will eliminate the need (and salary) for an instructor.

Customers from various locations could log in and receive instructor-led and multimedia training on the Web, or instructors could provide training in classroom-type settings and have wireless content distributed by infrared stations as part of the course materials. Then you can proactively deliver follow-up lessons wirelessly or provide wireless access to them and enable people to quickly refresh their memories when they have product problems rather than calling your support lines.

If your products or services require just 30 or 60 minutes to master all of the features, and the only training you provide is a manual, wireless may only be valuable if you spend a lot of time answering support calls for these products. In this case, giving customers wireless access to a simple set of instruction materials may be an inexpensive solution that reduces some support costs.

When Service Is Your Product

If your organization's primary commodity is service, this second strategic dimension may be the most important. For instance, those of us in consulting know that the main thing we have to offer is knowledge and expertise. When competitors offer similar knowledge and expertise, then the timeliness and quality of the service delivery becomes a main differentiator.

Financial services organizations professionals are among the most aggressive in adopting wireless applications to deliver service because they know that their clients' personal and business decisions rely heavily on fast access to accurate information. Marketing, real estate, legal, business consulting, and other service organizations will come to the same realization soon.

Do not view using wireless to streamline costs as a strictly white-collar application. There are many blue-collar workers in service businesses who can benefit from wireless access, both on their business premises and at customers' locations. Cars, busses, trains, and other vehicles are being built with increasingly sophisticated parts that give mechanics fits. Wireless access to auto manufacturers' design specs and repair guides could help mechanics serve customers faster and more effectively. Apartment complexes are adding wireless applications to help gardeners, pool cleaners, and other service providers do a better job.

Many government organizations that provide emergency response services (i.e., fire, police, and disaster recovery) have moved to wireless technology to be enabled to respond faster, armed with more accurate information. Other government organizations will find that wireless gives them one more communication channel that reduces costs. However, it is more likely the appeal will be to improve the quality of their services.

Nonprofits will probably find this strategic dimension to be the most valuable too. One of the American Red Crosses services, for example, is helping people learn to administer first aid in emergency situations. Assuming I could maintain the presence of mind, it would be good to have wireless access to first aid procedures in case the person next to me on the sidewalk decided to instigate one of those high-drama medical moments.

Sometimes the Medium Is the Service

Some organizations have realized that giving people wireless access within massive buildings is a service in its own right that helps increase customer retention and enhance the organization's image with customers and prospects. If you've ever tried to use a cell phone or PDA inside a convention hall or big hotel facility, you know the aggravation of the "no service available" message on your screen.

OpenGrid's mobilePlanIt applications enables convention attendees with mobile devices to access content about exhibitors and conference sessions, schedule appointments with other attendees, and provide feedback to speakers during sessions. LGC Wireless's infrastructure technology (www.lgcwireless.com) enables people to have wireless access in the Venetian Hotel in Las Vegas, the Santiago Metro subway system in Chile, major sports stadiums, and other large complexes throughout the world.

Colleges around the country, including University of California, Berkeley and Stanford University are deploying wireless networks around their campuses as a service to facilitate learning and to make their campuses more attractive to both prospective students and faculty.

Personally I'm against cell phone yakking in buildings such as restaurants, theaters, and the like, but there is marketing value to providing indoor access for other devices such as two-way pagers and PDAs so people can quietly tap out messages. Port Discovery in Maryland is a museum with educational and entertaining exhibits for kids and parents. They provide not only access but also wireless devices as a unique service that enables the kids to interact with a recently launched technology exhibit.

Determining if this strategic dimension is right for you will be easier if you have spent some time developing web-based service and support systems because you probably have thought through a lot of the procedures that you want to automate. Most web-based systems are developed with the goal of giving people technology tools to solve their own problems. If you are deriving benefits from these tools, then wireless makes sense because you are increasing the value of these tools by giving people an additional means to use them.

If automating service and support is new territory for your organization, then you should do a thorough financial analysis of your service and support processes to determine where it makes sense to bring in wireless technology. The next section will help you with that analysis.

Calculate the Financial Impact of Providing More Effective Service and Support

The first step in this process is to get the appropriate managers to separate your service and support calls into two primary groups: in-bound and customer on-site. Then go one step further and categorize the calls within each group to make it easier to identify where it is logical to implement wireless applications.

Some organizations create categories according to complexity of support calls (i.e., Level 1, same questions asked repeatedly; Level 7, unique problems that require an hour to solve). Others categorize calls by topic, such as "Installation Problems" and "Electrical Problems." Add as many categories as you need, then evaluate each category to determine if it is practical for a wireless implementation.

You may find that Level 1–Level 3 support calls are simple enough that two or three paragraphs of text can answer people's questions. If that is the case, it make sense to provide wireless access to FAQs for people who would otherwise call in. But Level 4–Level 7 support calls are so complex that they can only be resolved through telephone support. Or it may be evident that installation problems can be resolved with wireless content or wireless access to support documents on the intranet, but electrical problems always require extensive telephone support.

For each of the categories that a wireless implementation seems practical, do a financial analysis to determine what is the average amount you are currently spending to resolve the support calls. How many service calls do you respond to per day, week, or month? How much staff time is spent handling the average call? Assign a dollar value to the time. This is one of the most important calculations to make because many executives are unaware how much each service call costs. Remember the Federal Express story in Chapter 1? A simple call to resolve the question, "Where is my package?" can cost $20.

How many calls can you eliminate by moving these people to wireless support? This figure should be based on your estimate of how many customers and prospects use wireless devices, or can be convinced to do so. Running a pilot program may be the only way to know how many people will actually use *and be satisfied with* your wireless support application. You may find that this will only work with existing customers because it's easier to motivate them to use wireless service and support than it is to convince prospects to do the same.

Assuming you have a tight grasp on your customer data, you should be able to deliver support information proactively, and if so, factor this into your calculation since you can eliminate some support calls just by being ahead of the curve. Also, if you can wireless-enable your products with devices that monitor the products' performance, calculate how much you can save in support costs by being able to do preventative maintenance and respond to support needs faster.

When you're finished with your analysis and estimating, you may create a financial objectives statement for your wireless business plan that is similar to the following statement.

> We answer 4,000 support calls per week that are easy enough to be resolved with wireless content. Each call costs us $10, for a total expenditure of $40,000 per week. Our research shows that 20 percent of these customers use PDAs. We will spend $25,000 to develop an intranet with wireless access capabilities for these support questions and $5,000 in promotions to get all of our customers with PDAs to use the intranet. This should reduce our support calls by $8,000 per week, so our investment will pay for itself within a month.

Additional Financial Calculations

Another component of the financial evaluation of this strategic dimension is the cost reduction that comes from eliminating a lot of the cost for support materials such as manuals, spec sheets, and CDs. How much are you spending to produce and distribute these materials? By making these materials web- and wireless-enabled how much can you save on production and distribution costs? In addition, how much do you earn by increasing customer satisfaction because customers have more opportunities for resolving their questions?

Often workers within their own office buildings are away from convenient Net access when machinery goes haywire and manuals are stored away someplace where you need an archeologist to find them. I do a lot of public speaking and sometimes my laptop has problems working with a particular overhead projector. I don't carry manuals for my laptop and it's unlikely the technician at the facility could find the projector's manuals fast enough for my needs. It would be very cool if the technician or I had wireless access to information from either the laptop or the projector manufacturer (maybe a Speaker's Technical Crisis Resolution page) that walks us through the steps to resolve the problem.

If you are a manufacturer, it behooves you to analyze the financial impact of facilitating wireless access to your support materials by third-party service and support operations. How many products get returned to you or how many calls do your support people have to answer because your resellers' service departments can't fix a problem? The more problems resellers can resolve from their locations, the fewer products and problems will be shipped back to your facilities.

While we're discussing resellers, how much of your service and support costs stem from helping distributors and retailers to resolve their own problems such as lost items and questions about special promotions? The same equation to calculate cost per customer service call and how much of this you can reduce through wireless support will probably work for resellers as well. Look at how much money you spend providing them with printed, video, and other media to train them how to sell your products and determine how much you can save if you can deliver this information wirelessly.

Manufacturers are the organizations most likely to benefit from embedding wireless devices into their products so they alert you or your customers about problems before or when they occur. Currently, the technology to do this type of monitoring is going to cost less than $100 for very simple functionality, such as the i-Pot described in Chapter 3. But you may spend between $600 and $1,000 per device for complex features such as monitoring multiple product functions and environmental conditions such as temperature changes. Prices will likely drop as the technology becomes more widespread.

To see if this investment makes sense, calculate how much it costs you to support your product if it malfunctions, and how much it costs the customer per hour or day in lost productivity or revenue if the product stops working. If the support cost is more than the device costs, buy the device. The amount of time to proactively fix a problem will be less than the time to fix a broken product. If the cost to the customer after a few hours of downtime is greater than the cost of the device, embed the device and bill the customer. Later in this chapter I'll show you why this is a good (and profitable) idea.

One last support cost that should be worked into the equation is training customers how to use your products. As the Web gained recognition among top management as an important communication tool, organizations started using it to deliver training online and subsequently reduced a significant amount of overhead for travel and renting facilities. Wireless provides an opportunity to take training to a new level and further reduce costs.

How much are you currently spending on printed materials, CDs, travel, and video conferencing for customer training? How much of these costs can you reduce by delivering some of your training through wireless content? This should be easy to calculate by reviewing past expense records.

One question that may be overlooked is how effective is your training, meaning how long do people retain what they learn in training? If your training is more effective it can directly impact support costs because for some products, good training can save a hundred questions later. Estimate how much you can reduce your support costs if you wirelessly deliver follow-up training materials, or provide wireless access to this material.

Don't Forget the Intangibles

As you work through the numbers to determine how much support is costing you and how wireless technology might improve your operations, there are bound to be intangible benefits that are hard to quantify. The amount of consideration that you give to these depends on how important service is to your organization.

In some cases, the tangible benefits are sizeable enough that they justify the investment in wireless, and the intangibles just become icing on the cake. For other organizations that already have web content, online training systems, and so forth already in place, giving people wireless access is not a major extra expense.

If yours is a government or nonprofit organization, the intangibles can have great PR value. Remember my example of saving someone's life if I could wirelessly access Red Cross emergency training information? Journalists eat up that kind of news.

After doing all of these calculations and estimates, you should have a good idea about the value of this strategic dimension for your organization. If using wireless to improve service and support makes sense, let's look at some of the strategic objectives you may want to establish for guiding your tactical planning.

Main Strategic Objectives

In developing a strategy for using wireless to enhance your service and support operations, consider starting with the following three primary objectives:

1. Reduce the time and costs of supporting customers, resellers, and others, while increasing the effectiveness of your support and service personnel.

2. Create wireless early warning systems that save you money by resolving problems before they happen and reduce the amount of time people spend reporting on, responding to, and resolving service or support issues.

3. Turn as many service and support calls as you can into opportunities to make a sale or generate new sales lead referrals.

As with the other strategic dimensions, you may find that your business needs dictate additional or different objectives, but the ones presented in this book provide some good starting points for your planning.

Reduce Time and Costs While Increasing Efficiency

As business operations go, service and support can be rather expensive in terms of overhead, and these costs increase as the number of customers and sales leads increase. Besides the rising expenses, a rapid and/or seasonal increase in numbers of customers and prospects often causes the quality of service and support to deteriorate when there's an upward spike in calls. A bad service experience not only can lose customers and future revenue from them, but it can also result in irate customers telling dozens of people who may be prospects not to do business with you. It's a ripple effect that can be very costly.

Create wireless systems that work together with your website to give people access to information when they need it, formatted for quick access, and structured in a triage fashion. This means you delivering wireless content that customers can use to stabilize the most critical situations until they can get to a website or to your staff for additional help.

For example, suppose you sell someone a piece of construction equipment that suddenly malfunctions at a project site. An operator with a PDA could pull up a service page that gives them five steps to take to keep the equipment from blowing up or running amok around the construction site and rolling over your slower workers. At the same time an alert goes out from a wireless device established in the equipment to a field rep who hustles to the customer. While in route, the rep wirelessly accesses the equipment specs and its service history so when they get to the customer, he or she can quickly resolve the problem, revive the equipment, and ride off into the sunset

At the same time you are reducing costs, you DO NOT want to cause a drop in the quality of the service that you deliver. Wireless can eliminate the number of people who call, but you may find that people will want to communicate more often wirelessly because it gives them more convenient access to you. So when you are thinking of tactics to move support from the telephones or the website to mobile devices, also decide what your staffing tactics are going to be in order to handle what could be a high volume of wireless communication.

When using wireless technology to streamline costs incurred by your people in the field who provide on-site support for customers, you want to make sure that you increase your staff's efficiency in equal or greater proportion. For applications to address these as well as in-bound support tasks, consider implementing them incrementally to 1) be sure wireless is going to work in this area, and 2) to refine your projections of the financial benefits you should produce.

If your field service people work in cities and regions that have Ricochet coverage, and it's practical to use laptops on service calls, your wireless solution could be as simple and as inexpensive as getting Ricochet modems. They will immediately be able to access your intranet, customer databases, and support applications without any modifications to these applications. You will need to add network access security measures such as a virtual private network (VPN) if you don't already have these in place. If the screen size does not present a problem, you can put Ricochet modems in iPAQ PDAs for high-speed access to give field staff more flexibility in where they can have wireless access.

Who Let the Dogs Out?! Woof!

The mayor of Lincoln, Nebraska is committed to serving constituents by making his city hall a 24/7 wireless-enabled organization. The first department to deliver this level of service is the Lincoln Animal Control Division.

Using wireless Palm VII PDAs and the Palm.Net® wireless service, Animal Control's staff can access their mainframe computer to get data on animal owners and pets and review previous dispatches from virtually anywhere within their jurisdiction. In its first year this implementation will decrease the cost of distributing information to the staff by 50 percent.

Switching to the Palms eliminated the need for monthly printed lists of pet license numbers that quickly become outdated. Now, when an animal control officer finds a stray dog or cat, locating the owner is as simple as entering the license number on the animal's tag on the PDA. The officers also get background information on the owners as well as a history on the pet.

The application is already enhancing public relations and constituent service for the department because it speeds up the response time by Animal Control Officers to citizens' requests.

The increased efficiency witnessed in Animal Control is catching on, and other city departments are just going to the dogs (you knew that pun was coming). When the department compared the 800mhz radio system in Lincoln police cars to the data speed of the Palm.Net services, they discovered that the Palm application was three times faster at transmitting data. Guess which vendor's in the dog house now?

Now Lincoln's Property Assessment office is using PDAs to get real-time access to current assessment records and updating information from the field. Weed control inspectors are using PDAs to track violations. The city's next project is working on a criminal justice application that searches databases for license plate numbers, VINs, and outstanding warrants.

Say what you want, will, or may about government bureaucracy, but this is a great example of the "logic-versus-hype" method of deploying the next big thing. These Nebraska folks picked a department that had a clear and simple need, established their objectives, matched technology with the need, deployed it, measured results, and expanded the program.

What's important to note (vendors, take heed) is that inspiration and vision came from His Honor at the top. But he let the benefits of the application self sell itself to other departments, rather than let vendors come in pushing too hard for the next big sale.

More Tax Dollars at Work—Deep in the Heart of Texas

On March 28, 2000, powerful tornadoes touched down in the greater Fort Worth (Tarrant County), Texas area. Homes were destroyed and surrounding communities damaged. Most of the communication networks were down. In order to serve and protect, county officials needed reliable communications during a difficult weather situation.

Lieutenant Robert Durko and his deputies of the Tarrant County Sheriff's Office brought in laptop computers equipped with PacketCluster Patrol software from wireless applications vendor Aether Systems (www.aethersystems. com) and wireless modems. This application that is specially designed for emergency response agencies runs on the cellular digital packet data (CDPD)-based AT&T Wireless service.

Lieutenant Durko and his posse were able to coordinate the placement of deputies for emergency traffic and crowd control in the county during the tornadoes using this application. The application's flexibility allowed officers and storm crews to quickly respond to critical emergencies.

A year before the tornadoes hit, The Tarrant County Sheriff's Office moved from a Motorola RF network system with dumb terminals in patrol cars to this more free-ranging wireless implementation, thanks to a grant to replace the terminals. It took the department just three days to deploy the application software on 45 laptops. In one week all of the personnel were trained.

In the initial phase of the project, computers were mounted in patrol cars. They were wirelessly linked to information from county, state, and other criminal and motor vehicle databases. Plans are in the works to organize field reporting and other applications for the offices and expand the application to more than 70 vehicles from several agencies, including fire and emergency department operations.

While the department's response to the tornado storms in 2000 provides a high profile ROI story, Lieutenant Durko points to less dramatic ways in which the applications justify their $130,000 investment.

"We see our ROI in the amount of work that the dispatchers don't have to do anymore. There will be additional ROI when we analyze reporting in the field and look at factors such as paperwork reduction and centralizing fragmented data, thus increasing efficiency in many aspects of the department. People already saw some of these benefits from using radio units before we switched to the current application," says Durko.

"You need to look at the person-hours spent writing reports and running data searches, the time invested in creating paper trails and moving documents throughout the business process. You also have to look at the response time of officers and their booking times. Officers will be able to send information from the laptops to the jail before they get there with a prisoner, so all the officers will have to do is sign the printed documents that will be waiting for them. Also ask, 'What are all of my repetitive tasks, and can I eliminate them with the wireless application we're considering?'"

Similar to how the city of Lincoln, Tarrant County started its wireless implementation with a small focused group that had modest objectives, then let the group's success fuel the expansion of wireless applications to other departments.

Take Me Home, Wireless Implementations

This last story covers the range of service and support needs of one company. Your wireless service and support needs may not be anywhere near as extensive, but it's important to note that one application can address a whole laundry list of needs. Home Finishes, Inc. (www.homefinishes.com) did a thorough analysis to uncover costs that could be reduced or eliminated using wireless communication, and responded with an implementation that produced ROI in 90 days.

Home Finishes services new home warranties, preparation, and painting as a contractor for homebuilders. When a homeowner takes possession of a new residence, he or she has a team of Home Finishes professionals to repair any problem during their first year of home ownership. If a breakdown occurs in the vital electrical, plumbing, heating, or roofing systems, emergency help is available 24/7.

The company has over 600 tradesmen working across California and Colorado who communicate daily with the Customer Service Center (CSC) in Livermore, California to get job schedules and customers service requests and to submit time and expense data. The primary communication tools were cell phones used for voice but not data, and the main back office applications include field support, time and expense, job scheduling, and ERP software.

Home Finishes's analysis found that the process of requesting and transmitting data between team members and the Livermore head office was slow, inefficient, and inflexible. Field team members would receive weekly schedules or directions to new sites/locations by phone. Software generated new service requests, but these were delivered by phone calls to the field staff and case details were delivered separately to the nearest fax machines, or by phone if no machines were available.

Schedule changes and directions to job sites could not be communicated to the field crew as they occurred, so customers had to wait a minimum of eight hours for service. Field staff could spend up to two hours per day completing time cards and expense reports, yet still produced errors because they couldn't access customer codes in the ERP system. Four thousand paper time sheets per week had to be delivered by hand or overnight delivery service and then manually entered into the ERP system, causing significant delays in approvals and payment.

To combat these inefficiencies and delays, Home Finishes called in a company named Xora (www.xora.com) to develop a wireless application that included a speech recognition system so field staff could access data electronically or through voice calls. Within 30 days, Home Finishes had its first implementation ready for field deployment.

Weekly schedules, driving directions, and updated service requests to new work sites now are delivered instantly to the field staff's mobile devices, which has improved customer service by enabling speedier response times. Now field staff can remotely access any other data that they need by mobile devices or regular phones, whichever is more convenient, and have eliminated hours of phone conversations. They're also entering error-free daily time and expense reports in just five minutes. All of the improvements resulted in significant financial savings.

In the home office, the wireless application has lowered costs by eliminating the 4,000 paper time sheets per week, along with overnight delivery charges and manual reentry of the data. The office staff that used to do time sheet data entry is now assigned to tasks that increase customer service. The company supplies its customers with web-based real-time accounting information that cuts one to two weeks out of the receivables process, which improves cash flow. This application will further increase ROI by continuing to reduce support costs even as Home Finishes opens new market segments and increases the field support workload.

Now that we've examined the potential benefits that wireless communication can bring to service and support operations, let's look at how you can use wireless to shorten sales cycles and lower the costs of sales to prospects.

Wireless Gives Professional Services a Bottom Line Boost

The following two professional service firms each take a slightly different approach to wireless enabling their staffs, but they achieve similar objectives. Both are good examples of how service organizations and service departments can use wireless to improve the bottom line.

Attorneys in the Houston, Texas law firm of McGinnis Lockridge & Kilgoe LLP use their Palm VIIs to access e-mail while on the go, check the status of cases, track billable hours, and keep their schedules with them at all times.

Before using PDAs, the attorneys would carry laptops wherever they went. It was an expensive and nonergonomic approach to mobile computing. Moving from laptops to PDAs reduced the costs (e.g., telephone charges, fixing software glitches, etc.) that IS incurred supporting remote dial-up users by 25–35 percent and eliminated a seven-pound laptop from the attorneys' loads. Now the firm's legal beagles can stay connected to the network but still do the footwork that comes with being a lawyer.

In addition, up to 30 percent of an attorney's time was not usually logged, and thus unbilled. The attorneys use Time Reporter on the Palm to keep track of billable hours in real time. This information is automatically synched with the firm's accounting system while attorneys are on the road. If an attorney keeps track of just one hour that might have been forgotten in the past, then the mobile device has already paid for itself!

Mann Consulting (www.mann.com), run by founder Harrold Mann, is a firm that provides clients with professionals who serve as outsource IT departments for companies too small to have their own. These consultants are in the field all day assisting with every imaginable IT task. Often they must log on to four or five networks in a day, and meet with 10 different people in the same building. Mann's laptops are not an option but a necessity with Mann's consultants.

"Either you configure the laptop for every client's network or stay on sin-gle network and bring it with you," states Mann. So he decided to get every-one Ricochet modems from Metricom and stay on a single network. The ROI wasn't hard for him to calculate.

Mann advises you to "Think of conventional remote access to computer networks as an expense that should go away. Use that money to put informa-tion on the Web and let people access it wirelessly. I also looked at our transit costs—how much time do we spend going from customer to customer that we weren't billing for? This could be 12 percent, so if you become more pro-ductive while traveling, you potentially can capture that much more billable time. Ricochet only costs $1,000 a year." And, under the new company, Rico-chet's annual service cost may be significantly less.

Yep, different paths but the same objective. Those of us who "live but to serve" really appreciate recapturing some of those lost billable hours.

Wireless Early Warning Systems
Make Sense—and Dollars

Creating product performance monitoring capabilities could require some changes in how you manufacture products if you install and configure com-plex wireless devices, but this is not always the case. Changing the level of wireless intervention in your product support efforts may also result in some operational changes. There definitely will (or should) be changes in your mar-keting once you have this new capability. However, all of these changes will have a positive outcome.

This Is Your Life Before Wireless

Many companies that sell complex and expensive products, especially prod-ucts such as printing presses, airplanes, and medical test equipment, have a support process that is expensive and time consuming for manufacturers and customers. At no time is this more evident than when something breaks.

First, the product has to malfunction. Depending on what part is getting ready to go code blue (medical term for "one step shy of death"), the prod-uct's performance could be impaired or other components damaged before the part finally stops working. Because you then have to fix or replace several components instead of one, the product will take longer to fix. Finally, some-one has to find out that the product's comatose. This could take hours or days if the breakdown happens during the weekend.

If the product you sell protects items from damage (for example, fire sprinklers and alarm systems), this delay could mean that thousands of dollars in losses if a fire breaks out while your product is not functioning. If what you sell causes your customer to lose money when it stops working, that's more money wasted. These losses aren't yours, but it doesn't help your image in the market when this kind of thing happens.

Okay, so eventually someone at the customer's location finds out that your product has flat-lined and needs resuscitating. That person has to call someone at your company, which can add more hours to the delay if whomever he or she calls isn't around to take the call, or it's a holiday. When your person does take the call, she has to dispatch someone else to go out and fix the problem.

If the person going out on the call doesn't have the right information because the message was garbled after passing through several pairs of ears, lips, and dispatch slips, he or she may not be prepared to solve the problem. So he or she has to go back to the office to get the right materials, adding yet more time before the problem gets fixed. (If you've ever tried to get a DSL connection in your house, this will sound very familiar to you.)

By the time you get the problem fixed, the customer's mad, you might be liable for damages, and the cost of the service call is much higher than it should be because of the miscommunications.

This Is Your Life After Wireless

Now picture this. Your product has a chip or some other wireless device embedded in it. In the best case scenario, the device that monitors your product picks up an early warning that a problem will occur shortly. The device immediately sends a message straight to a field rep's PDA with a description of the problem and what procedures or parts are needed to fix it.

The rep gathers together the necessary parts, goes out to fix the problem, and the customer doesn't even have to know. There's no damage to the customer's business and no damage to your reputation. Your overhead for the service call is minimal, plus you only have to replace a part rather than the entire product.

If you decide that you don't want an early warning system (some folks love to live dangerously), you can still use wireless technology to reduce the amount of human intervention after a problem is located. A wireless message can go from the product to your computer network and be relayed automatically to the rep who supports that customer so the rep can respond ASAP to the problem. Another option is to have software on your network that uses GPS to locate the field tech who is closest to the customer relay the message to them.

You Know It's a Chiller, Legacy Chiller Night

"I think the small company that is using technology, particularly wireless, can have a lot of advantages over the bigger companies. The large manufacturers are often slow at adopting technology to their product lines, but a small organization can decide in 20 minutes if they want to do something. This gives me an edge."

That is Martin King's assessment of the power of wireless technologies to help the little guy. King is CEO of Legacy Chiller Systems. Operating with just 12 employees, Legacy Chiller Systems is a company that is definitely one of the Davids among the many Goliaths. They make water chillers that cool down the hot water that flows through multimillion dollar semiconductor test equipment. They not only build and sell the systems, but configure, install, and repair them.

King has managed to use an embedded wireless monitoring device from Notifact (www.notifact.com) to create a competitive sales advantage, a disaster-prevention feature for customers and a service cost-reduction tool, all in one fell swoop. There are other vendors that a prospect can buy a chiller from, some with less expensive systems. But Legacy uses Notifact and its unique maintenance contract to win the deal.

"We hardwire a Notifact monitor into the chiller and set eight sensors to monitor critical functions," says King. "We also give the customer the option to use a website to set the notification parameters. At this point, we have a sales advantage because our chiller has the ability to automatically notify us before a problem occurs."

For a $2 million tester, every working minute is money. A company can lose $50,000–$75,000 per day if the test is not working, so every day a Legacy product saves a customer in downtime pays for two new chillers. What's more, in the days before a tester breaks, performance deteriorates so that's even more money lost. The final deal closer is Legacy's service contract that says for every 15,000 square feet in which it provides maintenance, the customer gets the Notifact device and six months of monitoring for free.

Besides helping to close the sale, Notifact also reduces a lot of the product support costs. The monitoring feature allows Legacy to see some of the things customers are doing that may cause the tester to malfunction. It also allows Legacy to diagnose problems. Sometimes the customer's facilities manager can respond to a Notifact message (i.e., blown fuse, thermostat turned off), saving Legacy a support call. Before installing Notifact, Legacy support people would go to the site not knowing what the problem was and sometimes they didn't have the right parts, so they had to make a second trip.

Legacy also found that the average tech person at the customer's site doesn't know how to install a chiller (it's not a common piece of machinery), so Legacy had to provide installation support for the equipment attached to its chillers. The staff used to spend additional time walking people through installation and troubleshooting procedures. The Notifact device enables Legacy to monitor the product and provide this service from its office.

There are opportunities for manufacturers to gain competitive advantages on many service and support fronts with the use of embedded wireless technology. The key is having a willingness to explore the possibilities and the ability to move decisively to take advantage of the opportunities that present themselves.

Turn Service Contacts into Sales Opportunities

Converting each service call into a sales opportunity or sales referral will require a little planning. But doing the same with a problem support call requires a lot of forethought because when customers are in your face and greatly annoyed, a poorly maneuvered sales ploy is similar to walking up on the blind side of a skittish horse in a barn. If you don't tread carefully, you could get kicked out of the door.

Conversely, here is someone who has come to you to make his or her life (or some small slice of it) better. If you can do this with thoroughness and efficiency he or she might be so happy that he or she will listen to what you have to offer.

A lot of the service content that you will deliver to a mobile device will be for answering simple questions, or you will be sending out proactive support information, so customers will probably be in a positive state of mind. The message that they receive should leave them satisfied with your company. If you know your customer well, and you can determine that the type of question or problem he or she has indicates he or she is an ideal candidate for a particular product or service offer, give it to him or her.

For example, if someone responds to your ad about a new line of lingerie and asks when will it be in stores, answer her and also ask if you can wirelessly alert her on that date and send the names of local stores that will carry the product. When you send the alert, include a discount coupon for perfume that might not be selling very well. Or when your field rep goes to an office to fix a broken copier, have the rep beam a special offer for office supplies to the office manager's PDA.

When you make someone happy, or reasonably so, but there isn't a good opportunity to make a sales offer, it still may be a good time to ask for a customer referral. Several people I interviewed are overjoyed by the quality of service from their wireless vendors and are prime candidates to offer a referral anytime they receive support, assuming it's done tactfully. If you know your audience uses their mobile devices extensively to communicate with friends and colleagues, deliver a sales offer or request for possible leads in a message that can be easily forwarded to others.

There are other scenarios in which good wireless support can lead to sales. I became a fan of Kyocera's Smartphone when I went to their website and saw their interactive demo for the product (www.kyocerawireless.com/kysmart/ kysmart_demo.htm). The demo divides the Smartphone's features into small, nonintimidating sections of product notes.

For each feature that you click, a screen pops up and three or four short sentences appear in sequence to teach you how to use the feature. In addition, an image of the phone and a stylus pops up, and the stylus taps out all of the procedures as each sentence appears. When you click on each of the sentences, the stylus will repeat the activity.

Typically I'll have a cell phone for years and use maybe only two or three of a hundred features. In 15 minutes, I knew how to use every Smartphone feature presented, even though I didn't have the phone. Not only that, I wanted to buy the phone in the worst way because the features were cool and I knew that using them would be easy. I also knew that any time after getting the phone I could always access this demo if I forgot how to do something.

These days it's not practical to use dynamic graphics on most mobile devices, but a wireless version of the Kyocera demo could keep the screens with the instructions for using each feature, and maybe add a one-dimensional, one-color graphic. What's important is that you can take a complex product, divide its features into bite-sized pieces of content, add some basic graphics, and deliver a wireless training course that subtly convinces people to buy the product.

A Little Feedback Is a Good Thing

Gathering feedback is one of the most overlooked opportunities to produce sales leads when providing service and support online. A lot of websites don't have a form asking what people think about the organization's service, what they want added to the site or the product, or taking specific questions about their products or company.

Sometimes there is the very generic message "Send us e-mail with your comments." But remember, a customer who's using a site to solve a problem or ask a question is usually interested enough in the company to answer one or two questions.

The other day I was at a restaurant with one of my best friends, Dwight, and his family. His twelve-year-old son Daniel was pecking away on a Handspring Visor and he pulled up a review of the restaurant where we were eating. After all the basic information about the restaurant, Daniel then showed me this screen where he could add his own review while we were waiting for dessert, which the restaurant will post as a service to other customers and prospects.

Imagine the possibilities!

Someone engages your organization in a dialogue, or at least accesses your content. They have some very clear impressions about your company, whether good or bad, and she is holding the means to deliver opinions, sometimes immediately. Your restaurant can post details on what menu items are being well received—or not—so guests can reconsider their orders, or even open an instant messaging window to encourage additional feedback while it is fresh in the customer's mind.

This customer (who is now sitting in your eatery) could forward the feedback form right on the spot to a bunch of friends with personal comments or recommendations, thus generating new customers and helping you develop a reputation as the king of good service.

In this new world of wireless communication, feedback is the lifeblood of successful applications. A lot of money will be wasted on service and support, as well as other applications, if organizations do not do an adequate job of listening to customers and prospects. Many organizations give lip service to the concept of one-to-one marketing, but execute from a reality of one-way data dumping.

You don't have to try to generate a sale or lead from every customer or prospect interaction. You can push content to some targeted customers that concludes with a sales offer. Other content that is accessed by prospects may include a feedback form with three or four questions, and this form concludes by asking for a referral.

If the Shoe Fits . . .

When I started consulting with companies about their websites, I occasionally met marketing executives who said, "Those people in customer service aren't my problem." My response was, if people have a bad customer service experience, especially people dealing with you for the first time, you have a marketing problem. Soon you'll have a sales problem, too. Famous Footwear faced such a situation.

Famous Footwear is a Madison, Wisconsin-based chain of 975 family shoe stores. Aggressive pricing is at the core of their business strategy since the company operates in an intensely competitive market. Constant pressure to attract and retain customers, while maintaining profit margins, makes correct pricing critical, so employees in each store would spend between four to six hours per week manually changing and verifying prices.

This time-killing, paper-based process also produced significant numbers of errors and resulted in marked prices that didn't match advertised specials or agree with the register at check out. Price-conscious shoppers, often mothers with young children in tow, had little patience for mistakes. And, since the lower price was generally honored, stores lost revenue.

To turn this situation around, Famous Footwear bought a PDA and wireless LAN station from Symbol Technologies (www.symbol.com) for each of its stores. Each station is linked to a Cisco router that connects back to the home office.

Employees indicate on the Symbol PDA that they want to change prices and enter the date they want these new prices to be effective. The employee then scans a shoe box using the PDA's integrated barcode scanner and the box's item number goes to the home office computer system, which immediately sends the color of the sticker and the price for the date requested to the store.

It took just six weeks to develop and implement this application, and pricing errors have dropped by 75 percent. Given the nature of their market, price changes must be rolled out quickly to stores, and executed flawlessly by in-store staff. This improved pricing accuracy has improved profits as well as made customers happier. There are other benefits as well: Giving store employees real-time access to enterprise systems also can improve coordination of other mission-critical tasks, enabling the company to manage its widely dispersed stores as a cohesive unit, and giving employees more time to serve customers.

When Your Support People Are Money Collectors

A Houston, Texas company named ServiceIQ (www.serviceiq.com) recently launched a service for field support staff in small air conditioning (AC) contractor firms. These contractors install and support AC units in homes and small businesses. If an installed AC unit breaks down, support people drive out to the home or business to fix the problem and collect the 1money (usually checks) from the customer right then and there.

A typical support person makes numerous stops all day before returning to the home office, so at the end of his or her shift, he or she has a lot of checks, credit card slips, and paperwork to sort out, reconcile, and file. A paper-based system like this can be time-consuming and prone to errors. This is a situation that is begging for a wireless solution.

However, if you're a four- or five-person business, it can be difficult to install and maintain a wireless application to streamline this process, assuming you want to commit to this large of a budget. Small organizations need a different type of wireless solution. ServiceIQ is a wireless application service provider (ASP). An ASP builds all of the application and infrastructure software needed to link a mobile device (which ServiceIQ also provides) to a wireless network and transfer the necessary data back to the home office.

So rather than spending thousands of dollars to buy, install, and manage software and hardware, the contractor only has to pay a set-up fee, a leasing fee for the device, and monthly usage charges to the ASP. The contractor doesn't have to modify the software that runs the business, there is minimal training of the staff (a day or so), and the contractor can drop the service at any time with no headaches.

ServiceIQ President John Reiland believes that "ASPs make sense for service organizations with revenues less than $20 million. If you have a bigger organization, you probably have the entire infrastructure you actually need already in place so you can bring these applications in house from the beginning. For a small company that is growing, though, it may be a while before they need to bring these applications inside the company."

An interesting thing to note about ServiceIQ is that they spent a lot of time on designing the UI for the mobile devices they lease (see Figure 4-1), one of which is the Fujitsu PenCentra using Microsoft Windows CE operating system. The company is currently spending a lot of time designing a new UI for the more common Palm and iPAQ PDAs. Organizations that are developing applications for their own support staffs can take a lesson from this company that's developing a UI for customers.

"We had focus groups of people from companies representing 5 percent of the total number of small and large contractors in Houston, plus product visionaries," comments Reiland. "The business knowledge and experience that these people have is the most critical element of developing a good UI. In any wireless application, devices will be smaller and this is frustrating to users. Making the UI as seductive and familiar to what they know is very important for adoption. We somehow need to have a way for users to see where they are even though they can only see a small chunk of the big picture."

Any application that you plan to use to make your field support staff more efficient will require that you spend a lot of time on UI design, a topic that is covered in detail in Chapter 15.

Figure 4-1. Service IQ's user interface.

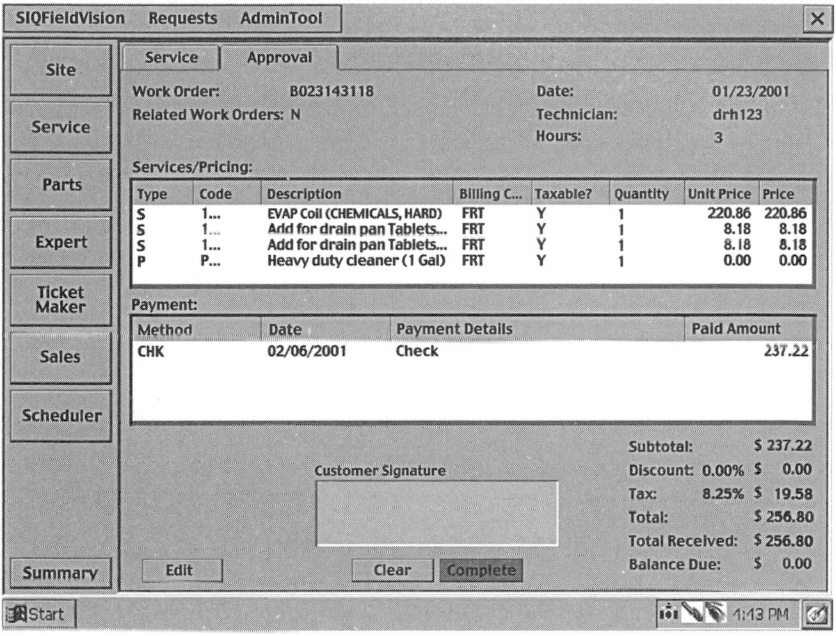

Food for Thought

This chapter addressed some of the major issues involved with using wireless technology to enhance service and support. Here are some questions to help focus your thinking and start your subconscious working on strategic ideas for your organization:

1. What are the routine service and support issues that you can resolve with wireless technology?

2. What information is needed to provide great support to people with mobile devices, from where in the organization can you gather this information, and do you have the resources to keep the information current?

3. How much printed support materials such as manuals, newsletters, and so forth can be converted to wireless content?

4. Can information you use to support customers also support business partners, field staff, and others with little or no modification of that information?

5. Can you get customers to help other customers solve problems wire-lessly, either through a message board or instant messaging as its relia-bility improves?

6. Can you provide support to e-mail inquiries fast enough by responding within 24 to 48 hours, even if you can only acknowledge their ques-tions and tell people you're working on resolving their problems?

7. Is it advisable to include wireless support as a feature of your service contracts?

8. Are your business partners who provide service and support to the people who buy your products open to adding wireless applications to support their efforts, or integrating their wireless efforts with yours?

CHAPTER 5

Communicating with Prospective Customers

This chapter addresses the third strategic dimension, using wireless technology to lower the costs of communicating with people who have not bought your products and services, or have not conducted business with your organization. Beyond reducing costs, wireless can shorten your sales cycles by facilitating the shopping process for prospects and improving the effectiveness of your sales force. When you finish the chapter you should know whether or not this strategic dimension is right for your organization.

Your organization may have the right product and market position so first-timers will feel comfortable enough to order from you using a mobile device. However, most organizations will integrate wireless communication with Internet and other business communication to move first-time buyers closer to a decision to purchase. Once prospects are ready to buy, smart organizations give them every method to place an order, including mobile devices. Smart organizations also put wireless technology into the hands of their salespeople and retailers to have a significant impact on closing first-time prospects.

That's what this chapter is about, influencing the sales process at the prospect level, the retailer level, and through your internal staff who interact with both groups.

Determine if This Is the Right
Strategic Dimension for You

When evaluating the potential value of this strategic dimension, here are several questions you have to resolve:

- Are the people who make up your base of prospective customers likely to be using mobile devices in the upcoming year or two?
- Are those with mobile devices using them at times when it makes sense to communicate with them wirelessly?

■ Rather than initiating wireless communication with prospects yourself, does it make more sense to give people the option to initiate wireless contact with you?

■ Are there steps in your product or sales cycles that could be eliminated or shortened if you use wireless communication?

■ Are the people who sell for you (both internal staff and third-party organizations such as retailers) mobile, or at least away from regular Internet and network access when they are in front of a prospective customer?

If you answered "yes" to any of these questions, you should consider developing wireless communication strategies to reach these prospects. This is particularly true for the first three questions. The more questions that you answer in the affirmative, the stronger the case that can be made for implementing wireless, as you will see.

Compared to trying to reach customers, whose names and contact information you may have in databases, reaching prospects initially using wireless is more difficult because these mobile device users are scattered throughout your target market. They may comprise just small percentage of your total prospect base, and they probably aren't on a list that you can buy.

If you sell technology products to IT people, for example, the likelihood that a large percentage of these individuals will have a PDA is high enough that it might be cost justified to send them wireless ads if you can limit the ad delivery to IT managers. However, if only 10 percent of your target market of 1,000 plumbing contractors owns mobile devices that can receive ads wirelessly, this approach may not make economic sense. Once you add up the costs to develop the ad and pay for the service that delivers the ad through a wireless carrier's network, you may find more efficient ways to spend your resources.

Conversely, if you send out a direct mail package that gives prospects the option to contact your wirelessly and the 10 percent of your audience that have mobile devices use them to respond, perhaps you can trim marketing costs by 5 percent or 10 percent. It is less expensive to deliver follow-up materials and answer questions wirelessly than by mail and telephone. The trick to determining if this strategic option makes sense is to focus on understanding your audience, how you currently communicate back and forth with prospects, and how you manage your internal business operations that facilitate the selling process.

In terms of understanding your prospects, you can apply many of the same criteria you read about in Chapter 3 for determining if this audience is the right one for you to reach wirelessly. For example, location and context are as important in assessing the value of wireless strategies for reaching prospects as it is for reaching customers. When prospects are most in need of your add-on products or services, are mobile devices the best or only way for you to reach them, or for them to reach you?

How closely the demographics of your target market match those of typical mobile device users is another determining factor. If your best prospects are technology people, upscale professionals, young executives, mobile workers, well-educated, or generally folks who tend to be the first in their company or social group to buy the latest technology, they are most likely to be mobile device owners. You should research your current customers or purchase market research data to be more accurate in your assessment.

Organizations that determine there is a sizeable portion of their target market using mobile devices need to review their current methods of communicating with prospects to further assess the value of this third strategic option.

Bring members of your sales group early into the process of determining if this strategic dimension makes sense. I cannot emphasize this enough. I have worked with companies that have ignored the sales force when developing business strategies for using new technology, which was detrimental to the successful implementation of the technology. Your sales reps know the sales process better than anyone else, so they can give you good insight into the value of using wireless communication. They know where in the sales cycles wireless can be applied most effectively, and what kind of impact it will have.

Your mobile sales reps often know best where most of the bottlenecks and inefficiencies lie, even if they don't know what might be the best wireless solution to the problems. Their feedback about what market data, industry news, background on competitors, and details about prospects they need will help your IT people determine if it is technically possible to implement a wireless solution.

When assessing the potential for wireless within the retail world, things are a little more complicated. On the one hand, if your products are in the retail channel you probably know a lot about how the stores operate, what their staffs need, and how prospects behave when they're in the stores. But since you don't directly manage these staffs, you need to talk to them to determine how wireless can help them and what potential outcomes they can expect.

How Are You Currently Communicating with Prospects?

Practically all organizations draw from the same well of conventional communication tactics—direct mail, trade shows, telemarketing, advertising—and the Web. And whether you're trying to sell a new product or convince some-one to make his or her first donation to your charity, for many organizations there is a sales process that involves meetings, phone calls, and a lot of waiting for people to make decisions.

Wireless makes sense if you implement it to extend the reach of your con-ventional communication activities and, in some cases, reduce the costs of these activities. In a tight economy, there is constant pressure to produce more results with the same or less money. At the same time, the competition for each new customer is fierce, so you have to look for new ways to engage prospects so they stay with for the entire sales cycle and not get scooped up by someone else.

By using wireless technologies, you can reach thousands of prospects with much more information for a fraction of the cost of reaching them through conventional tactics. A direct mailing to 10,000 prospects can easily cost you $20,000–$30,000 or more for expenses such as graphic design, printing, as-sembly of the materials, and postage. With wireless you still have to design the materials, but you eliminate most of the other costs, and the costs for deliver-ing the materials may be a few pennies per person.

By giving people the option to respond to you wirelessly when they see your ad or receive a mailer, you might pick up leads from people on a bus or commuter train who might forget about the ad by the time they get home. Unlike materials that are passive, such as brochures, you can use wireless tech-nology to engage these people in immediate dialogue through instant mes-sages (IMs) and audio presentations you can deliver to prospects with high-speed connections. Once you have a prospect's permission to send follow-up information wirelessly, you have a new communication channel to keep the prospect in the sales cycle until the prospect closes.

If your sales cycle involves several meetings and mailings to give prospects a lot of information, or there are several people within the prospect's organiza-tion who influence a sale, wireless can deliver the information faster and more economically. You may need to limit graphics and maybe forget about multi-media for the near term unless prospects PDAs support this kind of technol-ogy. But the value and convenience of giving prospects access to so much information may still make this a valuable (and viable) project.

Wireless offers added value in that prospects give you feedback from loca-tions where they can't get regular web access, plus they can carry your infor-mation with them to access again when it's convenient, or pass it on to colleagues. At trade shows you see people hauling shopping bags full of bro-chures and other promotional materials. Many of them would be happier to have all of that information tucked away in their PDAs instead, and you would be better served because your material is less likely to discarded.

Wireless Can Remove the Barriers of Time, Space, and Cost

All conventional communication has a limitation of time, space, and cost. There is only so much time, either in person, on TV, or through the radio that you can communicate with a prospect. Even if you write a book, you don't have enough space to say everything you want to say. And yes, even the biggest of organizations have a ceiling on how much money they can spend to say what they want to say. The smaller or more cash constrained your organization is, the greater these limitations become.

With a good website and wireless content delivery, you can take ten dollars and get $30, $100, or more worth of value because you can start a dialogue with prospects through conventional means, then continue it online and on mobile devices. Take billboards as an example of one of the most space-limited communication media there is. You can print ten to twelve words (for maximum impact) and a picture, which doesn't let you say a lot. But wireless can increase the value of your billboard advertising.

Use outdoor campaigns such as highway and bus billboards to deliver a strong opening message, then direct prospects to use their PDAs to get details from your website, or complete feedback forms with their e-mail addresses or phone numbers. The billboard ad that under the best of circumstances might have a ten-second impression can now have a minutes-long impact. People can learn about you in a no-pressure setting and then initiate two-way communication at their own discretion.

Trade shows are another communication channel where you can use wireless technology to break the barriers of time, space, and costs. At a typical show, you spend a lot of money for three or four days of exposure and an average of two minutes with 90 percent of the prospects who stop by your booth. Does it make sense to use a web and wireless promotional campaign to generate interest in your product prior to the show and schedule appointments for booth personnel?

When prospects get to your booth, and after you speak with them, have them use their laptops or mobile devices to access a second promotion such as a game or contest through a wireless LAN or an infrared station in your booth. Beam the prospects take-home content that they can review while they're at the show or back at the office. Your personal interaction goes from two minutes to potentially hours over a period of weeks as they play the game or participate in the contest, review your materials, send you e-mail, and so on. You also save money by distributing digital rather then print material.

Retail sales people are nice, often competent, and usually courteous, but they have dozens or hundreds of products to represent and not enough time to learn about all of them. Prospects often have more questions than sales staff have complete answers for. Does it make sense to give these sales people PDAs or outfit the store with wireless kiosks so the salesperson can beam everything a prospect needs to know directly to prospects' PDAs, along with a discount coupon redeemable on the spot? This type of wireless capability can give your retail channel more muscle to raise your products above the crowd.

Another time, space, and cost restraint that wireless removes is the limitation on the number of new markets that you can open up, particularly in new states, regions, or countries. Some small organizations found that once they had a website up, orders started coming in from regions or countries they normally could not afford to mail or advertise to because of costs or the time required to talk to prospects. Once the site was up, people from almost anywhere in the world could access the information. Wireless offers similar possibilities, in large part because of the Web itself.

You can use a service such as AvantGo to reach prospects in any country where there are wireless networks and web access. Unimobile markets software that you can use to, among other tasks, build an application that allows prospects to sign up to use their mobile devices to receive information from your organization, regardless of what wireless carrier they use. With this you could use your website to promote to a following of prospective customers in another country, and wirelessly deliver information for pennies per contact.

Start reviewing your conventional communication tactics to reach prospective buyers, donors, new employees, or journalists with the thought of using wireless to increase the impact, reach, and duration of those tactics. For each of your audiences there are conventional activities that are constrained by various limitations. If wireless can free you of these constraints there is probably a case to be made for pursuing this strategic dimension.

Calculate the Financial Impact of Communicating Effectively with Prospects

The following financial exercises and calculations will help you determine how much you're spending now to reach perspective customers, and isolate areas where wireless can play an important role in reducing costs. This is very similar to the process in Chapter 3 for calculating the potential impact of using wireless to reach current customers. The definition of prospect includes resellers, journalists, and others with whom you want to do business for the first time.

As with the previous strategic dimensions, some of these numbers may be rough estimates until you launch a pilot project or two to verify the numbers. But you have to have some sort of starting point because a "best guess" is better than having no clue at all.

Analyzing the Cost of Sales for Prospective Buyers

Let's start with your prospective buyers and determine how much you are currently spending per year on conventional communications activities targeted primarily to generate qualified leads. Then we'll explore how wireless may be able to reduce some of these costs.

What are your annual costs for each of these activities to make the initial contact with prospects and generate a lead? (The costs of conventional communication to follow up with leads will be addressed when I discuss the cost of the sales cycle.)

- Print materials (brochures, newsletters, etc.)
- Direct mail (postage, materials, creative) and special promotions such as contests and discount sales
- Telemarketing, including staff and phone costs
- Hosted seminars/conferences
- Promotions (contests, special offers)
- Advertising (placement, creative, copywriting)
- Administrative costs (support personnel and project managers)

These costs collectively represent your total annual prospect communication costs.

Next determine approximately how many prospects you reach, how many leads you generate, and how many leads become customers. The number of prospects and leads is important for determining the potential value of wireless, as I will demonstrate soon. Finally, divide the total annual prospect communication costs by the number of leads and you will see how much you are spending per lead.

Now answer this question: By how much do you estimate you can eliminate or significantly reduce the total cost to generate each lead if you can beam the same information to prospects wirelessly? The answer hinges on how many of your target market have mobile devices AND will be receptive to receiving your initial communication—the higher the number, the higher the amount you can potentially save. If the answer is 10 percent, then potentially you can reduce your costs by 10 percent.

There is a caveat, however. You may be spending $100,000 monthly on conventional marketing to reach 50,000 people ($2 per contact) and generate 5,000 leads ($20 per lead). Cutting costs by 30 percent to replace conventional with wireless communication doesn't make sense if you only reach 20,000 people ($3.50 per contact) or generate only 500 equally qualified leads ($140 per lead). Conversely, if you cut costs and maintain or exceed the number of prospects contacted or leads generated, then wireless communication is a good option.

Therefore, when you do a pilot project, you not only need to observe how much you are cutting costs, but also consider the number and quality of the leads that you are generating wirelessly. This may be a complicated process for some organizations, but it is the type of effort that needs to be done so you don't waste a lot of time and effort.

You may decide that the potential savings are so small that it doesn't make sense to try to reduce costs of lead generation. That's okay because there are two other calculations to consider.

Take a second pass through your list of lead-generating communication activities and determine how you can use wireless technology to increase the reach, and subsequently the number of leads generated for each of these conventional activities. You may find that, for a few dollars more than what you're already spending, you can expand the reach and duration of your communication activities.

For example, assume you're spending $25,000 for a trade show and for $1,000 in extra costs you can execute a thirty-day post-show wireless campaign that gets prospects you meet at the show to pass your information to friends who also become prospects. While you may not be able to gage with certainty the number of final sales that you will close, when you look at the numbers in this context the risk might seem small compared to potential benefits.

Can You Reduce the Length of Your Sales Cycles?

The third set of calculations you do should determine the value of wireless to communicate with prospects in a way that reduces the cost of the sales cycle. What is the average length of a sales cycle from the point a prospect responds to your lead-generation efforts (or from when he or she initially contacts your company on his or her own) until the prospect finally closes? You can do these calculations for as many products as you want, or by product line, service category, or business unit if it is more convenient.

List the main steps of the sales process that consume the time of your staff and/or delay the close of the sale. By examining each step of the sales process, determine if wireless communication can eliminate or reduce the time or expense of the particular step. Expenses associated with your direct or telemarketing sales force are considered in separate calculations in the next section, so do not include them here.

As an example, assume that a company sells a $50,000 high-end copier. In the sales cycle, once a person becomes a prospect, he or she needs to receive a $15 sales kit with a brochure, spec sheets, and other materials, which consumes a week from request to delivery to the prospect. Then the person makes an average of five calls to clarify questions that he or she, his or her manager, and the purchasing department have. Besides the time a salesperson spends on the phone, internal discussions eat up another two weeks. Then a sales rep has to meet with the prospect's decision-making committee, which is scheduled a month later. Finally, two weeks and three phone calls later, the prospect buys.

If the prospect has a mobile device, you can wirelessly deliver the promo packet as soon as the prospect makes the call, saving $10 and one week of time. Give the prospect wireless access to content that answers most of the questions that everyone who influences the purchase decision has, and you may eliminate four phone calls and save another ten days of time. You probably can't avoid the in-person meeting, or the lost month to schedule it. However, with e-mail or access to additional wireless content you can probably eliminate the last three phone calls and another week of time to get to the final buy decision.

In this scenario, wireless communication saves you the cost of a $10 promotion packet and seven phone calls, plus 24 days that are eliminated from the sales cycle (which means you get paid 24 days faster). Your organization will have different metrics and costs associated with your sales cycle, but this shows how the calculation process works and the benefits that you might uncover. Once you have calculated this information, you can determine the financial impact of the shortened sales cycles (i.e., increased cash flow, greater revenue per year, cost savings). Nonprofits that recruit donors or government agencies that attract new constituents have similar sales cycle costs that can be affected by wireless communication.

Now that you've calculated the savings you can achieve by communicating wirelessly with your regular customers, you need to use these same calculations to determine the value of wireless to reach your other types of prospects.

Resellers

For calculating the potential of wireless activities to reduce the costs required to bring new resellers on board, use all of the same calculations as you did for prospective customers, or modify as necessary. At the conclusion you should have a clear picture of the potential impact of wireless on reaching this audience.

Journalists

Journalists present a bit of a challenge because the value of new relationships can vary widely depending on factors such as which publication the journalist works for, how much coverage the journalist gave your organization, and who knows what else. Probably the best thing to do is look at this as two calculations.

First, how much can you reduce costs without reducing the effectiveness of your PR efforts, and second, how many new journalist relationships can you potentially initiate using wireless activities? The first exercise estimates quantifiable benefits, while the second estimates results that are harder to quantify. After you have a wireless strategy in place for eight to twelve months, it should be easier to establish measurable PR objectives.

In terms of cost reductions, how much are you currently spending per year on conventional communications to reach new journalists to get coverage and build relationships? These expenses include producing and distributing printed materials such as press kits and briefing papers, telephoning, press tours, operations costs (time creating and responding to press opportunities), and administrative costs. How much of these costs do you think you will be able to reduce through wireless communication? How many new relationships do you think you will be able to initiate?

Prospective Employees

How much are you currently spending per year on conventional communications targeted primarily to prospective employees, including the costs from when they first contact you until they sign a job offer letter? This may include printed recruiting materials, outbound and inbound telephone calls, advertising, attending or hosting job fairs, and executive recruiters. If you look at how many new employees you hired over the past year, you will get a sense of how much you're spending on average to recruit employees.

By creating a frequent wireless dialogue with prospective employees, or giving them wireless access to materials on your website or intranet, how much can you lower costs for each of those activities? As with prospective buyers, you may also find that the biggest advantage of wireless is extending the reach of conventional activities such as ads or attending job fairs. If someone going to lunch sees your billboard that promotes the job of a lifetime and directs them to wireless content, he or she may be more inclined to respond then and there by PDA rather than waiting until he or she returns to the office.

Analyzing the Impact of Wireless on Your Sales Force

To determine the potential impact of wireless on your mobile sales force, you need to consider how this technology can reduce the cost of managing salespeople, enabling them to operate more efficiently and helping them to shorten the sales cycles.

How much does it cost IT to support each salesperson's remote access to your organization's network? The telephone charges alone can be staggering if a salesperson has to dial in to the network every day. Many times salespeople need technical support to get their modems or network connection software to work. How much can you reduce this cost by using wireless mobile devices? Using Ricochet or RIM's BlackBerry devices can give salespeople unlimited access for fixed monthly fees.

Are there conventional communication costs incurred to keep salespeople in remote or home offices informed about important company developments, such as overnight shipping, faxes, and phone charges? Product changes or inventory availability, new prices, or general company news are in great demand while on the road, so you should give serious consideration to how much of the costs of delivering this information can be reduced through wireless communication.

Calculate how many sales opportunities from prospects are lost because of lost or delayed messages, or poor general communications, and how many of these can be turned into sales if your salespeople have appropriate wireless hardware and applications. You can cost justify the expense of giving your sales force PDAs the same way you justified giving your customers PDAs. If a $500 BlackBerry gives a sales rep always-on access to e-mail that results in each rep responding to ten, twelve, or more additional prospects per month, the evidence would indicate this is a viable option.

Analyze the role that your sales force plays in the sales cycle. How many meetings do they average per prospect, and how many of these can be shortened or eliminated if a sales rep can wirelessly access answers to questions that otherwise would have to wait until the rep returns to the office? Can your salespeople shorten your sales cycle or increase their close rates if they can wirelessly access your databases of product, customer, or other information while on a sales call? How much will this impact your business? You may not produce definitive numbers the first time you do this calculation, but after a pilot project you should see more quantifiable benefits.

Will wireless technology increase your sales staff's effectiveness if you give them wireless access to product-training, sales support materials such as PowerPoint files and general sales skills training? How much do you estimate this will impact your organization in financial terms? In many organizations the hardest (and most expensive) thing to do is get salespeople into the office for training because salespeople view every day in the office as a day not selling. But they also have downtime between meetings, in airports, and in hotel rooms where they can access training and product materials.

Other Financial Considerations

There is another financial consideration you may want to include in your calculations, which is to determine if you can use wireless to open up new markets and generate additional prospective customers. By using a service such as AvantGo to set up a channel for your business, can you have an international presence and open up the potential for worldwide prospects? Compare the annual cost of communicating with these prospects ($5 per person) using this method with the cost of expanding communication to international markets through conventional methods.

A word of caution, though. Roswell Books, a Canadian bookstore I interviewed a few years ago, built a website and the sudden onslaught of leads almost put them out of business. Quite a few dot-com companies had this same problem and did go out of business. When you calculate the potential increase in prospects from new markets, be sure to do the math to determine the financial impact of a sudden surge in leads and sales. If you are wildly successful, there is bound to be a strain on service and support, purchasing, shipping, and accounting staffs. These are good problems to have, but only if you have adequately planned and budgeted for them.

Main Strategic Objectives

Since there are several possible benefits that wireless offers for communicating with prospective customers, your opening charge into this new frontier should focus on just two or three objectives for this strategic dimension. As you start to achieve successful results, you can expand your efforts in this strategic dimension. Here are three efforts to consider:

1. Increasing the reach of your conventional communication activities

2. Reducing the cost and increasing the speed of each sale

3. Enhancing the effectiveness of field or retail sales people

Build on Conventional Success

For many organizations using wireless to build on the success of your conventional communication is a good strategic objective. If you have communication projects already in motion, it may not require much work or expense to add on a wireless component.

The same way that smart marketers use direct mail to drive prospects to their websites, use direct mail or a trade show appearance to motivate people to use their PDAs to access wireless content, provide you with feedback, or add their e-mail address to your data base. It doesn't have to add costs to your direct mail, and you're already spending a lot going to the trade shows.

If you use a wireless ASP and your web design team is on the ball with creating content that can also be accessed through wireless devices, the additional costs of implementing the wireless activities shouldn't be prohibitive. I will, however, caution you to not skimp on quality to save a buck or two. You can have a simple execution and still present a polished professional image.

After you execute a couple of projects and things go very well, expand on what already works. Collect data that provides guidelines for future efforts and a basis for comparing results when you start adding variables to new campaigns. Use this success to build political support from key people within your organization that results in access to more resources and extra muscle when you need to move roadblocks out of your way.

Conversely, should the initial results be disappointing, you can refine your implementation without a major disruption of prospecting efforts because the direct mailings and trade show appearances will keep on keepin' on, as we used to say in the 70s. More importantly, you minimize the potential public damage to your organization's image and prospects' receptivity to future wireless efforts you may launch. It is better to release a dud and have only 1,000 people see it than to drop a dud on a million people's mobile devices, especially while wireless is so new.

McDonaldland—There But for the Grace of Good Planning Go Ye

Some organizations' strategy to use new technology to extend their conventional communication is merely to digitize brochures and ads. If you adopt this as your strategic approach to wireless, I think you will be very disappointed with the results.

I remember when McDonald's extended their advertising campaign to the Web by posting one of their TV ads on their site around 1995, then made such a big deal about this you would have thought that it was the harbinger of great things to come on the Net. As if! Let's see, that's a bazillion bytes of data for an ad that's already run on TV, and most Net surfers only had 28.8 bps or slower modems.

I don't know what was worse, the fact that McDonald's did it, or that people tried to download it—an experience slower than watching grass grow. Well, people online and off got a good belly laugh from that. Worse, mainstream newspapers wrote stories about how bad an idea it was. I predict that a few companies will try something similar with wireless.

Now, fast forward to 2001. BMW (the high-end auto maker) builds a website they call BMW Films (www.bmwfilms.com) and posts a seven-minute short movie called *Star* that features recording artist Madonna and a BMW 530i. Madonna plays a spoiled rock star taken by a hired driver on a wild ride on winding roads (a la James Bond movies).

Note to MickeyD: You can't watch the movie (i.e., BMW ad) on TV. This boosts online interest. The movie actually has a plot, and there's a star. Subsequently, over 7 million people have watched this and other films on the site. Also, the BMW movie is in all of the web media formats for easy downloading and viewing regardless of what type of computer and media software you have.

And what is the lesson for you, the reader? If you're going to chart new wireless waters for your communication efforts, build the right boat, test the winds of change, and don't throw the bon voyage party until you're reasonably sure you won't sink 30 feet from the dock. Even if your strategy is to extend your ad campaign, wireless offers you a different way to communicate. Make sure that the wireless content you build optimizes the unique capabilities of the technology, and that the content isn't adversely affected by wireless' limitations. And one other thing: Don't tell *The Wall Street Journal* what's going on until you're sure your audience will be receptive to your efforts.

Reduce Costs and Shorten Your Sales Cycles

The objective to reduce the cost of each sale is a winner because it's clear how to measure your progress and, when you're successful, you deliver a benefit so compelling it should be easy to get resources to expand your efforts.

This does not have to be an extensive undertaking. If most of your prospects spend 15 minutes with a call center person asking the same 10 questions, you can proactively deliver to prospects' PDAs the answers to those questions, a 10 percent discount coupon, a link to your web order page, and a unique phone number. If only 500 prospects read your message and then order online, or call just to place an order without the usual chit chat, that's about 7,500 minutes saved or $28,125 if your call center people make $15 an hour.

There are numerous variations on how you might save money depending on what your costs are to move prospects through the sales cycle. However, the more complex your product, service, or sales process, the less likely it is that a wireless application may be effective as a stand-alone tool.

This is neither good nor bad. I just mention it so you will maintain realistic expectations for the potential. Too often new technology gets so much hype that people deploy it isolated from other applications or business activities. Then they are disappointed when the technology doesn't perform as hyped. There is a strong case to be made for integration.

More organizations are using CRM software and Internet tools to compile customer and market data, enhance the selling process, and gain a competitive edge, as I mentioned in Chapter 3. If you are using these tools to measure and predict customers' shopping behavior, also determine if and how they use mobile devices. Extrapolate this data about mobile use to your target market of prospects since their wireless use should mirror your customer base. This should help you decide when to use wireless communication, or what wireless content is best suited to convince prospects to take the next step in the sales cycle.

Vendors of these CRM tools are adding features that enable your sales staff to use wireless devices to access company data and product information. When possible and practical, take this capability one step further by configuring these same tools to enable prospects to have wireless access to the some of the materials your staff accesses to present in sales calls. If this feature can reduce the number of sales calls to each prospect and maintain or increase the close rate, this is good.

Another way to cut cost and time from the sales cycle is to wirelessly deliver content that enables prospects to calculate for themselves what financial benefits your product or service offers specifically for them. Then get prospects to beam the results to the other decision makers' PDAs during their next management meeting. This can result in fewer meetings that your salespeople have to attend, and it should definitely speed up the decision-making process.

If you sell expensive and complex products or services, there is likely a point when your salespeople have to work with prospects to do a needs analysis to figure out the ROI of buying that product or service. This could involve a lengthy question and answer session, or maybe extensive number crunching. If there are different departments or individuals within an organization affected by the purchase, this needs analysis can take days and several meetings to complete.

Extensity (www.extensity.com) markets time and expense, procurement, and travel planning applications, which can cost a significant amount of money, but also deliver a high ROI for customers. From their website qualified prospects can access a tool to measure the products' soft and hard dollar savings potential across key operational areas by performing a full analysis based on industry benchmarking data. Give prospects wireless access to this type of needs analysis tool, and give yourself one more opportunity to save time and money.

Building Relationships Can Shorten Your Sales Cycle

A good way to shorten your sales cycle is to use wireless applications to build on-going relationships. Most prospects will not jump on their Palm or iPAQ to begin looking at information when they're shopping for their first boat, a new printing press, or a hospital for triple-bypass surgery. But if these individuals respond to a phone call, a magazine ad, your website, or a referral, be ready to create a wireless umbilical cord to nurture them through the sales cycle until the birth of the sale.

The longer your sales cycles, the more meetings, mailings, phone follow ups, and general aggravation you have to deal with to get to the close. Sometimes during this process an interloper may cut in and steal the prospect from you. Use wireless technology to occasionally intercede throughout the sales cycle to keep prospects informed, to answer questions, and to make them feel good about doing business with you.

Relationship building can be pursued wirelessly by government and non-profit organizations, even though there may not be a dollars-and-cents sale at the end of the dance. Organizations at all levels of government have new constituencies they have to win over (close) such as newly elected politicians, newly appointed bureaucrats, or people new in the neighborhood.

Here's an example from the commercial world that local governments can adapt to really roll out the welcome wagon for new constituents. Portland CitySearch in Oregon (http://portland.citysearch.com) is a dot-com business run by Ticketmaster. The website provides up-to-date, locally-produced descriptions of area businesses, government agencies, restaurants, schools, community events, recreational activities, and attractions as well as maps, reviews, and other features. Original editorial content with a local flavor is featured throughout the site.

CitySearch encourages all types of people, including newcomers to the Internet, to become more involved in the community. The ability to demonstrate this online resource to the public is critical to the company's success of CitySearch, so they used wireless technology to take it to the streets.

The staff acquired and cleaned up a 22-foot monster 1967 Cadillac ambulance, and outfitted it with a 21-inch monitor, a CPU rebuilt by high-school students from used computers, and a wireless modem and named the vehicle Webster. Webster cruises the streets of Portland Wednesday through Sunday and attends community events and festivals, giving the public a hands-on introduction to CitySearch and the Internet. These introductions lead to an ongoing online relationship with people in the community.

Any municipality can partner with CitySearch, or create their own community site if CitySearch is not in their particular city, and put their city vehicles into neighborhoods to introduce new residents to city services. But enhance this tactic by using computers with infrared ports so people with mobile devices can download content from the site that's designed specifically to foster an ongoing dialogue with citizens who have not used services they may need later.

Additional wireless content can be created for these road shows for distribution to visiting executives in town for a convention whom you want to convince to hold their companies' sales meeting there next year, or to move their companies to your city. You might want to involve the local chambers of commerce in this effort. Once you start tossing the concept around your office, many creative ideas will pop up.

Build Relationships with a Variety of Audiences

There's a generation coming into its own, with one following closely on its heels, that uses mobile devices more than just about any other communication medium. And they use it for more than buying CDs and playing games. Nicole, the two-year-old daughter of close friends of mine immediately grabbed my iPAQ one day, totally fascinated with tapping the screen and watching things happen. In ten years PDAs will probably be the communication and shopping tool of choice for Nicole and her friends (Guard your digital credit cards, Mommy!).

Companies that market to the teen and young adult market will do well to explore ways to use wireless technology to develop a relationship with kids who may not be customers today, but are likely prospects for the future. Kids also have a great influence on parents' purchases. Hosting educational and entertainment content that enables kids to get more value from their mobile devices should create a favorable image for your company that translates into eventual business relationships. For maximum impact, deliver the type of content that can also involve parents so they're assured you're not exploiting impressionable youth.

The demographics of people who contribute to nonprofit organizations and patronize the arts fit rather snugly into the demographics of adult PDA users—financially secure, college-educated, managers and executives. While the costs are relatively small and there is still a novelty to the technology, this is a good time to experiment with using wireless to do relationship building that enlarges your constituencies.

According to research conducted by the Carolina Hurricanes hockey team, many people don't make their weekend entertainment plans until Wednesday or Thursday, which sometimes results in missing events that sell out days or weeks earlier. If you create a wireless service that delivers news about upcoming weekend concerts or art shows, with maybe trivia quizzes about music or art history, you can build a interactive relationship that results in new donors or patrons.

The value of relationship building applies to prospective resellers, journalists, and employees as well, particularly if you're in a smaller organization. Distributors and retailers carry a lot of vendors' products and some of those products may contribute more to their bottom lines that you do. So you have to work as hard to build relationships with them as you do with prospective customers, maybe even harder. Wireless can play an important role in that effort.

The sales process doesn't end when a reseller decides to carry you for the first time. You have to sell individual sales reps who may already have favorite products they like to promote over others. They have to be convinced to add you to the already crowded list of products they must know about.

Wireless content that helps sales reps understand not only your products, but also the type of person who buys your products, can be the deciding factor in your success throughout the channel. The insights that you pass on about your target market can also help the salesperson sell other products to a prospect, which increases commission income and thus tightens the bond with you.

Building an initial relationship with journalists can be a most time-consuming and expensive process, and here, too, the right wireless strategy can play a role in your success. Chapters 12 and 13 focus on the tactical topic of PR because good media coverage is a great equalizer for any commercial, government, or nonprofit organization that has to fight for customers, constituents, donations, or other resources important to your prosperity.

Even though we are going through some rough economic times as this book goes to press, things will no doubt swing in the other direction, and convincing good people to come work for you will become another area in which effective communication will have financial consequences. Costs for finding, recruiting, and hiring top talent can run into the thousands of dollars when the economy is good, and costs are still a factor even when the economy dives.

If the type of individual you want working at your organization is the intelligent, tech-savvy, forward-thinking person who typically owns a PDA, then your wireless strategy should have a relationship-building component for job candidates. People who are job hunting tend to do so most often when they're not in the office, so mobile devices are an ideal platform through which to reach these folks. Once you get a good candidate interested in your organization, you want to have a two-way line of communication open to him, and wireless is a good channel for this also.

Give Your Sales Force an Edge

With the ascendance of the Web, the intranet, the virtual private network, and sales force automation (SFA) software, the big potential value of these technologies is that mobile salespeople need only to carry a laptop to close more sales at faster rates. Whatever information and applications aren't on the laptop can be pulled up via a modem connection back to the intranet.

This actually works pretty well—as long as the prospect's property is blessed with an easy-to-find, easy-to-use phone line for the modem. Have you ever been in a meeting with a prospective customer, retailer, or rookie journalist who doesn't know you from Adam, or Eve, and tried to find a line for a modem connection when you really needed it? You'd probably have better luck finding a leprechaun.

Use wireless technology to take this final kink out of the sales force automation process. All of that fumbling around looking for a modem line in front of people who barely know you does not help your image. At the very least, it can increase your salespeople's personal efficiency and productivity to levels that justify the investment. As with field service staff, Ricochet offers great value with minimum costs because once that modem is in the laptop, your salespeople will have speedy access to everything they need without requiring changes to your applications.

The Cobbler's Kids Finally Get New Shoes

You probably know the well-worn phrase about the cobbler's kids never having any shoes because he's so busy making shoes for everyone else. It's one of those corporate *Aesop's Fables* often used to show how we folks in the technology business don't use technology very well for ourselves. Well, Aristasoft doesn't fall into that category.

Aristasoft is an ASP that rents ERP, CRM, and engineering document management applications. Rich Reynolds, the company's IT manager, says that they used Ricochet wireless modems to enable Aristasoft's sales staff to demonstrate their products at prospects' sites using a web browser. Reynolds reports that, "The biggest benefit of Ricochet is that we can get to the Web without wasting time. Before we had these [wireless modems], our field support personnel, who are located all over the country, would have to stay near a phone and provide remote support to the salespeople through telephone dial up in case there were problems." And the problems, they were aplenty.

"Prior to leaving our office we spent time on the phone with the prospect to set up his network to talk to ours for the product demo, which took up a lot of engineers' time and our people hadn't even arrived at the prospect's facilities. Then getting connected was its own nightmare for salespeople because they had to first log on to the prospect's network, and go through there to our network in order to simulate using our product. Salespeople would show up and couldn't get logged on to the prospect's network, or the network would drop the connection between his servers and ours, so that was a lot more work. Plus, we're not only talking about meeting delays here. It's hard to inspire a lot of confidence in your product or your people if you're having a Raggedy Anne and Andy show like this for a prospect."

Reynolds says that now their presentations are much better. Field support staff get a notification by pager when a demo starts and they go online. Ricochet enables the IT staff back in the home office to access salespeople's laptops to facilitate demos remotely when necessary. Presentations are much smoother, and field support people have more flexibility, which is important for those on the after-hours shifts who otherwise couldn't leave their computers. Everyone is a lot happier.

Reynolds brought up an interesting point that you should consider when implementing any application that gives people access to important organization or customer data—security. "Our biggest concern was security for us and for the client. We tested to see what issues there might be. We tried to attack [digitally] the laptops to make sure the modems didn't open us up to problems. When you're connected to the Net, your machine could be attacked if there are vulnerabilities in the connection applications you use."

If you have the security well under control, having that access to the home network and software, such as sales force automation applications, has great potential advantages.

For example, Reynolds says, "I'm visiting Cisco for a presentation, but when I get there I see that one of our current customers is right next door. I can use the wireless connection to jump online quickly to scan that customer's file in our database server and find out that they made a call an hour ago asking about one of our new products." Or ideally, a wireless notification drops into your PDA right after the call comes in.

Wireless—You Make Me Feel Like a Surgeon

Getting high-speed and full-screen access to applications and data is a preferred option for many. But there are those places and times when a laptop just isn't practical (like, maybe managing the herd on a cattle drive in Nevada). The mobile sales group for U.S. Surgical is a cut above many in terms of having rough sales environments.

U.S. Surgical, a division of Tyco, develops, manufactures, and markets a line of surgical wound closure products and advanced surgical products to hospitals throughout the world. About 400 salespeople are on the road meeting the demand for a range of products from surgical and cancer detection tools to surgical staplers. These sales representatives are often required to go into the operating rooms of hospitals. Before converting to PDAs, it seems there were problems with laptops causing sensitive medical equipment to malfunction, or the laptops proved to be too bulky to use and got in the way.

Since it was important that the salespeople capture and access sales information efficiently and quickly regardless of where they were, something had to be done. U.S. Surgical called on NetReturn, LLC (www.netreturnllc.com), a technology consulting firm. They developed a web-based application called ExpertSeller that enabled salespeople to access a wide variety of corporate data, including sales reports, product, pricing, customer, and related information.

AvantGo provides the technology to convert the server data that ExpertSeller generated into formats that any devices using the Palm OS or Pocket PCs can access, and also enables sales reps to interact with the data in wireless or offline mode. Salespeople can subscribe to reports that can be automatically generated from data in any database stored anywhere in the company, and then delivered to their PDAs.

Sometimes, your salespeople need wireless access for simple tasks. A buddy of mine told me that at one point in his last job, it would have helped to have a PDA with Net access solely for the purpose of getting to the company intranet that held stock quotes and other data for their customers and prospects. Before some important meetings, he would have to phone the office and ask someone to scan the up-to-the-minute data for that prospect because knowing those figures gave him an additional negotiation edge in the meeting.

While salespeople typically need more data than stock quotes, simple access to the Net can be a lifesaver. With prospects, it is often unpredictable what they might ask about, so wireless access to general information can be as important as access to the office intranet. There is also the issue of getting information to salespeople who might not have land-line access to the Net or e-mail all day once they leave their office or hotel room. There are some organizations that have equipped their worldwide sales force with wireless devices such as the RIM BlackBerry just so these people can get and respond to their e-mail.

Yo, Wanna Philly Cheesesteak with That Car?

If you run a retail operation, your salespeople work most of the time within your facility. However, wireless can still play an important role in making these individuals more efficient. The Brandow Group (www.brandowgroup.com) is a car dealership with three locations in the Philadelphia suburbs whose salespeople use wireless technology to close new buyers.

"We are committed to being understaffed with good equipment, rather than have a lot of people underequipped." This sums up Brandow Group CEO Peter Brandow's philosophy on wireless technology as a sales force tool. In 1998 he purchased software from Aether Systems and PDAs to enhance the company's wireless capabilities and reduce its cell phone bills. But Mr. Brandow was after more benefits than that.

Typically you need salespeople to be in a dealer location all day long until 8:00 p.m. or 9:00 p.m. However, from 1:00 p.m. to 5:30 p.m. a few shoppers show up, which means you have a lot of people sitting around with nothing to do. This costs both the owners and the salespeople money. By giving everyone PDAs, salespeople can go home or run errands during the downtime, but still manage the e-mail that comes in from the company's website. The staff doesn't limit themselves to one technology, though, using both PDAs and laptops.

Brandow says, "They use PDAs for 'call to action' activities, such as receiving messages while meeting prospects away from the dealership or rescheduling appointments, but the laptops help when people need to access a lot of details that are best displayed on a bigger screen. If mobile phones increase screen size, these can play a bigger role in managing information sent back to prospects in response to a query." It would be nice if there were wireless-enabled chips embedded into cars that contained details just about each car so his people could pull information to their PDAs from a specific car as they walk by it in the lot.

Brandow does have what I consider a different approach to retailing than many people I know. "When I know you want to buy, I don't want you here. I just want to finish the process. When you [the customer] can coordinate online or wirelessly with the retail outlet, this is a great thing. You can do all of the process online so you don't have to waste time coming in. An in-store experience can cost as much as $1,500 for each party." So many people today use the Web to do all the research that they used to do through a dozen conversations with salespeople, that it makes sense to integrate wireless technology into the process to shorten the sales cycle even more.

Zoom, zoom.

Supporting the Retail Environment

Manufacturers who rely on the retail channel for all or most of their sales may approach wireless applications differently than retail businesses. In retail environments, employee turnover and technology limitations make any wireless strategy a challenge.

Famous Footwear, the shoe store chain presented in Chapter 4, carries many brands of shoes for women, men, and children. A new salesperson could lose his or her mind in the first weeks trying to remember which shoe is best for what type of individual. These stores already have PDAs and wireless LANs that they're using to accurately manage pricing information. The home office could easily beam product briefings, frequently asked questions (based on wireless feedback from salespeople), and other content that will help the sales staff learn and retain more details.

If you're a shoe manufacturer, you should provide wireless content about your products to Famous Footwear's headquarters, which passes it out to their retail stores. Rather than give the wrong or no information about your shoes if a prospect asks about them, your content helps salespeople answer these questions accurately so they can concentrate on providing general service and taking the order.

When prospects go into a retail store and suddenly remember an important question that could remove their last barrier to buying your product, enable salespeople to open a wireless link through an IM to your sales desk and get the answers they need. Even though the sales staff may offer to help, some people prefer to shop around the store on their own and have as little action with the staff as possible. There are a few bugs that need be worked out of IM technology, most notably getting the different vendors' IM products to work together, but still explore the potential it offers.

You Don't Know Jack? You Should

The Jack, from a company named WideRay (www.wideray.com), is an incredible tool for delivering content into a retail environment. The Jack is the size of a moderately thick textbook, and it contains all the intelligence and computing power to enable you to beam content to the Jack, which then enables people with mobile devices to download that content through infrared ports.

The Jack is a portable, self-contained device that retail outlets can build into point of purchase (POP) displays and information kiosks, mount in company lobbies and on counter tops, and integrate with LANs and point of sales systems. These units can beam product info, customer testimonials, FAQs, discount coupons, and promotions directly to prospects' mobile devices. Retail staff can just smile and take orders. You could even slap a piece of Velcro on the back of a Jack and hang it in the employee lounge so you can beam the crew training materials and product updates.

British Motor Car Distributors (www.bmcd.com) is a Bay Area California purveyor of fine automobiles from England such as the Rolls Royce, Jaguar, and the ride-of-choice for Tomb Raider's Lara Croft, the Land Rover Defender. There is a WideRay Jack in each of its three dealer stores that contains pictures, specs, background information, and lease agreements for the Land Rovers.

Sales Manager Gordon Blackstock reports that, "These Jacks are great. About 20 percent of prospects who come in download the Land Rover materials, and we're starting to trace sales to these people. This is better than printed brochures because after someone leaves, he or she may throw the brochure somewhere and never see it again. But once he or she has information on his or her PDA, it's with him or her everywhere he or she goes, anytime he or she wants it. Also, if a friend says 'I've been thinking about getting a Land Rover,' the person who downloaded the information from us can beam it to his or her friend."

British Motor Car takes most of the material directly from the manufacturer and adds specialized content such as contact information from the various stores. They also have occasional lease specials that they make available to download. The company expects to add content for their other product lines and explore other promotional possibilities.

There's a lot of hype about location-based services that allow retail outlets to zap the mobile devices of people as they walk down the street, which I think is absurd, intrusive, and not likely to happen anytime soon. However, technology that enables a retailer to reach out and beam someone (or vice versa) once he or she enters the premises is a more effective approach. It can be very profitable for you to help retailers implement this type of application.

Food for Thought

Here are some questions to ask yourself about implementing wireless to communicate with prospective customers:

1. What are the steps within the sales process that can be supported or eliminated through effective use of wireless technology, and will the subsequent cost or time savings be worth the investment?

2. Are your prospects likely to be using wireless mobile devices?

3. What sales strategy and technology is already in place and how will wireless fit into this strategy?

4. Has wireless been overhyped internally in terms of sales expectations (unrealistic expectations can cause real problems later)?

5. What printed material, such as brochures, research data, and newsletters, can be converted to wireless content to facilitate prospects' online shopping and possible sales process?

6. What materials can you make available for prospects who have to "sell" others within their organizations on buying your products or services?

7. Do you have the adequate staff and technology resources to monitor prospects as you are moving them closer to the sale through wireless activities?

8. Is your sales force already using PDAs (with or without Net access), and if many are not using the technology, how difficult will it be to get them to adapt to using it?

9. How can conventional sales strategies support your online efforts or vice versa?

10. Are there incentives for the sales staff to incorporate wireless applications into their efforts to close prospects?

CHAPTER 6

Reduce Costs and Improve Efficiency of Internal Business Operations

Wireless technologies for internal communications are deployed to reduce costs and increase operating efficiencies. It also increases personal productivity and improves management of your physical assets (e.g., equipment, vehicles). This may seem like a tall order for a technology that some people consider to be in its infancy, but there's a lot that can be done with it internally.

The jury might still be out on the question of how much value there is in wireless communication to the outside world until your external audiences increase their use of the technology. But by the end of this chapter you will find a few compelling reasons to at least test the wireless waters with a pilot project or two for internal communication.

Implementing new technologies to facilitate internal communication is probably the easiest concept for your organization to understand, financially justify, implement, and support. There is relatively easy access to data for analyzing the potential positive impact of the project, and senior management collectively has more daily contact with internal communication processes than with the external ones. Once everyone agrees on a plan of attack, managing the technology implementation is easier because it's easier to manage internal audiences than external ones.

Determine if This Is the Right
Strategic Dimension for You

In order to assess whether this is a good strategic option for your organization, it will help to divide internal wireless communication into two categories: communication between people and communication between physical assets and people.

For the first category, do not limit yourself to evaluating workers who are mobile outside of the office. Sales staff, service people, and other road warriors who work outside of the main office most of the time are often away for days at a time. It's easy to chart the difficulties they have keeping in touch with the home office, and you can clearly quantify the costs they incur when they do contact the office, particularly through remote dial-in to the network. However, there are numerous people who never leave the physical premises, but are frequently away from their desktop computers.

Executives at RIM (manufacturers of the BlackBerry PDA) refer to these employees who spend 20 percent or more of their time in meetings, lectures, solving problems, and more meetings as interfacility roamers. Project managers, IT staff, nurses, warehouse and shipping staffs, assembly line workers, facilities managers, and even custodial workers play vital roles in the internal communications of an organization. Subsequently they need to be considered in any discussions of the potential benefit of wireless.

In this chapter the term road warrior refers to employees who travel away from your facilities, and mobile workers refers to both road warriors and interfacility roamers.

In the second category of internal communication, there are enormous benefits to using wireless to manage physical assets. For example, building tools, vehicles, and medical devices are assets that need to be tracked better so workers can get to them when they're needed. It may seem trivial if a driver spends 10 minutes looking for a forklift because someone on the previous shift parked it in a remote corner of a warehouse the size of Maine. But 10 minutes per driver per shift five days a week for 50 weeks amounts to 40 hours of salary that you're paying for someone to wander around the warehouse.

Tom Nogles, vice president of strategic services at wireless application vendor ThinAirApps (www.thinairapps.com), states that, from his company's perspective, "We're seeing that the value of embedded wireless can be greater than the value of human interaction with wireless. Because you have so much automation capabilities built into assets that these wireless applications can monitor, trigger, or control, organizations can get a great ROI. This technology may need to improve a little, but embedded wireless could be the biggest growth area in terms of dollar volume."

The value of pursuing this strategic option will be dictated as much by the size of your organization as the amount of cost reduction you want to achieve. Some smaller organizations will find that the amount of money saved does not justify the expense of buying, installing, and supporting wireless software applications because the cost of employees communicating to each other is low. However, you may find that just giving people mobile devices can be cost justified.

If everyone at a 10-person service firm is an occupational therapist that contracts out to local hospitals, maybe the biggest internal communication expense is the hour that a $60 an hour therapist spends each day coordinating who goes where. Giving everyone PDAs with access to a web-based group calendar may be all the wireless technology that the firm needs because everyone can access and manage their own calendars. However, a 300-person organization that provides services in 20 states will likely have a variety of communication costs and this will justify a more complex implementation.

As you evaluate the potential of this strategic option, don't let the fact that your organization is growing prevent you from moving forward because you're worried about outgrowing your implementation. In the 10-person operation, this solution I described might cost $7,500 for the first year ($200 each for the PDAs, plus monthly service fees), but the hours saved each day at $60 an hour pays for everything in six months. If the company added 200 people after a year and became too large for this solution, they can drop it and still be $7,500 ahead in terms of money saved.

Assess the Potential Impact on Business Operations

As you examine how your business operates, are there inefficiencies and costs that wireless can potentially eliminate?

Dial-In Remote Access

Do mobile users have to rely on laptops with modems to dial into your networks to access and send e-mail, or to access general documents? There is a high cost to pay for these capabilities. There are stories aplenty about road warriors accidentally deleting files, losing e-mails, and creating general havoc with the networks because remote access software is difficult to use. Besides the migraine headaches this produces in the IT department, road warriors' blood pressure levels and telephone charges go through the roof because connections are repeatedly dropped.

You can achieve significant cost reduction by replacing dial-up remote access with wireless remote access. This is one of the reasons why BlackBerries are so popular. You pay a fixed monthly charge for each user to get a connection that is "always on," so users don't have to dial up the home network or use a wireless dial-in to the Net to get their e-mail. Some people report that their laptop dial-in time after six months of BlackBerry use dropped from 12.3 hours to 6.8 hours each month. This saves phone charges, dial-in costs to the network, and a lot of tech support.

Intranets are popular in part because organizations still can save paper and production costs by digitizing documents, manuals, and forms for remote access (which is why remote dial-in became popular) but people can use Net browsers rather than dial-in software. You may discover that mobile workers still have to access the Net with modems or from their desktops, which still can be a problem. Wireless enables mobile workers to get what they need from wherever they are when regular intranet access is not possible or practical.

Get Off Your Knees and Be Free of Network Cabling

Many organizations are finding that using wireless LANs saves them a lot of money and aggravation. Wireless LANs can reduce the amount of network cabling you need if you're opening or moving to new offices, plus you can add or eliminate people from the network without spending time adding or pulling out cable.

A wireless LAN is an inexpensive way to give people network access in conference rooms, auditoriums, cafeterias, and other locations where they work, but are impractical for wired networks. Quite a few laptops and other computer products are sold with wireless LAN cards built in, so now you can eliminate this network hardware expense from the cost of going wireless.

If your organization has a lot of contractors who work at your site for weeks or months at a time, this can justify using wireless LANs to provide temporary access. Be careful about security since these LANs technically can be easy to access by some n'er-do-well in the neighborhood with a laptop and a wireless LAN card. But since you will have extra security precautions anyway if you have "guest" employees accessing your regular LAN, it shouldn't be too difficult to add security for the wireless LANs. Consider wireless LANs if, conversely, your organization is the consulting group that's going to live at someone else's location and you need to have access to your clients' networks.

If you want to have a good contingency plan in case you lose power or some other disaster strikes your organization's facilities, add wireless LANs to the mix. When the World Trade Center in New York was destroyed after the terrorist attacks, nearby ThinAirApps lost its Internet connection. ThinAirApps installed a wireless LAN in a company's office across the street that still had a high-speed connection, set up a laptop with a wireless modem in the window facing that company, and provided Net access to other ThinAirApps employees.

Another way to reduce networking costs is through the Ricochet network. If this coverage is available where your facilities are located, and the building's steel or concrete does not block transmission, you can deploy Ricochet modems and reduce the need for wireless LAN stations. If you're thinking about giving mobile workers Ricochet service as part of your strategic plan for enhancing field service or the sales force's efforts, internal communication becomes one more benefit to justify the investment.

Assess the Potential Impact of Wireless Department by Department

After looking at your general business operations and how wireless technology might impact them, do an analysis by reviewing how each department specifically operates. Involve the managers of these departments in this analysis to get their assessments of how they see wireless playing a role.

Give IT the Support It Deserves

IT people probably burn through more pairs of sneakers than the average interfacility roamer. They are constantly on the move answering the mournful pleas of the technology challenged from all corners of the stone, steel, and cubicle jungles. Often while the IT staff is in the middle of one rescue and repair mission, new pleas keep coming in as the techno-beasts continue to snarl, snap, simper, and die.

Wireless access to manuals, repair records, and vendor support sites can keep IT on top of problems, reduce response time, and make it possible to take a decent lunch break or go home at a normal hour. Buy software that monitors network and computer performance and alerts IT before these systems give up the ghost. IT staff will spend less time doing crisis management and more time enhancing technology productivity.

Keep Marketing People Connected

Marketing people, particularly those who deal with the day-to-day execution of marketing campaigns, are responsible for keeping their fingers firmly on the pulse of market change. Reality, however, often dictates that they keep their bodies firmly planted in seats from one meeting to the next all day. Seriously consider equipping them with mobile devices plugged into up-to-the-minute sources of market, competitor, customer, and marketing campaign news.

In the short and volatile history of the Web, we have seen the pace of product life cycles, and business in general, accelerate to an insane speed. At the same time the attention span of the average human being has diminished dramatically. Marketing opportunities are short, sometimes measured in days, so your marketing people need an edge if they are to take advantage of those opportunities.

Human Resources

Human resource people, responsible for keeping your talent supply line full, are also the purveyors of policy, paperwork, benefits knowledge, skills development, company news, and other information vital to the well-being of your employees. If you want to increase their effectiveness in this role, give them the ability to push wireless content to the road warriors and interfacility roamers.

There's an HR consulting group that provides organizations with wireless-enabled HR portals that tie into the various employment records, benefit packages, and other data that employees occasionally need to access. So if you're a bank executive in a hospital emergency room because your child just got hurt, you can wirelessly access details about your insurance coverage, forms you need to complete, and so forth.

Explore how HR can reduce costs for employee training materials by converting them into wireless content that mobile workers can access when they have stretches of downtime. Otherwise that material can become just one more stack of paper buried in a larger stack engulfing workers' "In" baskets when they return to the office.

You can also use wireless-delivered materials for those off-site training and professional development sessions held in places where individual Net access is often difficult (hotels, cabins in the woods). If you do several of these a year, it may be worth considering getting WideRay Jacks just for this purpose. Before leaving the office you can load them up with training materials that employees can access with their PDAs. Office staff can regularly beam updates, messages, and other information to the Jacks during the training sessions.

Choose Wireless When Time Is Money

If you have a department that provides consulting services to support the products you sell, Nogles sees wireless benefiting them also, particularly if you charge customers for that time. "Giving professional services wireless capabilities can increase the accuracy of accounting for their time, plus they can process the necessary paperwork for a client engagement while still at the site and speed up the invoicing process. If they are dispersed across geographies, there's an ROI you can derive from better deployment and management of these people."

Your customer support staff can benefit from the same capability, even if you don't bill customers for their time by the hour. (Some organizations provide this as part of the product price, or as a separate annual service contract.) Several months of tracking in detail how much time support people in the field spend on different support tasks or with various customers can be a real eye-opener, showing you numerous places to streamline efficiency. You may even find that you need to charge some customers more for the support they're receiving.

Connecting to Employees Without Desktops

The assembly line, warehouse, and shipping staffs collectively are the crux where supply meets demand. These employees have to keep products coming off the line and moving through the storage facilities to shipping docks in a rhythm to match the sometimes erratic demands of customers. Companies automate every other part of the supply chain but some fail to provide automation tools here.

Since most of these workers are rarely in front of a computer, are mobile devices the best way for them to plug into sales force automation, supply chain management, shipment tracking, and other software running this part of the business? Mobile devices can help these workers get wireless access to the automation systems of suppliers, contract manufacturers, and other third-party organizations that are part of the chain.

Using wireless technology to increase efficiency working with third parties is not just a manufacturing issue. There are PR and advertising agencies, freelancers, executive recruiters (headhunters to you readers over the age of 40), consultants of every stripe, and vendors of every hue who can benefit from using wireless. All of these people can be integral elements of your business operation. As you uncover various areas within your organization where wireless can play a role, explore extending that role to help the hands that help you.

Putting Wireless Where the Rubber Meets the Road

Wireless access also holds significant benefits where the rubber meets the road—in the hands of the drivers of your trucks, vans, forklifts, cars, and bikes—the real road warriors who facilitate your product and service delivery. Truck and bus drivers rarely come into the office and many others don't return after they leave in the morning until the end of the day.

If knowledge is power, then wireless power is knowledge[3]. Power to improve their efficiency by getting to their destinations with less wasted time since they can access up-to-the-minute maps, traffic reports, and directories.

Power to supply better service by having more customer and product data at their fingertips. Power to create new business opportunities, thanks to managers at the home office who can better direct or redirect drivers to respond to calls by wirelessly tracking their locations.

I spoke with Televoke (www.televoke.com), a company that "connects people to things," to get their take on the benefits of using wireless to manage fleet drivers. This is a case where you have people-to-people communication intertwined with asset-to-people communication. Televoke is a wireless ASP that also markets a product that enables a customer's business applications to interface with tracking devices from various vendors.

John Caner, Televoke's vice president of marketing, says, "If you look at fleet tracking applications, wireless brings new benefits to diagnostic data collection, dispatch, and routing. There is a dramatic potential for productivity increases. If people are held accountable for their whereabouts, they perform better. With the Internet this type of technology is now affordable even for small organizations and even easier to implement. Another benefit of fleet tracking includes finding out where mobile support technicians are and directing the closest one to a customer site to handle a problem without actually needing to call the person. You can also pinpoint a salesperson's position so you can feed her information about customers in her area." As technology evolves that will enable an individual's location to be tracked through technology in cell phones, this type of wireless application won't require the expense of embedding wireless devices inside of vehicles.

The Mobile Executive

Don't forget to consider wireless communication's potential impact on your decision makers on the move. Many organizations score their first major success in wireless implementations by equipping the traveling high command with mobile devices.

Even if they only use the devices to receive and respond to e-mail, productivity on the road often raises dramatically. How can you be sure? Put wireless technology in your senior executives' pockets, then go back six months later and try to take the devices away. I have five bucks that say when you leave, the device stays with the exec.

Make Meetings More Efficient

Meetings are the bane of many employees throughout an organization, but you may find that some departments have a heavier burden than others do in this regard, such as marketing, product research and development, and professional services. For these departments wireless technology can facilitate meetings involving mobile workers if you can find applications that don't hog bandwidth or storage space on the devices.

A company called nTeras (www.nteras.com) has a collaboration software program that allows PCs and mobile devices to access a single server and conduct a virtual meeting in which everyone sees the same documents, presentations, and other files. nTeras uses programming techniques that minimize the amount of data that actually travels to the devices, but gives you the feel of running the application from an office desktop computer.

One person can control what everyone sees on their screens, so someone from the home office can manipulate a massive spreadsheet so that all the mobile devices display just the data cells being considered. The mobile worker doesn't have to fumble around trying to scroll every which way trying to find the appropriate part of the display.

Suppose some last minute changes have been made to the budget, and they need to be approved before the board meeting later in the day. Some of the executives that must approve the changes are on site, but several are on the road, carrying mobile devices.

All of the executives connect via the Internet to a central server running the online conference application. Since some of the participants are at PCs and others are using mobile devices, the application adjusts its interface for each user. The person conducting the meeting walks through the budget changes, highlighting and verbally explaining the important changes. Each participant follows along on their handheld or PC and can provide feedback by telephone or through online interaction and telephony.

It's possible that one day wireless technology will eliminate some travel costs by enabling people to do online video conferencing with one of those webcams (mini-video cameras that broadcast images across the Net) attached to a mobile device. BUT, you will need one super-fast wireless connection and a mobile device on serious techno-steroids(pocket PCs are moving in this direction), which means maybe by 2003. Or when the Ricochet Phoenix rises from the ashes through Aerie Networks.

Cover Your Assets

I mentioned before that putting wireless devices in some of your more valuable assets is not a bad thing. It's not just the time that is wasted by employees looking for equipment that's been misplaced, or hoarded by one department to keep it from being misplaced that you have to worry about. Have you figured out how much theft eats away at your bottom line?

Asking a few discreet questions of your facilities managers and purchasing staff might reveal that you're replacing a lot of equipment, vehicles, or various odds and ends every year because they're mysteriously walking away in the dead of night. If this is true, it's time to consider embedding wireless devices in those valuable assets. It may seem like an expensive proposition, but it's true what they say about an ounce of prevention being worth a pound of cure.

And while you're out and about around your facility, ask department managers how much time people spend each day trying to find a $100,000 piece of medical test equipment, or a $50,000 tractor. Then add up the minutes. Whatever the total is, that's how much you lose, twice. The first loss is each person's productivity that's wasted on such meaningless tasks. The second loss is the number of hours a major piece of capital equipment is not being productive at helping you earn money, save money, or run a more efficient business operation.

Technically, you can use wireless to track practically anything. But practicality should dictate your actions. Wireless devices that you embed in objects may cost a few hundred dollars each plus the time it takes to connect them to an asset, program them for specific tracking tasks, etc. You may want to limit their use for assets such as test equipment that are costly (more than $1,000), easy to move, and/or play a vital role in business operations. You can put bar codes on less expensive items so you can use wireless hand-held devices with scanners to record and track the location and quantity of items such as inexpensive machine parts, consumer electronic goods, and office supplies.

Wirelessly Monitor Business Processes

There are valuable business processes that need to be monitored so someone knows immediately if the process stops unexpectedly. It's even better if a person can get advanced warning so he or she can fix things before they become problems. If an automated section of an assembly line stops, even for an hour before someone is alerted, it can cost thousands of dollars in decreased production. Likewise, undetected software or web server failure can be expensive.

These days you can electronically monitor everything from room temperature to electricity consumption to the number of candy bars left in a vending machine. If you can monitor the location or performance of something with a chip or software, then you can send that data through a wireless connection.

Add the capability for two-way wireless communication and one asset (computer program, for example) can then monitor another asset (nuclear reactor cooling system), receive a distress signal (Help me, I'm mellllllting!), and in response send a command to shut down the cooling system before Armageddon hits.

You might think this type of technology is only suitable for large commercial organizations, but companies with five or six people and definitely nonprofits can benefit as well. To a local nonprofit, the loss of one car or computer is going to have a more adverse impact than that same loss will to Ford Motors. The same is true for small business owners.

Wireless Helps Employees Work Effectively with Business Partners

I mentioned earlier that you should consider wirelessly linking assembly line and warehouse staffs to third parties in your supply chain. Here's an example of how you can do that and keep better control of your physical assets. Where-Net (www.wherenet.com) markets wireless devices that enable you to track assets as well as monitor their functions such as temperature and fuel levels. These devices can tell people where assets are and how long they've been there. All of this information can be made available up and down the supply chain to impact its overall performance.

"Suppose you're a tier-one auto supplier that makes transmissions," says WhereNet's Tom Turner. "You ship these to manufacturers in containers that may cost $1,000, so you want the containers back ASAP. The manufacturer's plant manager wants the transmissions, but may not hurry to return the containers, or even know where they are at the plant. If you can wirelessly 'see' where the empty containers are and how long they've sat there, you can get the items back faster."

This is a pretty good benefit, but the potential goes beyond protecting your assets.

Turner commented that the vision of some auto manufacturers is to have a system developed which enables customers to go to a dealer that has wireless access to the factory production and delivery chain. The dealer's system will tell customers when their cars were "born" and give them a URL where they can monitor their car from the assembly line all the way to the dealer. The technology needed for this kind of application is coming together now.

Imagine the possibilities. You're now not only protecting your assets, you're improving the operating efficiency of your employees and your business partner's employees who use those assets. It goes beyond the manufacturing process to include the retail level. Turner says you can take the car deal example one step further.

This same technology that enables customers to see when their cars arrive at the dealer can enhance the service provided by dealerships for the lifetime of the car. As the customer drives the car, monitoring systems can track what auto parts need to be serviced, check past service records, and so on. When the customer returns to the dealer for service, a wireless network in the shop knows what needs to be done before the driver steps out of the car.

Now that we've looked at a few of the general potential benefits of this strategic dimension, let's do some calculations to get a clearer picture of some specific financial possibilities.

Calculate the Financial Impact of More Effective Internal Communication

In this first section we'll calculate the potential positive effect of wireless technology on your costs for general communication of information (such as company news, employee benefits, rules, and regulations) that impact all or most of your employees. The next section addresses some department-specific communication and asset management costs.

Calculate Costs for General Employee Communication

How much are you currently spending per year on conventional communications tactics specifically for your employees? Do you deliver company news via faxes, printed calendars, newsletters, and memos? Calculate how much you're spending on other printed materials such as reports, company or government rulebooks, and direct mail to employees working at home or in branch offices. What about other costs for communication between branch offices, such as wide and local area networks?

You also want to calculate the costs to train employees about your organization's products and services, as well as the costs for providing professional development courses. For each of these categories, determine if it is practical and economical to shift some or all of this communication to wirelessly delivered content.

Calculate the Potential Impact on Department-Specific Communication

You should meet with each of your department managers to evaluate how much they're spending for conventional communication. This might involve doing some of the same calculations as you did above. But you also want to concentrate on increasing efficiency. Organizations with just a few dozen employees may not cut enough expenses to justify the cost of wireless technology, but a 20 percent to 30 percent increase in efficiency that enables them to respond faster to customers' needs can give them a major advantage over larger competitors.

Marketing

What is the value of your marketing staff keeping current with markets, customers, competitors, and news specific to your industry? (This may be an intangible but important benefit.) Based on that estimated value, will wireless-enabling applications such as CRM software increase the responsiveness of the staff significantly enough to outweigh the expense? You may not be able to answer this now, but when you contact wireless application vendors, you definitely need to work through this calculation with them.

Are there contractors (e.g., advertising, PR, design) and vendors who provide services and products that play a time-sensitive role in your marketing campaigns? If so, will there be significant increases in efficiency and marketing success with wireless communication that includes alerts when projects are completed, or wireless e-mail and instant messaging? Estimate how much this is worth in terms of fewer calls made, fewer meetings, or time saved by launching marketing or PR campaigns faster.

IT

IT people resolve problems and enhance the performance of all things digital used by the rest of your employees. Calculate how much you can improve IT staff efficiency if they have anywhere, anytime wireless access to e-mail, message boards, and software tools. Don't forget to estimate how much time IT staff spend supporting the physical computer network of cables and hardware, and determine what percentage of this you can eliminate with wireless LANs.

Also estimate the company-wide productivity increase if employees don't have to sit around waiting for software or hardware support. Besides enabling interfacility roamers to be productive when they're away from their desks, mobile devices can enable these individuals to keep working if their desktop computers or software crashes.

HR

If your HR staff frequently gathers and processes information from employees (i.e., data for benefits programs, EOE requirements, vacation requests) using printed forms, how much time and money can you save if these forms are completed and submitted wirelessly? Don't forget to factor interfacility roamers into the equation as well as your mobile employees. Employees in the warehouse or IT staff who rarely see their desks may have the most difficult time completing paperwork.

Calculate all of the expenses for time and materials associated with training both new and long-term employees. How much can you save by adding wireless access to materials and training software? And if you can deliver training reinforcement materials to employees' PDAs, will this increase efficiency in a way that you can measure?

Assembly Line and Warehouse/Shipping

Wireless enabling your assembly line, warehouse, and shipping staffs is a topic that probably merits its own book, or at least a significant portion of books devoted to supply chain management. I will do the best I can here to give you a little guidance in financially analyzing wireless possibilities in these areas.

You do not need to be a manufacturer to benefit from wireless. Distributors and retail operators may also find several of the following calculations beneficial, as well as government organizations that manage sizeable warehousing and shipping operations.

Can assembly line managers run a more efficient and profitable production process if they are wirelessly tied into databases with sales forecasts and customer orders? Subsequently, will they have more accurate data on how much of what items to produce by specific times? What is the possible financial impact?

Next, estimate the financial benefits if your assembly line and warehouse workers are wirelessly connected. Will the production process improve through faster and better delivery of parts and components from the warehouse to the assembly line? Conversely, can wireless communication from the assembly line allow warehouse staff to better manage products coming off the line and headed for the warehouse?

Can wireless communication channels between assembly workers, purchasing staff, and suppliers streamline parts and components purchasing? What is the potential financial impact? Manufacturers expect wireless technology in this supply chain management process to have the combined benefits of reducing costs and improving competitiveness, so be sure to factor both into your financial calculations.

Will wireless communication enable the warehouse staff to provide marketing and sales with valuable information such as inventory availability data on product returns that result in more profitable relationships with customers and prospects? It might take a while to evaluate the financial impact of this particular application, so to give yourself some time to prove success. You may want to make it part of another wireless application whose benefits are easier to measure.

Finally, are there customer service cost reductions or increased customer satisfaction that can result from wirelessly linking the shipping department with various aspects of the business? These links may be to CRM, sales, or accounting software and to outsourced shipping or delivery services.

Calculate Costs for Asset Management

What is the cost each year in physical assets lost or stolen from your facilities? How many of those assets could have been bar coded or otherwise embedded with wireless tracking devices and probably not lost? This calculation should reveal if your annual losses are significant enough to justify the investment in these wireless devices.

By department, how many people frequently (over two times a week) spend more than five minutes trying to locate equipment and other important business tools? What does this amount to in personnel cost per week (total amount of employees' time multiplied by their average hourly salary)? Then calculate the lost productivity cost for equipment when you calculate the time it is not in use while people are trying to find it.

If your organization owns major pieces of capital equipment (include here computer networks) create a list of these assets, and then for each asset calculate the hourly or daily cost if it stops working because of a mechanical or other problem. These figures should make it easy to determine if monitoring software or hardware with wireless communication capabilities that alert you to a problem is a good investment. What are the potential savings if your support staff (or contractors who provide support services) can receive instant wireless notifications before this equipment malfunctions?

Add to all of these departmental and general business calculations ROI estimates for applying wireless technology to internal communications needs that are unique to other departments or your organization in general. When you have a clearer picture of the potential financial impact, you can start to develop your main strategic objectives.

Main Strategic Objectives

Some of the objectives that your organization sets for this strategic dimension will be different depending on whether you're in the commercial, governmental, or nonprofit sector. Most nonprofits, for example, may not worry about manufacturing, warehousing, and shipping issues (except the Girl Scouts when it's time to sell those cookies).

There are three objectives that can be appropriate regardless of your industry or size of the organization:

1. Decreasing communication costs

2. Increasing employees' personal productivity

3. Enhancing your overall business operating efficiency.

Save Some Money, Honey

As with the previous strategic dimensions, cost reduction seems to find its way to the top of the list. After many organizations got burned by large and questionable investments in early web technologies (technologies promoted by outrageous hype and fear), they put the brakes on. Reason began to overrule reaction in the decision-making process. So let's be reasonable from the beginning and avoid that mistake.

If you can show specifically where a new technology has measurable financial impact in the early days of its use within your organization, you will likely get the financial and political backing you need for more aggressive deployment. In some cases, the savings you produce can fund wireless efforts to launch applications that have valuable but harder to measure benefits.

There is another value to focusing on cost reduction of internal communication. You can test new ideas and specific technologies away from the public eye. When it comes to things such as interface design, mobile device performance, and determining what is good or bad content, people are pretty much the same whether they work for you or they're a potential customer.

So experiment with different content design and layout styles. Give employees different mobile devices so you can see how content looks on the respective devices. What causes people to stand up and take notice? What causes yawns? Which activities really trim communication costs, and which ones just shift the cost from one point (printed newsletters) to another point (printed e-mails) within the organization?

For small organizations that have only one or two people with full-time IT responsibility, you not only have to look at reducing costs after the application is in place, but you also have to be as attentive to how much you spend implementing it. I'm a big fan of using ASPs. You have low start-up and on-going costs, you don't have to sweat a lot of the details about what devices people have, and if things don't work out you're not left holding a lot of useless hardware and software (those mobile devices are still great personal productivity tools). Here are two companies that use ServiceHub, an ASP based in northern California that I first mentioned in Chapter 1.

Rollin,' Rollin,' Rollin,' Keep Those Truckers Rollin'

Aggregate Haulers in San Antonio, Texas owns a herd of 150 trucks in their area that haul concrete and asphalt, plus another 750 trucks across rest of the country. Their approach to finding the right wireless solution can be summed up as, "If at first you don't succeed, try, try again."

Kyle Kellar, Aggregate's terminal manager, says they used to have a system in which one or two guys would take a stack of shipping orders and make a lot of calls to drivers telling them where they needed to be the following morning for pick ups and deliveries. Often they would have to make several calls to each driver before reaching them, and sometimes call again to confirm that the driver could pick up and deliver the orders.

This "dialing for drivers" approach led to a lot of confusion, missed assignments, and irate customers. It also led to dispatcher burnout. Dispatchers had to wait until the last shipping order came in at 5:00 P.M., work on a schedule until 6:00 P.M., and then spend several hours calling the drivers. All of this was after a full working day doing their other tasks.

"We started with a paging system, but there was no way to confirm that drivers received the messages," recalls Kellar. "So we still had people missing assignments. We upgraded pagers, but all they did was confirm that the messages were sent, not received. Also, there were areas where we couldn't get coverage."

In the midst of this madness, AT&T referred Aggregate to ServiceHub, and life has been much better ever since.

"Now when we send messages drivers' phones beep, they read the messages, and we get notified automatically that the messages have been read," reports Kellar. "Drivers send confirmation messages back to verify that they understand the orders and have accepted their missions. We have complete confidence that messages are getting delivered and assignments should be completed. Customers are happy, dispatchers are less stressed, and they get home sooner, and our drivers are happy because the increased efficiency means they can haul extra loads which means more money for them."

Kellar says that to implement this system they only needed to invest in a $100 phone (which they lease to each driver) and $40 a month per driver for unlimited data delivery. ServiceHub set up all the technology needed to facilitate communicating the messages in multiple languages and also provides Aggregate's dispatchers with a web page where they enter and manage messages.

Since they use ServiceHub, the application works with any back office system or with anything on the front end in terms of the wireless network. Aggregate can switch vendors and go with other carriers and telephones, or switch their entire back office system without changing their ASP service. Even if they drop the system there's no loss of money because they haven't invested in any infrastructure.

Since they've had success with their first phrase of wireless technology implementation, Aggregate now plans to have bar codes on their trucks to know where they are in the quarry pit. The company can then give construction companies access to tracking information via the Web so they can see where trucks are or when they're supposed to arrive and be able to give drivers new orders based on their location. There's expense up front for this application, but Aggregate believes it will pay off down the road.

Maybe I'll get a chance to check out Aggregate's wireless application personally one day. Kyle is trying to convince me that I want to leave this consulting life behind and start up a new life driving big trucks. Hmm, intriguing thought.

Meanwhile, Back at the Farm, They're Saving $50,000 a Year

Fifty-thousand dollars a year isn't exactly chicken feed so you probably want to check out what's happening in California farm country.

Borba Farms is a third generation, family-owned farm with 180 employees. They grow row crops, which means that every year there's something new such as cotton, tomatoes, or sugar beets. Their land totals 17,000 acres, but there can be as much as thirty-five miles of other farms between Borba properties.

We're not talking little house on the prairie here. Borba Farms has a standard corporate structure with executives, managers, foremen, and employees. The line foreman used to spend a lot of time driving across the vast properties to meet individually with four or five area foremen to give them sheets of paper with assignments for their people to do the next day. The area foremen then would work out all of these details with their respective workers.

"One day in 1997 the main foreman came in and said there had to be a better way to manage this communication process," recalls Roy Martinez, Borba Farms' controller. "We were considering wireless options when our AT&T rep recommended ServiceHub, who worked with us to develop a solution that would work. We felt our big problems were going to be learning how to use software, finding an application that could be used by foremen who spoke mostly Spanish, and getting coverage in remote areas. ServiceHub assured us that learning to use the software would be simple since it's run from a browser using forms that the company set up. They could also configure the application to automatically translate messages into Spanish."

Borba Farms paid $8,000 for a laptop and five cell phones that could receive text messages, and ran a test with the main foreman to be sure the ServiceHub application would work. Though the display screens were small and more difficult to use than PDAs, they settled on cell phones because these also allowed the foremen to make and receive voice calls.

The back end set up consisted of a simple spreadsheet with workers' names, the fields they were assigned to, and a list of farming operations. Everything was number or letter coded (i.e., Field A, 2 = Till the soil), which resolved most of the language issues. The phones can't print out messages, but they are saved so foremen can verbally pass them on to employees or write out instructions.

Martinez states that, "Once we tested and made sure it would work, we brought everyone together to train them how to use the application. It took several hours, but they were ready to try it the next day. The positive feedback was great right from the beginning. It has saved a lot of wasted drive time by foremen, and we have not modified the application much in this time. If someone found a dead spot in coverage, they just moved a half-mile or so, plus AT&T eventually added another tower in the region. We calculated the time we used to spend before ServiceHub, plus wear and tear on vehicles, and determined that we now save in a range from $20,000 to $50,000 per year (the farming operations vary with the change of crops). One of the intangible benefits was that all of the foremen saw that management was listening to them and cared about what it would take to make their jobs easier to do. It was a great morale builder that we responded in the way that we did with the technology."

While Borba Farms hasn't changed the application much over the years, they are always evaluating what other technologies are out there. When you deal with perishable commodities, you only have a few days to get these products to market, and they're lost forever if you miss this window of opportunity. When facing this type of situation always be open to evaluating new techniques or technology that can help improve your ability to get to market on time.

Borba Farms is considering wireless tracking devices for all the equipment so they can monitor location, fuel consumption, electrical problems, and other functions. If a tractor runs out of gas because the service truck didn't make the connection, they can correct the problem quickly, plus have data to use in a meeting with the trucker. Some of this equipment costs $100,000, so if there's an engine problem, it's good if the farm can be notified so they can shut the system down.

Increasing Personal Productivity

If you look at many of the wireless applications, a central component consists of PDAs, which were originally developed to help individuals be more productive. At a basic level, adding wireless capabilities to PDAs offered another level of productivity by giving users access to mountains of information available from the Web and back office software applications.

What you need to do from a management perspective is harness and expand that personal productivity so you ultimately channel it into your other objective, which is to increase the overall efficiency of your business operations. To accomplish this, it's not enough to buy software that creates wireless links between employees, applications, and your physical assets. You must also commit to going down in the trenches where your line managers and employees work to observe how they do their jobs. You have to actively gather their feedback and then act according to that feedback.

As you read about various wireless implementations, notice that many are influenced by feedback from employees who must use the technology on a daily basis. I chuckle when I read about companies saying they are going to mandate this or that regarding the deployment of PDAs.

Those most likely to have successful wireless strategies are people who say, "We're deploying iPAQs to our field service team because they determined that they need color capabilities to reference color-coded wiring schematics." Or "We're giving e-mail pagers to our custodial staff who said they only need to get e-mail alerting them to problem areas." Because these hardware deployments are based on individual or department needs, as well as the organizations' overall business needs, more employees will actually use the device. And you don't overspend buying more features than people need.

In terms of what your employees do on their PDAs, your organization's business needs and back end software often dictate what many of your wireless software applications will be. But how employees interact with these applications with their mobile devices will determine their productivity levels.

Just because you can give your consulting team wireless access to a 200-page briefing document about your client, which saves printing costs, doesn't mean that they need to see every page when they're at a client site. Spend time with the team to determine what top five or ten items they need to access, then develop wireless content to deliver those items in the fastest way possible, thus increasing productivity.

Simplicity in the Name of Humanity

The comparatively small business processes are often the ones that produce big payoffs in the wireless world. Here's one case in point.

Sigma-Tau Pharmaceuticals, Inc. is the U.S. subsidiary of Sigma-Tau Group, Italy's leading research-based pharmaceutical company. The subsidiary develops what are called orphan drugs, meaning there are less than 200,000 possible users of these particular drugs because they cure or treat such specialized medical conditions.

Since income potential relative to the money spent to research and develop these drugs makes profits slim or nonexistent, you might call this a humanitarian rather than a commercial venture. Sigma-Tau is committed to helping ensure that no patient anywhere is overlooked.

Providing new or improved treatments worldwide for diseases that are complex and difficult to diagnose is a major challenge as employees travel to urban as well as remote areas to inform doctors and patients about treatment options. Mobile executives, sales people, researchers, and others need to constantly receive and send e-mail, and laptops aren't the most practical tools to schlepp around as you're dodging flora and fauna in the back country.

Even though e-mail access was the main need, mobile workers still had to keep a lot of data handy. So Sigma-Tau decided to use Palm VIIs and ThinAir-Apps technology to give people in the field access to scheduling and contact data. Based on their initial success and rapid acceptance by the mobile workers, Sigma-Tau plans to add new wireless applications and expand the hardware to include Pocket PC devices and mobile phones with Net access capabilities. *Va bene.*

Personal Productivity—Not Just Another Pretty Interface

Whatever applications you implement to increase personal productivity, remember that it takes a lot of work to create an application UI that people will actually use. Since this is a priority, plan to commit to the necessary effort. The upside of this extra work, though, is that employees will use the applications more effectively. As productivity increases, employees will start to find other uses for their PDAs or the applications. I will discuss UI development in more detail in Chapter 15.

Increasing productivity with technology often produces a feedback loop among employees and sometimes between them and management. As one person finds a new way to resolve a particular issue and reduce headaches using a PDA, the person next to him or her will want to learn how to do it. This is how software user groups became extremely popular in the 1980s. Create an active wireless feedback channel or user group between the people responsible for deploying your applications and those that use them so you replicate and expand upon productivity gains.

Don't forget that substantial productivity gains also can come from the applications that are included with PDAs when you buy them or come from sources outside of your organization. For example, the occupational therapists in the example I gave earlier could access a public wireless portal that provides advice for helping people to recover from a stroke. This resource improves the therapists' professional skills, which in turn helps the firm better fulfill its mission and increase customer satisfaction. The result is additional income.

You don't have to create all of the wireless content that improves employees' productivity. Actively help them take advantage of what the wireless world has to offer in terms of personal productivity services and tools. Or, at the very least, foster an environment in which the people using wireless technology are encouraged to seek out and share these services and tools with each other.

The decision to use ASPs to implement general business applications might also make sense for applications that enhance personal productivity. EarthLink (www.earthlink.com), one of the largest internet service providers (ISP), offers small and mid-sized businesses a wireless service that combines e-mail hosting and BlackBerries. Customers just order the service, and EarthLink staff does all of the set up, configuration of both the e-mail system and the BlackBerry devices, and service management. Individual users get their devices delivered to their offices ready to go.

Improve Operating Efficiency

If you can use wireless to increase the ability of both people and machines to work together more effectively, then you will be well on your way to truly impressive improvements in how your organization runs its business. Of course, therein lies the challenge. You have to actually get people and machines operating together at some higher level of integration than most organizations have ever experienced.

It's not that organizations don't understand the potential benefits that this integration offers, but the task can seem so daunting. I can't say that this task will be easy, fast, or inexpensive, but it doesn't have to be viewed as entering Dante's Inferno either. First you have to increase people's productivity, then your machines' productivity and conclude by uniting both wherever possible and practical.

The individuals using wireless technology can drive much of the effort to increase personal productivity. But what about the physical assets? Well, that requires someone with a keen eye and a broad vision.

The keen eye is required to look at an engine assembly, medical testing equipment, a forklift, or a network server, and answer the question: How can we improve the way it operates, or reduce the times it fails to operate? How can we improve the way employees work with the parts in the warehouse or the shipping containers on the loading docks? How can we better manage our technology or our business processes so that we are more proactive than reactive?

Many times the answers will come from the people who work directly with these assets and business processes. Sometimes the answers will come from the vendors of various wireless technologies. Great things will happen when you bring together the visionaries, employees, and vendors to explore the possibilities.

When you figure out if and what wireless technology is practical for improving the productive use of your various assets, it is the time to consider how to integrate your people and assets into a unified wireless implementation.

You may be tempted to do everything in one fell swoop, but start by building infrastructure and applications that will allow you to implement projects in successive stages that may take as much as a year or two before the complete vision is realized. Always think long-term, but take one step at a time. This is also the point at which you need to turn up the hype filters. Do not substitute vendors' claims or industry analysts' predictions for your business objectives.

Use outside input from vendors and industry analysts to establish boundaries and best case scenarios, but the objectives you set for your business operations need to be realistic and practical given the capabilities of your organization and its resources. Measuring cost reductions and even productivity gains can be straightforward. But quantifying improvements in operating efficiency can be tricky.

In the Web's hype heyday, it seemed everything and everyone associated with the Net could deliver quantum leaps in business efficiency. A lot of good money chased bad investments and produced questionable results. When it comes to wireless technology, your organization's mantra should be "Know first ourselves and our mission. All else shall follow in due course."

Shifting to Tactics

This concludes my discussion on strategic issues. In Chapter 16 I will discuss in detail how to develop your written plan that includes strategy and tactics. Part of that discussion will address how to prioritize these strategic dimensions and determine how to balance the implementation so you don't overwhelm your resources. I also want to reinforce the fact that you must have specifics—specific objectives, specific benchmarks to measure your progress, and specific expectations of executives, managers, and employees.

Food for Thought

Before you move on, here are a few questions to ponder on internal communications:

1. Where can you streamline internal communication costs by digitizing printed material for intranet posting and wireless access?

2. As an alternative or supplement to internal e-mail, does your IT staff recommend giving interfacility roamers wireless access to intranet message boards and using wireless instant messaging?

3. Is management committed to allocating similar resources to your internal wireless communication activities as it will allocate to the external wireless communication?

4. Can you double the payback from your wireless content developed for customers and prospects, particularly product information, by also using it for internal or remote staff training?

5. When cellular networks improve bandwidth capabilities, or if you are within the Ricochet network, is there a way to incorporate technology such as audio and video broadcasts into wireless applications that reduce the number of in-person meetings?

6. Is it practical to create systems that allow your mobile workers to wirelessly shop and order from your organization's suppliers while still keeping purchasing staff in the loop?

7. Can you put a system in place for mobile workers to access your intranet to communicate, exchange documents, and otherwise collaborate with others who are at the home office or on the road themselves?

8. Do you have someone assigned to keep pace with new embedded wireless technologies that you may be able to use for asset management?

PART III

Tactics

Let's move on to the topic of tactics, starting with using wireless to increase brand awareness and loyalty. In each of the upcoming chapters on the seven specific tactical options I described in Chapter 1, my goal is to stimulate your creative juices so you start to think of great ideas for tactics that can help you reach your strategic objectives. The seven options are:

- Building brand awareness and loyalty
- Directing response communication activities
- Educating your various markets and business audiences
- Demonstrating products or services
- Researching—keeping wireless fingers on the pulse
- Enhancing your PR effectiveness
- Developing operational tactics to facilitate successful wireless implementation

The building brand awareness option addresses how you can use wireless tactics to enhance the current image or build a new one for your organization and its products or services. It goes beyond recommending wireless banner ads to address creating and delivering significant messages that inform your audiences and paint the right picture of your business. This option includes tactics that help you build relationships and motivate people to spread the word about the value of doing business with your organization.

The direct response option is all about getting people to take action today, right now. Whether the desired action is to call a toll-free number or to call the White House, wireless has a role to play because by its nature, wireless communication conveys immediacy. This option also involves integrating wireless with conventional tactics because there are times when the most cliché offers delivered wirelessly—get a free gift, call before midnight tonight, write today to save the planet—still motivate people to rise up and rally 'round the cause.

Educating your audiences is a tactical option based on the premise that the more people know about you, your service, how to use your products, the history of your company, etc., the more inclined they are to do business with you. The Internet Age delivered a channel to knowledge into the hands of the average consumer, worker, and executive, and those that understood how to pack this channel with valuable information prospered. Wireless extends this channel to more people to access at more times than possible before, and if you understand how to prime it with valuable information, you too will prosper.

Product demonstration may be the most difficult of the seven tactics to implement until wireless technology advances a level or two, but it has the potential for the biggest impact on your bottom line. If you can use these tactics to give people a direct experience using your service, seeing your product being used by someone else, or hearing your expert advise, you have the greatest chance to persuade people to buy what you're selling.

Research tactics that enable you to uncover information and gather valuable feedback from customers, prospects, business partners, the press, and your own employees can provide the lifeblood of your organization—knowledge. The more knowledge that you can gather through wireless surveys at the moment when people are most willing and able to give it to you, the more competitive your organization will be.

The nature of PR has changed dramatically as print, TV, and radio journalists have come to rely more and more on the Net for getting and communicating information. What's more, the general public is increasingly turning to the Net first to gather stories. As a result, stories that sometimes took days to surface in the media are now being posted on the Net a few hours, if not minutes, after they break. Wireless technology as a PR tool gives you your best shot at keeping pace with this breakneck speed of news delivery so you don't lose complete control of the coverage your organization receives.

Wireless implementation can be a tactical nightmare. There are so many logistical and operational issues that stretch from the senior executive level down to the rank and file employees that you need to give serious thought to your tactics for resolving these issues. Executive commitment, budgeting, vendor selection, application design, and UI design are some of the major areas of concern. Plan well and you'll survive a lot of potentially deadly pitfalls.

As you read about each tactical option and activities that others have executed, some of these will be more applicable to your organization than others. That's okay. The important thing is that you explore all the options so you can have a broad picture of the possibilities. Afterwards you can narrow your scope to address those activities that offer you the greatest potential benefits.

Keep a pen and pad handy so you can jot down ideas as they come to you when you're reading. In Chapter 16 I will walk you through a specific brainstorming process that you can use with other executives and managers. The ideas you jot down along the way will provide a good catalyst for your brainstorming.

Many of the tactics presented can be used to support any of the four strategic dimensions, with modifications to address the respective audiences. For example, a direct response tactic to generate immediate action such as embedding a secret code in a wireless message may be used to get customers to buy accessories for products ("Find the secret code and save 15 percent off your next order!"). You can use the same tactic to get mobile employees to complete forms ("Decipher the secret code hidden in the expense form to qualify for a special prize!").

The seventh option may seem like it is only for the fourth strategic option since it stresses tactics targeted to your employees, but the end result is helping them develop applications for pursuing all four strategic dimensions. The public relations tactical option is the only one of the seven that is pretty narrow in its strategic implementation, addressing mostly communication with customers and prospects, with journalists being the primary audience within both of these strategic dimensions.

When you go to the book's online supplement (www.wirelessinconline.com), you will find additional stories, brainstorming ideas, and information that your management team can use. You may also find other readers with whom you can exchange ideas. Because tactics will continually change as wireless technologies evolve or are replaced by newer technologies and more organizations start using wireless, it is important to reference this supplement that I will evolve to keep pace with these changes.

Without further ado, let's dig into some wireless tactics.

CHAPTER 7

Building Brand Awareness and Loyalty

A number of companies wasted millions of dollars for interactive branding campaigns whose successes were measured solely by how many people clicked on a web banner. While organizations fixated on the click-throughs of these campaigns, it has taken several years for them to start to understand the multifaceted role of interactive media in shaping the brand image that customer and prospects have of an organization.

This chapter has two goals. First, for those of you who don't use this word brand and all of its derivatives on a regular basis, I want to clarify the concept of building brand awareness. Reviewing and reading about organizations' interactive branding campaigns uncovers a definite lack of understanding of what it means to build a brand. Simply speaking, branding, brand awareness, brand loyalty, and all of the other "brand" words boil down to developing and influencing the images that people have of your organization, products, and services.

The second objective of this chapter is to help you understand how wireless tactics can help with this branding process. It will present the role that wireless technology can and should play in a branding campaign so you don't waste a lot of time, money, and talent. The tactics here will be most helpful for pursuing the strategic dimensions of communicating with customers and prospects.

Before going into a definition of building brand awareness, let's dispel one particular misconception before it has time to take hold in the wireless realm. Kate Everett-Thorpe of Lot21 states that, "The click-through has become the digital media planner's heroin." Some planners know of no other way to measure the value of interactive communication to branding campaigns, so they desperately cling to this method of measurement to justify their budgets.

The smart veterans of those heady days of unbridled web spending have learned that 1) a brand is more than a spinning digital logo, 2) brand awareness is more than clicking an ad, and 3) you can't use wireless communication by itself to execute a successful branding campaign. A brand may take months or longer to establish and requires ongoing efforts in a variety of media to maintain.

What Is a Brand Anyway?

The successful use of wireless as a branding tool requires that you have a good grasp of what some of the brand-related terms mean and understand the realistic capabilities of the technology to impact your brand image.

If you look at the earliest use of the word "brand," it originated back in the days when a logo was burned onto the backsides of horses and cattle to designate who owned the branded livestock. As advertising evolved in the first half of the twentieth century, the term brand referred to the logo of a specific company, product, or service. Even government and nonprofit organizations created logos.

With the age of television came an accelerated effort by numerous organizations to increase the awareness and influence of those logos. In a short time the brand became more than just the logo, it became synonymous with everything good and bad that people thought about a product. The definition now includes everything good and bad that people personally experience when they come in contact with any part of the organization.

This latter point is very important to the discussion of wireless. Organizations discovered in the past few years that they can spend a fortune for ads, printed materials, and PR to create a brand image, but lose customers because the experience of navigating their website was horrendous. Interactive media is not just another piece of marketing collateral material. It is new technology that changes how people interact with your organization. Subsequently you cannot divorce from the branding process the experience that people have with your organization through a mobile device.

A brand for a product, service, or organization consists of three things:

1. *The Visual Representation.* This is the logo for your brand. It can include stylized text and graphics associated with a product or organization that is always displayed along with the logo. In a wireless campaign, it's important to maintain as consistent a "look" to your logo as is practical. However, for a wireless branding campaign to be successful, the next two elements are much more important.

2. *The Brand Message.* The brand message tells someone why he or she wants to buy whatever it is you're selling. The message is everything communicated by AND about a product or organization. It is not just a catchy slogan or a jingle you create (i.e., The United States Army's "Be all you can be."), though the slogan often captures the main thought that you want to convey. Everything that you communicate supports that main thought and is part of the message, from the slogan and retail store displays to wireless ads and stories about how customers use your product or service. Even how your employees dress and act toward customers contributes to the message.

3. *The Brand Experience.* The brand experience is made up of people's collective experience with everything associated with your organization, products, or services. A brand alone is neither good nor bad. What makes the image you have of a brand good or bad is determined after you and other people are touched by it in some way.

You may or may not know a lot about cars, but it's likely that when you see one with a BMW logo on it, you immediately have one or more emotional responses that can range from envy to distaste. The logo is the visual representation. The primary message communicated by BMW the company is summed up as "the ultimate driving machine," and most of their print-, visual-, and audio-delivered messages support this main message. There are other secondary messages about the BMW brand that include what is written or said by journalists, dealers, customers, and your friends.

The customer (or prospect) experience is whatever direct interaction a person has with a BMW car, whether through owning, test driving, or just drooling over one on the showroom floor. In a broader sense, the brand experience with the BMW company encompasses someone's interaction with the car, the corporate officers and employees, the dealers, and BMW's websites and wireless content (if they develop any).

All three factors—the logo, the message, and the experience—contribute to the success of the brand. The BMW logo has the instant recognition and emotional response that it does because it is unique, world-renowned, and has been seen countless times by many of us during our lives. The message is simple to grasp, has strong emotional appeal, has been consistent over the years, and is reinforced by a very high price tag. And it seems everyone who owns a BMW has great things to say about their experiences with the car and the company.

Additional Definitions

There are other brand-related terms you should be familiar with as you develop wireless tactics to enhance the branding process.

■ *Brand Awareness.* You have brand awareness when your audience recognizes your logo, is familiar with the brand message, and has some firsthand experience with the brand. In an organization's ideal world, just seeing a logo triggers a strong positive message and motivates a person to live or relive the experience with the organization or product. This would be strong brand awareness, or what some might also describe as strong brand identity.

■ *Brand Loyalty.* Brand loyalty occurs when people who buy your product or service, like it, and buy it again, even after trying a competing product or service. My stepdad drives a Buick and he is brand loyal. He's driven Buicks since before I was born. The man is eighty-years-old! Yet he plans to buy another car, and as sure as the sun rises over Philly, it will be a Buick. Anyone unclear on the meaning of brand loyalty?

■ *Brand Building.* A brand building (also called branding) campaign is aimed at increasing your brand awareness and brand loyalty so that you increase your sales. Typically the campaign consists of all of the activities that:

■ Create a new brand
■ Change or expand the attributes of an existing brand
■ Develop or expand brand awareness among various audiences

The better-executed campaigns, particularly for influencing an organization's brand (rather than just a product's brand name), are those that involve not just the marketing department, but also salespeople, customer service staff, and practically every department in the organization.

■ *Brand Consistency.* Because so many things influence the message that people receive about an organization, you have to be careful the message doesn't get distorted, making it difficult to establish a strong brand identity. For example, you receive marketing materials from a company that presents the message of "Great customer service and satisfaction!" but then the wireless content you access is inaccurate, feedback forms are confusing, and no one responds to your e-mail. The latter message is inconsistent with the former one and weakens its impact.

So, what is the role of wireless technology in all of this? It can be quite diverse, actually.

When Your Logo Goes Wireless

You can use your logo in your wireless communication tactics. However, the bad news for those defenders of the corporate logo (affectionately known by some as logo cops) is that it probably cannot be reproduced in all its colorful glory and splendor or exact micron-level measurement as specified in the logo cop handbook. My advice to logo cops: Get over it.

People need to accept the limitations of the medium and create a new set of guidelines for using the logo for wireless communications. For the moment you can't reproduce a four-color logo in digital format for a low-resolution monochrome screen just slightly bigger than a business card, and deliver it quickly through 19 bps wireless networks. You can digitize your existing logo as close as you can to the print version and run with it. All of the logos I've seen on mobile devices so far are clearly identifiable with the organizations they represent.

Of course, if you are rolling out a new product or company, the digital challenges to visual brand do not have to be a major issue. When you hire a design group to create a new logo (including layout for stationary and all the other elements of the brand identity), make sure they also design representations in digital format for the Web and for wireless. Even if you don't think you will run a wireless marketing campaign for a while, it's best to deal with these issues from the beginning with the original designers. It will take less time and cause less aggravation and you'll have something that will work better in every medium.

Wireless communication can be effective for delivering your logo in a way that enhances its image, but the logo should remain consistent with how it's presented in other media. Some organizations got caught up in the web frenzy and decided that their logos needed to be jazzed up in this new medium. Occasionally you visited a site where the logo zipped and spun around the screen, morphed into 3-D artwork or burst into flames. (Ever see the IBM "flaming logo" commercial?)

When wireless technology advances, these digital enhancements can be okay if your organization has the image of being cool, hip, and leading edge. But there's a potential problem for organizations with years and millions of dollars invested in creating a particular image. If people see your logo in a wireless context that is so disjointed from your "usual" image (i.e., your image in print and television) that it creates confusion about your brand, this is not good.

The Wireless Medium Can Be the Brand Message

Wireless is a medium that can help you define and reinforce the strength of your brand in how you use it as well as what you say through wireless communications. Providing wireless access to your customers reinforces the message that your brand is on the leading edge technically or that you are very service oriented. One way to do this is to provide access in places where it is difficult for people to use their wireless mobile devices.

The Venetian Hotel is a luxury theme hotel in Las Vegas that tries to recreate the experience of being in Venice, Italy, in part by covering nearly as much land as the city of Venice. When you build a steel and concrete structure that huge, there are bound to be places inside it where wireless services don't work.

LGC Wireless of San Jose, California (www.lgcwireless.com) provided the Venetian Hotel with hardware and infrastructure that enables guests and visitors to have complete access to any one of five major national wireless services (Sprint PCS, Nextel, AT&T, Cingular, and Verizon). The Venetian promotes this benefit as yet another reason to stay at their hotel, and since providing great service is a big contributor to their brand's strength, the wireless service enhances the brand.

There are various locations where lots of people congregate, but wireless services are poor or nonexistent, so enabling them to get wireless access can be good for your brand. LGC has a diverse customer base that includes SAFECO Field, the Seattle Mariner's baseball stadium, the 413,000 square foot Dadeland Mall in Maitland, Florida, and the subway system in Santiago, Chile.

The University of California at Berkeley plans to deploy wireless LAN access campus wide as another feature to enhance their brand message as a college that uses leading-edge technology to enhance learning, and attract potential students.

Wayport (www.wayport.com) provides fixed-location, high-speed, wireless access hardware and infrastructure that Starbucks Coffee, American Airlines, and several hotel chains are deploying to give their mobile customers a fast lane to the Net using laptops and wireless modems. This gives these companies using Wayport another service that they can use to attract more customers.

Provide Access to Specific Content

Consider providing wireless access only to information that is related to a specific location or events being held at a particular location. For organizations that want to project an image of being on the leading edge of business or social trends, this is a great way to strengthen your brand while avoiding the infrastructure costs of providing complete access to public wireless networks.

A Little Bit of Tokyo in Downtown San Francisco

In 1999 Sony opened in a four-story mega entertainment center called the Metreon in downtown San Francisco that is similar to Sony's Mediage Multimedia Center in Tokyo. The Metreon is a flash and dazzle complex that contains movie theaters, retail shops, and restaurants as well as The Discovery Channel Store.

What really gives Metreon its flash and dazzle are establishments such as the Microsoft SF store where you can preview all kinds of new technologies, not just computers, and the Airtight Garage where you can play unique interactive games. As you might expect, there are also PlayStation and Sony Style stores where you can play with all things Sony.

Communications Senior Manager Kirsten Maynard says, "Metreon is a place where companies come to test new products because the people here are early adopters who are willing to try new things. WideRay created Metreon-specific content that visitors can download with their PDAs from WideRay's Jack infrared data stations located in several areas of our complex.

"This content opens several categories of information—movie times, general information about the Metreon, restaurant information, and as you go deeper into the content you get more details about the various retailers, special attractions, prices, hours that they're open and so on. We have special promotions that run for a week or two and a map of layout on each level."

The Metreon doesn't distribute coupons or advertisements as part of the opening screens, but allows them to be posted as part of the content within categories by the different establishments, though not too many take advantage of that. "We want people to know what the Metreon is and what it has to offer, but we don't want people to feel as if they're being sold a lot of merchandise or bombarded with ads," says Maynard.

Metreon believes that being able to deliver content wirelessly is a beneficial branding exercise because it enables guests to try something completely new, which is a key part of the company's mission

There is a valuable lesson to learn here for many types of organizations. All of the feedback about the Jacks is positive. Maynard says, "Visitors feel that finally someone is beaming them information that's useful. People carry around PDAs and use them for basic productivity tasks. But people feel that they've spent money, learned how to use something new, and now they're wondering what's the next step with the technology."

Metreon reaps the benefits of presenting a consistent brand image by providing wireless access to people who come to the facility specifically to try new things. They deliver content that helps people get the most of their brand experience while at the Metreon. The content expands brand awareness because people beam this information to their friends later and use the content to coordinate meetings with others at the Metreon's different establishments.

And the content contributes to brand loyalty because the more people access it, the more they are inclined to visit the Metreon again.

You could even say that Metreon is helping to strengthen the brand identity of wireless technology in general. Maynard explains, "It's exciting for people to see new developments with technology, especially when they can accomplish something important. Maybe it's up to companies like us to try to create new content and new uses for the technology. Not that people expect us to be responsible for this, but they're happy when we do."

A Port in the Storm Builds Brand Loyalty with Kids

It's not just the commercial world that can get a boost in the brand by providing wireless access to content that enhances customers' brand experience. On the nonprofit side, Port Discovery in Baltimore, Maryland, is a museum of exhibits focused primarily to children, and they recently added some very interesting wireless capabilities.

With funding from the State of Maryland, the W.K. Kellogg Foundation, and Aether Systems, Inc., Port Discovery opened a new exhibit, the PD Kid Club in July 2001. The PD Kid Club is Port Discovery's sixth and final permanent exhibit and culminates the museum's initiative to integrate community and technology.

Port Discovery's staff believes the digital revolution is changing the landscape of opportunity for kids, allowing them to express themselves, interact, create, and communicate in powerful ways. Essentially, this is Port Discovery's brand message. PD Kid Club membership introduces youngsters to several digital technologies that give them the experience they can apply to their own pursuits in everyday life.

To show kids how technology can empower them, The PD Kids Club showcases high-tech methods of creative expression. Children can use computers to create their own digital music mix. Members also can use computer software to create elaborate animated pictures and digital movies for playback on a PC.

Wireless interaction is enabled through the Kid Club Communicator (KC²), a modified RIM BlackBerry that allows members to interact on a deeper level with the exhibits at Port Discovery. Kids use KC²s to access more interpretive content in all of the museum's exhibits, interact with the physical environment in new ways, and keep track of the accomplishments they make in the exhibits.

According to Port Discovery's Marketing and PR Manager Michelle Stetz, the KC²s are a fabulous success. "The kids and parents are very excited about using the KC²s because they're unique. We do exit surveys and find that adults like them as much as the kids do. One reason is that the devices get parents working together with their children rather than just sitting down while the kids go off and explore which was our goal."

Stetz says the museum benefits because they're now widely recognized for bringing new technology into this environment and using it in creative ways. The wireless capabilities are also valuable because the museum can significantly change all of their exhibits just by changing content. They avoid the expensive and time-consuming task of dismantling and replacing the physical exhibits, plus they can promote new programs more frequently, which increases visitor traffic.

The museum has a five-year plan to further enhance their use of web and wireless technology. "We're a prototype for other children's museums that want to implement similar programs. We intend to expand how we use wireless capabilities in other exhibits, and we also want to increase the capabilities of our website so kids can use it interact with exhibits and activities at other museums. Who knows what the future holds? Someday wireless capabilities may enable our kids to interact with kids in other states," says Stetz.

Wireless Enables CMP Media to Help the Second-Oldest Profession

Since ancient times, people have gathered in great numbers to hear orators orate and to wander down aisles of merchants merchandising. Today we call these gatherings trade shows, and surviving some of them puts a real strain on your patience, your brain, and your feet. From merchants' viewpoints, these shows are a real strain on their budgets too.

Providing wireless access to facilitate all of the communication that goes on among and between attendees, vendors, journalists, and the people running the show can be a big brand booster, as well as possible new revenue source, for the show organizers.

CMP Media LLC (www.cmp.com) produced the WEB2001 and Internet-+Mobile Conference and Exposition and they put this theory to the test in a big way. While implementing a wireless application at an event for wireless tech people might seem like a slam-dunk branding effort, this was actually risky business because no crowd is less forgiving if you screw up than a bunch of technology experts.

CMP used OpenGrid's mobilePlanIt, wireless LANs, and infrared sync stations to help attendees build a personalized agenda of what and whom they wanted to see at a show. Besides being able to participate in conference polls and complete evaluations of conference sessions without dealing with paper forms, attendees could also choose to receive conference or exhibitor materials in electronic form using their PDAs' infrared ports.

"We wanted to demonstrate a real-world deployment of a mobile solution to the attendees of WEB2001 and Internet + Mobile because they're exactly the type of tech-savvy people who rely on mobile devices to network and gather information in their day-to-day businesses," said Simon Tonner, the show director. CMP also wanted to use this innovative application to reinforce their image as a leading-edge source of technology information and insights.

CMP maximized attendee participation by using the wireless LANs, which enable laptop users with wireless modems as well as mobile device users to access the application. This application produced the additional benefit of creating a way for exhibitors and sponsors to distribute promotions, marketing materials, and press releases to attendees and the press, services that CMP can personalize and sell.

In terms of brand loyalty, CMP's application draws people back to other conferences, plus it is a vehicle that helps exhibitors and sponsors increase brand loyalty among attendees assuming they do effective follow-up with the contacts they make.

Communicating Your Brand Message Wirelessly

Not every organization can provide wireless access capabilities to its various audiences. These organizations need to consider using the wireless medium to deliver branding messages directly to their target markets. This requires more planning and effort than the previous tactics since you have much less control over where and when people will be using mobile devices, but executing wireless branding campaigns is similar to traditional branding.

You must have concise, clear messages, target the right audiences with the right messages, and be prepared for a process that may take months to achieve success. Wireless offers the advantage of being able to instantly communicate with customers and prospects, but do not assume that this means you will achieve instant results. These expectations cause some marketing people to use the wrong metrics to measure success, or abandon the medium too soon when initial results are not what they expected.

Keep It Short and Sweet

I highly recommend that you read *How to Get Your Point Across in 30 Seconds—or Less* by Milo O. Frank (Washington Square Press). Then put the following sign on your desk: *I Will Adhere to the 30/90 Rule When Executing All*

Wireless Branding Campaigns. The 30/90 rule is that you should deliver your key branding message in no more than 30 seconds or 90 words.

Thirty seconds, or 90 printed or spoken words, is all the time and space that you have to make your wireless branding campaign an awe-inspiring success, a colossal failure, or a monument to mediocrity. Reading Mr. Frank's book will show you how to make your point and convince people to take action within 30 seconds. On a mobile device, 90 words and four, maybe five graphic elements are about the most someone will endure before he accepts what you're saying or discards your message. Do you want to succeed or fail?

The previous paragraph was my 90-word branding message for Mr. Frank's book. You still may have a couple of questions about the book before you buy it, but is there little doubt as to the intended purpose of *How to Get Your Point Across . . .* and how it will help you develop your brand messages?

The typical wireless device is small and slow, and even when bandwidth is faster, the devices will still be small. Many devices do not have color screens. These factors make reading text hard on the eyes. Also, most wireless mobile device users are people who are busy all day. Busy people with eyestrain don't have a lot of time for poorly targeted and written wireless messages.

Intraware Uses the 30/90 Rule—Reduces Lead Acquisition Costs 95 Percent

Intraware's mission (www.intraware.com) is to provide IT professionals with a package of services that manages the complete software life cycle from product research to deployment and maintenance. They used a wireless branding campaign in 2000, one of the first of its kind, to introduce three new service lines to the corporate IT market.

Figure 7-1 shows the design and copy for the campaign ad that was created by Lot21 and delivered through AvantGo's advertising network to IT professionals who received the ad when they accessed AvantGo channels targeted by Lot21.

This ad generated a hefty number of qualified leads that cost just 5 percent of the typical $10 per lead generated through direct mail and other marketing activities. Rudi O'Meara, Intraware's creative director, managed the effort. Lot21 came up with the initial idea and they helped O'Meara sell it to a management reluctant to send ads to people's PDAs.

This campaign was particularly challenging because it had to achieve so much. Intraware was offering new services that included evaluating enterprise software, purchasing it, delivering it electronically using their technology, and maintaining it for Fortune 1000 client companies. Outsourcing these services

Figure 7-1. Intraware's wireless branding campaign copy.

You and are the
better way to IT

Intraware is the logical
approach to software
management because it
works just like you do.

$A+$ **Smarter**

Intraware's services are
web-based. That means you
can evaluate, try, buy and
master software—all online.

 Faster

Electronic volume licensing
and deployment to all your
desktops on our time
schedule.

Innovative

If being first is important to
you, check out the Intraware
site for new tools and
services that keep you
ahead of the IT curve.

philm@lot21.com

submit

Tap here if you'd like us to
send you a free Intraware
Tee-Shirt.

Intraware
Control your technology
www.intraware.com

was a new concept for companies, so prospects had to be both educated and reassured about the value of the services and the reliability of Intraware. Intraware also did the training and asset management.

"We had to brand the company and three services, plus acquire new customers, on a medium that didn't have a marketing track record, recalls O'Meara. "Lot21 had to tell people who we were, then talk about deployment technology that was a very new concept and e-learning (training). Even AvantGo was a little worried, given that we were a small, new company."

Instead of leading with details and features, Lot21 led with benefits and focused on partnership—the "You and i" (i.e., the "intraware") that you see in the ad. This piqued people's interest enough so that they would click on the link in the ad and go into content at Intraware's website to find out more details. If they entered their e-mail address in the space provided in the ad and clicked "submit" this gave Intraware permission to automatically generate an e-mail that detailed the product and how to get the t-shirt by providing a snail mail address. Recipients didn't have to call or buy anything, but if they were interested in the product they needed to submit more information.

"We were wary of being seduced by technology for the sake of technology. Unless it could be proven that there was an inherent advantage to using wireless, we were hesitant," says O'Meara. "One of the reasons we went with Lot21 was because their entire organization is centered around finding new technology and bringing it to their clients. They pointed out to us that many users of PDAs were perfectly matched with our target audience, upper level IT executives and managers."

The Intraware campaign is an example of the direct delivery of a primary brand message. They had the advantage of a powerful message for the audience, an audience that included their primary target market, and the "newness" of the medium.

Sometimes, though, you will need to deliver more than 90 words to your audience to reinforce the initial message, answer questions, and so forth. You need to determine what your follow-up messages will be and whether you want people to receive these through additional content that they click to wirelessly, a phone call they make from their mobile phones, or some other means.

It is best to immediately move people into a dialogue in addition to giving them a link to other content whenever possible. Intraware followed-up the initial ad with e-mail that was triggered by people sending their e-mail addresses, thus quickly engaging prospects in a dialogue. There is an expectation of immediacy in wireless, so a fast e-mail response enhances your image as a responsive organization.

Also note that Intraware gathered information from prospects in segments rather than all at once, thus increasing response rates. First, they requested just an e-mail address and promised something in return, the t-shirt. Then they asked for the mailing address, optionally, with the reply e-mail. Then, if people were still interested in the company, they were asked for the major information that qualified them as a lead. People are intimidated by long forms, particularly busy mobile people.

Deliver Your Brand Message Through Sponsored Content

Sometimes it makes sense to deliver the brand message indirectly by sponsoring content. For example, a pharmaceutical company can sponsor a quick guide to treatment options for diabetes that doctors can access and download. When a doctor finishes reading the guide, there will be a message such as "This guide was sponsored by Bart's Pharmaceutical Emporium," along with a link to Bart's website. While this tactic may not be as easy for some to execute wirelessly as it is on their websites because of bandwidth limitations, careful planning can still open up good opportunities.

In essence, sponsoring content means that you provide information about a topic that's related to your product or service and a logo or tagline that says this content was sponsored by XYZ organization. For example, I get financial news on my iPAQ that's sponsored by CNN Mobile, which is a news service for mobile people worldwide. Because the financial news has value, I read it frequently. The CNN Mobile logo is small and doesn't get in my way.

More importantly from a branding perspective, people equate the logo with bringing them valuable news. If some of these people decide they want more than just financial news, and they want to access this from wherever in the world they may be, then they're likely to subscribe to the service and recommend it to friends.

Wireless industry research firm Telephia's John Dee Fair advises that, "If you can attach a benefit to the content, sponsor wireless content. An example might be a luxury automaker sponsoring game scores and stats from March Madness basketball finals. The target market of mobile device users lines up well with the advertiser's best prospects, and the timeliness and repetitiveness of the sports information being delivered is perfect for reinforcing the image."

Some people promote running online ads that feature just the logo and maybe a tag line rather than sponsoring content. "The limitations of mobile devices will require more creativity on the part of advertising and marketing people," Fair continues. "Moving ad banners from the Web onto mobile devices is probably not the best way to use these devices." I don't recommend this either, particularly for smaller organizations with limited budgets because you have to run so many ads of this nature before a brand identity develops. I believe small organizations can use their money in more effective ways, and both small and large organizations will get much more impact per dollar from a sponsorship rather than a simple banner ad.

WideRay CEO Saul Kato concurs. "If your task is something that a sponsor wants to help you with by providing valuable information, you're happy because that sponsor is providing a needed and wanted benefit. In wireless, the form factor of mobile devices is bad for banner ads. People are going to get tired of seeing a basic ad constantly in the corner of their screen. The real success-potential lies in the fact that you can open up a dialogue. People can specify what they want and drill down and start a dialogue online, or you can get people to call on the phone."

Whether you use sponsored content or deliver 90-word messages, do not assume that wireless alone will carry the message. You can have great interactive ads that win nice awards, which is okay, but customers and prospects must have other contacts with your organization. Human beings need to touch paper, feel products, or interact directly with other human beings.

The wireless branding campaign works best when people have seen (or will see) print or TV ads, trade show booths, brochures, or articles about the company or product in other sources. If you are introducing a brand to an audience wirelessly, you probably will do well to move people from the initial message to another medium quickly, even if it is just your website, so they can gather additional information.

Target the Right Audiences

Besides crafting the right messages, one of the hardest aspects of using wireless as a branding tool is hitting the right audience. Intraware had phenomenal success because many of the people using PDAs at the time were perfect candidates for their services. You have to do a lot of work defining your target audience as well as keeping tabs on the rapidly changing demographics of mobile device users.

You should have the easiest time targeting your existing customers if you keep good tabs on their locations when they use wireless devices, how they use the devices, some of their other habits, and their needs relative to your products or services. Of course, the intended results from delivering it will be different than with people who haven't done business with you.

Targeting prospects will require more research work and more diligence in evaluating the results from each of your efforts. Lot21's Everett-Thorp says,

"You must look at objectives: Move 'x' units of products, get 'y' people to the website, and make them regular visitors. Then have each medium, promotion, and ad track back to the objective and measure how many times these were accessed. We care who saw it, how many times, and who actually reached the objectives. However, just because acquisition costs drop 30 percent doesn't mean you should automatically do that activity to an audience 10 times larger in size, or triple the run rate. You have to constantly analyze how you got results."

You should do another test or two to make sure that the results you got were not random. In fact, most direct-marketing professionals say that you should test repeatedly as you continue and expand your campaign.

Using location-based technology, (i.e., sending a particular ad to someone because you know he or she is walking by one of your retail outlets) has great potential for creating a negative rather than positive reaction from people. If you're in a cab racing to the hospital, getting a beep on your mobile phone for an ad when you expect to get a call about the condition of the person you're going to see will likely annoy you. There is an exception to this, which is when people are in a particular location for a specific activity.

If there are 50,000 screaming Madonna fans packed into a steamy arena for her concert, this is probably a good time for a music retailer to beam in coupons for her *Music* CD, t-shirts, and other Madonna items that create a brand identity or loyalty for the retailer. There are many times when certain events will bring together large gatherings of people who have similar interests and subsequently are prime targets for messages appropriate to the demographics AND the event.

This convergence of action (being at a specific location at a known time), context (the reason everyone is together), and appropriate message is the sweet spot of location-based marketing. As long as their PDAs are not overwhelmed with messages, the numbers and predictability of people's mindsets work in your favor. You have a better chance of engaging the people you contact in an ongoing dialogue.

The reason using the same tactic on individuals walking or driving past a bar is a flawed tactic is that you can't be sure of the context in which the action is taking place. Are they late for a meeting? Are they even old enough to drink? My advice is go with the numbers or hit the individuals after they enter a location such as Metreon.

Branding Powerhouse Procter & Gamble Goes Wireless

Hiugo (www.hiugo.com), based in Milan, Italy, is a company that combines technology that enables clients to do location-based wireless ad delivery with professional services to develop interactive wireless marketing campaigns. They executed some interesting branding promotions for several Procter & Gamble products including Pringles potato chips.

Pringles is a fairly popular snack food here in the United States. But in Europe Pringles is viewed as a cool, hip product and subsequently, brand-building promotions and events that Pringles sponsors are targeted to eighteen- to thirty-year-olds with a particular emphasis on those who like extreme sports.

One wireless brand campaign in Italy involved integrating a special code that was attached to Pringles boxes as a silver scratch pad similar to those you see on "scratch & win" lottery tickets. This was one of the first promotions that was executed nationwide, and it involved 7 million Pringles packages. People who bought the Pringles scraped the pad and sent in the code using SMS messaging on wireless phones. They were then sent in reply a short set of questions to answer. A prize generator assured that most people won something.

P&G knew this campaign (message) reached people whenever they're handling the product (action), usually to eat some, so it is likely people were relaxed and had time to respond to the promotion (context). Since this was a joint promotion with one of the wireless carriers, the possible prizes included free minutes of calling time, mobile phones, and other goodies from the carrier. So this message was contextually relevant since the carrier knew that everyone had to respond to the promotion with a mobile phone.

This was a very simple wireless interactive campaign that you could easily do here in the States, but give people the option to use their PDAs as well as cell phones to send in the code. You can also have people directly access your web content using a mobile device and enter the code this way, thus giving them a more immediate interaction without the delay of sending messages back and forth. People can enter the code that then triggers a pop-up screen with the survey for them to complete.

Your application can determine if the customer is a winner on the spot (preferable option) or send contestants a notification by e-mail with additional information about your product. The former option requires that you have some back end database systems in place that can do fast calculations and support large numbers of people at one time, but the instant gratification for respondents produces better results in the long run.

Some direct marketing veterans might wonder why not tell people as soon as they scratch the ticket if and what they've won. The purpose here, however, is to use a location-based promotion to increase the response rate of people who you want to draw into a closer, ongoing relationship with your organization that increases the exposure of your product or service. If I just scratch, win, and collect a prize at the check-out counter, I'll be happy, but you won't have a dialog with me.

A word of advice regarding any promotion that includes contests and prizes: Unless you run game contests for a living, outsource the contest logistics, from collecting entries (e.g., names, codes) to selecting winners and distributing prizes. In the United States, many states have different rules governing contests, and any web-based contest has to conform to all of these. If you search for companies that perform this service, take steps to ensure that they're a reputable company.

A Second Pringles Promotion Has Personality

There were two big extreme sports publicity events in Rome and Naples in September and October of 2000 that drew 90,000 teens for these 48-hour nonstop parties that also included music and contests. Pringles was one of the sponsors. In a second location-based promotion that was more interactive, Hiugo created a wireless chat room and message-posting forum (with the Pringles logo prominently displayed) so teens could use their mobile phone at the event to meet up with friends and make new ones.

The most popular wireless promotion was the personality surveys that were distributed on the Web during the time of the event, and wirelessly to the cell phones of people walking through the crowds. People answered questions and, depending on their answers, one of the several Pringles flavors was deemed most appropriate to that personality type.

There were prizes of Pringles merchandise and, as you can imagine, a promo to go buy the flavor that matched respondents' respective personalities. Forty-five thousand people viewed the wireless Pringles content and 9,900 completed the surveys.

A very important point to note about this Pringles promotion is that the content was not only targeted to a specific age and interest group, but also written in the dialect of the people within each city. As with many countries, in Italy there is a common language, but people in different regions speak with distinct dialects that are subsets of the Italian language.

Because of development costs, many companies rarely address a second language, never mind the distinctions within a language itself such as the many shades of Spanish spoken in different Hispanic communities in America. However, the more you can leverage the capabilities of wireless, web, and related technologies to increase the personalization of your content, the more effective will be your branding campaign.

You should also keep tabs on the development of wireless chat room and instant messaging technology. America Online is the preeminent success that it is in large part because of its chat rooms and IM capabilities. In an event such as the one in Italy, giving people this additional communication option with their mobile devices will increase your campaign's effectiveness.

The Brand Experience—You Only Get One Chance to Make a First Impression

The wireless brand experience is where a lot of organizations will require extra coaching. If you're spending millions of dollars to create and fortify a brand that many people recognize, respect, and respond to, why risk damaging your brand image through poorly executed wireless activities? You can sabotage your strong offline brands with poorly developed wireless content.

Consistency is important, but how people interact with your wireless content can help or hurt your brand. Before you develop new content or use existing web content for wireless delivery, impress upon everyone who is involved with this project that everything they do on the Web and wirelessly is part of a person's experience with your brand.

If the people who view your website or wireless content have little or no previous dealings with you, this content is the first in-depth communication with you. A series of TV or radio ads give people just a glimpse of what your products are like, or what it's like to do business with you. Wireless content give people a more detailed picture and the website is where these people really take time to look you over, satisfy their curiosity, and seriously consider if you can meet their needs.

Your content must be as clear as the ad, brochure, or personal referral that sent people to the content. They may not spend a long time with your wireless materials, or they may read and interact with quite a bit of it, but decide not to do business with you because they are disappointed by this brand experience. If people come to you for the first time as a result of nothing but a wireless message and they find the content is confusing or incomplete, they will leave and probably never come back.

Bad navigation will be the kiss of death to people's wireless brand experience. With all of the hyping of the term "wireless Net" a lot of consumers have bought mobile devices with the expectation that their wireless experience will be the same on their mobile devices as web surfing on their desktop computers. Of course, this isn't possible, so you must minimize the disappointment that some people feel by presenting them with just the right amount of content that is well-structured with logical links.

Web design philosophy has been that you give people as many ways as possible to browse a site because each person has different information-gathering styles and interests. But there will be cases where you have to structure wireless navigation so you lead people where they need to go. This is not only because of the size of the devices, but because mobile people are often in a bigger hurry to get what they need.

Respond Quickly to Inquiries

The wireless portion of people's brand experience holds another opportunity, or peril, depending on how you approach it. A dark cloud over the Web as a branding tool is that organizations do not respond in a timely fashion—within 24–48 hours—to e-mail or other types of communication that websites' visitors generate. This tells both first-time prospects and your oldest customers that you don't care about them, even though you may have spent years building a reputation as an organization with outstanding service.

Not too long ago the Fisher-Price toy company had a problem with their Power Wheels and Barbie Jeeps, battery-powered vehicles that toddlers could drive around the house. Some of the toys would catch fire without warning, which, needless to say, caused concern among parents. Taking on the guise of concerned parent when the news stories first came out, I went to the company's website.

First, finding any information about the situation or what to do about it if I was worried about my kids' safety was incredibly difficult. When I did find a page buried a few levels down, it only had a vague reference to the problem and an 800 number to call for more details. I wrote an e-mail saying I had kids and I was worried because a friend of mine mentioned the problem with the toys, so what should I do.

About a week or so later I received a reply. Helpful, but just a tad late if you're a stressed parent (luckily, in real life, I don't have kids). Of course, I wasn't surprised since many of the largest companies with the biggest brand marketing budgets don't reply to their e-mail for weeks, if they reply at all. But this seems like a lousy way to increase brand loyalty.

People are getting the message that, in the wireless world, organizations will be able to communicate with them even faster than through the Web. "Instant communication anywhere, anytime" has become the mantra for wireless capabilities.

In fairness to you, it's not your fault that people have this expectation for their wireless experiences, or the expectation that wireless Net surfing is the same as the desktop experience. But because you have, or will have, a wireless presence and you are opening a line of communication through this medium, people will extend this expectation to you when they access your wireless content. A painful fact of marketing is that perception is often as strong as reality, and very difficult to change.

The best way for you to neutralize the potential downside of these perceptions is to plan for them ahead of time. Once you make the decision to use wireless applications for more than communicating to your employees and business partners, you must carefully plan AND execute the wireless component of your brand experience. If you're going to communicate wirelessly to the outside world, do it well or don't do it at all.

The Wireless Branding Campaign

The specific wireless tactics you use in your campaign to build brand awareness, as well as pursue the other six options, will be dictated by whichever strategic objectives you have. You need to identify all of the people who will be involved with executing your tactics and the roles they will play in the branding campaign to get their input on what tactics make sense. This means people inside the organization plus those outside of the organization that you're trying to reach. They can be your best source of feedback.

In this section I will offer some general guidelines to help your branding campaign be more effective. Let me start with a question: How much baggage are you bringing to your wireless campaign?

Leave Your Baggage at the Gate

If an organization called me tomorrow to run a wireless branding campaign, I would start by preparing them to shed a lot of baggage from conventional and web branding campaigns gone by. As each new communication medium is born, marketing people initially stick to the tactics that worked in the previous medium.

The early days of radio ads (someone reading print ads) were pretty bland before people figured out that they could add music and sound effects. The first TV ads consisted mainly of actors reading copy to the camera (with occasional music and sound effects) before they started taking advantage of visual action, drama, and humor.

Web ads were initially driven by print ad standards (i.e. cost per thousand), with the promise of TV-type productions once cable modems became widespread. Eventually web advertising evolved to campaigns that were driven by how many page hits and click-throughs were generated. As people contemplate wireless branding, some wonder how much weight we should give to wireless ad click-throughs. Alas, the sins of the fathers threaten to afflict the children.

As you develop wireless branding tactics, try to view this technology in a new light not dimmed by shades of the past. That means you should buy or borrow several mobile devices, lock yourself away for a day or two, and access sponsored content. Click on ads, navigate through pages, and complete forms to get a good feel for the unique capabilities that this medium offers. Then you will be ready to start developing tactics.

And by all means, make sure the people planning your branding campaign aren't focusing on the wrong metrics. "To me, relying on ROI numbers or web stats and traffic reports are questionable tools," states Intraware's O'Meara. "Part of my issue with interactive advertising is the focus on traffic and how many people visit a site, which tends to ignore the aspects of a brand campaign whose results are harder to quantify [do people understand what our product does, our competitive advantages, and so on]. This leads to campaigns that don't communicate compellingly about the benefit of the brand, or they miss the more abstract aspects of effective branding."

Guidelines for Your Branding Efforts

Here are some general guidelines to follow as you form your branding tactics.

■ *Know how people perceive your brand.* Before launching a wireless campaign to increase or improve brand awareness, it helps to know what people think about your brand. What are the predominant impressions that people have of your organization, product, or service? How many people have these impressions? How much do you want to increase those numbers? Either buy research companies' existing data on the level of brand awareness about your brand, or conduct your own research.

Your research can be as simple as having salespeople ask two survey questions of every prospect they meet for 60 days, or conducting full-blown mail and telephone surveys. Whatever option you take, repeat the same research during and/or after your wireless campaign. If you make progress, continue the brand campaign, if not, make adjustments and relaunch the campaign. Keep the following in mind.

■ *Don't try to revive a dead brand.* A brand image is not always positive. If you're having image problems, it might make sense to change it or shoot the product and put it out of your misery. Don't spend a lot of resources on a wireless campaign to make more people aware of a weak brand. In the late 1950s a majority of people in the United States were aware of the Edsel automobile, even nondrivers. But the number of drivers who had a positive impression of the Edsel was so small that the car was a dismal marketing flop.

■ *Measure success by more than sales.* A successful wireless branding campaign often, but not always, equates with immediate or high sales volume. A lot of people can think your product is the greatest in the world after they access your wireless content. But they may not buy the product for another two years because they are not ready to replace what they already have. This is why constant research to keep abreast of what people think about you is important. Otherwise, there is the danger that senior management could kill a very good campaign because they're expecting sales tomorrow.

To assess the actual effectiveness of a brand awareness campaign, make sure you link it to as many tangible results as possible, such as an increase in leads, more shelf space, more volunteers, or an increase in constituent diversity. Even when you can't prove a direct connection to sales, it's good be able to say something like, "When we ran this wireless campaign, sales increased 20 percent, and when we stopped it for two months, sales decreased 10 percent."

■ *Track customer retention.* You should also track customer retention so you can measure brand loyalty. If your branding campaign closes but cannot retain customers, some part of the campaign is flawed. Find the problem. Fix it.

Transparent Language (www.transparent.com) sells software that helps people learn foreign languages. I own one of their programs and I subscribe to their daily e-mail service that drops an Italian "Word of the Day" on my BlackBerry so I can practice when I'm on the road. Transparent can easily track how long I use the service, plus they embed their e-mails with subtle links to special offers and hint that you can forward the e-mail to friends. (This allows them to equate loyalty with referral sales or leads.)

Another success measurement can track how many people navigating through content, take additional action, and complete forms that indicate how satisfied they are with the experience. It's not only important that people see and respond to content. They have to be happy with the process because if they're not, they will tell 100 of their closest friends. Not very good for positive brand awareness.

■ *Don't do something just because it's cheap.* Just because something costs less doesn't mean you should do it. I vehemently oppose spamming, that exercise guided by the philosophy "because it's cheap and fast, send them a million [fill in the blank: e-mails, wireless ads, pop-up windows]." This kind of silliness just irritates people, doing your image more harm than good, and it costs time and money that can be better spent.

■ *Remember the value of integration.* Integrate your wireless efforts with as many conventional and web activities as possible and practical. Comments Lot21's Everett-Thorp, "Before the Web, companies used to have a media mix, in which you made ad buys for various media (print, TV, radio) as part of a coordinated campaign. But web advertising often was done in a vacuum and not tied into a media mix. Advertisers are finally seeing the Web and wireless as valuable parts of the mix."

To get maximum value from wireless content, ads, or promotions, give people every opportunity to find out about these activities, and then move them to other media to enhance their brand experience. Use direct mail or print ads to push people to your wireless side with the promise of interesting information. ("Go to our AvantGo channel to find ten new ways to improve your golf game.") Or move people from wireless content to web content ("Go to this URL for the complete report.")

These recommendations apply whether your campaign is for new organizations, products, or services, or for ones that are already in the marketplace.

Help Employees and Business Partners Present Consistent Brand Messages

So far, we have looked at wireless as a medium for delivering your brand message and building brand awareness. But you should also look at how to use wireless technology to help your internal staff become a more integral component of the branding campaign, because there are several potential internal problems that can undermine your efforts.

Get Everyone's Message in Sync

When everyone isn't singing from the same songbook, you can undermine your own branding campaign. Employees who are often out of the office or are in branch offices and don't get enough brand-message reinforcement are most likely to have this problem. In meetings with clients I've heard the president describe the organization or a product one way, the marketing person describe it another way, and the engineers describe it a third way.

Maybe the root of this problem comes from the fact that some organizations have rambling, convoluted mission statements that say nothing. If they don't have a clear branding message on paper, wireless isn't going to make it any clearer. If your mission statement can't fit on one-third of a PDA screen or less, it's too long.

Take a cue from Cisco, which builds hardware and other technologies that link and manage the many components of massive computer networks to keep the networks running smoothly. When they were a start-up, wooing venture capitalists in the "dash for cash" in 1984, their mission statement was "Cisco networks networks." They now have employees all over the planet who present a consistent brand message whenever they represent the company, even as the company expanded from supporting the PC revolution to the Internet revolution to wireless.

If you have a comprehensible brand message, wireless can help get the message to mobile workers, occasionally remind them of the message, and deliver information such as customer stories and press clippings so mobile workers keep singing the same song.

Facilitate Communication Between Departments

A second way that employees can hurt the organization's branding effort is through the lack of communication between the groups that produce the products, sell them, and provide the service and support. Say, for example, that marketing doesn't accurately convey to product development what prospects want. Consequently, the product features fail to live up to the prospects' brand expectations that marketing has created. Product developers don't warn the salespeople in time about a serious problem, so product sales become branding headaches as products break, and the headaches only get worse because the service staff wasn't warned either.

An internal wireless communication channel between these groups that facilitates planning, proactive content delivery, and problem resolution will go a long way to keeping your branding campaign on track. Communication between marketing and operations, fundraising and volunteers, or accounting and shipping may be other areas where wireless can play a role to ensure a positive brand experience when customers deal with your organization.

Using wireless to enhance communication between your employees and third parties also can have a positive impact on customers' and prospects' brand experience. When you look at communications with outside contractors, suppliers, resellers, and others, you may find other potential weak spots in your branding efforts.

As more and more manufacturers are finding, keeping as tight a communication link as possible between assembly line, purchasing, sales staff, and third-party contract manufacturers will determine if the right products get to market at the right time. Product delays are not the impression you want at the top of people's minds when you measure brand awareness.

Your marketing staff may work with various agencies such as advertising and PR or freelance designers. These people placing your ads or schmoozing the press are on the front line of your branding campaign, so use wireless to help keep everyone as current on information as possible. When possible, also encourage these contractors to use wireless technology to improve their efficiency. When they're performing at their best, your image can't help but look good.

However competent the sales clerks are in the retail store, unless you own the store these people are not going to know and communicate the brand message as well as your staff. Any wireless tactical plan for your branding campaign should include the reseller organizations in general, and the floor sales staff in particular. This plan should extend to sales rep and telemarketing firms, as well as the sales reps of organizations that can influence your sales. If you sell high-quality, low-cost copier paper, use wireless to keep copier salespeople up-to-date so they can recommend you to their customers.

Service organizations, be they commercial, governmental, or nonprofit, that rely on third parties to deliver a key component of that service should consider a wireless link to these contractors because your reputation can suffer if they don't deliver. An executive at a Canadian gas utility company told me that when customers can't get any heat, they don't call the supplier that didn't deliver in time, or the contractor that accidentally damaged a pipeline. Customers call the company that sends them their bill.

Food for Thought

By now your tactical subconscious should be working on ideas for using wireless communication for brand building. Before moving on to the next tactical options, here are a few questions to help crystallize your thinking on the subject of wireless and branding.

1. Do you have a clear picture of what your organization and product brand images are (or what you want them to be)? Do the people who will be developing and contributing to your wireless efforts have the same picture?

2. What conventional activities are your organization conducting to build brand awareness? Can you build wireless content and activities that will extend your conventional brand-building activities?

3. Would it help your overall brand image if you provided general wireless network access to people who visit your facilities or, alternatively, provide wireless access to specific content? Will this be practical for you to implement?

4. What content can you create (i.e., industry briefing papers, research reports, monthly tip sheets) that gets people to keep coming back to your site? Do you have the time and resources to regularly update this material?

5. Is there content you can create for people that has "pass along" value so you can encourage recipients of your message to extend your brand to their associates, family members, and others who can influence the decision to do business with you?

6. Do you have good opportunities to sponsor content for your various markets?

7. Do you have access to resources that can help you target the right people to receive your wireless messages?

8. Do your IT people have technology in place that can help you personalize content so individuals feel they're getting information specifically for them? Sometimes this can be accomplished by personalizing web content that your audiences can then access wirelessly.

9. Are there areas within your organization that can use wireless technology to improve the brand experience that people have with your organization?

CHAPTER 8

Generating Immediate Responses from Your Audiences

With branding campaigns, you're working toward a long-term objective of building loyalty to your organization, product, or service. It's okay if all of these tactics don't generate immediate responses, such as having people sign up for your newsletters or buy products today, as long as you develop strong relationships and eventually sales. Metreon and Port Discovery in the last chapter fit into this category.

Direct response communication has the goal of generating immediate results today, right now! You want people to access your information in droves and quickly download background papers, product specs, and samples of your products (if your products can be digitized). These activities can be part of a broader effort to build brand loyalty, or they can be a "here and now" effort to boost end-of-quarter sales or generate publicity on a college campus to find temporary workers for the Christmas shopping season.

There may be times when you want people to take action not online or through wireless devices, but by telephoning your office, attending a political rally, or racing off to a fix a broken pipeline in the wilderness. Because of its ability to deliver messages instantly, it is easy for wireless communication to take on an air of immediacy in the right situations such as emergencies or announcing events with impending deadlines.

The bottom line here is that you use direct response activities to generate immediate and tangible results to achieve current goals.

A note of caution: If you do execute a direct response effort as an isolated event, be sure to remain consistent with your brand image and message. For example, a financial services company may want college students for temporary positions at tax time, but it shouldn't run an ad that attracts anyone with a pulse. The ad still needs to project a conservative, service-oriented image so the company attracts people who will be representative of that image.

Direct response activities can have a wide range of goals. For example, you might want to:

- Entice people to read your information so they will be motivated to buy, even if they buy after dialing a phone number or running to the nearest retail outlet that carries your product.
- Get your employees to take action in response to both internal and external communication needs.
- Get contractors or other business partners to move quickly so your organization can resolve problems or take advantage of new business opportunities.

The ideal direct response tactics are those that motivate users to take some kind of action before they leave your wireless content or message.

Don't focus on generating sales via wireless devices. Instead focus on fostering two-way communication. Enable people to find and review additional information at their convenience after your initial contact with them. Be sensitive to the context in which people are receiving your message. Always have clear calls to action in your messages. If you do these things successfully, often sales will follow through one channel or another.

Use Direct Response to Motivate External Audiences

There are many direct response tactics that can support your strategic objectives that involve communicating with customers, prospects, and others with whom you want to do business.

Organizations of all types often need to motivate their customers or constituents to take action. Some use direct response tactics just to distribute as much information as possible, as quickly as possible. For example, a sporting goods store might post a notice on their AvantGo channel that says "Click here to access our Guide to Better Windsurfing, and get a $20 discount on our new wetsuit."

This ad has the benefit of getting people to quickly (motivated by the $20 incentive) read information that may indirectly lead to sales of any product related to windsurfing, plus it has the added bonus of getting people to specifically buy a new wetsuit. Other wireless ads and content may need to motivate people to take actions that require more effort and commitment, such as go to a store, write to the board of directors, or "bring a friend."

Regardless of how much or how little effort is required of the recipient to respond to your message, one element that will dictate the success or failure of your tactics is the offer that you make to people.

The Value of the Offer Pushes People to Take Action

Direct marketing specialists will tell you that the offer is one of the most important parts of any marketing activity, whether it's direct mail, TV ads, or sales presentations, when the main objective is to produce an immediate response. The offer can be simple—"$19.95 per month and the best wireless service on the planet is yours"—or it can be complex—"Just $199.99 and you can take this power mower home today. Save 10 percent if you pick it up by Saturday! But wait there's more!"

I describe these two offers as, respectively, a basic offer and a special offer. The basic offer boils down to what is it that you want me to do, what will it cost me, and what do I get. In the first offer, you want me to buy your service, the best wireless service is what I will get, $19.95 is what I have to pay for it, and it doesn't matter when I buy the service. It's obvious that YOU want me to buy today, but since there's no special offer, there's no reason for ME to buy today.

In the second offer, there are still the key elements of what you're selling and what the customer is getting, but the "special offer" is the 10 percent discount that customers can get if they take action quickly.

In the wireless environment, using basic offers is fine. But we're talking about getting people to take action quickly! By virtue of where and how people use mobile devices, many of them are probably not near a fast Net connection, they're busy, and probably getting ready to do something else or go somewhere when they see your message. Go with the special offer. Greed and urgency are good motivators to catch people's attention.

You can lead with the offer, close with it, or state it several times in the body of the message. The offer can be as creative as you want, and you can change it as often as you want. The offer can be used to try to motivate whatever action you want: Get a free Teddy bear (or a free teddy) when you "call today," "submit this form," "visit our website," and so forth.

Sasha Pave, Lot21's director of technical design, has good insights on how to develop your offer to make it more effective at generating quick responses from recipients. "Make sure you know not only whom you are talking to, but in what context," Pave says. "Mobile users are on the bus, train, or plane and generally use their devices for information retrieval. Messages must be quick and the information must be relevant and to the point." Pave believes that special offer digital coupons are ripe for mobile platforms.

Allowing the user to bring in the PDA to a retail outlet to redeem a coupon is an effective way to reach prospects and motivate them to take action that results in a sale. The marketing team at CompUSA generated impressive results using a digital coupon.

Clipping Coupons in the Digital Age

CompUSA is a national retail chain of 225 stores in 84 major metropolitan areas that sells computers, software, peripherals, and accessories. In 2001 they decided to break new ground and create the first mobile coupon. It was redeemable for a 10 percent discount on PDA and cell phone accessories. (See Figure 8-1.)

By clicking on the CompUSA coupon ad that ran on a rotating basis on AvantGo's network, people were greeted with a message promoting the discount, along with photos and descriptions of eligible products. People saved the coupon as an AvantGo channel to their mobile devices and brought the devices along when they shopped at any CompUSA location.

At the stores, shoppers selected the items they wanted, then showed the onscreen coupon to the cashier upon check out. The cashier input the code and the discount was instantly applied.

"The results were amazing," says Tony Weiss, CompUSA's executive vice president of merchandising. "Having the ad on AvantGo ensured that we reached a very large and targeted audience that mapped exactly to the people we wanted to reach. For us, every AvantGo user is a customer or a potential customer. The response rate was far better than what we had expected."

Eighteen thousand users saved the coupon to their handheld devices or mobile phones. Of those users, a full 5 percent used the coupon at a CompUSA store. Not too bad for a mobile coupon that was created and deployed in just one week, especially when you consider that developing and placing traditional ads or coupons often can require lead times of several weeks.

"Being able to place a digital ad or coupon in a matter of days provides us with a whole new level of flexibility and market responsiveness," Weiss says. "And we saved a significant amount of money, too, because we didn't have to print and mail the coupons. This campaign definitely met all of our marketing goals."

And don't make the mistake of thinking this approach will only work for technology products. Nontech organizations can do the same things. The

Figure 8-1. CompUSA's first mobile coupon.

question here is demographics. Any commercial, governmental, or nonprofit organization can do some variation on this direct response tactic, as long as the demographics of the mobile device user fit the profile of your target audiences.

All you need to do after you work out details with a retailer is use the discount coupon as bait to lure people into taking the action you desire. "Access our wireless catalogue for lawn mowers, and get a discount coupon." "Call us to pledge a donation, we'll e-mail a wireless coupon." "Complete your 1040 tax form with your mobile device, we'll give you a link to the coupon for a free bottle of Bayer aspirin."

For your offers to be special, they don't always need to be for monetary gain, but they must be compelling relative to the audience and the action you want them to take. If you're asking someone to access a particular message or section of content, it probably doesn't make sense to offer $5. Instead, offer people the chance to win a prize. "Click here for our special report on rice cookers. You may win a gold-plated CookRite rice cooker!"

To offer someone $5 to complete a form makes sense if it costs you $20 using any other means to get the same data from a similarly qualified person AND $5 is the minimum offer to motivate your target audience to complete the form. If a buck and a smile will get the deed done, save yourself four dollars.

In light of some of the dot-com madness that went on at the turn of the century, do not make the kind of offer that will send you into bankruptcy court. Offering someone a $100 product for $80 only makes sense if it's done for a limited time, or you have additional items to sell the person at 300 percent markup. A compelling offer does not mean a fiscally ridiculous offer.

How Do You Know When the Offer Is Right?

Gauging what is the right offer depends on more variables than I can cover in one chapter, but the things you have to keep in mind are:

- What action do you want people to take?
- Is the person you're trying to motivate someone who has a business relationship with you already, or will this be his or her first contact with you?
- How much is that action worth to you?
- How much effort will it require on the part of the recipient of your message to take action?
- How much resistance will this person have to taking this action? (He or she may have no problem answering six questions about random issues, but will refuse to answer two personal questions.)

It is vitally important that you test, test, and test again. What's special for one audience could bore another one to tears. Use the conventional and web world primarily as an idea generator for special offers, but don't assume that if an offer worked like gangbusters on the Web it will be affective on a PDA.

In some cases, you can bring in the usual suspects of direct response marketing such as t-shirts, coffee mugs, free trips, or a chance to win a million dollars. At a certain level people are still people, regardless of their occupation, and human beings respond similarly to "free" stuff and "special deals."

Grab a couple of direct marketing magazines and specialty/novelty catalogues to see what type of giveaways are working. When you go to trade shows, look at which knick-knacks seem to be the most popular with attendees.

Don't be surprised if stupid gimmicks work best with an intelligent audience. Sometimes those button-down executives need an excuse to relive their inglorious (but fun) youth. You may also find that, even though free t-shirts move people to take action, you need to use Polo shirts rather than t-shirts as an incentive for presidents of Fortune 500 companies.

Information Can Be a Potent Special Offer

Your special offer doesn't always have to be for something tangible. People see and hear offers for intangible benefits all the time. "Access these 10 tips on healthy eating and we guarantee you will add years to your life!" However, the less tangible the offer, the more likely it will be perceived as a basic offer.

Information might be viewed as an intangible offer, but it can be a great motivator if you put some thought into how to make it compelling information. This tactic has added value because you can deliver it immediately once a person takes the action you want, thus providing instant gratification. People respond faster if they know they will get a reward sooner rather than later.

Financial services companies that offer new customers PDAs are really offering financial information delivered quickly (along with a free PDA, of course). As customers get addicted to receiving one type of information such as stock quotes or financial reports, it will be easier to use other information to motivate various actions. For example, "If you like what you received from us so far, renew your service today and we'll send you a special report on how to spot bad investments."

Offer Professional or Personal Improvement Information

In general, people who use PDAs bought them to get control of certain aspects of their business or personal lives, so they are likely to be motivated by business or personal information management. Teenagers and college students who have PDAs are motivated as much by coolness and communication with their friends as by personal management, so they're likely to be motivated by information on how to manage their cool.

IT professionals might respond best to an offer such as "Complete this short survey and receive seven tips on how to get more productivity from your software contractors." Marketing people may respond to this offer: "Visit this URL and receive our guide on how to enhance your ad campaign." Real estate agents might take action if they get a message to "Call this number and we'll e-mail you our weekly newsletter *Advice You Can Use from Successful Real Estate Agents.*" And teens, unattached single adults, and senior citizens returning to the dating circuit may all respond to "Subscribe to our online magazine and we'll send you the video *How to Be Cool Without Being a Dork.*"

Offer the Key to Unlock Details on Special Topics

Sometimes you can keep people coming to your digital doorstep by giving them the ability to search for information on specialized topics. In these early days of wireless, information in general is going to be hard to find as people sort out what from the Web is valuable to make accessible to those of us wirelessly connected. Consider setting up a directory or resource tool of some sort that hooks people by helping them search for a particular type of information.

If your market is optometrists, maybe you can set up a directory of eye care supplies and equipment providers. If your prospects do a lot of work with the federal government, set up a directory of government information sources (various government agencies are quickly popping up online). These directories can do a lot to generate frequent visitors. Once you establish frequent visits and hopefully start gathering some demographic information on visitors, you can plan occasional special offers.

While the main goal of a direct response offer is to get people to take action immediately, one of the goals for any tactical campaign should be to establish a pattern of frequent two-way communication. That's how you increase customer retention, generate referrals from prospects and customers, and maintain active relationships with business partners.

The Right Lists Can Reel 'Em In

Consider offering lists of items, events, or facts that people can't easily get elsewhere in exchange for them downloading information or referring your product to friends. A lot of people seem to be addicted to lists. David Letterman's book *Top Ten Lists*, in various incarnations, has been selling strong for over ten years.

To attract TV junkies, maybe you can offer a list of TV trivia. "Answer these five questions about your travel plans to Hawaii and we'll send you the list of the ten most popular episodes of the TV show *Hawaii Five-O.*" Whatever list category you offer, be sure it changes on a weekly or biweekly basis if you want people frequently responding to your activities. Hook 'em, Danno.

Of course, this type of targeted message is best when you have a qualified database of customers or prospects, but as the wireless industry evolves there should be tools or services that allow you to better pinpoint audiences.

Creative Messages Spur Constituents and Customers to Action

Many organizations in all levels of government are in the business of distributing information, sometimes within specific timeframes. Tax-filing deadlines represent the ultimate crunch time to get information out to huge constituent audiences. These agencies rarely have money to offer cash incentives for people to read the information, so they have to rely on creative messages to spur their constituents to action.

If people sign up specifically to receive wireless notifications about a particular topic, such as tips on how new legislation will impact city services or state tax rules, they already have some incentive to get this information. All you have to do is send the alert, point to the information, and make it easy to retrieve the information. There are many times when organizations need to get people to take actions other than just gathering information.

A regional or federal park service might announce a special event for the upcoming weekend, such as a concert or pony rides, that is an incentive for parents of young children to bring the family to a park. Perhaps this is to create photo opportunities that in turn generate news coverage to influence a city council meeting to approve an increase of funds to the park.

You occasionally read about nonprofits that are on a mission to save something or other: the trees, the whales, a historic monument, etc. A carefully-crafted message delivered wirelessly can inspire donors and the journalists who cover them to contribute money, write articles, or write to their congressional representatives. If the wireless world starts to offer the equivalent of the public service announcement (PSA), these kinds of activities will be more affordable for nonprofit organizations.

Anne Riser, president of the Personal Communications Industry Association (PCIA), a telecommunication industry association, sees wireless as a great mobilization tool. "If a professional association has sophisticated members who use wireless devices, wireless applications can be a real boon for contacting and staying in touch with these members. For example, getting them to contact their congressional representatives to take action on an upcoming vote. Wireless is good for grassroots action-prodding campaigns."

When you plan product launches, use wireless campaigns to reach customers who you believe will buy the first units of your new product. This tactic feeds into the more long-term tactic of building brand awareness by getting a core group of customers to buy early, then encouraging them to spread the word to other customers and prospects.

You may need to quickly mobilize customers to rally in support of objectives other than generating sales. Whether to fight a hostile takeover attempt at next week's board meeting, or to create a public display of loyalty to counter tomorrow's weak quarterly earnings announcement, wireless communication can play a role. Wireless can be the latter-day trusty steeds that bring corporate Paul Reveres to spread the alarm through every wireless village and farm, for the customers to be up and to arm (my apologies to Henry Wadsworth Longfellow).

Direct Response Tactics Specifically for Prospects

If your primary strategic objective with wireless is to reduce the cost and length of your sales cycles, then getting people to take swift action is a key component of the tactical execution of the strategy. Aside from the cost of marketing activities and materials to generate leads, the other big costs of the sale are time and timing. The time your salespeople have to spend with prospects, the weeks it takes for someone to make up his or her mind to buy, and the lost sales opportunities because your message reached an audience after they lost interest in your service.

Every step along the sales process, look for ways to use wireless communication to ask for and get a response that can shorten the time it takes to close a sale. When your ad or other marketing materials reach someone when they're mobile, have wireless content available. For the person who comes into your retail store, have wireless access available so even if he or she doesn't have a PDA with Net access, the device's infrared port can access your information.

Whether a prospect makes contact with you either conventionally, on the Web, or wirelessly, have several means ready to deliver wireless "take action now" messages. As the first rumor of a concert hits the street and someone calls your box office wanting to know the second when Bruce Springsteen tickets go on sale, offer to deliver the information to the prospect wirelessly. And when you contact the person, send him or her a seating chart so he or she can pick out his or her seats.

A popular tactic with some retailers is to give people who place orders on-line the ability to have their goods waiting at the check-out stand. Giving this tactic a wireless spin, suppose someone wants to be notified on their mobile device when your new car safety seat for twins is available. When you contact the prospect, send a quick form to complete so he or she can arrange to have the seat packed and ready to go when he or she gets to the store. This gives the prospect an added incentive to order right then because he or she can pick up the product with minimal delay on the way home from work.

If you have analyzed your sales process, you should know various points after the initial contact when it makes sense to deliver a message or a gentle reminder wirelessly rather than getting a salesperson to make the contact. This is true of commercial organizations selling products or nonprofits soliciting first-time donors. For both groups, reducing the time between contact and final close significantly impacts cash flow.

Warning: Sometimes Restraint Is the Better Part of Communication

Using wireless as the initial contact activity with a prospect is not advisable unless you can be fairly certain that at least a few of the demographics of your audience match your target market. Draw a lesson from previous experience on the Internet. A driving force in some e-mail and banner advertising was that it didn't cost much, so companies thought they could spam a billion prospects. If only two dozen people bought the product, it was okay because the campaign only cost a few thousand dollars, maybe less.

Today many organizations feel that, even though spam is less expensive than many conventional marketing activities, there's creative talent and time they have to commit that could be put to better use elsewhere. More importantly, the negative backlash to spamming is considered harmful to organizations' images. Those evaluating wireless communication are more demanding about targeting, market segmentation, and other sound marketing practices that were not made obsolete by the "new economy."

As the number of mobile devices increases, and wireless technology improves to the point where you can monitor demographics and user behavior with a high level of accuracy, organizations may use wireless to spearhead direct response activities to prospects. In the meantime you should rely on conventional and web communication to introduce your product or service, then use wireless to motivate and facilitate follow-on communication with prospects.

An exception to this might be if you develop a wireless campaign to motivate customers to forward your message to the wireless devices of people who have never bought your product. In this case the initial contact is being made by a trusted source, so there will be less resistance to at least opening the message. Response will be determined by how enthusiastic your customers are when they deliver the messages.

Howard Sadel, Director of New Media & Graphic Communications for the North Carolina Hurricanes hockey team, is contemplating this tactic. He talks about the fact that a lot of people become devoted hockey fans after attending just one game, and they start introducing all of their friends to the sport. One woman bought two season tickets and invited a different friend or colleague who had never watched the Canes play to 41 games.

Send Your Messages in Waves

"If possible, split your messaging up into an initial call-to-action, then follow through with more information if recipients ask for it," advises Lot21's Pave. For example: A message to purchase a book could be the main focus of the ad, with a book description and review available if the user has time to dig in. Chances are all PDA users are also desktop computer users with Internet access. Whenever possible, follow through with e-mail messages.

"Give people options, options, options," says Pave. "You're not going to hit the person ready to buy each time you send a message, so give them choices of action to take. (See Figure 8-2.) For example, provide them with a directory of stores, the option to read more right then and there, and whenever possible give the prospect the ability to have more information sent to them via e-mail."

Even after you've been given permission to send prospects e-mail, you don't want to bombard them with a lot of ads or with ads that are huge relative to the screen size. Screen real estate is small, so a small ad commands much more attention than the same size ad on a full size monitor. Also, a huge ad can annoy some people if it interrupts their reading of other material.

Direct Response Tactics Can Improve Service and Support

If one of your primary strategic objectives is to be more proactive to resolve problems before most people even know they exist, direct response tactics will be your lead tool. Again, this will likely be more effective for reaching customers because you already have a relationship with them, and you have wireless communication channels that customers have volunteered to use.

If you have systems in place internally that enable product development, marketing, and customer service to communicate with each other more effectively, it should be relatively easy to extend that wireless channel to customers. That way, when the product development team realizes they need to replace a defective part, marketing can immediately deliver an appropriate message

Figure 8-2. An example of how to offer a customer choices.

to customers before rather than after products start malfunctioning, causing you legal, financial, and PR headaches.

Notify Customers How to Improve Efficiencies Using Your Products

The people who develop a product, or sometimes even other customers, are frequently discovering ways to make the product operate more efficiently. You want to get this news out to customers as soon as possible, and by so doing, show them how much you care.

Software companies often make small improvements of existing product features, what they call "in-line" upgrades. These upgrades are made available on websites, and are popular with users who download them without a lot of time and hassle. These companies can implement a direct response tactic, which is to wirelessly deliver service as soon as it becomes available and extend the value of their web communication.

Wireless gives you a fast way to deliver tips on improving product performance, or in the case of software, maybe even the actual improvements. If you sell products or services that customers depend on daily, then delivering information to them that they can immediately take action on (and benefit from) makes good business sense for you.

Sometimes you can use wireless to make it easier for people who are already motivated to take quick action to communicate with you, in essence creating a direct response channel from external audiences into your organization. Since you can't catch every problem before it happens, you have to give your customers every opportunity to take action to either reach a person who can help resolve their issue, or to solve the problem themselves. Wireless offers great value as a communication tool to speed up problem resolutions.

This need to create a direct response channel into your organization transcends customers and prospects to include even people who do not do business with you. For example, someone may not own what you sell and never will, but he or she might be upset about your employee-relations practices, your expansion plans into his or her neighborhood, or what he or she sees as poor government policy.

Subscribing to news reports is popular with mobile device users. If they read about your organization discontinuing services to a particular market, be prepared to start a dialogue with them should they go directly from the story to your wireless content. While you may not want to commit the resources to deal with noncustomers, it behooves you to offer them the faster path to addressing their issues because noncustomers can still influence the behaviors of customers and prospective customers.

Use Direct Response Within Your Organization

There can be numerous situations that merit the use of direct response tactics as part of your internal wireless communication, particularly when they involve people with frequent deadlines. Murphy's Law (whatever can go wrong will go wrong, usually five minutes before a deadline) and communication glitches are collectively the dark side of the force that haunt many organizations' business operations. Wireless technologies are the light sabers that can help your people rise above this adversity.

Project teams equipped with PDAs should have wireless capabilities tied into their project management and e-mail applications so mobile workers and interfacility roamers can respond faster to each other and to events that will delay or derail projects. For example, line workers could get a wireless instant message from a field sales rep alerting them that a deal just closed for a gazillion components, and subsequently make quick adjustments to ramp up production so this new deadline as well as old ones are met.

Add a news service to the application that tracks your organization's main suppliers. Project managers could find out quickly, for example, that a supplier's plant has burned down, and they will be able to immediately take action to keep production on schedule. Round out your wireless deployment by embedding wireless sensors into the plant machinery and your facilities managers can receive alerts so they can fix problems before they affect other deadlines.

Any type of organization can use these "rapid response" wireless applications. Many groups at every level of government use contractors that are integral to the groups' ability to deliver services on time, or at least in a timely fashion. Nonprofits often rely on outside talent for marketing support, and delays in communication between these groups can delay execution of key elements of the marketing campaign.

Of course, your organization may be in the consultant or contractor role, so your wireless tactic may be designed to increase your responsiveness to your clients' needs. If it is difficult for you to get clients to go along with the program, a pilot project with clients might be advisable until you have a couple of success stories to prove its value. Unless the client has a wireless capability that you can tap into, you probably want to make the application simple and use a wireless ASP to keep costs down.

There may be times when a direct response tactic needs to address just a few individuals or a single group within your organization, such as:

■ Administrative assistants who receive messages from specific individuals that must be forwarded to their managers
■ Research staffs that need to distribute reports based on market surveys as soon as that data comes in from web-based sources
■ Dispatchers who have to assign rescue teams at a game preserve as soon as reports come in about animals in distress

For other organizations, there will be entire departments that can benefit from these type of tactics.

Marketing

Marketing people have a constant need to get rapid responses from internal staff and the outside contractors who are vital to the success of marketing campaigns. A late-breaking industry crisis, for example, requires an immediate response to journalists. The PR department or agency has to be called together as soon as possible to plot strategy and implement it, sometimes within hours. Wireless can be the rapid-response tool that guarantees this turn-on-a-dime operation.

Investor Relations

Investor relations staffs, particularly during economic or industry upheaval, need to maintain a steady stream of communication with their investor community. Wireless communication, in conjunction with time-sensitive web content, can keep this vital audience in the loop. With so many financial services companies giving away PDAs to their customers to wirelessly conduct transactions, it may be safe to say that a lot of your investors are prime candidates for your direct response activities.

Public Relations

When you have unexpected crises (product recalls, natural disasters, Scrooge suddenly threatening to foreclose the mortgage on the orphanage), those who communicate with customers or the general public must be as proactive as possible. Wireless can give them the edge they need to ensure maximum responsiveness. PR people aren't the only ones who should be part of this wireless tactic, but also customer service staff, senior management, and even receptionists.

Reseller Support

You can use location-based direct response tactics to provide product management services to your resellers so you can keep them better stocked with the right merchandise at the right times. Federico Aloisi of wireless application vendor neXui in Italy describes such a scenario. "You can create a location-based service for a company that sells products with short shelf lives through retail outlets. Using a GPS system or technology that wireless carriers already have, plus CRM and mapping software, delivery vans can be automatically matched with customers in their vicinity and sent information about which items are at the end of their shelf lives. The drivers can then make a delivery during that trip."

Aloisi believes that the scenario of a person being beeped as he or she walks by a particular store is possible, but may not be pragmatic unless you can somehow create a profile of the person. However, you or your resellers can give people the opportunity to subscribe to a service so that they are targeted to receive messages based on what they want (i.e., to receive an alert when specified products go on sale, or when a new book comes in) or at certain times.

If you use wireless to automatically send up-to-the-minute product availability, price changes, favorable news stories, sales incentives for in-store sales people, and even market analysis data, this could quickly trigger local marketing efforts by the retailers. The result is a competitive edge in an environment in which product sales are driven by changing customer's demands and frequent sales staff turnover.

Human Resources

HR staffs often need to quickly distribute information, and just as quickly get responses back from employees. With so many road warriors and interfacility roamers in some organizations, this is not an easy task, so wireless can make HR's job easier. Sometimes HR needs quick responses from job candidates who may be all over the world.

IT Staff

The IT department provides the life blood to your organization's automation systems, and it is an integral part of the productivity gains that IT systems deliver. When your employees can't work because their computer or software suddenly stops, you need action fast. Besides IT, any department or outside party that provides vital computing operations support service to others within your organization needs to be in the direct response loop.

Senior Management

Direct response should be a tactical consideration even at the highest levels. The reason many organizations equipped all of their managers and senior executives with mobile devices is so they can receive and reply to e-mail which, along with instant messaging, are some of the most immediate two-way direct response tools there are.

Asset Tracking

Using wireless technology to track assets or monitor LANs, cooling systems, and other equipment is, at the tactical level, direct response communication. If a vehicle malfunctions, a wireless alert goes out so someone can take immediate action, or if the room temperature reaches 90 degrees, a wireless command turns on the air conditioner. In many cases, wireless enabling assets, facilities, and various business operations means giving wireless devices to a range of employees and third parties who have to use, service, or otherwise interact with these inanimate objects.

Exploring Other Direct Response Tactical Options

The remaining tactical ideas in this chapter can be applied to all four of the strategic options, though some may be easier to apply to customers and prospects than to your employees. The important thing to keep in mind is that each idea and example of what other organizations have implemented that is presented here is a stepping-off point to what could be an avalanche of specific ideas that meet your particular needs.

Indirect Direct Response

Although much of direct response revolves around approaching people with a sense of urgency, sometimes the subtle approach can work wonders. It does require establishing ongoing communication with customers or prospects so once in a while you can slip something in that lets people lead themselves to a particular action. Other times you may be able to use the events around you that create a sense of urgency and motivate people to take action.

One of my services is onsite speaking and training seminars for organizations. I keep a database of contacts, but it would be counterproductive to send them monthly messages asking, "Hey, do you need me now?" So sometimes sending out a notice about an item I read in the news that will help their professional development can indirectly inspire them to take action and hire me to do a presentation for them.

The rationale is that if I meet these people at a professional development conference, they're probably interested in enhancing their professional skills. Also, they attended and liked my session, and they might be interested in hearing me again. Therefore, by sending the news item, it catches their attention, provides a small but valuable service, and subconsciously says, "Hey this guy knows what's going on in our industry. He's a pretty good speaker and our managers need some guidance."

This tactic really isn't a newsletter and it doesn't have to be delivered on a regular schedule. It's an FYI (for your information) service that I do as a way to keep in touch and provide value beyond the sessions I gave. You can execute variations on this tactic using late-breaking news stories, changing economic, industry or social trends, pending scientific developments, or "little-known facts" that might interest your audience.

If you run a hardware store in Ohio, you can send customers a news item that warns them to expect a really harsh winter and includes a recommendation that "extra roof insulation is advised in older homes." This valuable FYI should motivate immediate insulation sales from recipients because the first snows are already falling.

A state tax board can send out news regarding a recent business tax law passed by the legislature, with the hope of getting companies to visit the board's website immediately where there are not only details on the new law, but new tax forms as well. The office is much happier when companies respond and file weeks ahead of the deadline rather than at the last minute.

Look at the nature of people's jobs, their industries, areas of personal interests, geographic locations, and so forth, then determine what related information you can provide that indirectly motivates an action favorable to you. You may have noticed in my examples that these are long-term tactics in that it may be your fourth or fifth FYI that moves someone to call you or visit your website that day. But you can make indirect tactics more immediate.

Use Events to Create a Sense of Urgency

Another approach to motivating immediate action is to use the timing of events around you. Few things drive hordes of people into flower shops and card shops like the sudden realization that it's the day before (take your pick) Mother's Day, Valentine's Day, or a significant other's birthday, and someone forgot to buy cards, flowers, and gifts. Part of the popularity of websites such as Blue Mountain Greeting Cards (www.bluemountain.com), FTD.com, and similar online enterprises is that they send out reminder notices so people can take immediate action before it's too late.

Their reminder services are considered extremely valuable by recipients because otherwise customers might forget an important event and be in the doghouse for weeks. (You may know this from personal experience.) This builds brand loyalty plus, when people are in a panic mode, they most likely will turn to you if you give them a wireless lifeline to a solution. Consider this tactic regardless of the industry you're in.

Whether dealing with customers, prospects, journalists, resellers, or contractors, there are often dates by which certain actions need to (or should) be taken, and wireless-delivered messages can be the motivator. Provide a reminder service for those events, and when practical, include with the reminders links to special offers or other materials.

A local symphony orchestra can send its donors a reminder to this week's gala fundraiser where "all the stars will be out," and format the message for easy entry into PDA calendars. This should motivate recipients to check their schedule right then, and once the item is in the PDA calendar, it serves as an ongoing motivator that hangs in the background.

Sometimes the reminders can be about an event or activity that you don't control such as Father's Day or a trade show, but that you have a vested interest in because you offer products or services related to the event, or people attending the activity are your target audience. For example, "Just 10 shopping days left to take advantage of our special Christmas sale. Download our catalogue today!" "Order our special Mother's Day bouquet. That special day is just five days away." "Winter's almost over. Have you taken advantage of our special ski vacation package?"

Unsolicited reminders may be okay, but you should know the audience you're contacting pretty well before doing this. Sending additional information with reminders can be insurance to get more people to take the action you desire, but you have to carefully gauge how you do this. If you find that after the fifteenth time you send someone a reminder of your summer solstice sale you're starting to get some particularly nasty replies to bug off, maybe you should consider reducing the number of reminders you send to, say, three or four.

Build Anticipation by Creating an Event

Sometimes you can launch an entire direct response campaign that is coordinated with a time-specific event that you create. For example, you can encourage people to take action within a short time period (e.g., "Order by [specified date] and save. Get two-for-one, reserve your seat, etc.").

Another way to go about this is to build up anticipation by promoting something for a specific date. "Be here January 27 to get research information on medical advances that will dramatically change how you provide health care." By regularly promoting this event to the right audience, you should have people lined up (figuratively speaking) on that date waiting to get the news.

An alternative way to build anticipation is through the uncertainty of a "mystery tease and deliver" campaign. Hollywood studios often use this tactic to promote movies. Deliver teaser messages to the effect of "Be here June 1! Something really special and exciting will happen. You don't want to miss this!" Of course, what you deliver had better be worth the anticipation you build. It will also be effective if you are a well-known reputable organization so people won't think the promotion is a scam.

Organizations often combine an offer, which you should make very compelling, with the deadline, which should within a few days. "Save 10 percent on everything in the store if you arrive before noon this Friday!" Another variation on this tactic is to deliver a "get it before you run out of time" message, special offer optional. "Send your donation today to save the whales before they're gone forever." "Visit our store this weekend before [item] is sold out." If you're going to motivate a busy mobile user to make time to take action, pull out all of the stops.

Being a most devout and loyal Bruce Springsteen fan, all that's needed is a message that says "Springsteen Oakland concert tickets, sold at this URL, today only!" and, unless I'm on Mars, I'm all over that site like jam on toast. This particular tactic, the more extreme of the deadline-motivated tactics, gets best results when you know your audience well enough to predict results with a high degree of certainty. An offer that reads "'Lawrence Welk's Greatest Polka Hits—one day only! Order before midnight tonight!" is probably doomed if you broadcast it to teenagers at an *NSync concert.

A Tale of Two Sports Cities Shows How to Create a Sense of Urgency

Regardless of which country you visit, you will find that sporting events are a big part of life for many of the people who live there. The following two stories show how sport teams in different countries used wireless communication to motivate those who embody the true meaning of brand loyalty, sports fans. Both relied on specific events to create a sense of urgency for the fans receiving their messages

Nothing Could Be Finer Than Wireless in Carolina

The Carolina Hurricanes hockey team (www.caneshockey.com) in Raleigh, North Carolina has jumped on wireless communication with both skates. They ran three wireless campaigns during the 2000–2001 season to reach both fans and people who had never seen a game in their lives.

The initial campaign ran from November to December 2000. The Canes' Howard Sadel saw wireless as a huge opportunity to communicate with people in a different way and give them a new point of purchase. "A lot of people miss our games because they don't know about when the games are, or they get the information at time when it's not convenient to call. We did research to find out what was the best opportunity to push out ads since we knew we could target ads to specific geographical areas. In focus groups our fans said that they don't make entertainment plans any further out than three days because of schedule uncertainties, family events, or other issues. We saw wireless as the best way to get something to them."

The first campaign consisted of ad banners on various wireless sites that just said, "Purchase tickets for upcoming Canes games." The Hurricanes estimated that 15 percent of people who saw the ad called the ticket office, but they didn't have good tracking mechanisms in place to accurately measure sales results. They compensated for this with the second effort.

The next campaign was an ad with a promotion code so ticket sellers could better track sales. On three Saturday's in February, the Hurricanes offered a five dollar discount if the ad recipient called as he or she was looking at the ad. Callers got right through to a salesperson on a toll-free number and could place an order. Again, 15 percent of those who saw the ad called and one third of them (5 percent of the people who saw the ad) actually bought a ticket.

The third wireless campaign was part of a bigger marketing effort designed to double season ticket holders from 6,000 to 12,000 in an eight- to ten-week period. Sadel states, "We used everything: TV, print, radio, the Web. We had a Friends of Canes fan club in the corporate community promoting season tickets, and a local radio DJ broadcasting from the roof of our office building.

"On the last eight days of the campaign we used wireless advertising. The phones became swamped during this last week and made it impossible to track leads to specific media sources. We do know that seven-game season ticket packages skyrocketed. We had 35,000 wireless ad impressions within a 90-mile radius with a 6.5 percent call-through rate. There were too many calls received to sort out conversion rates."

Technology from WindWire (www.windwire.com), a company near Raleigh-Durham, North Carolina, formats, stores, and later delivers ads to mobile devices through the wireless networks. WindWire helped to design and execute all three of the Canes' wireless campaigns, charging $80 for every 1,000 messages sent out. Windwire's Director of Marketing Billy Purser described some of the mechanics of how the campaigns were executed.

"WindWire has three ways to do demographic analysis before showing ads to a particular device. The site that people are going to, for example, ESPN versus USA Today, identifies their demographics for us [income, gender]. Searches that a person does on a site can help us identify additional aspects of their demographic. And the cell phone tower of the wireless network sends a signal that tells where the person is located. Our technology mixes these three data feeds to fine tune the analysis, automatically select an appropriate ad from our client inventory, and serve it to the device. Cell towers have determined what device the user has so we send the ad properly formatted."

Messaggio Diverso, Stesso Linguaggio (Different Message, Same Language)

Hiugo, a company in Milan, Italy that is similar to WindWire, was responsible for executing a recent wireless campaign to promote a brand awareness-building event tied to the debut of new shirts for one of Milan's soccer teams, Inter.

Italian soccer fans are every bit as devoted, enthusiastic, and vocal as any sports fans you will find here in the United States. Inter wanted to capitalize on this support to gather and fire up the faithful as well as recruit new fans, so they set up a big rally in downtown Milan to draw people to see the Inter team players. They also wanted to sell newly redesigned team shirts.

"To attract people to the rally, we ran ads in the *Gazette della Sport* announcing the rally and a drawing for prizes that would be given away at the rally," states Hiugo President James Carter. "But to be eligible for the prizes, people had to send Inter a text message via their mobile phone using SMS (short message service).

The only requirement for the message was verification that the sender planned to attend the rally and their mobile phone number, which in Europe is the equivalent of sending someone your e-mail address. The people who won prizes could give the organization more personal data for future communication from Inter, but this data wasn't mandatory. "Inter gave us a free hand to set up and execute the campaign," states Carter. "Their main directives were to target the wireless campaign to a local audience and to keep costs low. We used our technology to set up the SMS interaction. The campaign was a success given that the interest generated was much greater than expected, which was due in large part to the requirement for the message being so vague. We didn't limit their responses so Inter fans expressed themselves beyond what they were asked. The feedback we got can be posted on the Inter website, and we expect to see more even though the rally has past."

The ad ran on a Monday and Tuesday, and generated 1,500 messages. Hiugo generated replies to all of these people with more details on the rally and encouraging recipients to spread the word, though the company doesn't know how many of these were forwarded to others. There was also a pop-up banner on Inter's website and e-mail was sent from two Inter sites to an existing mailing list. Because the measurement for success was rather limited, there was no tracking system put into place to learn how many people who sent messages bought the shirt.

What's the Final Score?

Although both sports teams had different messages—"Buy tickets" versus "Show us you care"—their wireless tactics conveyed the same language of urgency. They used specific events and delivered messages within days of those events to motivate people to take immediate action. They also combined wireless with other media to get maximum impact from their efforts. The Canes used wireless messages to move people to conventional communication—the phone calls—while Inter used conventional newspaper ads and the Web to get fans to send wireless messages.

These stories make another important point. I mentioned in Chapter 2 that you can't use the same tactics in the United States that you can in Europe or Asia because of the differences in wireless technologies, cultural factors, and so forth. But what I probably should say is that organizations in different countries are pursuing similar tactics, such as the Canes and Inter, but how they are executing these tactics is different.

In North Carolina, people will read a short text message on their cell phones, but they're going to place the ticket order through a voice phone call. In Europe, people will receive AND send text messages with a phone as often as they use the voice capabilities. In the United States, some companies seem fixated with trying to implement wireless communication tactics on cell phones the same way companies do in Europe and Asia. In the United States, you can learn from what the Europeans are doing with text messaging and determine how to imitate this with the devices that Americans are most comfortable using.

There are some other lessons to be learned. States Hiugo's Carter, "Our company is beginning to develop the wireless metrics for measuring efficiency and ROI, and learning how to reward customer loyalty. We have been able to give clients a tool for targeting one audience on one day within relatively small geographic areas, within a context that makes them receptive to messages that organizations want to deliver. And our campaign are totally opt in."

Create a Mystery or Contest to Generate Quick Responses

There are many ways to combine conventional communication with your wireless tactics. How about using radio ads to direct people to where they can get wireless content for more details? But to get people to act quickly, add a little pizzazz to your campaign. Have your ads or other traditional communication materials and your wireless content contain elements of a puzzle that people solve to win prizes.

For instance, your ads or brochures can have clues to a mystery (murder, theft, name of a new product that hasn't been announced yet, whatever catches your audience's attention). Scatter answers to the mystery throughout your wireless messages. Your traditional marketing materials will have more impact because readers have to constantly reference them to decipher the clues. Your wireless content gets thoroughly examined because users are busy searching for answers. Neat, huh?

Denise Villa, my friend and colleague who works with me in Italy, has kept me up to date on Telecom Italia Mobile's (TIM) TV ad campaign that used a similar tactic in a recent set of ads that generated a lot of immediate wireless responses. In the spots, three women from Venice sail off together in a boat, but end up getting lost. It is presumed that they are stranded on one of the many islands off the Italian coast.

Two men and a woman are hired from an important magazine to find the missing women and are promised a journalist position at the magazine if they succeed. Each person heads off in a different direction, east, west, and south. People watching the ads were offered a chance to win prizes if they sent an SMS message (only one per person) forecasting the right direction the three women took when they got lost. Everyone who selected the right direction then had to guess between three different island's names. Those who guessed right again were eligible for a drawing to win a trip and other prizes.

In this promotion, TIM generated a lot of attention for itself by using conventional media to deliver a series of ads that create a mystery story line that captivated people's attention. Then they added the wireless aspect to get both customers and noncustomers directly involved with the story, which people responded to quickly. By making the contest two parts, TIM generates back-and-forth communication that the company can expand into an ongoing relationship. How many variations can you add to this campaign?

Never Underestimate the Value of the Weird and the Wacky

It's healthy to resort to the wild and wacky when you want to get a good and swift response from people. So it was with great sadness that I read the other day about the demise of the U.K. coffeepot. In a Cambridge University computer lab known as the Trojan Room (fight on!), someone set up a Polaroid camera in the room with the coffeepot. They engineered a system to take frequent pictures of the coffeepot, then automatically digitize and scan the photos onto the lab's Internet site. People at their desks were able to go to the Net site and see if there was coffee in the pot before they walked over to the room.

Not exactly my cup of tea, but once word got out around the Net about this site, 2.3 million online visitors since 1993 stopped by for a look-see. (Yes, that's really 2.3 million—Ya gotta love it, mate!) I'm not sure what in the wireless world will be so ridiculous, yet so popular, but I think some of you have an obligation to push the envelope to the far reaches of imagination—or simplicity—and see what flows out.

(Author's note: The Trojan Room Coffee machine was finally switched off at 09:54 UTC on Wednesday, 22 August 2001, when the lab officially moved into its new facilities in the William Gates Building in West Cambridge. Cheers.)

The tactics in this chapter are just the tip of the iceberg of possible tactics you can use to get customers, prospects, employees, and business partners to take action. You need to reach out to customers and others on a regular basis to get an idea what will work. They will be some of your best marketing partners if you regularly communicate with them.

Remember Kirsten Maynard's observation at the Metreon, as visitors downloaded information from the WideRay Jacks? Some visitors responded, "Wow, finally something useful you can do with a PDA." It's not that people feel keeping tabs on appointments and contacts isn't important, but for all the articles about the great potential of wireless, there isn't a whole lot that's exciting for average consumers. Actively solicit feedback from vocal people such as these. They will tell you what they like because they want more of the same.

Another recommendation is to keep your wireless activities fun and interesting. No matter how staid an organization may be, there should still be a little fun and excitement associated with their content. This is what keeps people talking about your areas to other surfers, and encouraging them to visit your area. A person is more apt to part with information or his or her money while he or she is having a good time.

Food for Thought

Well, now that you have some ideas that should keep your subconscious busy for a while creating direct response tactics, here are some questions to consider before moving on to educating your various audiences:

1. What are the specific actions that you want recipients of your communication to take immediately (i.e., access a document, complete a form, call before midnight tonight)?

2. Do you spend time talking to people such as customers, colleagues, friends, and family to find out what types of offers might motivate them to respond in the way that you would like?

3. What incentives are you willing to offer for taking quick action that are also valuable to the potential recipients?

4. Are you doing something fun to motivate people to respond?

5. What conventional promotions are effective at getting people to take quick actions? Can you duplicate these promotions through wireless tactics, or at least make wireless one more response vehicle for those promotions?

6. Are there external events that can be used as deadlines to motivate quick action, such as Mother's Day, Christmas, the Super Bowl, etc.?

7. What other organizations can you get involved in a direct response campaign? (Maybe they can provide products or services that you, in turn, can use as a special offer.)

8. Are you building e-mail lists from your website that you can use for wireless direct response activities?

CHAPTER 9

Educating Your Markets and Various Business Audiences

I feel that wireless is a great tool for educating the many audiences that need or want to know more about an organization, its products, and services. For one thing, you can give people wireless access to a mountain of data on your website or intranet that includes text, charts, diagrams, and eventually audio and video files. You can proactively distribute any portion of this material to millions of people for less than the price of mailing a postcard to each person.

Another value of wireless is its anywhere, anytime flexibility. You have numerous possibilities for delivering dynamic market education, individual self-paced learning and professional development, and corporate training to people sitting around in airports and waiting rooms.

This chapter will explore these wireless possibilities, looking at education in two broad categories: 1) educating external audiences, and 2) educating the audiences internal to your organization. Chapter 11 will discuss wireless tactics for gathering information from outside sources through research that educates the people within your organization.

What Does Education Mean in a Wireless World?

Education includes not just classes and training, but also activities that give customers, prospects, and others with whom you do business an in-depth understanding of your organization, product, and services. Information as brief as a two-sentence new product announcement can be part of the education process, but I will focus mostly on using wireless technology in more extensive education efforts.

Wireless technology can be used:

- To extend the reach and value of web content, a way for people to access web data when they're away from their desktops

- As a conduit to move instructors' materials on network servers directly to recipients' laptops or mobile devices
- As a communication channel for keeping internal and external audiences educated on the latest company news

All four strategic dimensions can benefit from the education tactics. Customers often want to learn more about organizations' current and future products or services. Customer support staff must provide product education through training, either in person or through print, audio, and video materials, and some nonprofits' service staffs are called upon frequently to educate people about historic facts or community issues.

I believe that the more you educate prospects about your organization and product, particularly complex products, the greater chance you have of converting a prospect into a customer. As you analyzed your organization's sales cycles using the exercise in Chapter 5, you may have found that a fair amount of the cost of each sale comes from all the calls and meetings to educate prospects in one way or another. Therefore, you want to find ways to do this wirelessly to reduce costs and speed up the sales cycle.

Internal communication applications can address the many situations in which you need to educate employees or business partners about the company and upcoming products, or train employees how to use different pieces of equipment or business systems. If you want to get more value from employees and executives, you have to foster their professional development while controlling the costs for that education.

Educating your audiences is a communication tactic for commercial, governmental, and nonprofit entities. The tactical opportunities are fairly evident for businesses of all sizes. Federal, state, and local government groups have one main mission and that is to provide a service. Often this is done through proactively delivering, or providing access to, information that educates a broad array of audiences.

To hear some people in nonprofits describe their business, for at least one person life is a continuous process of educating audiences about what the organization is, why it exists, and what it has done for somebody lately. Having done some fundraising for a nonprofit myself in my youth (no, I don't mean Boy Scout candy sales), I can testify to the reality of that job description.

Wireless Lessons from the Hallowed Halls of Academia

There are organizations whose entire business is education, and wireless can play a key role for these companies to improve the value they deliver to their customers, the students. Saul Kato, president of WideRay, believes that, "Academic environments are where wireless applications can have a significant impact because people constantly are moving around a campus, but they need access to information from wherever they are. A high school we know uses wireless to deliver school-wide information, and also allow students to develop wireless content.

"The progression of wireless applications will start with teacher-to-student communication in which students will use mobile devices for in-class note taking and following presentations. Next will be communication from administrators to the various people who visit the campus—prospective students, parents, etc. Then you will see student-to-student and faculty-to-faculty communication increase rapidly."

One word of caution here, though, comes from Dr. Todd Lowe, a professor of engineering at the University of California at Santa Cruz. "Mobile devices potentially can benefit students and faculty, particularly laptops with wireless modems, but the handhelds that are available today have limitations. Note-taking, for example, is very cumbersome. You can't just give everyone PDAs and expect immediate benefits. You have to review your curriculum very carefully to determine where and how this technology makes sense."

Let's look at how two leading universities are tackling the question of wireless technology in academic settings.

Big Game Week—Two College Rivals Tackle a Common Challenge

In my college days at UC Berkeley, I spent many a Saturday afternoon on the football field. Um, no, I wasn't a running back. I was one of those Cal Marching Band folks. Regardless of how good or bad the football seasons were, we all lived for one thing—Big Game Week when Cal played our arch rival Stanford University.

The Cal-Stanford rivalry has gone on for over a century, and to hear some students and alumni talk, you would think that any endeavor the two colleges pursue will be a clash for dominance and bragging rights. But the two guys heading major wireless projects at the respective schools say, "Not really. We're more than happy to collaborate on ideas that help each other benefit every way we can from this technology."

So let's take a look at what these schools are doing. The Stanford story represents many of the department-specific efforts taking place at colleges nationwide to enhance classroom learning. Cal's story covers the broader scope of implementing technology to make an entire campus wireless-enabled so students can have access to campus network servers and the Net from wherever they may be, an endeavor also being pursued by schools nationwide. As you read both stories, look for ways to translate each school's activities into tactics you can use within your organization.

I'll let Stanford take the field first.

Down on the Farm—Stanford School of Medicine

In 2000 the Stanford School of Medicine (www.med.stanford.edu) received money to buy the preclinical medical students Palm 5x PDAs. Several wireless application vendors donated software and services so they could get valuable feedback from the field regarding how their products worked.

Todd Grappone, director of computing and network services for Lane Medical Library, heads up the wireless effort. "The first content we rolled out was histology (microanatomy) class materials and class schedules. Because the first year of medical students' lives is heavily scheduled with classes and information intensive, we wanted to give them the ability for anytime-anywhere studying, and have greater control of their schedule."

The school already has an online curriculum website, so they added an AvantGo server and created a channel for each class. Students can get pop quizzes created by teaching assistants, flash card files, and lecture-specific content for studying.

Microbiology students, for example, will get a study list of 40 different microbes, their environmental conditions, and details on how to treat diseases that they cause. Grappone's staff developed a game to teach microbiology (i.e., infectious viruses and other microscopic organisms). Students play the game, then get a score at the end with feedback that tells them what answers they got wrong. There are also multiple choice questions that reinforce learning.

The school found that 30 percent of students liked reviewing this information on their PDAs. Students don't study lecture notes or syllabuses on PDAs, but these files are passed around by students and then transferred to PCs at their dorm rooms. "When you can share notes this way it makes them much more useful because many people's handwriting is so bad," says Grappone.

Grappone has a laundry list of benefits from the wireless implementation. Many are intangible, but important nevertheless. "We think that PDAs will soon be just as important to doctors as a stethoscope, so getting students used to this now will make them better in the future. We decrease mistakes by having safety checks built into tasks such as writing prescriptions, which not only benefits patients health, but also reinforces lessons about correct dosages and correct or adverse drug combinations. We also wirelessly deliver up-to-date relevant hospital data for physicians while they are on duty that makes them more effective since they don't have to wait until they can get to a PC.

"We can provide more billable hours by having better logs of what happened. Right at the time you do a certain procedure or have a conversation with a patient, you will record exactly what you talked about. You can put a patient's entire treatment routine on a PDA and be sure that all the right tests are run and billed for appropriately."

Roll On, You Golden Bears of UC!

Up the road from Stanford in a radical town named Berkeley, some discussions of revolution focus on the rapid changes in technology, and how these revolutions will improve UC Berkeley's mission of education, research, and public service. Cliff Frost, director of communications and network services, has the challenge of converting the wireless revolution into practical applications.

Frost sometimes wonders if he won't have the slightly enviable problem of implementing a technology so popular that his resources won't be able to keep up. His team is currently running a pilot program that is the forerunner to giving the entire campus of 31,000 students and 20,000 faculty and staff wireless access.

"The thing that drove us to start this pilot was a research project the computer science department is doing," states Frost. "They have set up wireless LANs in two buildings that house Electrical Engineering and Computer Science classes and offices. Everyone found it very useful because students with laptops can access materials on the school's networks as well as from the Web, while faculty and staff can bring their laptops to meetings in different locations and not have to bother with connecting to the network."

One of the campus departments is measuring the value of wireless to students so they can determine if students learn more because of it, and if the technology is cost effective. For example, Cal has a web-based program in which classes are videotaped and digitized for future online access. Implementing a wireless access project is a lot less expensive than creating and digitizing videotapes for each class, and wireless access to class material may achieve the same or more benefits.

Some departments find that it's better to have wired network access within classrooms in their buildings because so many students congregate at one time (50 to 100) that wireless transmission from all of the laptop modems would interfere with each other. The School of Optometry, on the other hand, is interested in wireless communication within its complex of buildings because students are dispersed throughout the facility and don't work in such large clusters.

Frost continues, "We also don't see wireless replacing wired connections because faculty will still use wired network access in their classes and residence halls where they have Ethernet, modem or DSL access. However, at any given time students in these locations represent only one fifth of the total student population. We expect the wireless network to be popular with all of the students."

Like Stanford, Cal received technology donations for this project, though not from a wireless vendor, but from a corporation that is considering deploying wireless technology and is looking to the Cal project for valuable feedback. For any organization that is considering adding wireless LANs to their internal operations, there are many important lessons to learn from this pilot.

Frost reports that there are serious logistical issues. "Because of the scale of everything we do, we have to worry about maintaining the network. Whenever the access points [relay stations that transmit to wireless modems] need an upgrade, someone has to go to every unit because not all upgrades can happen wirelessly. This is very labor intensive and not a task you have to worry about with wired networks.

"The access points have to be physically linked to a wired cable at some point, so you have to figure out where to put them. You have to worry about building construction, power sources, and health and safety issues, plus you have to make sure your access points are not stolen. If this technology is campus wide, what happens if someone uses equipment that interferes with RF transmission? Phones and microwaves can interfere and slow network performance."

Unauthorized access to the network can become an issue since 802.11b wireless LANs don't provide access control. Cal's network is not built for the general public, but anyone can come onto campus with a wireless LAN card and be on the network. The school's servers are protected and systems manage user name and password distribution, but the wireless access makes it that much easier to people to get into a situation where they can anonymously attack the network.

Privacy issues can also be a problem since anyone can "listen in" on someone else. There is standard encryption in place, but you have to assume that things are visible, so users need to be sure that they use a secured socket connection. This isn't hard to do but people have to be cautious in order not to expose credit cards and other personal data. Because people don't perceive eavesdropping on a wired network as a big danger, they are not used to taking this safety precaution when they're using a wireless LAN.

In spite of the challenges of wireless LANs, there are still many wireless tactics for educating those within your organization.

Educating Outside Audiences—To Know You Is to Do Business with You

As a web and wireless tactic, educating audiences outside of your organization is the process by which you leave virtually no stone unturned to give people a thorough understanding of your product, organization, and industry. The driving goal is to make individuals feel great about doing business with you.

A good branding campaign can quickly catch people's attention and convince them that they should seriously consider what you have to say. However, it may take some time and repeated contacts before they absorb your information and fully understand all the benefits that you offer, or why they should do business with you. Maintaining your information online and delivering it wirelessly is less expensive than paying someone to be on the phone constantly with the same people.

Educating these audiences may help you successfully reach several strategic objectives. Give customers a better understanding how a new service that you're offering can improve the value of a product they already have, and you may convince them to remain your customer longer, or inspire them to refer new customers to you.

Give the vice president of a company a detailed picture of how other members of your professional association have been able to improve their business operations, and this will help the vice president convince her executive team to join your organization as well.

This tactical approach can help companies with complex products, such as technology companies, and also real estate agents, photo processing services, ballet companies, government agencies, and others with easy-to-comprehend offerings. Even for simple products, you may need to educate people about the many ways that it can be used, your organization's operating procedures, or even industry trends that impact people who use your products or services.

To determine if market education is a tactical avenue you should follow, begin by asking a few basic questions. Will market education help close more sales at a faster rate if prospects have an in-depth understanding of our products or services, or how they come to market? Will education about senior executives' industry expertise help us to better differentiate our services so we gain a competitive advantage?

Are there opportunities to improve fundraising if we take the lead in educating the market about new developments in tax laws that affect contributions to nonprofits? Can market education boost our agency's credibility so the state or federal legislature will appropriate more money for us in next year's budget? If the answer to some of these questions is yes, than market education is a tactical option you should explore.

Some Basic Tactics to Educate External Audiences

If your product fits into the new or advanced technology category, or if it has complex features, do not underestimate the value of market education in moving people closer to the sale. Before someone plunks down hard-earned cash for new technology, even if it's just a $19.95 pager, he or she wants to have a good understanding of what it does. The person who has to buy several hundred of these pagers for her organization will want to know even more about the product. No one wants to be the sacrificial goat if it turns out he bought the wrong product.

Complex, by the way, does not necessarily mean difficult to use. A car is fairly simple to drive—you put in the key, turn it, press the gas pedal, and you're off. But the machinery that lies under the hoods of recent model cars almost requires rocket scientists to understand. I'm sure there are many car salespeople who spend hours answering the "why's," "what's," and "how's" regarding cars' underlying complexities.

Given the limits of mobile devices, you don't want to try to deliver thirty pages of web content to describe the complexities of your product. You want to become the master of the 30-second (90-word) message that sums up that complexity. So what you do is condense those 30 pages down to 20 pages that are delivered in small chunks categorized according to what the mobile user needs for at any given time.

This way, if a person sitting on a bus wants to refresh his or her memory about a particular feature, he or she can. A sales rep in a meeting with the accountant and tech staff can pull pages describing features that will save the organization money and the pages that show the product is easy to install and support, then beam these to the respective people's PDAs.

A government official meeting with local politicians to sell them on a federal project can do something similar, but maybe the official needs to access Environmental Protection Agency (EPA) data for the local area and summaries of scientific studies from MIT to beam to the pols in the meeting. The more you think about the inquisitions—oops!—I mean meetings in which you've been wrung dry for details you wish you had at your fingertips, the more you should start to think of new ways to use this tactic.

The key to the success of educating audiences is to understand not only why someone needs the information, but also the context in which someone is going to access and use it. It also helps to know what technologies will be available.

If your audience will be in places where there are wireless LANs, then maybe you can guide them to access your website directly. If people in your audience are predominantly iPAQ users with 56K bps modems, then you can proactively distribute color images such as diagrams, charts, and simple graphics (but keep the file sizes small), or direct people to where they are.

In some situations, it may be impractical to deliver anything more than one or two pages of data, so you will need to deliver high-level summaries of your information, then list URLs where you have more details. These URLs can be uploaded to someone's desktop computer when they sync their PDA, or the recipient may be able to get to a computer with Internet access.

Sometimes Education's Just a Game

Product benefits, rather than features, may be the focus of a market education campaign. If your company offers people new ways to use old products, you might boost revenues or customer retention by increasing people's comfort level with these new benefits.

Most consumers have a checking account, but not everyone is comfortable paying bills each month automatically from their accounts. Here's a situation in which you can create a wireless campaign to educate customers about how much better their lives will be with automatic bill paying. The amount of information you need to deliver is relatively small, plus you can add a short feedback form that customers can complete to get an automatic assessment of how much time they will save with the new service.

In the next couple of years you may see faster and smarter technology in place that will let you deliver to general consumers a detailed description of benefits accompanied by video clips, and then have someone send an IM for a live conversation. As technology capabilities improve, you may even be able to execute an educational program similar to one my company launched for AT&T.

In 1995, we promoted AT&T's PassageWay computer-telephony integration (CTI) system online. Our challenge was to help people who had used phones and PCs for years to understand that linking the two devices offered significant new benefits. Without market education, it was going to be a difficult sell. Although comfortable with phones and PCs by themselves, prospects feared they would be overwhelmed by the "new" CTI technology.

We developed a briefing paper for PassageWay that explained CTI benefits in an easy-to-read manner that didn't intimidate people, and presented examples of how different types of companies could benefit from the technology. To make the briefing paper come alive for people we used the PassageWay Solution Game.

This funky little interactive game with wild New Age graphics puts players in the role of stockbroker at a small brokerage firm (stockbrokers were a main target market for PassageWay). In the game, players competed with a giant brokerage firm in a race to raise $100,000 for a new venture.

Each step of the way, they encountered a selection of people to call and approaches to use to get them to invest in the venture. If players made the right choices fast enough using simulated PassageWay CTI features, they won. Together, the briefing paper and interactive game helped people understand CTI and got consumers excited about buying the PassageWay product.

If you look at the iPAQs and other PDAs with multimedia capabilities, you can see there is potential today to deliver this kind of educational campaign wirelessly, though you would likely want recipients to play the game offline. Unfortunately, what's missing is the bandwidth to make transmitting a one megabyte game feasible, plus the required storage space could be a problem for people who keep other data on their PDAs.

On the other hand, if you trim down the complexity of the game and accompanying document (you can play solitaire on iPAQs, to give you a hint of what's possible), you may be able to execute a similar campaign. Or people could download the game when they sync their devices, and then get wireless updates or communicate wirelessly with you regarding your products.

A Twister Game for a Digital Age

A couple of years after the AT&T project, we got a similar assignment in which we had to likewise focus on product benefits, but for a product that was much more complex than PassageWay.

Lotus Development (now IBM) (www.lotus.com) approached us just three weeks before the Spring Comdex trade show in Chicago and said they needed a major promotional campaign for their integrated messaging product being announced at the show. Lotus needed publicity not only for their product, but also for their business partners such as Siemens and AT&T.

Integrated messaging in this product let companies integrate voice, fax, and e-mail communication so you could pick up e-mail messages as voice mail when you called your office, or get voice mail (converted to text) and faxes when you picked up e-mail. We decided to launch an Internet-based promotion at the trade show that ran for 30 days following the show. We used a *Twister* (the big movie hit at the time) theme with a Chicago focus to take advantage of the movie's popularity and Comdex's location.

We created a website scavenger hunt, secured handheld tornadoes as show giveaways, designed handout cards to publicize the site, negotiated with companies for dozens of prizes, and coordinated publicity with Lotus's business partners. The plot for the scavenger hunt was based on the premise of a tornado whipping through Chicago, blowing away the portable fax machine, cell phone, and laptop of our two main characters.

To play the game, people had to follow clues about locations in Chicago where they could find the missing items. Each clue they got right, besides qualifying them to win prizes, delivered a key benefit statement about the Lotus product. Bonus questions led people to information about the partners. Once people collected all of the answers, they completed a form and were eligible for the prizes, and their information went into a database. They also received an entertaining education that made a very complex product easy to comprehend.

Although the promotion netted nearly 500 qualified leads, today we could add a wireless component and subsequently educate more people while increasing the number of leads. In addition to giving people a printed card with the URL (which I'm sure a lot of people lost or threw away), we could set up a WideRay Jack in the show booth and beam the whole game to people's PDAs.

People could then play the game on their PDAs while waiting in those endless lines for food or cabs while it's fresh in their minds, and they could pass it on to colleagues they meet elsewhere on the trade show floor. The game would likely stay on a lot of PDAs until attendees left the show, and since this was a 30-day promotion, prospects could beam the game on to others on the plane or back at the office.

Education is more than features and benefits. Sometimes it's not the product that you should educate the market about, but the process by which you deliver it to customers. Do you sell products or services with few features and benefits that distinguish them from competitors, or are you in a business where speed and efficiency of service is your competitive advantage? Consider showing people the design and production process you use to develop your products, or the unique way you provide service if these processes result in greater benefits for the customer.

Burger King is one company that effectively executed this type of educational tactic in the 70s. A hamburger is not a complex product, nor is one raw burger much different than another. But Burger King generated lots of sales with ads that showed how the process of flame broiling a burger, only after a customer ordered it, made their burgers better than the ones competitors fried and left to fossilize in a warming bin. "Hold the pickles, hold the lettuce, special orders . . . [Can you finish the jingle?]"

If you offer a service that prepares crucial documents for trial lawyers, you can win sales by educating them about how your research process is more thorough than your competitors' and why that matters. If you operate a non-profit group that provides services to the homeless, but you have a method that serves more people with higher quality, then your goal might be to educate government funding sources about how your methods make you a great candidate for funding.

In both cases, this tactic builds prospects' comfort levels about doing business with you because your internal processes set you apart from others. Since lawyers and government bureaucrats practically live in meetings, wireless delivery makes sense for those audiences, and once you get this information into people's PDAs they can beam it on to others during these meetings.

Educate Audiences About Your Organization

Another strong card to play is educating people about your organization, particularly if it's new. In many industries, prospects feel comfortable dealing with organizations after they learn more about the management team. Perhaps knowing the financial strength of your organization or its financial supporters may encourage more people to do business with you. This information indicates that you have the financial resources to stay in business for the long term.

There are many aspects of your company you can use as the focus of this tactic. How about the diversity of your employees, or your commitment to hire the best and the brightest scientists for your R&D department to ensure that customers will always have access to the best products?

You can also consider keeping people informed about partnerships with well-known companies or your key customers. Hans Gomez, a former IT manager with ImageX.com, says "My perception is that this type of information helps customers feel like they are making the right choice since other industry leaders are also using the same product."

For wireless purposes, you might want to take your web content and morph it into a newsletter or news service format. However, the newsletter format is only helpful if you push out really meaningful information. I've seen more than a few newsletters that are filled with mainly self-congratulatory pieces.

A one-page story on Joe Blow's promotion to senior vice president that is 90 percent biography details barely gets a yawn from readers. A better story is one about Jane Brock's rise to vice president of operations that includes her vision for taking the organization in a new direction that has significant implications for customers.

Too many companies put out content that is great chest-thumping prose about an organization, but offers little of value to customers' or prospects' main interests. Pushing that kind of fluff out to busy people's mobile devices will be mostly an exercise in futility.

Perhaps the best way to think about wireless as a tool to educate your audiences is to position yourself as a news service, albeit one that is not totally objective, but you can work around that. Find someone in your organization (or hire someone), who can report on your company with as much objectivity as possible, and who will also spend time with customers to understand what information they want to know.

Once you meet these parameters, set up a six- to twelve-month plan of "news coverage" that is tied into known future events such as new product launches or fundraising drives and has the flexibility to report on news as it happens. Give the person responsible for developing wireless content a budget, access to resources that can facilitate the content delivery, and a certain amount of autonomy to create a loyal following.

Integrate this activity with your web content development so that your wireless efforts not only have stand-alone power, but can also move people to your website where you can present more details. You also want to build feedback capability such as surveys into your wireless content.

In the Jane Brock example, this feature would allow you to gather immediate and valuable feedback about the direction in which she wants to take the organization. The feedback itself can be turned into news that expands your education efforts. While details on your organization's future will be of interest to different audiences, knowing that current and potential customers are wholeheartedly supporting you makes the education effort much more successful.

Helping Others to Educate Themselves

There are significant potential financial benefits in helping people improve themselves through self-administered education. Consider the millions of dollars people spend each year going to seminars and buying books to become better sales professionals, truck drivers, moms, or just better human beings. By being the source, or "host," of personal and professional self-help content and applications, you provide a valuable educational opportunity for recipients, and give yourself opportunities to generate additional business.

Point-of-Sweat Education

FitSync (www.fitsync.com) markets an application to gyms and fitness centers to help people pursue the mother of all personal development endeavors, fitness training. It not only provides valuable knowledge about how to make one's body healthier, but it also gives people the tools to apply this knowledge. The beauty of FitSync's product is that it gives gyms (such as Sports Club/LA in Los Angeles) several ways to increase their revenues, it makes the gyms' training staffs more effective, and it increases customer loyalty by enabling people to improve their fitness training on their own.

FitSync's application consists of a database of general fitness data and software that lets members enter personal details about their weight, age, fitness goals, etc.; receive a workout regimen; and then track their progress as they're working out. This technology, which sits on FitSync's web servers, also includes software from Aether Systems and other components that enable the gyms to set up infrared stations. Members and trainers with PDAs can access the application through a wireless network, the stations, or when they sync the devices to their PCs.

Once members download software and enter their personal information in their PDA or a loaner unit supplied by the gym, they do their regular workout routine. As they complete each exercise, members enter data into their PDAs that access FitSync's web database to update member information either in the gym or later at home or in the office. (See Figures 9-1 and 9-2.) Members can manage their workout programs and chart their progress from anywhere.

FitSync president Paul Wittrock describes the various ways that his technology helps the gyms. "Nondues revenues such as those that come from personal training is are big money makers as membership fees drop. We help by replacing paper systems that the trainers use, making them more efficient and members get better service. Gyms subsequently can sell more training services and more effectively manage their trainers. FitSync increases member retention by enabling the gyms to implement loyalty programs such as points earned for using the gym, and keeps in touch with members by delivering information when members sync their PDAs. Members are already buying items such as vitamin supplements and workout gear elsewhere, so our systems lets them buy from the website and gyms share this passive revenue."

The hardware investment for gyms and fitness centers is modest, between

Figure 9-1. FitSync's wireless application lets members of fitness clubs enter workout data easily on their PDAs.

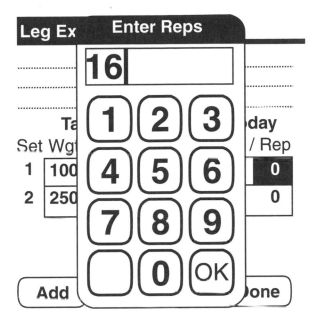

$500 and $5,000 depending on the size of the gyms, and installation is relatively simple. Once you have a wireless pipe like this to your customers that provides strong personal development value, you build a strong loyalty and frequent communication that opens the door to deliver other services.

"A system like this allows you to send out global messages with less hassle than sending e-mail, and more targeted because you know the context in which they're receiving the information," Wittrock explains. "'Running low on Power Bars? Reorder now!' It's easy for the member because the gym already has their credit info already on file, so they can order without worrying about personal data being stolen."

You don't necessarily have to provide as extensive a system to your customers for this training tactic to be effective, though you might consider something like FitSync as a benefit to help keep your employees healthy and loyal. You can provide a similar wireless application that enables your audiences to improve their language, parenting, management, cooking, scouting, or other skills.

The trick to finding the winning self-help, skill-building tactic is to determine what motivates your target audience. To maximize your benefits, make the program complement your product. If you sell office supplies to office

Figure 9-2. The FitSync application allows fitness club members track the progress of their workouts.

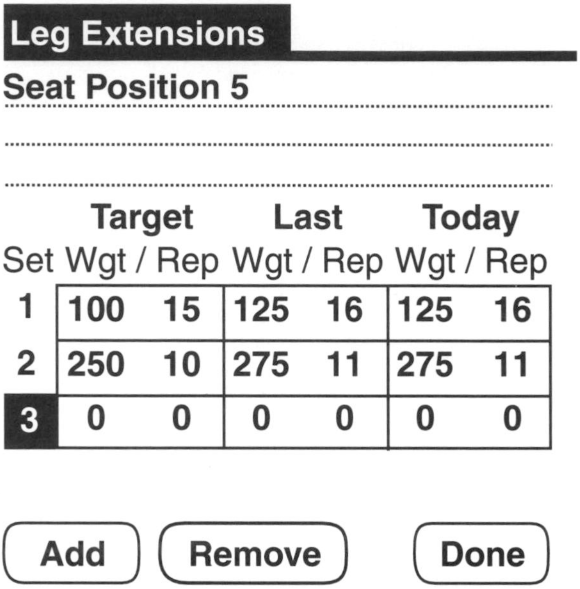

Leg Extensions
Seat Position 5

Set	Target Wgt / Rep		Last Wgt / Rep		Today Wgt / Rep	
1	100	15	125	16	125	16
2	250	10	275	11	275	11
3	0	0	0	0	0	0

(Add)   (Remove)   (Done)

managers of small companies, provide a training application that improves their stress management skills.

If you're in a local orchestra, provide a service that helps patrons improve their knowledge of contemporary composers. A state unemployment agency could provide a service that helps people improve their job interviewing skills. These services do not have to be complex. They can be as simple as sending out five facts a week with a short quiz to test how much the recipient learned, with links to more background material.

One-Hit Wonders, a Variation on the Self-Help Tactic

A variation on this tactic of helping people help themselves can be a one-time or short-term education effort that teaches people how to address an immediate issue, or gives them access to online content and tools that can solve a problem. Unlike regular service or support that helps people fix your product, this effort is for a problem or issue that is not directly related to anything that you sell. The people receiving the information may not even be customers. An example that illustrates this happened to me recently.

Sharka Stuyt is a business coach I know whose computer was infected by one of those viruses that, unknown to you, takes control of your e-mail and sends out a message with an attached virus to everyone in your e-mail address book. Within a day of discovering what happened, she sent all of us an apology (though it wasn't her fault) and a two-page document that detailed procedures to get rid of the virus and how to undo some of the damage that the virus might have done. There were also links to different software tools to help with these tasks.

The benefit of this tactic from the recipients' viewpoint is that most of us on her mailing list are not technical people and so we probably don't know a lot about fighting viruses. And while we could go to an antivirus company's website to get similar information, her e-mail was proactively delivered and faster to absorb than going to a site and surfing around for the information. The value of the tactic to Sharka is that her effort created a lot of good will, even for those of us who hadn't been infected because it showed a willingness to help solve a business problem. I wouldn't call her company if my computer crashed, but if I need a good business coach who I feel will go out of their way to help me, Sharka will get the call.

You can't plan per se for those random situations in which this tactic may be used, so the best you can do is make your marketing people aware that this is a valuable tactic and have them monitor news events. They also should have e-mail addresses and wireless contact information you have received from customers and prospects set up in a database so you can immediately contact them if the need arises. Insight, tact, and good judgment will have to guide you in deciding on when to pull the trigger on this tactic.

Since this is an unsolicited message you would be sending, make it informative without being too wordy, and give recipients directions that are easy to follow and will produce positive results with a minimum chance of them causing more harm than good. In case of the virus for example, you can send out information that educates people how to take the right safety precautions, and give them five specific steps to remove a specific virus. But in those instructions you don't want to tell people to do extensive repair work on their operating system where one mistake can critically disable the entire computer.

One last word of caution: When you execute one of these one-time hits, do not include promotional information about your company (just add a contact phone number). Do not send it to people other than those who are customers or have for some other reason been in contact with your company. People receive "helpful" spam e-mail daily from companies they've never heard of and these go unopened straight into the digital dumpster.

Educating Business Partners

This tactical option gives you an opportunity to improve the level of expertise among business partners that handle some or all of your retail sales, customer service, support, or other business operations. Whether your business is computers, engineering, medicine, finance, or other fields that require a high level of education or skill by sales people, the technologies and techniques in these industries advance so fast that even the experts can barely keep up.

Enlisting sufficiently competent third-party sales and support organizations is a monumental and somewhat costly challenge. First, you have to recruit them. Rep firms with people knowledgeable enough to understand your product and markets are increasingly hard to find.

Next, you have to train them about your particular business, which is time consuming and expensive. Once you get them up to speed, you have to worry about competitors stealing their people. There are also the logistical problems of training retailers scattered across the map. You have to deal with the fact that retail operations are responsible for many products besides yours, and their sales and customer service people often don't have time to learn the intricacies of your products.

Wireless education tactics can counter these shortcomings by delivering technical information and other content that can educate retail and other third-party personnel faster, less expensively, and more efficiently than conventional training. Consider deploying WideRay Jacks or helping these companies set up wireless LANs that the sales staff can access when they have some time between serving customers.

The core information you send to business partners can be the same as you would send directly to customers and prospects, but you will need to modify it for your partners. Retailers, for example, can use tips to overcome sales objections associated specifically with your products. The ultimate objective should be to enable third-party organizations to present as strong a case for your products and services as your internal staff. Getting to this level could take some time and a lot of effort, but an organization's grasp should exceed its reach.

Another group you want to educate are the people who influence your industry. They can be analysts, directors of associations that represent the people or organizations in your market, industry speakers, or top executives of the leading companies in your target market. These types of individuals are typically in meetings and on the road a lot, so wireless is a good way to communicate with them.

You can deliver the same content you deliver to other audiences, or if you have a way to isolate your contact with them (i.e., a database or special mailing list), you can create special briefing papers just for them that accompany your own materials. As technology such as wireless instant messaging improves, there are possibilities for short real-time briefings while these people are waiting for their next flight or are between meetings.

One of the most powerful ways to educate an audience about your product or service is to give them a hands-on demonstration. Impossible with wireless, you say? Maybe not. The next chapter gives you some ideas how this tactic might work for you.

Internal Education Tactics

Education of the troops is an ongoing process that happens at many levels. When a person begins employment, they have to learn about the organization's policies, procedures, key people in the organizational chart, employee benefits, and so on. Then they have to learn procedures and other information specific to their respective departments. This may include learning how to use office equipment, plant machinery, etc.

Once employees complete their "entry-level" learning, they require ongoing education to keep abreast of new developments within their industry, market, and profession, as well as new projects and activities within their organizations. Also a part of continuing education is the type of learning that comes from tapping into the collective experience of others within the department or organization.

There is often general information that people only access occasionally, such as policies and procedures manuals, directions for completing travel and medical expense reimbursement forms, or lists of the retailers carrying your products. Since mobile workers don't need to get to these materials all the time, it may be all right to just provide simple access to an intranet with the materials via their wireless devices.

For information and skills that are critical for employees to do their jobs, such as customer support procedures, or product assembly processes, spend time with your mobile workers to carefully plan both what content to make accessible and how to deliver it. If you provide extensive conventional training of mobile workers or interfacility roamers before they are sent into the field, then your wireless content might include refresher materials that serve to reinforce what workers learn. But, if you hire people one day and put them on the road or into plant vehicles the next day, you might want to consider creating a full-featured training program that you can deliver wirelessly.

Of course, you may have decided when you were evaluating the fourth strategic dimension that you want to use wireless to reduce the cost of training. In that case, you should do a review of all of your training programs to determine the particular tactics you will use.

David Koehn, AvantGo's director of educational services, helps customers develop extensive wireless-enabled training courses. He also managed the development of a course that AvantGo staff use to train third-party developers who write applications using the company's technology. (It's always reassuring to know that vendors use their own technology.)

Koehn made several good recommendations that can contribute to the success of your efforts, whether you plan to create traditional training courses, or you are developing content to facilitate the distribution of policies, procedures, and general information.

Effective Design and Deployment Mean a Lot

Here are some of Koehn's recommendations:

■ *Mobile learning is a blend of a product (a knowledge application) and a service (knowledge transfer).* Because of this blend, m-learning needs conception, graphic and/or layout design, application development, and deployment planning. Whenever possible, use those with mobile expertise to manage your mobile learning implementation.

■ *Use whatever you can from existing courses or materials.* Don't forget the m-learning mode is an extension of existing learning systems, whether online courses accessed on PCs or instructor-led classes, and not a separate pool of information. Use whatever you can from existing web materials such as page design, navigation, and search features, but modify these for the mobile user. The search feature is especially useful for reference materials like a Peterson Guide, though your material may not be that extensive.

■ *Make your mobile courseware cross-platform so it works on all types of devices.* Students may want courseware on their iPAQ one day and on their RIM BlackBerry the next.

■ *Give a lot of thought to the design choices that you make.* For example, decide if you are going to provide images for high-end mobile devices that you hope will work on low-end devices, or if are you going to use images that work well on low-end devices, but don' t use all of the capacity of the high-end device. Because the people receiving training may be using devices with different graphics capabilities, there will always be trade-offs on what looks good, what is needed, and what is practical. You have to find the right balance without sacrificing the main objective, which is to deliver effective training.

■ *Stick to HTML and JavaScript for creating your courseware.* This will make it easy to develop, easy to deploy, and easier all around for the people who have to use it. Your courseware should be interactive on mobile devices, even when the users aren't wirelessly connected.

■ *Publish the lessons from a dynamic syndication server rather than manually writing all of the pages.* This is a publishing tool that allows you to create training modules in a SCORM-compliant (standardized) format and publish them to the Web in an automated way that does not require hours and hours of hand-coding.

■ *As users input data into a particular course or interact with a trainer, be sure they can reconcile the data between their desktops and mobile devices using the devices' sync feature, web surfing, or having it pushed from your servers.* Students do not want the progress of training on the handheld version of their course to differ from that of their desktop course.

■ *Make certain your m-learning course creates value.* And, in turn, make certain you look to charge an employee's department for an m-learning product, even though the application is for internal use. People will take these more seriously if there is a price tag attached, even if the money is primarily a paper transaction between departments.

■ *Always be aware of the context in which people will use your courseware.* Mobile learning is a "point of activity" application, meaning people likely will be doing whatever the course material is trying to teach them while they are taking the course. If users will be outside when learning or reviewing materials on horse breeding, it may not be a good idea to use fonts and font sizes that are hard to read on PDA screens in outdoor lighting. You also want to use a lot of diagrams because users won't have a lot of time for reading when they're working with a couple of frisky equines.

■ *The situation and conditions under which people will use the courseware should also determine your hardware selection.* Brad, a friend of mine who drives heavy construction equipment, is shopping for a PDA. He's very conscious of the hardware design because the sand, dirt, and moisture in the areas where he works can ruin the internal components if the outer casing is flimsy or allows particles to slip in.

■ *Don't use fill-in-the-blank text fields.* Use select lists and drop-down answer menus (see Figures 9-3 and 9-4) or buttons (see Figure 9-5) so a pen tap or a click can make the lesson interactive. Someone who's brushing up on a couple of product features while sitting in the customer's lobby before a repair visit doesn't have a lot of time to etch long essays.

Figure 9-3. A select-list menu.

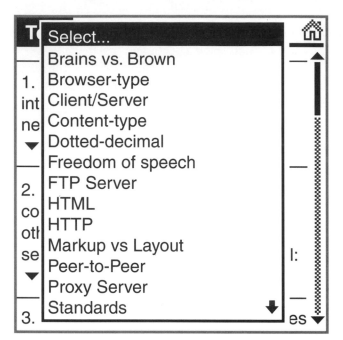

■ *Your courseware should have occasional "e-mail for help" and "phone for help" features.* This is especially valuable if people will be in locations where access to online help may not be available.

■ *Create pages that require as little up and down scrolling as possible.* Never expect students to scroll left and right.

When you finish developing your courseware, make sure that everyone who will use it gets hands-on experience guided by an instructor during the class or at some time before they go into the field. This is to ensure people use the application. If you just hand people a PDA and send them on their way, or let them download the application on their own, it's likely that people won't use the courseware.

Remember that m-learning, the same as in many other uses of mobile devices, often changes the behavior of the people using it in the organization and thus affects the behavior of the organization itself. If employees are learning on mobile devices, try to determine how this will impact instructors and managers, since the technology can increase the pace at which people learn,

Figure 9-4. An example of a screen that leads to a drop-down answer menu.

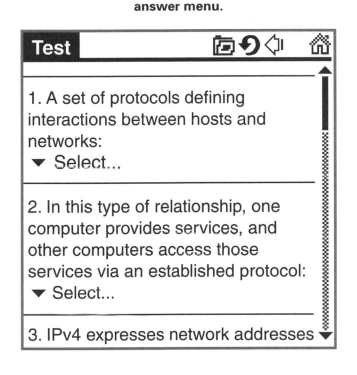

the type of questions that they ask, or even the way they perform their duties. These may all be positive changes, but to maximize the value of this new way of doing business you can't have these people caught off guard.

When Does It Make Sense to Use m-Learning?

You can use these guidelines to develop mobile courseware that teach people to do all sorts of things including teaching people how to assemble, use, maintain, and/or repair equipment, depending on the person's actual job. You may have employees hired to specifically do these things, but your mobile workers might be able to fix some things that break faster than it will take for support staff to arrive.

You may also need to train people how to use software applications, complete complex business operations that occur in the field (i.e., processing customer's loan or insurance forms), or promote key features and benefits of your products. Mobile learning can be effective if your organization markets services or products from several companies and it's hard to remember all the

Figure 9-5. Using buttons to make lessons interactive.

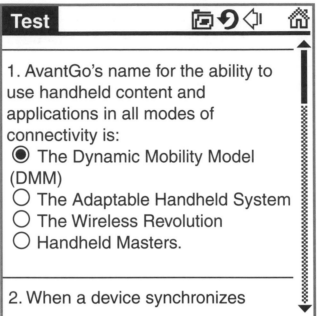

details about each one, or for your resellers and sales reps who also carry your competitors' products.

Wireless training programs also make sense for mobile workers who have to keep track of a broad range of procedures and processes, such as doctors, lawyers, and financial services professionals. It's not so much that you want these people to be learning on the job, but there are times when someone needs a quick refresher course for procedures they haven't done in a while.

Some organizations have six-figure (or more) budgets to create "knowledge bases" on servers to store details on best practices, selling tactics for large accounts, documents that are designed for certain proposals, or negotiations. Your mobile workers may not need training programs for these, but they probably can benefit by having wireless access to this intellectual capital.

As a closing thought, I recommend that you explore ways to use your training and other employee education tactics for your external audiences as well. The design and implementation expertise you learn from these applications for your employees can be applied to training for customers, possibly without a lot of modifications. Subsequently your investment will produce greater returns. And conversely, some of your tactics for educating external audiences will work for employees as well. In fact, self-help and professional development may produce more immediate financial returns among employees than customers and prospects.

Food for Thought

As you consider using wireless technology to educate your audiences, keep these questions in mind:

1. How much of your product or service sales process involves educating prospects about your company and product?

2. Do your sales staff, research department, or other departments have information already produced that you can use to create wireless educational content?

3. Do you want to password protect some of your educational material so it becomes a reward for customers, or an incentive to get people to take a specific action?

4. What topics will your target audience be interested in learning more about? (Topics need not relate directly to your products or industry.)

5. Can you create and provide wireless access to a centralized area on your website for educational information from other Net sources, preferably some of which is updated regularly to encourage repeat access?

6. Can you get credible people who may not be in your organization to provide educational materials (e.g., lectures, audio clips, articles)?

7. Do you have the internal resources to create your own educational content?

8. Do you have the technology, and internal support, to create interactive presentations in chat rooms or message boards as this technology improves?

9. Are there resellers or business partners who can benefit from your educational content, perhaps after some modifications?

10. Have you considered creating online games and puzzles as vehicles to educate people about your product or company?

CHAPTER 10

Demonstrating Your Products and Services

In its purest form, previewing (demonstrating) your product or service is one of the strongest ways to communicate the value you have to offer.

Those of you over age 35 may be familiar with the term "the puppy dog sale," which refers to that fine sales art form of giving someone a product to use for a couple of hours or a couple of days. If you want to sell a family with little kids a puppy, give them the puppy. "Just for one night," you tell them, "to see if you and the puppy like each other. If you don't like the puppy, bring it back tomorrow. No obligations." You know what happens, don't you?

By sunrise the next day, the puppy and kids have bonded for life, and unless the parents want to deal with weeping and wailing that would make Ghengis Khan misty-eyed, that dog is SOLD. Stop by and pick up the check! You see this happen every day to varying degrees with cars, furniture, CDs and other products.

The question that this chapter answers is, "Can I do that with wireless?" Of the seven tactical options in this book, product demonstration is the most challenging, and it is not practical for every organization. This chapter is specific about what types of businesses can use this option.

Also, wireless technology capabilities will have to evolve in terms of bandwidth and PDAs' computing power before some of the tactics presented here are possible. If your product or service can benefit from these tactics, it still makes sense to consider these options as these evolutions occur so you can have a general plan in place when the technology is ready for you.

Another thing to keep in mind is that many of these tactics are heavily dependent on the Web, since most of the necessary content will sit on your website. And the tactics that are interactive, such as allowing people to preview various feature options for an automobile before buying it, will be driven by web-based software or software access through your intranet. Subsequently, you need to have your web act together before you can execute effective wireless tactics, or at least provide wireless access to some of your current web product demonstration features.

Prospects and customers will be the primary target audiences for these tactics, but it is probable that variations on the same tactics can help your employees and business partners in certain aspects of their jobs. For example, an interactive video that lets prospects preview the different ways they can have a car customized can also increase the knowledge of your dealers' salespeople so they sell these customized features more effectively.

What Kind of Organizations Can Use "Try It Before You Buy It" Tactics?

The Internet enables various types of organizations to execute the digital version of the puppy dog sale, and wireless can become an extension of this tactic. Demonstrate all or many of your key product features online and you will move prospects closer to ordering that product, either using their mobile devices or through conventional options such as the telephone or retail outlets. Other organizations may be able to offer only a general preview of their products or services.

Most companies don't let prospects take items home to try out as in the true puppy dog sale. Prospects just get to spend time on test drives or in retail stores trying on new outfits, listening to CDs on in-store headphones, and otherwise getting a feel for whatever it is they are interested in buying. If you let people spend enough time in the store actually demonstrating a product or watching it work, a decent percentage of them will eventually buy it. These businesses have found that, as technology improves, it becomes easier to shift these in-store demonstration tactics online.

The obvious companies that can demonstrate their wares online are those with products that can be digitized, such as software, music CDs, printed materials, and your brain. That's right, demonstrate your brain online. If your business is selling the knowledge of you and your staff, such as consulting or legal services, or general information such as research data, industry-specific reports, and newsletters, you can demonstrate or preview these for prospects. Later in the chapter I will show you specifically how to do this.

Some of you may be wondering how a company that sells products such as office equipment, fine china, real estate, or hotel suites can demonstrate their goods online. Hey, believe me. It can be done. These companies have found that they can use a combination of audio, video, and photos to give people an online preview of their products, and these tactics potentially can be extended to mobile devices as wireless technology evolves. This applies to more than just products.

With the exception of your doctor, many service professionals let you try it before you buy it. Lawyers advertise "the first hour is free." Creative agencies bring in portfolios so you can see how their creative minds work, and some even create a mock ad or promotional campaign for your organization. Consultants offer you the first issue of their newsletters for free, and sometimes the entire subscription is free so you can experience their awesome powers of problem solving. Expect to see these professionals extend these tactics using wireless.

It's likely those hearty dot-com survivors that have viable web-based services will be among the first to give wireless prospects the ability to test their services before committing any money. In fact, dot-com companies probably have most of the back end software and infrastructure in place to make it easy for them to add wireless access capabilities. CDNow, the popular music dot-com, makes music downloads available for preview. When a sizeable number of their customers have PDAs capable of playing RealAudio files, CDNow should be able to offer a wireless download option.

A Viable Tactic for Government and Nonprofit Organizations

Government organizations do not sell products, but most provide services and some of these are candidates for this particular tactic. Public libraries are part of the local governments in their respective cities and they often have services and special programs that they promote to the general public.

The Oakland Public Library (in Oakland, California) has a business information center that specializes in providing free resources and research services for businesses and individuals. One of those services is a set of materials on international trade. A creative mind could think of a few ways to make this information searchable from wireless devices so mobile workers can experience firsthand the benefits of using the library on a regular basis.

As you wander down the hallowed halls of local, state, or federal governments you will find valuable resources that more people would use if they knew what these agencies and departments did. By their nature, mobile workers don't have much time to wander, so provide these citizens with a sampling of what information or services they can get (details on wills, birth or death certificates, probate information, and other public records, for instance), and you may convert them into "customers."

This is particularly true if you can enable people to request or retrieve the information and even the complete services with their devices rather than having to come into the agency offices. In some cases, the amount of data may be so large that it is more convenient to retrieve it when they sync their PDAs with their desktops, but if someone can at least order the materials while waiting for the train, it saves valuable time.

Nonprofits such as associations and educational institutions can give you a sample of what those fees and tuition will buy you. Associations let you come to a meeting or two, or a monthly dinner with stellar speakers, usually for a higher fee than what regular members pay. A tactic that might be described as puppy dog sale meets "carrot and stick" coercion.

During the summers at some of our finer colleges and universities you often see bored students-in-waiting tagging behind parents on a tour of the premises as everyone in the family tries to decide which school their child will attend. This usually is not a total preview of what lies ahead, but then, you don't want to scare the parents off before they write the first check.

Nonprofits can use this tactic if, similar to government agencies, they provide information or services as their main charter. Some book clubs are national in their reach and have websites. If you were shopping for a club to join, wouldn't it be nice to be able to peek in on a few while sitting in O'Hare Airport?

A couple of book reviews written by members and an excerpt from an online chat discussion delivered to my PDA could help me decide. When instant messaging (IM) technology becomes a general consumer tool on mobile devices, the book clubs could hold scheduled wireless meetings and invite potential members to meet and greet current members.

When more mobile devices get multimedia capabilities, it may make sense for museums, orchestras, theater groups, and others in the visual and performing arts to use wireless graphics, video, and audio clips to preview performances for potential patrons. This is the kind of wireless vision that the Port Discovery museum has for its PD Kids Club.

Associations can make some of their members-only services and industry research data available wirelessly to prospective members on a trial basis. The PRSA has a free service for members it calls PR Works, which is a database of case studies from successful PR campaigns. Wireless access to a 30-day trial or five searches for free could be quite effective. Many a PR professional has sweated through planning meetings trying to develop a winning campaign, so the ability to search PR Works from their PDAs to find an idea that works can sufficiently impress someone and inspire them to join.

Three Ways to Make Your Products Come Alive Online

You may have sat or stood through product demonstrations that consisted predominantly of one-way, high-pressure communication from seller to prospect. When using wireless technology the demonstration needs to be an interactive, two-way communication process whenever possible and practical. At the very least, you want people online and with mobile devices to preview things for themselves, at their own pace, and be able to communicate with you at various steps throughout the process should they choose.

There are three types of demonstrations you can implement online, depending on what products or services you market. Wireless can be an extension of this effort, given the factors I've already discussed. I have a feeling that by the time this book hits the shelves, there will be a new generation of PDAs with greater computing power that will make some of these tactics more viable.

1. *Direct Experience.* In this type of demonstration, let people hold and use your product, usually for some limited time. Computer software, visual products such as videos and digitized artwork, information services, and consulting services are some of the products with which prospects can have a direct experience.

2. *Limited Experience.* This type of demonstration lets prospects use the features of a product, but not take possession of the product. For example, a service company that provides information from a medical database may let prospects access data. But the access will be very limited and data can be viewed only on screen and not downloaded.

3. *Simulated Experience.* Companies with products that cannot be physically accessed from a mobile device can use this option to strut their stuff online. A cruise line, for instance, can use a combination of still shots, an interactive data base, video, and audio clips to let prospects see and hear what life is like on one of their deluxe vacation cruises.

Let's look at these in more detail to see how to make each of these types of demonstrations effective.

There is one type of wireless technology that will enable you to take full advantage of this tactic's potential and that is fixed broadband wireless. A company such as Wayport can set up RF networks in fixed locations (i.e., airports, hotels) to enable laptops and PDAs to surf the regular Web at DSL speeds or faster. There's also the Ricochet network, which delivers fast wireless Net access to mobile users.

I don't talk about fixed or mobile broadband much with this tactical option because you can't do much to take advantage of it other than have the right content on your website. It is also hard to fit fixed or mobile broadband into your plans to reach external audiences until there are tens of thousands of subscribers, or at least until enough people in your target audiences are subscribers. For example, if you want your online product demonstration applications for external audiences to also be used as training tools for employees, wireless LANs can deliver this access to interfacility roamers.

Direct Experience Demonstrations

How well you can use wireless technology to give prospects and customers a hands-on demonstration of your products or services depends on what it is that you offer. Here are some ideas categorized by type of product or service. You technically may not fit into some of these categories, but there are possibly ideas that you can get from them nevertheless.

Software

Software is great to demonstrate and deliver online. For one thing, people can download full-working versions of your software as easily as downloading any other file. Once they get the software, they can use it immediately. If they like it, and your online area is appropriately equipped, they can order it and download the finished product.

I've looked around on a couple of websites of software companies that sell applications specifically for PDAs, including Handango (www.handango. com). Handango offers trail versions of many programs they sell, though their file sizes generally start at two megabytes. If your software files are collectively over one meg, I think downloading them from a mobile devices is going to be a problem until a lot of people have 56K or faster modems and wireless access charges drop. There is, though, the option to download this software by synching a PDA to a PC.

In an ideal situation, the software demo will have the capability to access the device's modem, dial a website, and automatically walk users through an online ordering process. You should develop a demo that is a fully functional piece of software, but with limits on the amount of data it will store or the number of days that a person can use it before it stops working. The ability to turn the demo into a "real" product with just a phone call should also give the demo more appeal.

Another direct experience option for software companies is a pay-per-use feature, which is the business model of software ASPs. The software sits on a web server and people use their web browser to pay to use the software for one task, one time only. KnowledgePoint (www.knowledgepoint.com) sells employee performance management software called Performance Now for computer networks, individual PCs, and also on a pay-per-use basis.

With the third option, customers get to experience the software in a way that is valuable to them. KnowledgePoint receives revenue (always a good thing), and a portion of the people who use the product on a pay-per-use basis end up buying the single user or network version of the application.

Depending on how extensive the application is, it may be possible to format it for pay-per-use delivery to a wireless device. The limiting factor is the speed of individuals' wireless connections. Even though the software processing happens on the web server, the user has to stay connected while waiting for the processing to finish, then send back the results of the task. When we get to high-speed wireless networks, this should work well.

As with other tactics, you have to be in tune with the context of the application's use. If your customers are mobile or away from a wired Net connection when they do tasks such as performance evaluations, then an application like Performance Now makes sense. Until this concept catches on in a big way, the companies that can be most successful with pay-as-you-go software for wireless devices are those that sell basic personal productivity software.

Information Services

I define information services as companies that market either packaged information (i.e., research reports, newsletters, financial analysis), access to data sources such as legal or medical data bases, or the means to track data such as news reports and stock prices.

It's fairly easy to let prospects take these services on a "test drive," if you will. One option is to give prospects a free trial for a limited time. This tactic is particularly effective if you market an information tracking service (i.e., the stereotypical wireless services of news, sports, and weather).

Typically the information being tracked changes rapidly. You subsequently can give away enough to get people addicted to the service. But there's always new information that you can convince people to buy. Biomedical research data, market tracking services, and real estate listings for agents' use are examples that can be added to the three services I listed. After a one-month trial period of experiencing the benefits of receiving up-to-the-minute property listings, I think many real estate agents would find it difficult not to continue using the service.

Two possible direct experience tactics for companies that sell information through subscriptions, such as medical or insurance industry newsletters, is to give away samples of older materials or use a limited trial offer. Ragan Communications (www.ragan.com) offers seminars, newsletters, and consulting services on various PR, marketing, and Internet communication disciplines. The section of their website that promotes newsletters contains complete newsletters that are several months old. These could easily be pushed out to wireless devices or formatted to facilitate wireless access.

In all of these tactical options for information service companies, the demos should have built-in mechanisms for prompting orders. When my company tested a particular news service (it has since gone to dot-com heaven), we received daily reminders to order the full service during the last ten days of our free trial.

Consulting Services

When you first think about it, delivering a demo of a consulting service may seem far-fetched. But you can do it quite effectively with some careful planning and forethought. The biggest challenge is to provide enough service to make it valuable for the recipient, but without giving away the entire store.

An easy tactic you can use is to wirelessly distribute briefing papers or summaries of research reports you've written that educate prospects about aspects of the field in which you consult. You can also distribute articles written by senior members of the firm and published in well-known journals. These documents demonstrate your firm's competency and breadth of knowledge.

J.P. Morgan (www.jpmorgan.com), the Fortune 500 investment banking firm, used an interesting tactic in 1998 to demonstrate their consulting services online. Many firms in their industry use computers to calculate the potential risks of various investments, but only employees of the firms actually manipulate the data. Bankers advise their clients based on these calculations, but clients never learn how bankers arrive at their conclusions.

J.P. Morgan set up their own analysis system, called the Event Risk Indicator (ERI), on the firm's website so people can do their own calculations. An econometric model covering 26 markets in four separate regions, the ERI reports an "Index of Likelihood" of a currency crash ranging from zero to 100. In sample tests from 1993 to 1997, the ERI had warned of seven out of ten crashes one month before they actually occurred.

Besides giving people more control over the data they accessed (building brand loyalty), this ERI system gave people a demo of how J.P. Morgan's staff processes data and arrives at the advice they give clients. By making it easy to understand a complex financial calculation, J.P. Morgan demonstrated competence and the fact that clients would not be subjected to that "experts in the ivory tower" attitude that drives some clients crazy.

It is possible that you can develop a slimmed-down version of a financial calculator or business problem-solving application that can be pushed to mobile devices. You might be able to have someone run an application like ERI while connected, but if you can distribute something that works on its own while stored on PDAs, you get great "pass it on" value. When a recipient meets a colleague, they can beam your tool over the infrared port.

When perspective clients are reviewing your firm, they often want you to demonstrate competence in their particular industry or meeting their specific type of business need. Rather than have consultants get into lengthy discussions about what they have done and for whom, at least while prospects are still in the "just looking around" mode, these firms have relied on posting case studies on their websites. The more these stories mirror a prospect's size, industry, business needs, or geography the better. This can be effective as a wireless tactic.

Of the companies that I researched for this book, Palm, AvantGo, and Aether Systems use this tactic the best. They're not consulting firms in the strict sense of the word such as Arthur Andersen and Ernst & Young, but the professional consulting services that they sell with their technology products play a major role in customers' decisions to use these companies. Consulting firms could learn a lot from them.

All three vendors have more customer stories than I see at much bigger companies' sites. The stories are in short and long versions and they are categorized so you can find ones that demonstrate the vendors' competence in many specific industries or in meeting various business needs such as sales force automation and supply chain management. I give Palm the edge for having the best implementation of this tactic because their customer stories are easier to find and search through.

Lot21 doesn't have a lot of customer stories on its site, and they execute advertising and branding campaigns as well as provide general consulting. However, the stories in their portfolio section are laid out well for the person who wants to get the key points and move on, or spend some time learning more about a particular project. The text and graphics are laid out in a size and format that can be easily ported to a mobile device.

If your consulting firm only solicits one type of client, this is a fairly easy tactic to implement. You prep six to ten stories for easy access or push delivery, exchange some of the stories with new ones every now and again, and that's pretty much it. But if you have a diverse target audience, you need a diverse stable of stories. Create a mini home page so people can quickly find what they need.

A tried and true way to demonstrate your consulting expertise is to bring your senior staff online to interact with people live through wireless instant messaging (as more people get access to it) or by e-mail. To do this in a way that shows you're competent, but without giving away too many details, establish guidelines such as one question per organization, or limit questions to a topic that represents a small portion of what you do.

For taking the IM approach I recommend that you do this at a scheduled time, and for maybe an hour at a time. For example, send an announcement to prospects that your senior consultant is going to answer IM questions on "ABC" topic at 10:00 a.m. and 4:00 p.m. on whatever date you select.

For the e-mail option, announce that this consultant will answer e-mail questions on the topic for some specified number of days. Either respond just to the people sending e-mail or set up an AvantoGo channel to distribute answers to all the questions you receive. The latter is better because it saves time if you get the same questions from many people, plus you can use the channel to reach additional people with each answer so they have broader impact.

Limited Experience Demonstrations—Stretch Your Imagination

In the mid-1990s, Digital Equipment Corp. (now owned by Compaq) executed an incredibly creative project on the Net that really defined the indirect experience in product demonstrations.

Digital developed a new line of high-powered computers with significant speed and performance advantages over competitors. But the problem was every computer company claimed to be bigger, better, faster. How do you prove your machine works best without putting one in every prospect's office? It would be a financial and logistical impossibility, right? Maybe not.

In a beer-based brainstorming session at a Silicon Valley microbrewery, a Digital marketing executive and a couple of engineers decided using the Net to deliver their new computer (called the Alpha) to any person's desk who wanted it. Simply stated, Digital would set up an Alpha at its office, give people Net access to load software from their computers to the Alpha, and put the machine through its paces.

The Alpha project worked out better than anyone had expected. Thousands of people accessed the Alpha, including people from smaller companies that wouldn't have been able to get a loaner computer to test (and who otherwise may not have become customers). Digital attributed a sizable number of sales to this promotion as well as dramatically shortened sales cycles.

Digital also received several indirect benefits from the program. Knowing that many people were using the system simultaneously, users were more impressed with the Alpha's speed than they would have been using the computer alone at their offices. Others were so impressed that Digital took such a big risk by letting the world use their computer that they accepted the company's claims without even testing the Alpha.

This kind of tactic is primarily suited to heavy or expensive equipment that manipulates electronic data, such as medical diagnostic equipment, computers, and test equipment. These would likely have to be simple tests because uploading a lot of data from a mobile device could be a problem. However, even a simple demonstration is okay since the more interaction you can encourage that involves prospects to enter their own data into your product, the greater your chance of shortening the sales cycle.

If you have long sales cycles that include several presentations for prospects, get your contact from the prospect's organization to send you the data on a CD that you can load up on your equipment. Then, when your sales reps do their presentations at the prospect's office, the people in the room can use their PDAs to access and run your equipment.

If you market access to information databases, another limited experience tactic is to give prospects the full-working service, but give them old data to use. A few years ago Ziff-Davis used to market Computer Select, a CD-ROM-based database of technology articles from numerous publications.

The Computer Select demo was a fully working CD-ROM with five-year-old data. Prospects who received this demo got a true feel for how efficiently the CD-ROM searched for and retrieved data. They saw the depth of information the service provides, and they could perform all of the software tasks, such as printing. They could try the service for as long as they wanted without the company giving away what was most important—current information.

There are some logistical issues with demo delivery that you need to work out, such as do you let people search while connected? This is probably best since running a database application on a PDA could cause the device to have a digital aneurysm, assuming you can trim down a database application enough to run on a PDA and still hold enough valuable information. But then you will have to determine if running the demo will cause prospects to run up a big cellular bill for the time connected. As you can see, you continually have to weigh the pros and cons of each approach you consider since there will always be trade-offs between great ideas and the cost of implementation.

The Entertainment Industry Can Benefit

I include among eligible candidates for the limited experience category the entertainment industry—movie producers, theater groups, rock stars, etc. Promoters want you to experience full-working features of their "products," but they certainly don't want you to experience entire products on the Net before you buy them.

The video and audio playback capabilities of some of the newer PDAs will enable people to preview excerpts from any live performance, whether it's a local production company or international rock concert tour. Together with liberally intermingled still shots, companies can effectively demonstrate the flash and blast excitement of *Pearl Harbor*, the intensity of *Hamlet*, or the steamy excitement of the singer known once again as Prince. The one restraint is the modem speed of the PDAs trying to access this information.

One of my cousins, Christian McBride, is a widely acclaimed acoustic and electric bassist on the jazz scene and is emerging as a key musician in the pop and R&B music arenas. His website (www.christianmcbride.com) provides a good lesson that can be carried over into the wireless realm by young performers who want to preview their credentials. There's a good sprinkling of music clips, a video clip, and photos of Chris with just about everybody who's anybody in entertainment. By creating promotions with some of the Avant-Go's music channels, or creating his own channel which links to his site, Chris can have a wireless stage to demonstrate why he's the "go-to" guy when heavy hitters like Sting, Chick Corea, and Pat Matheny need a good bass man.

Of all the companies online in the early days of the Web, several movie studios seemed to do the most to push the online technology envelop to its outer limits. They recreated movie scenes with intense graphics, included every imaginable background detail on movies, offered interactive communication with movie characters, and executed a range of promotions that drew repeated visits to the site.

The music industry indicates that it plans to become aggressive in its use of the Net as a product demo vehicle after that whole episode with Napster. It will be interesting to see how they capitalize on the potential of wireless communication now that some PDAs that can double as MP3 players are hitting the market.

The Net is also a good venue for budding entertainers to demonstrate their talents. They may be small-town dance troupes, waiters, or waitresses waiting for their big acting break, or junior Spielbergs in training. As with any small business, these future stars can go online and leverage the Net as effectively as the big guys to tell (or sing) their story to the world. Wireless can definitely become a part of that effort since talent scouts will likely be carrying mobile devices capable of accessing the deft digital displays of demonstrable skill. Let's do lunch, sweetheart. Hollywood & Vine, baby!

The Simulated Demonstration

Probably the majority of the organizations using wireless communication will need to simulate the experience of using their products. Don't consider this a poor cousin to the first two demonstration options. You can create some rather engaging simulated demos, especially as new technology matures, that allows you to create graphics-intense wireless presentations and more sophisticated interactive capabilities.

Reaching for New Hyatts with Demos

Many products are inert, nontechnical, relatively unexciting, and about as far removed from electronic show-and-tell as you can possibly get. Or are they? The people at Hyatt Hotel will definitely tell you "no way."

In 1995, I spoke with Steve Yastrow, who was then Hyatt Hotel's Vice President of Resort Marketing. He went on the Internet one day and saw the future of hotel marketing. "When we evaluated the Net with a long-term perspective, we saw this as being the way the world is going. By getting online early, we're learning something new every step of the way. We'll have much more experience than other businesses that come online later," he said.

Steve envisioned making the Hyatt Hotel properties come alive for people online as website development tools matured. He wanted be able to create 3-D room displays so travelers could "walk" through hotel lobbies and into restaurants, then click to get pictures of different menu items. Visitors would be able to "ride" the elevators, see the rooms and suites, and even check out the view from those rooms. For a few months in fact, a Hyatt site in Hawaii had a camera mounted on the roof that sent pictures from the beach to the website. Potential vacationers could check it out to see when the "surf's up!"

Yastrow's vision included the business meeting side of the hotel industry. At the click of a mouse, meeting planners would conceivably be able to compare different meeting room layouts to determine which setups best met their needs. Jerry Michalski, an industry analyst at the time, suggested developing software that tabulates the costs of the various setups (including items such as projectors, screens, tables and chairs versus just chairs, meals, etc.). As planners modified their arrangements, they could automatically see how the changes impacted the costs.

And how well has the vision evolved into reality, and how will wireless technology play into the vision?

The 3-D images of the facilities and menus are not available yet, but you can get a pretty effective slide show of many features at all of the Hyatt properties, including the restaurants. The rooftop video camera feeds have been replaced with a very slick feature that lets you click your mouse on images, then drag the mouse to get full 360-degree panoramic views of cliffs, beaches, and rooms that make you want to pack up now and go.

There are also meeting room-planning features that let you search the worldwide network of Hyatt hotels and resorts for rooms and auditoriums that meet your needs. You can preview floor plans and capacity charts based on the type of seating (i.e., classroom or auditorium) you want for a meeting.

Wireless will let you extend these product demonstration capabilities to the mobile prospect. A company named VisualGold (www.visualgold.com) is overcoming some major technology barriers so you can deliver visually arresting images wirelessly to your audiences. Their technology not only does significant file compression, but it has the smarts to take your web content and automatically format it for the best possible display on whatever PC, laptop, or mobile device is accessing your information. All this happens unknown and unnoticed by the user.

VisualGold adds in technology from another company, RemoteReality (www.remotereality.com), to enable the 360-degree view of images, even on mobile devices. With this type of technology in place, and the arrival of multimedia PDA capability, you can create wireless simulation demos that effectively give people a detailed sense of real estate, restaurants, museums, amusement parks, or any "product" that consists of land and buildings.

For this tactic to have maximum impact, link your visual to audio files that add the element of sound that completes the feeling of being right there on the beaches of Maui or in the house of your dreams. And be sure to have content that directs people to where they can get more details and an opportunity to buy, make reservations, schedule a meeting, or take some other action that moves them closer to making a "buy" decision.

Saturn Rocks the Demo World

When his first cars came off the assembly line, Henry Ford would tell people "You can buy our Model Ts in any color you want—as long as it's black." Well, times have changed. Many products, including cars, come off the assembly line in every color imaginable since there are so many people with diverse tastes.

However, it's one thing to be able to deliver a product custom-tailored to meet your customer's needs. But it can be highly impractical to show every prospect a custom-designed product before he or she buys it. Unless, of course, you push the Internet and wireless envelopes.

If Saturn (www.saturnbp.com) ever makes a convertible with a serious engine, I will probably be one of their first customers just because of their online product demo feature. The reason is that I can sit at my desk and select a car model, then check out every possible feature and accessory, from the paint job to the seat covers and wheels.

All I have to do is click a color and the car changes to that color. Don't like that one, click again. Then when I want to select the interior I get more choices, and all of the choices are color-coordinated to match the exterior color I selected. Want a bike rack? Select the option and a bike rack appears—with a bike. Curious about a sun roof? Click "sun roof" and poof, there it is.

Most important for Saturn, after you spend hours exploring all of the possibilities, the demo moves you gently into the selection of financing options, dealer selection, and so forth while you are most excited about creating exactly what you want. Most important, the prospect has complete control over the demo process without a salesperson hovering over his or her shoulder. Of course, a person also might want to access this demo with his or her PDA while in a Saturn showroom in case he or she thinks about last minute adjustments to make to his or her dream car.

It may be 2003 before you can recreate as awesome a product demo tool as Saturn's on a mobile device, but you owe it to your organization to start moving in that direction now.

Clothing companies can use a demo like this to create online areas where people enter their bodily dimensions (e.g., height, weight, skin tone), pick clothes from a catalog, then change colors, patterns, and so forth until they design the outfits that they like. A word of advice, though: Take a cue from Saturn. When someone picks an item, limit the color choices for the matching clothes to what really works. Do that, and every male in America who hates to shop (me included) will lock your demo site into his or her PDA.

Any business that markets products which come in a variety of colors, shapes, styles, and sizes can use the power of Net and wireless technology to let people demo the many options before they buy these products. To address some of the bandwidth issues in the short term, you can upload these demos to WideRay Jacks or other infrared stations in stores so people can access the demos to do this "mix and match" drill. This makes the in-store salesperson's job a lot easier while ensuring that prospects get what they want.

Granted, some people are genetically disposed to accept nothing short of the in-store shopping experience, such as my buddy Miranda. But if your prospects are comfortable with catalog shopping, then wireless devices and simulation demos should pay off quite well for you, as long as you can get them to access your demos.

Product Demonstrations in the Marketing Mix

Take a few minutes to consider how product or service demonstrations can be used in combination with other wireless tactics, such as direct response activities, press relations, and research. You also should publicize your online demos in all of your conventional marketing materials and ads.

In some situations you should offer people immediate rewards for accessing and using your demo. For instance, offer a valuable report or article to people who view your demo and deliver this reward to individuals' mobile devices. Or people who try out your different clothing outfits can be rewarded with a discount coupon and special offer.

Contests or special giveaways (the tried-and-true mugs and t-shirts) are also good tactics to use to encourage people to access your demonstrations. If you're really adventurous (hint, hint), you can design a contest so that people have to use the demo to get answers to clues in your brochures or other conventional communication materials.

Within the product demo itself there should be a specific direct response call to action at the end of the demo. At various places throughout the demonstration you can put subtle reminders to place an order. Practically every screen on the Hyatt Hotels' site has a hyperlink to the hotel's online reservation center among a list of general information links.

In every press campaign, either online or off, alert journalists about your product demonstration. Although they understand that these demos are promotional pieces for companies, a well-produced demo can still give editors a better understanding of the basics of what your product does.

You can also develop a product demonstration to help gather research feedback on new product designs or to solicit ideas for how to market the product. Set up an area where you can password restrict entry, unless you don't care if your competitors know what you're up to. Then invite people who are your valued customers to view the demo and e-mail feedback, complete a feedback form, or come into a web chat room for real-time discussions.

If you give people free products or free access to some of your services in return for them taking time to look at your demo, you should generate a lot of responses for your research. Another way to build up high levels of interest in your research is to ask for feedback as you design your demo. Then let the people who give you feedback see the demo before you release it to the world.

These are just a few ideas for integrating product demonstration with other tactics. As you read through the following chapters, and think back on previous ones, more ideas should come to you. Let's move on to research and see how you can use wireless communication to increase your education from your external audiences.

General Do's and Don'ts

Here are some general guidelines for creating effective online demos. If it's possible, your demonstration should enable people to experiment and explore at their leisure and examine features in whatever order makes sense for them.

If you give people the opportunity to personalize the product or service to meet their specific needs, you can increase the impact of your demonstration by keeping their data rather than letting the prospects have it. FitSync technology gives gyms the ability to create demos that support personalized information since a lot of what powers the application is web-based software and a database. Gyms could create three or four different previews of the service so a potential member can track his or her weight training for a week or so. Then the prospect has to sign up or the service disappears after deleting all of his or her accumulated data. It will be mighty hard to let a service go if you've entered two or three weeks' worth of data.

Whenever practical, don't restrict prospects' use of the product demo, though you do want to put time limits or copy restrictions on the use of digital merchandise.

Always try to provide an easy way for prospects to go from the product demonstration to actually buying the product or service. Remember, you want to give people every opportunity to order the your product while they're most favorably disposed to purchase it (e-mail, telephone, mail). You also want to give customers several options to pay for the product. Accept credit card, check, money order, or whatever else is legal and makes sense.

If your organization regularly sells new reports or other information to existing customers, keep their credit information, shipping address, and other details that are constant in your database. That way, people can get the sample of a new report and be able to order it with minimal data input required from them, possibly just by entering a personal customer code. Again, the technology to manage this type of transaction will have to be in place before you make this option available to people wirelessly.

It is logical that, if you can effectively demonstrate your product online, you should give people the option to order the products after their demo when their interest level is highest. Taking this thought one step further for those organizations that sell digital or information products, why not deliver your product to the same devices customers use to buy it?

As with the other tactics, this will be more practical as wireless technology evolves to facilitate these types of transactions. But in the meantime you should test your ability to deliver products or services, as well as methods to manage the billing and payment process. A wireless ASP might be able to help set up an application to manage transactions that won't cost a lot of money.

The number of potential buyers may be small, but remember that your exposure to potential embarrassment is also small if things don't work out—as long as you don't tell the whole world what you're doing. For some reason, companies want to let the entire universe know when they do something on the Net that they think is cool.

Food for Thought

To recap, keep the following questions in mind as you begin to think about using wireless to demonstrate your product or service:

1. Does your product lend itself to demonstration in its original form directly through wireless communication (i.e., anything that can be digitized, consulting services, information access)?

2. If you are going to make a part of your product accessible wirelessly, how much can you give away or show off before you cross the line of giving away too much?

3. Once you get people to demonstrate your product, can you make it as easy as possible for them to order the product, either wirelessly or conventionally?

4. If you sell tangible products, such as appliances, hardware, and clothes, can you put the product designers online to "demonstrate" the talent and expertise that went into the products?

5. Do enough of your customers and prospects have mobile devices capable of playing video or audio files to justify using these as means of showing off your product capabilities?

6. Is your product comprised of physical locations, such as real estate, vacation resorts, concert halls, and so forth? If so, can you set up live broadcasts of video or pictures from these locations?

7. In your potential product demonstrations, is there some level of inter-activity so people can have some control over what they see and experience online, or will they be able to input information that makes the demonstrations more personal to their situations?

8. For those really hard to demonstrate products or services, do you have writers available who can bring these pictures to life with text?

9. Do you have a way to demonstrate products under development so you can gather feedback that helps you fine-tune the products?

CHAPTER 11

Reducing Costs and Enhancing the Value of Your Research

In this chapter I will talk about how you can gather information from secondary sources to increase your employees' ability to make your organization more competitive. I will also advise you how to enhance the education you receive from the marketplace through wireless research tactics that gather primary data from customers, prospects, resellers, and others important to your organization.

Tactics for educating your various audiences, presented in the previous two chapters, are important for enhancing the communications that come from within your organization and go out to others. But your organization has as much, if not more, to learn from your various markets: the press, business partners, and others. As the world becomes a more competitive place, wireless technology can increase your ability to listen to the people who buy your product, allocate your budgets, donate funds, or otherwise help your organization thrive.

One of the big values of the Web is its ability to engage people in two-way communication so we can break away from that old world habit of organizations bombarding people with one-way messages until they buy or die. In the new Internet world order, active dialogs rather than monologues, are better for both organizations and the people with whom they communicate. Wireless enables you to extend and increase this dialog with mobile individuals.

I will start with tactics for gathering information from various secondary sources on the Net because these may be faster to execute while you put the necessary systems in place to collect primary research.

There is such an incredible wealth of data on the Web from a myriad of

251

sources that you can find information to meet many business needs. If the current amount of online information isn't enough to stagger the imagination, new information is added to Net with such speed and intensity that you practically need a small army to keep up with everything. Wireless can help your troops keep pace. As wireless services such as AvantGo and Handango flourish, the deltas of digital data will deepen.

Research information comes in two forms. First, there is secondary research, data, and information that is already collected and available for you to pick up. Some of this is categorized and packaged neatly for easy access on the Web, such as with the LexisNexis research service. But, a large portion of information that is potentially valuable to you is scattered across the Web and requires some effort to centralize in a way that will help you.

The second form of information is primary research data, which you collect directly from people online. You can gather primary data through surveys you conduct at your website or with surveys embedded in wireless content that you push out to people. In some organizations it's difficult to sell top management on the concept of doing any kind of formal primary research, particularly since conventional research costs so much (due to printing, mailing, data collection, and data entry costs). However, I believe that doing research online and wirelessly makes sense because it's so easy and it can be inexpensive to do.

Secondary Research Tactics

Why do secondary research online? Well, research is gathering information, and there's a heck of a lot of information to be gathered on the Net.

Create Links to Research Databases

There are research databases you can scan for information, such as LexisNexis (www.lexis-nexis.com) which is the premier source for legal, corporate, governmental, and academic data. They provide fee-based, searchable access to more than three billion documents from thousands of sources, and they provide software tools for managing this content. I've used them to research which journalists and publications have covered companies similar to our clients.

Your mobile users can get to these services and do document searches directly from mobile devices that let you browse the entire Web. If they frequently gather specific documents (i.e., 1995 court files from all litigation cases in the state of Montana), consider creating an agreement with the data supplier to distribute these documents from a server where you store data for-

matted for mobile devices. However, unless your users have laptops with Ricochet, or wireless modems such as those from Sierra Wireless that access cellular
data networks, this tactic may not be advisable for retrieving long documents
because reading them can be tedious on PDA screens.

There are also databases for specific subjects. The National Institute of
Standards and Technology (NIST) is a government agency whose website
(www.nist.gov/srd/online.htm) lists several dozen free and fee-based databases just for scientific subjects. Single-subject databases narrow down your
search quite a bit, and they have search features that enable you to fine-tune
your search to find just the information you need. You can focus on your area
of interest without wading through unrelated materials, which is practical for
mobile devices' small screens.

Many database providers charge you to search through the information,
but the cost is often justified because it would take people days of constant
searching to otherwise find the same information. Over the years these fees
have become quite reasonable. You can do a LexisNexis search at their website
for under $30.

Sometimes professional associations, such as the American Trial Lawyers
Association, use the Web to provide its members with access to the association's research database. ATLA members need immediate access to all aspects
of trial and legal information that can be customized and organized, depending on their different needs.

Members initially had to contact the association's staff, who researched
500,000 legal documents and resources from ten different databases and sent
the information back to members by fax or snail mail. Now members can
search and retrieve their information themselves using the Web.

Jerry Miller, the Director of ATLA Exchange explains, "Our members will
have better service, and receive their information within seconds. The research
staff does not need to become involved and guess the search subtopics that
members need, which can take up to four weeks to deliver. By having the online search option, members will be encouraged to use this service more often
and at a lower price."

A large number of associations are aggressively using Internet technology
to provide better services to their members. As a result, pursue some associations in your industry that you may be able to work with to build wireless communication links to these services so your mobile workers can have more
sources of valuable data.

Reach Out to Directories, More Directories, and Portals

Internet directories are another seemingly endless source of research data.
There are the top-tier directories that you already know, such as Yahoo,

Google, and AltaVista, that have catalogued the hundreds of thousands of websites on the Net. But there are also hundreds of smaller directories world-wide maintained by organizations and individuals that provide access to in-dustry or topic-specific information.

One day when you have a couple of minutes to spare, go to Yahoo and type "directories" in the search field. You will access a universe of directories categorized and subcategorized. There are bound to be a few here and there that your mobile workers should have handy access to from their PDAs.

Directories are another resource you should ask about when you check out what your professional associations have to offer. Sometimes associations only have links to companies in their respective industries. The Wireless Com-munications Alliance (WCA) is a California-based nonprofit business league for companies and organizations involved with wireless technologies. WCA has a directory of wireless companies in Northern California (www.wca.org/compa nies.htm). If you're a salesperson on the road and one of your markets includes wireless companies, PDA access to this directory can be quite handy when you need to find information in a hurry before meeting with a prospect.

You should include portals when you're lining up research sources. These are essentially directories that can include articles, online services, and even the capability to buy products. Some are accessible for free by the general public, and others are only available through paid subscriptions. You should keep tabs on portals and make them wirelessly accessible if they provide a val-uable research function for your organization. AvantGo has a number of direc-tories and portals, such as DocCheck, which is a free directory service for healthcare professionals that gives them easy access to over 280 medical web-sites.

Here's a directory just for you because I'm pretty sure you're a busy execu-tive that doesn't have a lot of time to waste—CEO Express (www.ceoexpress. com): "Designed by busy executives for busy executives." You'll find links to other sites categorized by topics such as Business Magazines, Daily News, Mar-ket/Demographics Research, and Competitive Intelligence. It looks like the place to go first when you need to find important business news or do some quick research on a variety of topics.

Make the Most of Secondary Research

Before you wade in the waters of wireless research, planning is key. You and the managers of various departments within the company (marketing, cus-tomer service, business operations, R&D) should sit down and determine what kind of secondary research information will be valuable to the respective de-partments.

Marketing people, for example, typically need information that's different from customer service or human resources. And marketing often needs information delivered much faster than other departments because marketing opportunities can come and go within days online. Research and development may require research data just near the beginning and the end of their projects.

While you're discussing who needs what, determine which format they need it in. Some people may prefer to get key data extracted from survey reports and represented with charts and diagrams, while others may want to see specific types of comments and no numerical data at all. A few people may want only summaries of data from reports or other sources and a link to the locations of those sources. Mobile workers may find that their needs when they're on the road are different than when they're at the office.

Once you and your department managers decide what kind of information they need, your organization may want to use a data management approach similar to what financial services company J.P. Morgan did several years ago. They set up a four-person team whose primary job was to scour the Net and find databases and other research sources that were valuable to the company's various consultants and analysts.

Once the team found appropriate information, they posted it to easy-to-search intranet pages. To increase the size of this repository, all of the firm's employees were encouraged to also search the Web on their own for such sources of information, which would be funneled to the research team for categorizing and posting.

You can create your own team to develop a similar central intranet of web and wireless sources, then give mobile and interfacility roamers wireless access to the repository. Instead of creating an in-house team, you and a professional association may be able to jointly develop a centralized source of databases for your specific industry, or you can contract with a company that provides access to these types of databases as a service.

Make sure your research intranet includes directions for how to use the various mobile devices to get to the resources listed. You also should have instructions for retrieving the information once people get to it if any of these sources requires fees, passwords, and so forth. Then schedule meetings with managers to make sure that all departments know what information is available.

Your research team or an individual coordinator should keep abreast of online search tools (which I will discuss in a few paragraphs) and new online areas that may be of value to the company. More people can be assigned to work with the research coordinator as the need arises.

This is a good time to discuss the issue that still seems to have a lot of executives skittish, which is giving Internet access to all or most of the employees. Some executives hesitate to do this because they worry that workers will fritter away the hours searching out porn Web sites and playing games. Fifteen years ago, some of these executives also discouraged a PC on every desk for similar concerns about time-wasting.

My advice? Don't worry about it. For one thing, you're not going to be able to restrict where mobile devices can go on the Net, though you can jump up and down and scream a lot if wireless access charges become excessive. More importantly, you will find that employees who have free reign to roam cyberspace often find valuable software, contacts, and information that help them or others do their jobs better. Since there is more data online than an army of workers can track, the more pairs of eyes you have scoping out the terrain, the better. The work time that may be lost by a few goof-offs will be offset by the increased productivity of those with a wider array of information at their fingertips.

I feel it's advantageous to give everyone access to cyberspace, but don't do this as a way to avoid some element of centralized management of the information-gathering process. This reduces duplication of efforts and ensures that data that is useful for several groups won't stay on just one person's desktop or mobile device.

Automate, Automate, Automate

Once you begin to uncover information sources, consider automating every part of the data collection process that you can. There is so much information online, and it changes at such incredible speed, that the only way to ensure that your organization doesn't get swamped with information overload is through automation.

Software search "agents," whether custom designed or off-the-shelf from software vendors, should be the backbone of your automation efforts. Establish a schedule of how often various people need particular information, then schedule your agents accordingly to pick up this data.

Your agents can deliver the information to a list of the appropriate people or just bring it in to the research team who can post it on the intranet or push it to the appropriate people with notes and recommendations. However, you may find that you need wireless and other applications to facilitate information delivery.

When you subscribe to information providers, such as eWatch from PR Newswire for example (www.ewatch.com), use their search agents that filter out information according to your needs, then deliver it automatically to your e-mail or mobile device. As new wireless technology comes to market, you should find more options to automate the data retrieval process for your mobile workforce.

Before I move on to primary research, one point to think about is that all of this effort to create a research intranet not only benefits your employees who work at their desks and around the office, but maybe even some of your external audiences. Thus, you can further justify this particular wireless investment by making a significant component of your wireless application benefit audiences beyond mobile workers.

Takin' It to the (Wall) Street

To facilitate the building of your research intranet for potentially all of your employees, you can go out and buy, rent, or borrow a ready-made intranet that addresses one specific area of research. Someone else does all the initial research and creates the software applications that search for, retrieve, and package the data for various internal audiences. The good vendors will even add the wireless capabilities for you. Consider this a wireless "portal in a box" that eliminates a lot of the up-front development costs.

WallStreetView (www.wallstreetview.com) launched in 1998 and soon received praise in the press for being the most comprehensive, expansive, and easy-to-use financial portal. It featured, among other information, real-time stock quotes, market news, analysis, and commentary on the world of Wall Street.

CEO Shawn Carpenter says that, "Originally our service was for individuals who wanted to track stocks, bonds' performances, IPO markets, and other national or international financial markets. But we made a strategic decision to target corporate employees with a portal that ties together internal and external systems, and that also can be accessed by clients and others outside of an organization.

"Organizations need to have a variety of financial information from the outside world so they can track industries, competitors, and, in the larger organizations, track their investment portfolios that an internal trading group manages. Right now organizations have a 'silo' of information on a dedicated VPN server that takes data from all sources and feeds it just to the trade group."

This is a problem for organizations, having many applications that dump data into a single database that only one or a few groups can access directly. Other employees could make better use of the data if it wasn't slowed down or screened by this bottleneck. The other problem with silos is that they make it difficult to integrate data that collectively could deliver greater value to an organization.

You can configure WallStreetView so that financial information is automatically packaged as it comes into the organization, then shipped to different constituencies, including mobile workers with wireless devices. "Everyone can have a single interface, what we call Financial Desktop, but intelligence in the system figures out who gets access to what. For example, sales people can find competitor data easier than searching the Net on their own," says Carpenter.

One of the wireless benefits to the portal is that it facilitates messaging and re-routing to mobile people. Its biggest value, however, is sending people automatic alerts about events that happen within the software, the market, in the news, or other areas that you designate. Currently you have to call people and try to find them, or wait for them to respond to e-mail. Instant messages in the wireless space will enable even faster communication when using the portal.

"Quantifying other benefits that wireless offer in an application like this can be difficult depending on the business," comments Carpenter. "In financial companies, knowing immediately that certain stocks are going south is an easily understood value. In general organizations, the value will be harder to find. Sometimes the data they get is only quarterly, so there isn't a real speed-of-delivery issue to begin with."

Wireless devices can be less expensive than giving everyone PCs, and then when they see you can pump data from wireless devices into main systems so people can get real-time analysis, the technology's popularity will increase. Wireless gives the portal more options for delivering information, which makes it even more popular with organizations.

One thing you want to be sure of is that the portal will run on all of the computer networks and support most of the mobile device formats, what Aether Systems calls "create-once, deliver-everywhere" capability. Aether Systems is a company whose wireless application technology drives WallStreetView's wireless capabilities. In addition, you must address security issues pertinent to wireless technology, such as preventing unauthorized access. WallStreetView does this by ensuring that only entering an individual password accesses personalized investment accounts.

Future plans include giving customers the ability to initiate relationships with resellers and stockbrokers, who in turn will be able to provide customers with entire packages of detailed and personalized supplemental information.

Now that you have an overview of secondary research options, let's look at primary research and how wireless tactics can help out here.

Primary Research Tactics

If you've ever personally managed conventional research projects, you know that the process is a righteous pain in the posterior. Hiring and managing data collectors, making hundreds of phone calls, mailing thousands of surveys, tabulating data, and so on. These are the trials and tribulations that cause people to avoid research like the plague. Internet and wireless communication will eliminate many of these hassles.

To conduct surveys online all you need to do is design, post, and promote or electronically distribute your questionnaires, then collect the data and tabulate it. Simple. Okay, maybe it isn't a twenty-minute job, at least initially. There can be a lot of setup work to do. But once you have the right software tools in place and provide a little training to the people administering the surveys, you can run post a new survey every hour if you want.

Perseus Software (www.perseus.com) markets both an ASP service that will create and distribute surveys from their portal, and software for organizations that want to install and run survey applications from their own servers. The ASP option is well-suited to smaller organization since Perseus takes care of all of the back end software issues, as well as collecting and tabulating the date.

I don't want to go into all of the technical details of creating online surveys, but be sure that you focus on planning and ease of use. Think about the following four points:

1. Plan for the needs of the people who ultimately will use the data.

2. Make sure the software tool that creates the actual surveys is easy for the tech layperson to use.

3. Insist, nay, demand that the survey is easy to use for the person completing the survey.

4. Make the user interface simple as possible for the software that tabulates the data and produces reports.

The last three points are vital because the Web has made it so that anyone can conduct surveys as often as they want. You can get departments and small organizations to do primary research that never would have been collected in the past because of the expense or the difficulty using research software (or research firms). Now anyone can gather more timely feedback at a faster pace as long as you make the tools simple to use. The Perseus website has a section of documents with tips and sample questionnaires that address a range of business uses for online surveys (www.perseus.com/surveytips).

You can set up wireless surveys that collect data on an ongoing basis and maybe tabulate the data weekly, or monthly, so you can track changes in attitudes or buying habits over a long-term period. You can also change your survey by the month or by the day if you need to get feedback on different issues, promotions, product prices, and so on.

Since surveys can be downloaded onto a mobile device, completed on the Web or completed by e-mail and then automatically tabulated, the ongoing administrative costs are limited to the time you spend to develop or change surveys. Even if your distribute surveys by e-mail or conduct real-time focus groups through wireless instant messaging, the associated implementation costs are still much less than with similar conventional research tactics.

Primary Objective: Better Decision Making

Just because something is cheap or easy doesn't mean you should do it. This directive actually came from an Internet dating guide, but it's just as applicable to research. There should be specific objectives if you're going to do research online or wirelessly. Companies find these research activities are usually generated by one or more of the following business areas: marketing, sales, customer service, or product development, but I believe that every department should look at using wireless to gather feedback.

Your marketing department can use wireless research for all of the traditional tasks such as gauging market attitudes and customer needs, and also to measure the effectiveness of various marketing activities. They can distribute surveys to generate valuable feedback on the potential success of conventional or online marketing campaigns, specific promotions, and ad messages that are being developed. You subsequently can make changes, if necessary, before these campaigns are released to the public.

One caveat here: Because respondents to website surveys are self-selecting, results you get may not be the statistically accurate picture of the general population that you would get with quantitative research surveys conducted by snail mail, in person, or by phone to carefully screened recipients. If you distribute surveys to customers' PDAs or by e-mail to a database you've developed, your results have greater statistical accuracy, assuming you have good demographic data on those people in your databases.

Your sales team in the field can access survey forms on their mobile devices to collect data during sales meetings at trade shows, while talking on the phone to prospects, or hand the device to prospects in a retail outlet to have them complete the survey. It would help team members if they can wirelessly access and query the data tabulation reports, or at least view the graphs and charts from completed surveys. This feedback can help them vary their sales presentations to better address prospects' concerns or offer different products based on the survey responses of the prospect during a meeting.

Your support and service staff can use a combination of wireless surveys and web chat room discussions to measure customers' satisfaction with your products and services. Some of this feedback (along with your responses) can be posted directly to your website or distributed wirelessly for other customers to read and learn from. Field service people can complete wireless surveys after each customer engagement to collect data that improves future service delivery. This feedback will also serve as an early warning system to alert you to problems before they become major business traumas.

The product development team can create surveys to not only track market trends, but also determine what new product features, or new products, you should develop to address emerging trends. This doesn't have to be solely an internal function since you can bring business partners such as retailers into the survey design and data-gathering process.

The HR staff can use surveys to gain insight as to why people accepted or rejected job offers, or what potential job candidates think about your organization's culture, benefits program, or any one of a dozen other topics. HR can also use wireless surveys to get a snapshot of employees' attitudes on policies, the effectiveness of training, the latest marketing campaign, and other issues important to them or to management.

A word of caution though: Unless the survey results can be delivered to management in a way that guarantees anonymity to any employee who wants it, the chances are low for getting honest feedback. Employees are very concerned about having their comments, particularly criticisms, traced back to them. CustomInsight (www.custominsight.com) specifically focuses on HR departments with ASP services and software for distributing surveys to employees that emphasizes privacy.

The shipping department can measure customer satisfaction with that operation by distributing surveys directly to customers or, if you both ship and deliver, have delivery people conduct short surveys with their mobile devices. However, surveys delivered directly to customers will likely produce more frank feedback.

Survey Tips and Tricks

I asked Gale Grant, a former executive with the e-Business applications company Open Market, what are some design issues you should consider. She has considerable experience developing systems for gathering web surfers' feedback

"People will not answer surveys that they don't find interesting or beneficial to them," Gale states. "Questions that ask 'How much money are you planning to spend' or 'When do you plan to purchase' are not very popular. However, people do respond to questions that ask for their opinions about existing products or services, or you can ask them to input suggestions. It also helps to tempt them with prizes.

"The question 'Are you the primary decision maker?' can be couched in wording that asks 'To help us develop web content that addresses your specific needs, what is your role within your organization?' Give respondents multiple-choice answers with one of the answers being 'primary decision maker.'"

Coming up with the right phraseology for questions requires a little extra work, but the right questions will generate better responses. Unless you have a fabulous prize to offer for completing a survey, don't make it too long. Six to ten questions should be the limit. You can break up a long survey and distribute sections of it to different audiences, or distribute one section a week.

You may want to turn surveys into games, such as a scavenger hunt, which are much more enticing than regular questionnaires. Games take the tedium out of answering one question after another. Scavenger hunts are also good because they get people to look at more of your content while they hunt for hidden items and clues. But you have to be careful that the content isn't too long or has too many graphics.

Gale concludes, "You have to be up front with people and tell them how their information will be used, or if you will release a report of the survey results. If you tell people after the survey how the company responded to their input, even if you disagree with their suggestions, those whose ideas you don't use will not get upset and feel they were ignored."

A Material Survey

Recently CNN had Madonna on its TV network for an interview. During the four or five days before the interview, CNN online ran a banner headline, a couple of background articles to feed the hype, a seven-question multiple choice trivia quiz, and a one-question survey with several answers to the query "What do you think Madonna's greatest asset is?"

When I checked an answer to the single question, a screen popped up with the number of votes for each answer and the total number of voters. The trivia quiz was set up to tell me immediately after each question if I was right or wrong. However, I didn't get to see how my score compared to others, or even how many people had taken this quiz, which I consider to be a short-coming.

Alrighty, fans. What lessons can we learn from this little item?

First, it helps when people can see the results of everyone who has taken the survey to date. It gives them a sense they they're not alone, plus folks like to compare their answers with other people's responses.

Second, sometimes the right survey not only allows you to gather knowledge, but it can have promotional value. If CNN wanted to have a hook for a short story about Madonna on one of their news shows, they could have led with, "A majority of people surveyed don't believe that Madonna's a great singer. We'll have all the details following this commercial." Think of ways to turn your survey results in a promotion that draws people to your website, get them to call or move them along in the sales cycle.

Third, if you do take web and wireless survey results and use them in some promotional effort, be sure to add a disclaimer that says this is a self-selecting survey audience that is expressed their own views (which CNN does). Online surveys can tell you a lot of useful things, depending on how they're implemented, but they're never going to be the same as those surveys where you take all the steps of good scientific data collection.

Fourth, if your web and wireless traffic is high enough, you can charge companies money to place an ad on your survey (which CNN also does).

Fifth, if you change your survey every day, you can start to build a following of people who come to your site just to take the survey and check out what other people are doing. You don't have to be an entertainment company for this tactic to work, just know what topics really interest your audience.

And sixth, unless you're doing surveys such as these just for the entertainment value to your guests, take the opportunity of getting people to give you feedback to also give you permission to continue a dialog with them. If a busy mobile person takes time to answer your questions, you should open the door to some kind of future communication.

By now, some of you more devoted Madonna fans probably are wondering what the results were to the Madonna single-survey question. Well, the four possible answers were, "She's a great actress," "She's a great singer," "She's a great self promoter," and "She's a great dancer." While only 1 percent of nearly 4,500 votes (at the moment I was there) felt Madonna is Oscar material, a whole bunch of people (71 percent) believe she's the self-promotion queen of the universe. Singing took a distant second place (21 percent). But hey, it was a self-selecting audience. Maybe the rest of the non–web-surfing world believes Madonna is an Oscar waiting to happen.

Data Tabulation of Online Surveys

As with collecting secondary research, you want to automate the online survey data tabulation process as much as possible. If you post surveys in your online areas, this is often easy. On websites you can develop a system that automatically drops each person's responses directly into software that does a running tabulation of data as people complete surveys. At any time you will have a tally of results as of that moment.

You can transfer the tabulations into a database program to do a complex analysis of the survey results. This option makes sense if it's important to have detailed statistical data, or you want to cross tabulate results. If all you want is a general idea of what people think about your products, or you just want to collect people's comments, you can forego the detailed analysis.

If you use different applications to distribute, collect, and tabulate wireless surveys, you have to be sure that your software that distributes or collects surveys enables the data to be easily transferred to the program that does tabulation and analysis. In general, research software that does complex data analysis has been upgraded to pull data from e-mail surveys with no problem. You may have to take some extra time to facilitate data transfer from web-based survey services or applications.

In-Person Data Tracking— a Major Burden Made Lighter

One of the more expensive aspects of research is the data-tracking process conducted by human data collectors. This is usually associated with observing scientific experiments, business processes, or mechanical operations. You watch a process, you record numbers and details, you may add a note or two, and then you repeat the cycle. Sometimes this goes on continually for months or years at a time, with people recording their observations and delivering this data (often in printed form) back to a central source for tabulation and analysis.

For a short time I worked for a market research company that specialized in transit studies. We had to field teams with dozens of people who rode California Bay Area subway trains and buses and count the number of people getting onto and off of the vehicles, while noting the time of day and locations of these actions. The entire data tracking procedure was paper-based, with another team manually entering all of the data into computers and then doing the tabulation.

There are quite a few other organizations that collect data on the location and condition of frequently moving people or physical items such as cars, shipping containers, and packages. There is also scientific data tracking such as though well-documented animal behavior and migration studies seen on the Discovery Channel, plus medical and drug studies of every kind. Rounding out this category of data tracking are those organizations that record huge volumes of numerical data such as sports team statistics, gas, light, and water meter readings, or census information.

Wireless technology offers opportunities to reduce costs and increase efficiency for all of these forms of data collection. The range of tactics includes everything from giving mobile devices to people who are in the field collecting data to embedding wireless devices that automatically send readings from residential utility meters to data collection equipment in vans that drive around the neighborhoods.

Performance Counts

One of the challenges of tracking data is putting an army of employees into the field to monitor how effectively people or machines perform work tasks. This is particularly difficult when data collectors have to record these tasks frequently and quickly. Generally there is one group of employees who collects the data and a second group that takes this data and does all of the analysis.

Some organizations still have paper-based systems because the conditions under which their data collectors work make it difficult, if not impossible, to use laptops. These conditions can include a cramped working space, inclement weather, or other factors. But using pencil and paper often leads to errors, duplicated efforts, and other inefficiencies.

Wireless technology can replace paper-based systems and significantly improve data tracking. Mobile devices can be used in many of the places where space is limited. Second, by creating a link from mobile devices directly to back end software on an organization's server, they can eliminate duplicated data entry efforts and dump the field data straight into the tabulation software.

Wireless Helps Postal Carriers Make Their Appointed Rounds

The United States Postal Service has worked with numerous airlines for more than 70 years to haul mail to and from international destinations. Unlike Federal Express, the United States Postal Service doesn't have its own fleet of planes, so they rely on other organizations' planes. However, this increases the chances for mishandled shipments.

Before the Postal Service developed a wireless application to streamline its operations, ramp clerks went from plane to plane when the mail arrived at a destination and completed a series of paper forms to document mail-handling irregularities. Clerks tracked everything from weather damage to mechanical problems that caused a flight, and therefore the mail, to be delayed.

These completed forms were later given to Post Office employees to process. Often not all of the information was properly recorded, or the handwriting was illegible, which made it impossible to decipher the forms. In 1999, the Postal Service decided that it was time to automate this data collection process to save time and improve service. They developed a wireless application and equipped ramp clerks with Symbol Technologies' (www.symbol.com) hand-held devices with bar code scanning capabilities.

International letters and parcels are placed in large containers before going onto planes, and each container has a bar code that lists the flight number's final destination. Clerks now scan each bar code with the Symbol device and process the container for delivery, making this information instantly available to the Postal Service's entire network. They also track carrier negligence and the related fines assessed for these violations. With the new system, executives can make adjustments online and quickly resolve minor infractions. If larger infractions occur that reveal airline negligence, such as weather damage or theft of parcels, then midlevel and national reviews take place.

Data collected in the system will be used to improve existing performance, identify routings that need to be changed, allow trend analysis on types of incidents, and enable the Postal Service to work with its vendors to provide better performance.

Wireless in Paris in Springtime

Centre Auto Sécurité (CAS) is one of five companies authorized by the French government to carry out mandatory inspection of vehicles that are more than four years old. This involves a technical evaluation of over ten million vehicles each year. CAS operates 500 inspection centers and employs 1,200 technicians.

To conduct a vehicle inspection, the garage technician used to capture a large volume of technical data using printed forms, evaluated the data, and then passed it to a secretary who typed the information into a report that was given to customers. This was difficult for technicians because they were writing data in cramped and dark locations. There were also errors by the secretaries as they transcribed the handwritten data.

CAS decided to equip their technicians with Psion Workabout mobile devices and the necessary back end software (www.psion.com). With this application, they enter vehicles' details then use the pop-up screens to work through the test procedure. The system offers a menu of optional phrases so technicians can enter results that don't meet test parameters. After the inspection the data is sent to a dedicated PC which produces a report, an inspection certificate, and an invoice.

Technicians' accuracy has significantly improved and they are much happier using mobile devices rather than clipboards and paper since they can now enter correct data even in dark areas. There are fewer data entry errors, and the printed reports are prepared faster, which is good for both the customers and the centers. One center alone may have to inspect more than 6,000 vehicles every year.

For certain portions of the inspection procedure (such as testing the braking system) CAS is exploring the possibility of plugging the Workabout directly into the test equipment that they use. This will eliminate the need for technicians to manually key in the data, further streamlining the inspection process.

Ahh, It's the Sportin' Life for Me

Soccer, Little League baseball, high school football, and summer league software are mainstays of cities and suburbs across the country. Collectively they generate a challenging sea of registration, scheduling, scorekeeping, and statistical data. We're talking about data on 35 million amateur sports athletes playing in 2 million leagues.

SportsPilot (www.sportspilot.com) in Dallas, Texas is an ASP that help coaches and scorekeepers with iPAQ mobile devices easily capture, analyze, and store this information, while giving coaches a better tool for managing their teams.

These individuals install SportsPilot's ScorePad software on their iPAQs that they can then use for basketball, baseball, softball, hockey, and soccer games. During a game, rather than mark a paper score sheet when a player scores a goal or makes a shot, the scorekeeper taps the screen that resembles the familiar paper score sheet and uses the same scoring symbols. Users can indicate where on the field, court, or ice a particular action occurred (i.e., a foul line shot, a corner kick).

These features not only give coaches a complete picture of individual and team statistics after the game, but during the game they can make effective strategy adjustments on the fly. After the games, the iPAQs upload all of the game data wirelessly to SportsPilot's servers, which apply an application called SportsWriter to automatically generate statistics and stories about the respective games.

Based on hundreds of sports story templates created by professional sports writers, SportsWriter produces quality "news" stories about the players' exploits in the game that are posted on SportsPilot's public Internet site in minutes. An ASP service manages all of the mundane chores that go with amateur sports, such as registration, recording payments, scheduling games, and posting updates.

SportsPilot now has a customer base of 35,000 athletes, and expects that number to grow to 300,000 and beyond very quickly. Key to their success is getting people to adapt to the change from paper to mobile devices, a transition that is helped along with the color iPAQ screens that are actually more appealing than black and white paper sheets.

Though it's applied to amateur sports, the feature in this type of application that offers extra value for business or scientific use is the ability to do a lot of the data crunching on the mobile device. This gives your employees the ability to make more decisions right there in the field as they collect data rather than waiting for the home office to compile data and generate reports. Depending on the need, this flexibility and speed can add significantly to your wireless implementation's ROI.

ScorePad has a couple of other features that you should consider with any data collection application that you implement. One is extensive help files. When I worked on that transit study we put the data collectors through a lot of training and gave them paper notes to take with them. If you can condense all of this training into easy-access help screens on the mobile devices, productivity will increase, while errors and inefficiencies decrease even further.

Man, I Want a New Drug—Wireless Helps You Get It Faster

PHT Corporation performs clinical trials for some of the largest pharmaceutical companies in the world. To streamline both the time and financial costs of collecting data from all over the planet, PHT gives patients Palm PDAs running a special data retrieval application that supports multiple languages.

Patients use the PDAs to note symptoms and any medications they take, as well as the time when these events occur. The application allows patients to add written details to more accurately describe what occurs. At end of each day, patients plug in a modem and press a button to send the data from the handheld to PHT's web server so it can be accessed securely by authorized personnel.

This application not only saves the costs of manual data collection but it also provides more reliable results, so drugs get to market faster and more safely. In PHT's business, enabling the pharmaceutical companies to save time is more important than saving money.

The real economic challenge for these companies is to get new drugs approved as soon as possible during the first round of evaluations by regulatory agencies. The likelihood of swift approval increases significantly when the agency gets better and more documented reports, which in turn speeds a drug into commercial use.

After a drug such as Viagra is discovered and patented, there is a fixed future date when the patent expires and competitors can enter the market with geriatric—oops!—I mean generic versions of the pill. During that time compounds go through animal testing, initial clinical testing, and finally clinical trials where companies devote hundreds of millions of dollars and several years to prove that each medicine is safe and effective.

If a company can do those clinical trials and arrive at compelling scientific conclusions six months earlier because of the wireless communication, it will earn an extra $500 million for a drug that is worth $1 billion a year in terms of gross revenue. That's over $2.7 million per day for a six-month advantage.

Regardless of the cost savings of automating a manual process, you can make a pretty good case that ROI is substantial if you can present clearer, more compelling, and better-documented data that shows a drug is safe and effective for patients worldwide. A reliable data collection and access system is the key to reaching this objective.

Doctor, Doctor, Tell Me the News

Sometimes you have to collect mountains of data, and not just the numeric type. You have to collect descriptive reports on the actions, behavior, or physical changes of large numbers of people, animals, or objects either in one location, or scattered over large geographical areas.

Wireless still can play a big part in reducing the overhead of managing such projects, but you have to give a lot of thought to the user interface for these projects. You are often recording complex observations, yet most mobile devices don't make it easy to enter pages of text in one sitting.

Another complication is that sometimes you find yourself working in situations that require quick data entry. If the cheetah that you're observing eat dinner for your research project suddenly looks up and decides that you look good for dessert, you may have to jump up and do a Carl Lewis track sprint to get out of harm's way. But you still have to make note that the cat's main course was a 70-pound wildebeest.

Medical studies fall into the "quick data entry" category (minus the cheetah), and wireless applications are a good way to improve the speed and efficiency of these data collection tasks. The following stories are more examples of the type of applications to implement when you really need to "git it and git."

Easily Track 'Em Coming and Going

Clinical nurses and physicians active in patient research at the Erlanger Medical Center Emergency Heart and Stroke Center in Chattanooga, Tennessee use Palm Vs to simplify the process of qualifying patients for research trials at the region's Level I trauma center. When a patient arrives, neurologists and research staff use the devices to reference the criteria of various research trials to see if a patient can be included in a research project that studies the prevention and management of strokes.

Clinical nurses use their mobile devices' infrared ports to beam trial protocols and patient information to the physicians' devices to determine if a patient can be included in a study that could potentially save lives. Before using the Palms, it took as long as 45 minutes to determine if a patient met the criteria for a study, then explain the clinical trial to the patient, obtain informed consent, and get the patient randomized into the trial.

Going wireless eliminated 10 to 15 minutes in this process by eliminating the time-consuming search for protocols in the midst of a busy emergency room. This time saved adds up to significant numbers when you're dealing with dozens of patients each week in the ER.

The valuable lesson here is that you should load up your workers mobile devices with as much background or supporting information as possible that they will need to assist their observations. You don't want people having to log onto your network every time they need to check a definition or review a data collection procedure. Also, if they will be observing a predetermined set of actions or data, create drop-down menus with multiple choice selections so workers can use a stylus to tap on the appropriate details. For example, "Patient's pulse was between: a) 60 and 70, b) 70 and 80, c) 80 and 90 beats per minute."

Researchers at the University of Toronto and Toronto's Sunnybrook and Women's College Health Sciences Centre use wireless communications to help in a study that provides crucial insights into bipolar disorder. This is a mental illness characterized by wide mood swings ranging from mania to depression.

The study allows researchers to track mood variations in two groups (individuals with bipolar disorder and healthy individuals) and compare the varied results. The goal of this study is to determine if fluctuations in mood differ over time, either in frequency or the extent to which they fluctuate, among people with bipolar disorder as compared to people who do not suffer from the condition.

The study is conducted using Qualcomm pdQ smartphones (www.qualcomm.com). Twice daily, study participants are prompted by the device to answer a brief questionnaire that appears on the screen. The questionnaire asks participants about their mood as well as a number of symptoms common in depression and mania. After completing the questionnaire, participants transmit the information wirelessly to a central database.

Unlike paper-based questionnaires, the pdQ device allows the researchers to track the exact time each questionnaire is completed and to also phone the participants quickly if a report is missing or incomplete. The researchers eventually hope to incorporate a global positioning system (GPS) chip that will enable them to factor environmental issues into their studies.

If you are conducting research in which voice contact between workers, research subjects, and others can help the accuracy, speed, or efficiency of your data collection project, a smartphone hardware product is a good call. And of course the GPS capability will provide added economic value. In case you don't manage to outrun that cheetah and end up as Desert Sorbet, the home office can use GPS to direct a team to retrieve the mobile device and the data it contains.

As voice recognition technology improves, and more PDAs come equipped with multimedia capabilities that allow audio recording, mobile devices will enable workers to make voice data entries. This will be particularly effective when people have to enter repetitive data, and the number of entries is fairly small.

All right, I don't want to eat up any more of your time on this topic. Let's move on to discuss the tactical role of wireless communication in public relations.

Food for Thought

Reviewing the following questions should help you to clarify your thinking about using wireless to enhance your research efforts.

1. What objectives do you have for online and wireless research?

2. Is there information that you want to get from customers that's different than what you want to gather from prospects or the market in general?

3. Do you want to buy off-the-shelf survey software, or build your own?

4. Who within the organization will get the information you gather from

the Net, how will they get it (by e-mail, directly from the intranet, or other method), and what will they do with it after they receive it?

5. Have you made it clear to the people who are giving you feedback what you will do with their information?

6. After you collect research information from people, can you later post results (or a summary of results) on your website, or send results by e-mail and wireless to the mobile devices to those who participate in the research?

7. If you plan to do information search and retrieval on the Web for qualitative research, is there technology you can put in place, or services you can subscribe to that will make the job easier?

8. Is there a person or group of people within your organization who can take the responsibility to find, retrieve, and catalog research information from the Net so it can be delivered to mobile devices?

9. To help make the cost of implementing research projects more manageable, is it possible to have different departments share and contribute staff to the same research projects, thus splitting the expenses?

CHAPTER 12

Taking Your Press Relations Effectiveness to New Heights

After seven years of executing, observing, and speaking about online press relations activities, I have to say that few communication tools offer greater potential to help build relationships with journalists than Internet and wireless technology. I also believe that few tools are as underutilized for PR as the Net. If your web efforts fall short of their potential, wireless will not reach its full potential to impact press coverage because a major benefit of effective wireless activities is to drive journalists to your site.

The issue is not one of competence, for there are many very competent and effective PR professionals at organizations whose online PR efforts need significant enhancement. So how do we turn this situation around? First PR people must understand that the ways in which journalists cover the news changed dramatically in 2001. With that understanding must come a change in how senior management and PR pros view the role of the Net for press relations, along with a firm commitment to subsequently change the way their organizations use the Net to fit that role.

A recent national survey of journalists revealed that 75 percent of them use the Net daily for article research. When a news story breaks or they receive releases, a majority of journalists go first to an organization's website when they can't reach a PR contact on the phone. A majority would run with a story initiated on the Net, and would rely on chat rooms and newsgroups as primary or secondary news sources.

The 2001 economic downturn accelerated these trends by reducing news staffs, resulting in fewer people doing more work. Because the Net makes journalists' working lives easier, they will use it more as workloads increase. Some major print and broadcast media's websites run news stories within a few hours, if not minutes, after these stories break. This puts yet more pressure on journalists to rely on the Web to research stories faster. So in this new millennium where news is both instant and global, how do you proactively maximize your PR efforts rather than constantly be behind the news curve?

This chapter shows you how to use the Net and wireless communication together to build and strengthen relationships with journalists, increase the impact of your PR efforts, and generate more media coverage. Chapter 13 presents feedback from PR professionals who discuss how to use wireless to boost your press and investor relations efforts, and deal with one of the nightmares of the PR profession—crisis communication management.

Walk a Mile in Journalists' Shoes— the First Step to Successful Online PR

Unlike my previous two books in which I wrote about developing Internet business strategy, this book project gave me a better hands-on perspective of how the typical journalist works.

In 1994, when I did research for my first book, it was easy to call a company, ferret out the person who did their web design and content development, then talk for an hour about every detail of their company's Internet strategy and tactics. I only had to work with a PR person one time to get an interview set up. Also, few organizations had websites, and there was little information on the websites that did exist, so using the Net for research on companies' backgrounds wasn't critical for me. Except for journalists who primarily covered tech companies, most other journalists did not use the Web much for research.

With this book, PR executives and agencies played a key role in getting me in front of the people with whom I needed to speak, and the Web was a key source of information before and after interviews. Every organization I researched has a site, plus the Web in general offered a lot of information that I used as stepping-off points for various book topics. What's more, my two-month deadline to research and write this book made me the stereotypical reporter on a tight deadline. I needed information in a hurry, and organizations with the most useful websites tended to get the best coverage.

Given this experience, I can definitely speak with true insight as to what journalists need online to make their job—and yours—easier. This insight is reinforced by research conducted by my company and others, which reveals how and how much journalists rely on the Web, and how wireless will factor into their jobs. Only by putting yourself into the shoes of a typical reporter on deadline, such as in a scenario in which you pretend to do background research for a story, can you maximize web and wireless communication for PR.

In addition to putting yourself into the role of a journalist, it also helps to spend time talking to him to find out what things are important to him. Once for Symantec (www.symantec.com), an Internet security technology company, my team created a resource guide in their press center with information specific to key cities that mobile journalists frequently visited. After developing some general ideas of what this section should contain, I called a few journalists to see what they thought would be valuable.

Some of their ideas coincided with ours, but they also added a lot of ideas for information we wouldn't have thought about providing because these journalists obviously knew all of the trials and tribulations of being a reporter on the road from first-hand experience. We also found that you can't assume that all journalists have the same needs. For example, the female journalists as a group had a few requests that were different than the males, such as adding a list of safe places to jog.

I recommend that you (if you have PR responsibilities) or someone in your PR department budget a day to call journalists you have relationships with and ask them for a blunt but constructive critique of your online press area. Also ask them if or how they plan to use wireless technology. Don't be discouraged if many of them are only planning to use PDAs to communicate by e-mail. The important thing is to determine if they are using mobile devices.

Once you beef up your online press activities, contact these same journalists once a quarter or so to get ongoing feedback about your efforts. Many journalists aren't on the "bleeding" edge of wireless technology use, but as it starts to become mainstream and they test the waters, journalists will move fairly quickly to adopt new technology if it helps make their jobs easier. You want to keep pace with that evolution.

Journalists Recommend Four Steps to Increase Online PR Effectiveness

"If a person has poor press communication skills in real space, then cyberspace won't help them much. They'll do the same bad job, only faster." This was the comment of one of the editors I surveyed in 1995 to find out how journalists used the Web, and to ask what advice they had for PR professionals to help them communicate more effectively with journalists.

For two years (1995 and 1996) my company surveyed hundreds of journalists, mostly those who covered technology and a few business news reporters. Journalists found that quite a few PR people committed online the same four cardinal sins that were (and still are) common in conventional press relations:

1. They didn't target the right press contacts.

2. They didn't send the right information.

3. They didn't know enough about the companies or products they promoted.

4. They would e-mail to ask, "Did you get that release I sent?"

If I were to send out this same survey today, I'm pretty sure that the comments would be similar, even when including wireless communication. As mobile device use increases, journalists will not want to receive communication about products and topics that they do not cover. And given the devices' technology limitations, journalists will be even more sensitive about receiving or accessing only the most salient details.

These four points may seem like excerpts from PR 101, but do not take them lightly. I worked in the trenches communicating with journalists for over 15 years before recently giving it all but the strategy development side of the PR business. I have heard editors complaining about the same shortcomings in PR professionals that entire time. More importantly, I hear editors constantly state that these four problems kill stories before they ever have a chance of making it into print, regardless of how good they may be.

If your PR staff or agency can't address these issues effectively, all the wireless technology in the world isn't going to help you. So the question is, what should good PR pros do to minimize these shortcomings and maximize the Net in their efforts, and how will this carry over to wireless communication?

Target Your Press Contacts

As one journalist summed it up, "The rules are the same online as with conventional media relations: PR specialists need to both understand the needs of their clients, as well as the specific characteristics of the publications they approach. Shot-gunning e-mailed press releases (especially with long cc: lists of other publications for all to see), pitching inappropriate companies or stories, and generally using electronic media to throw out more information in the hope that it will sticks only hurt perceptions of clients, not help."

Another journalist commented, "Don't use the Web to send even more blanket releases than you do now. If I recognize an annoying sender's ID, it's awfully easy to hit that 'delete' button." When journalists are mobile, time is precious, so they will be highly selective in screening e-mail that comes to their devices. If your organization is known or becomes known for blanketing the universe with e-mail, journalists likely will create software filters to automatically block out all of your e-mail from their devices including those that may have appropriate information that could lead to a story."

"I prefer (but others do not) press releases by e-mail. However, it is easy to abuse this too," warned one journalist. You should talk to your media contacts to know who wants press releases attached with their e-mail. Many mobile devices will have difficulty allowing users to view attached documents.

Some editors feel that PR people not only need to target their individual press contacts better, but they also need to do a better job at targeting publications. "Try to understand my needs," explained one editor. "For example, we are not really a product/news magazine. Our magazine is about broad technology categories, so I'm not that interested in new product announcements unless they are about some new technology or new application of technology."

Send the Right Information

People who don't spend the time to target their mailing lists are almost guaranteed to send wrong information to at least a few people. "Don't flood an editor's mailbox with a too-frequent stream of insignificant announcements," stated one journalist. "The writer who covers your new product announcement may have absolutely no use for your releases about financial achievements or newly hired executives."

Even after matching the right journalists with the right story, some people don't send the right information, or they omit important details. Some of the suggestions we received identified information that journalists prefer to receive by e-mail. "If vendors set up websites, I would just as soon they let me know where theses sites are and what they contain. When I want more information, I'll go to the site." This particularly holds true with journalists using mobile devices since these are not the best tools for general web browsing if you're in a hurry.

This kind of advice usually prompts PR people to ask what they are supposed to do when they have important news that an editor may not know about. The story could grow old waiting for an editor or writer to happen by the website and see it.

One journalist advised that, when you have something new or time-sensitive, "Make your e-mail information concise and accurate. Tell me what's out there, give me a precise location, and a sample of the content. There's too much going on to rely on blind luck." Another journalist wrote, "I'd rather just get a quick note about a particular topic, then ask if I WANT more information and let me decide."

If you're going to create a system to deliver wireless messages to your press audience, consider how you can personalize the messages that you send. The ease and speed of using e-mail lists to send announcements and notes lead many people to take the path of least resistance (blanket mailings) rather than capitalize on the ability of Net technology to deliver more effective targeted messages. You don't need to have each individual journalist receive a unique e-mail. But you should have your list of e-mail and mobile device addresses broken down at least by topics such as news, feature story suggestions, etc.

"Keep in mind the target readers of the various publications and try as hard as possible to personalize the pitch for that magazine," advised another journalist. "This saves time and ensures a better hit rate. In addition, provide clear positioning statements about product strengths and core technologies for whatever it is you are announcing. Pay attention to what we're writing about and make comments on what, in your opinion, we're missing."

Wireless communication will work best if you not only target the right person at the right publication, but also understand when might be the right times to use wireless. If you know a reporter will be at the location of a media event, trade show, or disaster, you should tailor information to the specific situation as well as the needs of the individual.

Know Your Product

Knowing about a company's product means more than knowing how the product works. To effectively present products to editors, PR pros also need to understand the product's role in the market place. One editor commented at length about how market awareness will help PR people to do a better job for their companies.

"Generally, PR tends to make one big mistake, and that is thinking about their clients from the clients' perspective, instead of from the perspective of the recipient of the information. While this may keep the clients happy initially, the failure to explain your clients within the larger perspective or the context that the public will perceive them can only lead to ineffective communication.

"Some thinking on the part of PR about why I should care about their message means that they have to think about where their clients' products or companies fit into the real world being described in my magazine. It isn't so much the fact itself that is interesting, but where the fact belongs with all the other facts."

One of the challenges that you will have to meet with wireless communication is the one I presented in Chapter 8 on building brand loyalty. You must be able to present your organization, its product or service, what it does, for which audiences, and then tell how whatever you're announcing in the press release will impact those audiences—all in 90 words. It's going to take a lot of diligence to meet this particular challenge. Once you catch journalists' attention, then you need to point them to additional information that puts your message into proper context.

Don't Ask, "Did You Get That Release I Sent?"

A number of people weighed in with advice about this issue that is pretty straightforward. "Send me e-mail and leave me alone. E-mail is a terrific method of communicating; why ruin it by annoying me with 'Did you get my release?' questions?"

Another journalist stated, "Send me e-mail. Trust that I got it. Don't call to follow up." And finally, "Send info, then don't bug me about it." Everyone else who commented on the "question from hell" said pretty much the same thing.

Remember your objective online—it's to initiate a dialog. If you have targeted your message to the right people and have given them links to sources with sufficient details to back up those initial messages, you should hear something from those you contact. It's a waste of time (for you and your contact) to ask mundane questions. To stack the deck in your favor, include dialogue starters in your initial messages such as, "This is some initial information. I can send you more details, or is there something specific I can point you to on our website?"

Another tact might be to offer options, such as multiple sources that are available for interviews. "The following information is a good overview of our service, and in addition to the details we have on our site, our director is available for a 10-minute conversation to answer whatever questions you may still have. Do you want to consider an interview after you've had time to review these materials, or would you rather speak to some of our customers?" Journalists are more likely to respond to news announcements if they have easy access to people to interview.

There were a few other tips offered by journalists. PR people should be sure to include their phone numbers with any e-mail that they send. (They should also put it in several places on the website where their press information is.) Any requests for copies of stories should be accompanied with a postal mailing address. And "each PR person should reply PROMPTLY and with alacrity to any e-mailed question from the press."

In the next chapter when you read about PR professionals who are using wireless as a key element of their communication with the media, you will see that many are heavily focused on capitalizing on the quick response capabilities. When it's 30 minutes before deadline on an industry story, either you respond quickly to a reporter's inquiry or your competitors may get the stage to themselves.

Additional Research Shows How Journalists Use the Net and Wireless Technology

While the previous four recommendations address some universal needs of journalists, there is more that you should know about press people and how they are using the Net.

For seven years Don Middleberg, CEO of Middleberg Euro RSCG, and Steven Ross, a journalism professor at Columbia University in New York, have authored an extensive survey of journalists to determine how they are using the Net for their work. Their 2000 *Middleberg/Ross Survey of Media in the Wired World* is based on surveys of more than 500 journalists who work at newspapers, magazines, and broadcast stations nationwide, and it shows a pervasive use of the Web by those who deliver the news.

Some of the findings of this report are:

- Practically every journalist goes online at least once a day to check e-mail and spends an average of 15 hours a week reading and responding to e-mail.
- Together with e-mail, article research is the most popular use of the Internet, with 81 percent of journalists searching online daily for information that they find primarily at organizations' and professional associations' websites.
- About one-third of broadcast journalists are interested in getting audio files from websites, with a smaller percentage interested in getting video files there.
- Journalists use the e-mail as much as they use the phone for conducting interviews with new sources.
- Seventy percent of journalists conduct e-mail or discussion group dialogues with their readers, and about the same percentage use incoming e-mail as a source of story ideas.

What These Research Results Mean for You

I think the most interesting findings of this survey are:

1. While journalists prefer to speak first to all of the interested parties involved in a breaking news story, they will go to an organization's web-

sites as the first source of information if they can't reach a primary source at the organization.

2. Over half of journalists would consider using web chat room or news-group postings as primary or secondary news sources.

3. Nearly half indicate they would consider reporting or spreading a story that started on the Net if it were confirmed by an independent source.

The results of this survey have significant implications for your organization if building relationships with the media is important to you. Journalists use the Web daily for writing news stories, so when they can't reach you on the phone they're going to your website first. If it's difficult to find information, or your press center doesn't have enough details that they need, journalists are either going to your competitors' sites, a discussion group, or to their readers with whom they already have a dialog. What's more, a lot of journalists are going to run with a story if they pull it from a chat room or their e-mail box first as long as they can find a second source to confirm it.

Think about it for a minute. If you're on the West Coast, an entire news story about your company can be birthed, nurtured, and turned loose on the world of online and conventional media before you have time to commute to the office. Someone posts messages on the Web that your organization cheats little old ladies of their life's savings. Three journalists get it, go to your website but can't find anything, so they send out e-mail to 10 grandmas they chat with regularly and find two or three who say, "Yes, that company did it." Two journalists might keep calling you until they can verify the facts, but suppose one doesn't. Next thing you know, you pick up a newspaper and there you are looking mighty bad in the public eye.

Can this happen to you? Let's look at a slice of PR history.

A few years ago, one of the biggest, most expensive PR faux pas came after someone in a newsgroup reported a problem with an Intel PC chip that potentially could have affected only a tiny portion of the PC-using population. Rather than addressing this story while it was still a minor speck on the news landscape, Intel let it grow online to become a bigger-than-life, negative, front-page story in major publications everywhere. It cost $400 million to re-place chips to enable a feature that most people never would have used.

While Intel had crisis control people trying to spin this beast back under control, newspapers like *USA Today* dodged the spin-doctors and went straight to newsgroups to interview people whose quotes ran in the paper. If this can happen to the big and mighty with their legions of PR people, then average organizations should have no doubt that they can suffer the same fate.

The bottom line is, news reporting is becoming an instant communication process that is catching a lot of PR people unprepared. If you are not spending time and resources to beef up your online efforts, you are leaving a big gap in your PR strategy that will result in missed coverage opportunities, or worse, negative press coverage. Wireless has an equal potential to impact news coverage, even though the Middleberg/Ross report shows that only about 10 percent of journalists use mobile devices.

Don Middleberg tells me that over the next year or two wireless technologies will change the way journalists cover the news and work with PR professionals. "What we'll be seeing is a wave of wireless technologies that extend currently available Internet tools. For example, journalists and PR professionals will be able to instant message each other without being shackled to a PC.

"Wireless is the wave of the future. As PDAs become more advanced, more journalists will use them. Communications between journalists and PR professionals will become more instantaneous, continuous, and more transparent. Wireless is just a new iteration of the same techniques we have used all along."

Middleberg believes that, to make the best use of wireless technologies, "PR professionals must find out which journalists are using PDAs and instant messaging and get their buy in, or 'opt in,' to be on your IM list. Then start using wireless to communicate with them. [But] it all starts with relationships; technology is just another tool to strengthen the relationship. High-tech without high-touch is meaningless." This brings us back to editors' earlier comments that you must have good relationships with journalists to begin with before technology can help you.

But even if journalists never increase their use of PDAs, having those within your organization use wireless communication as an extension of your online press efforts is the only way you're going to be able to keep pace with the rapid pace of news reporting. Your success in this endeavor depends heavily on the strength of the information you create on your website, and how effectively you equip and manage the people who will use both the Web and wireless technologies to execute your PR activities.

Building the Foundation for a Winning Online PR Effort—the Online Press Center

There were several additional findings of the Middleberg/Ross survey of which you should be aware. Journalists find that many press centers are underdeveloped and lack much of the information that is useful for their stories. Companies make it difficult to find information, both in press centers and on their websites in general. Even information as simple as phone numbers is difficult to find or doesn't exist. The websites that journalists consider most credible are those of professional associations and nonprofit organizations.

So, while journalists turn to companies' websites first for information, they don't always feel they're getting the complete story. Having an ineffective press center is similar to running a race with your foot in a cast—you can hobble around the track, but you can't compete. Maximizing the impact of your online press efforts requires a lot of attention on what information goes into your press center. There are several ways in which wireless tactics can influence PR, but all of them will directly or indirectly lead journalists back to your site.

The Objectives of the Press Center

When I counsel people on building effective press centers, my goal is for them to give journalists most of the information they will need to either complete a story about a client's organization, or to include useful details about the client in a broader story. Ideally, journalists will contact someone at your company to interview to get additional insights, quotes, and so forth. But if someone is on deadline and they're going to write something without calling you, or just skip you altogether to go to a better site, you do well to make the journalists' lives easier.

In addition to developing content that can result in a complete story about your organization, I recommend that you create supplemental material that makes the press center a valuable industry-related resource that encourages repeat visits. Why do you want to create industry-related content? Because it gives your organization the impression of being an industry leader and people from industry leaders get quoted a lot.

You also want to create an industry-related resource because it will become a one-stop center for journalists to collect materials for a wide range of stories. If a busy reporter can go to one or two websites and get all the background they need, rather than spend hours ferreting around a dozen sites for what they need, more times than not they'll take the first option. And if your site provides most of what a reporter needs for those impressive feature stories, your organization will likely be written about as well. Don't believe me? Let me tell you a little secret.

Faced with a 60-day deadline to crank out 300 pages of researched information, I became the reporter with the deadline from hell. The reason most of the wireless technology companies referenced in this book are here is because their websites had information that enabled me to get the customer stories, industry background, and the contacts I needed to set up interviews. These sites saved me literally days of hunting.

Smaller and midsize vendors fared better than very large technology companies, though quite a few vendors of all sizes never made it into the book because I couldn't decipher from their sites if they should be included. To be fair, the "people" factor caused others that were guaranteed coverage to miss the cut because whomever I contacted was not responsive. Conversely, there were a lot of PR people who were great to work with, and between them and their websites I assembled news I could use.

After developing content that keeps journalists coming back for more, the next objective is to engage them in a dialog with your organization. This is where agencies can really define their role and play a larger, billable role in online PR. In order to engage people in meaningful online conversation, you must have something to say (content), you must have news (it either happens or you make it happen), and you need to use some interactive tools, including wireless wherever possible. Let's start with developing the right content so that your press center has something to say.

I define a good press center as one that has (resources permitting): 1) core information, 2) supporting information, 3) value-added information, and 4) resource information. You may not be able to develop all of this content at once, so these categories are in order of importance—"must have" materials followed by valuable materials to add as soon as you have time.

Core Information

Core information is what enables reporters to write a basic and complete story unaided, or do some basic research to determine if they want to include you in industry stories and the like. This includes press releases, three- or four-paragraph customer stories, a company overview, and primary media contact people.

If your organization produces more than 12 press releases a year, give strong consideration to grouping these releases by topics (e.g., financial news, new products, community service news) and/or categories (e.g., product line one, product line two). A list of press releases only in chronological order is okay if a reporter is looking for details on a recent announcement, but it's fairly frustrating when there are dozens of releases, or when the reporter is doing a story on a particular topic.

The Middleberg/Ross survey reports that over 75 percent of journalists list contact information and search engines as important features they would like to see in press areas. You should categorize your media contact people either by product line, type of news (i.e., financial reports versus product news), or type of media that they serve if you have more than two or three PR people. It's a time killer to chase after a contact name on a website and after two rounds of telephone tag find out that you should have called the other person listed.

It's important to have the e-mail address of your contacts HTML-coded so journalists can click on them and pop up an e-mail form. Having to copy and paste an address isn't going to kill a story, but it's one of those little aggravations that contributes to subconsciously shading a reporter's impression of your organization.

On behalf of the journalism profession, let me vent one of the greatest aggravations about some sites—the lack of a phone numbers for PR contacts. Sometimes it takes a lifetime to find even the main office phone number! We may find 99 percent of what we need on a website, but at some point every good journalist needs to call someone on the phone, either to verify some facts, to clarify some points we don't quite understand, or just to put a human "face" on a story. Why do people make something this simple so difficult to find? You only increase the chances of erroneous details showing up in stories.

For journalists with wireless access, you should make most of this core information available for mobile devices. Press releases should be restricted to the most recent ones, with links older archived releases. Journalists working on breaking news are primarily going to look for the release specific to this story. If news breaks today that involves older products, or something that happened at your company a while ago such as a recall of products sold last year, then you might want to make available last year's releases pertaining to the subject. The wireless version of the company overview should be in condensed form with sections such as our market, our history, and management team written in 90-word blocks.

Supporting Information

Supporting information provides detailed documents that give background details about products, services, customers, and other aspects of your organization. These might be overview documents that explain in more depth how your product works, description of your target markets or competitive advantage, highlights of press coverage about you that reinforces the main messages of your PR campaign, and so on.

The core information should be the bait that answers the key who, what, where, and by whom questions, and your supporting documents should enable reporters to get to the meat of the matter as time allows. Your customer stories for this section should offer a lot more detail about how customers decided to select you, what was involved with getting your product or service to work, and the benefits they are receiving.

Even if reporters don't use this material in their articles exactly as written on the site, a well-written customer story answers a lot of questions a reporter might otherwise call and ask. It also gives them a better understanding of what you do so they can ask better questions in an interview. Aether Systems and AvantGo were two companies I interviewed whose customer stories covered a lot of details in a way that helped make complex topics easier to understand.

Talk to your media contacts who write in-depth news and industry stories and you may find there are other documents that should go into this section (details on your management team or board of directors, background on land management negotiations and regulations or local ordinances that dictate your agency's actions, management negotiations, copies of speeches by senior executives that pertain to topics covered in recent news releases).

Unless reporters are using mobile devices with high-speed connections, you may want to just have pointers to these documents so reporters can access them when they sync their devices. For wireless access use basic text files with minimal graphical enhancements, and consider making them a little shorter.

Value-Added Information

Value-added information are your heavy-duty documents really spells out details on products, your organization, the industry that you're in, or the markets you serve. These can be technology-briefing papers developed by engineers, or guides that help reporters understand and review your products in the context of customers who actually use them. So you minimize the biases that reporters sometime bring to the process.

This section might also include research reports on your customers, scientific and medical studies that support your products, or environmental impact studies that support your political positions. Sometimes this is information that is sequestered away in a section of your site that only personally screened media people can access.

PowerPoint presentations, industry analyst contacts, and other materials that you will use in press tours, press conferences, and other meetings should be included in this section. I've found that press meetings, particularly those on the phone, are easier to manage with everything on a website. PR people don't have to schlepp these materials from coast to coast, you don't get calls for materials from people who missed the meetings, you can better control phone presentations, and you rarely hear, "I didn't get that press kit you said you were going to send."

You can post these materials on pages that are not linked to any of your site's public pages, and then remove the content after a certain amount of time. Even though it's a small hassle, I would duplicate the material and have a URL for the primary media organization you are meeting with (i.e., www. company.com/NYTimes.html). Don't worry about others getting the URL since journalists are protective about their sources of information. Besides, if you don't want the world to know a particular fact, why tell it to a journalist?

From the wireless perspective, giving direct access to many of these large documents makes sense if the journalists have laptops and high-speed wireless modems. Making the presentation materials available is good if journalists have iPAQs or other PDAs with multimedia capabilities, you're willing to graphically neuter your materials, and journalists are willing to look at these on the small screens.

Creating Valuable Resources for Journalists

The resource information section helps you cement your relationships with journalists. Two things are important to make this work. First, the specific content, links, and interactive features have to be developed from the perspective of meeting journalists' needs, not just your wishes. Second, this content has to change frequently to continue to be relevant and compelling to reporters.

Based on what topics are covered by the reporters, who are likely to write about (or who you want to write about), your organization, consider posting an "idea generator." You might ask, "Are you writing about or planning to write about the following topics? We have executives and customers who can provide you with valuable background information." If you make boating supplies, some of the topics might be "boating safety laws the legislature will vote on next week," "favorite boating locations for new boat owners," or "new boat engine technology that reduces pollution."

The idea is to think of topics that are current, certain to be of interest to the journalists whom you want to reach, and something that someone in your organization or a customer can speak about with clarity. This information can be available for wireless access or pushed wirelessly to reporters' mobile devices.

A resource section can include trend reports written by your staff or other organizations, such as industry research firms. Post ongoing research on your website or distribute the information at trade shows. You can convert this material into a "Report of the Week" section, or make arrangements with other sites (i.e., a professional association) to conduct the surveys and let you publish their results. Have links to analysis reports written by customers or industry leaders that address trends, new technologies, market attitudes, and so forth.

There may be a wealth of information that you can provide links to that make a reporter's life easier. Just get into their head or recall questions they have asked in the past, pretend you're writing the type of story that you want to be included in, then go on the Web and do the research. When you find sites that have value, link to them.

It may take a lot of work initially, but these links should be easy to maintain and enhance (you don't want reporters going to dead links.) Don't worry about sending editors away from your site once they get there. If you make the resources valuable enough, journalists will bookmark the site and become frequent visitors. Provide the same URLs to mobile devices if they can easily access these pages.

As technology becomes available for searching content wirelessly, put it to work for you if there are a lot of documents in your resource section. Also, if wireless-only content becomes popular and you find information that may be valuable to reporters, add this to your list of links.

Develop Thematic Resources with a pcAnywhere, Anytime Twist

Another option to consider is what I call the "thematic" resource, such as the one I mentioned earlier that we developed for Symantec. One of their products is pcAnywhere software that enables mobile users to access their desktops through a laptop modem when they're in different locations. Since journalists who cover Symantec often travel to conferences and trade shows, they use laptops when mobile, and they need information that can be difficult to find when they're on the road, we decided to centralize some of this information.

We gathered details such as per minute phone charges in the leading hotels in the cities most frequently visited for technology trade shows (hotels didn't always post room phone rates) and good restaurants for quiet interviews. Most reporters at his time used CompuServe and AOL for e-mail, but trying to find out the local access number was very difficult, so we gave them a list of numbers for these cities. Reporters picked up these and other details on the Web before they left their offices.

In this case for Symantec, the resource is valuable to journalists in it's own right without having anything to do with covering the news or researching background material. It benefited Symantec in two ways: It increased the company's popularity with journalists, and it subtly reinforced the brand image of pcAnywhere as a mobile user application.

Your PR team may think of dozens of possibilities for a thematic resource. If possible, add wireless access to these resources. For example, the Merriam-Webster dictionary folks could create a journalist style sheet that's wirelessly accessible for reporters who are writing stories while away from the office. The Internal Revenue Service could create a tax-filing guide specifically for free-lance writers since they have tax calculations and filing procedures that may be more difficult than those of publications' staff writers.

Perhaps it's possible to make wireless access a resource in its own right. For example, at trade shows reporters file stories, research details on compa-nies, or meet with companies to verify information. A wireless LAN or a WideRay Jack in your booth can provide access to help journalists accomplish these tasks. The wireless LAN will enable journalists to get to your press center or the rest of the Net, while the Jack only provides access to information that you load on the device. Both technologies are particularly helpful if reporters show up at the booth looking for information when your executives and PR people are unavailable.

Interactive Features That Build a Dialogue with Journalists

Include in your press center's resource area interactive features that help you build and maintain a dialog with journalists. You can have these in several places within your press center. The simplest forms of dialog facilitators are e-mail links that ask reporters to "click here for more information." Some sites have forms that let journalists sign up to receive news releases and other infor-mation about specific topics.

These are good first steps, but to be truly interactive, you must give peo-ple a reason to want to talk to you, and you have to respond with useful infor-mation. For example, if you e-mail a press release about a new service, don't ask, "Hey, did you get my release?" To start a dialog, ask, "What do you think about this product?" "Is this product something that in your estimation will be popular with customers?" "We don't think we have any competitors, but what do you see in the market?"

For decades organizations have launched campaigns to push materials and spin events to try to get favorable press coverage. But in the midst of all this pushing and spinning, the really successful PR pros ask journalists ques-tions, get their take on the issues at hand, and then respond in a meaningful way to both reporters and organizations. Sometimes a conversation produces some coverage, other times it sets the stage or strengthens the relationship in a way that leads to a future story.

In addition to e-mail, organizations are using web broadcasts for special announcements to facilitate dialog. With streaming audio technology from companies such as RealNetworks (www.real.com), executives from their offices can deliver audio presentations over the Net, which are received by journalists through their web browsers. A variation is "auditorium software" from companies such as Placeware (www.placeware.com), which creates virtual auditoriums on the Web where journalists can gather for presentations that can include audio and PowerPoint slides.

Both of these technologies facilitate dialog with journalists because they are convenient for companies and the press (you can schedule several meetings a day and never leave your office), and they enable two-way real-time communication. If you have this technology set up on your servers, you can respond immediately to any news situation, and you have the flexibility to conduct one-on-one or group meetings.

The promise of the Web is that it will enable you to have unprecedented two-way communication with various audiences, so use it to initiate and maintain your dialog with the media. Use wireless to coordinate your executives and PR teams so the right messages and materials are being communicated through the Web, even when you need to respond to breaking news within hours, if not minutes.

You should be encouraging your PR staff and agencies to use technology tools to facilitate and manage a dialog with the media both to meet short-term needs and maintain long-term relationships. But there are executives who only care about getting more news coverage "right now," so they don't create a favorable client or provide the resources necessary to enable these technologies to be brought into play. In reality, it is in the best interest of your organization to focus on the tech tools that help you build the relationships because ultimately those with the strongest relationships will tend to have more frequent and more positive coverage.

This brings us to the "people" issue of online PR. Having the best press center and the most effective technology gives you the potential to do great PR. But it is the people who are involved in the execution of your PR campaigns who will turn that potential into reality.

Executives, Managers, and Staff Hold the Key for Online PR Success

I ask PR and marketing communications people in my online PR seminars what they think are the reasons why so many websites are not great PR tools. The feedback I get from people frustrated with their own organizations' efforts indicates that their managers or higher-ranking senior executives don't really understand the Internet and its capabilities. I agree wholeheartedly with this observation since I have called more than a few managers and executives over the years to talk to them about online PR.

Because of this lack of understanding, the PR people in the trenches don't get the support, guidance, and resources they need to create effective content for journalists. Also, if top management doesn't care, the troops aren't motivated to take the initiative online because performance evaluations don't depend on it.

Another factor contributing to press centers' poor performance is that PR as a business operation is undervalued in some organizations. When sales are booming, other business and marketing activities get the lion's share of the praise, when economic times are bad, PR is often one of the first areas hit with budget cuts.

Other feedback I've received from session attendees indicate that the politics of the Web in their organizations is such that content is dictated by people on a web team who don't understand the Net's potential to enhance PR. When you're up to your elbows in press releases, meetings, and deadlines, it's hard to siphon off time to lead an educational campaign to get others inside the organization to see the light.

Then there is the PR agency factor. Many PR people I have called to gage their need for online PR immediately deferred to their agencies who seemed less than enthusiastic about the possibilities. Though few people come right out and say it, I get the feeling that some (definitely not all) agencies view an interactive online press center that helps journalists write stories about their clients as a threat that will take away billing opportunities.

The problem here is that these firms' senior executives can't push past the fear of losing billable hours to see that a full-featured press center (that they manage) opens up new billing opportunities and a way to increase client retention. Either that or the agency people are put into the same straitjacket as in-house PR people because clients' senior management teams don't see the value of online PR. One very positive development I see happening is that agency people seem to be adopting mobile wireless devices rather quickly, which will be very helpful for executing tactics such as I will describe shortly.

If any of these scenarios reflect the situation at your organization, you have to take the lead to break everyone out of this box by showing them how proper use of the Net results in better journalist relationships that, in turn, produce more media coverage. Here are some steps to take down that path.

First, web and wireless technologies combined will produce the ultimate

PR tool for good PR people in this new millennium. However, as a senior executive you have to believe in the value of PR and be willing to commit the resources necessary for its success. Effective online PR requires a lot of effort (though not always a lot of money) and without your strong commitment to PR in general and online PR in particular, the spirit may be willing, but the online efforts and results will be weak.

Second, you must be willing to step in and take an active role in the way your organization or agency executes PR campaigns. You have to be a member of the planning team and where possible, a participant in the campaigns themselves. Without this willingness backed up with action, you will doom your online PR to perpetual mediocrity. Besides resources, your PR people often need a motivator and a visionary to set a plan in motion, and political clout within the organization to remove bottlenecks created by other departments.

I read in a recent issue of *Technology Marketing Magazine* that, because the Web is the source of a lot of nasty turf wars, senior executives are abdicating responsibility for stepping in and making decisions that are in their organizations' best interests. Sorry, but you cannot and must not do the Oscar Ostrich drill, and bury your head in the sand. PR is too important a competitive tool.

Third, you must define the role of your PR agency in your online effort, not wait for them to take the initiative. To start, make it crystal clear that a press room or press center on your website is not just a posting board for press releases. This is going to be the tool that makes the reporter's job of covering your organization easier and more productive, AND the means by which you are going to engage that reporter in an active dialogue.

Get Your People to Understand the Value of Web and Wireless Technology

In many respects, the success of any wireless tactic begins with a battle for the minds and hearts of the people involved with incorporating the technology with your PR efforts. Both managers and staff have to know and understand the capabilities of the web and wireless technologies.

I will assume that most of your PR staff uses the Web, but have they really looked at how sites are using press centers, chat rooms, and pop-up screens that permit someone within the organization to chat directly with someone on a particular page? Without first-hand experience, none of the potential of this technology is real in people's minds.

The same holds true for wireless. Unless managers, those at the vice president level in particular, use mobile devices, they will not understand how the technology can impact PR campaigns. Until the light bulb blinks on in people's minds, there will not be the vision that has to come from the top down to make web and wireless technology a key part of PR operations.

Until senior partners at PR agencies understand the full capabilities of these technologies, they cannot adequately articulate to clients the need and benefit of using them. Wireless is something new, which means clients have to take a little risk to test the water, so agency folks sometimes have to cajole, coerce, and (within reason) sometimes jump up and down in clients' faces.

Here are some press centers you should look at to get an idea of how others are creating valuable content for journalists. My firm worked with Symantec, for one, in 1995 to create one of the first Web press centers, and since then, the company has constantly evolved this area in order to meet their needs and the changing needs of the media (www.symantec.com/PressCenter/index.html).

Another former client is KnowledgePoint. They are a much smaller company, but they have a pretty complete center for their needs (www.knowledgepoint.com). BellSouth (not a client) has a good pressroom also, including a search engine and a good layout for their directory of media contacts (www.bellsouthcorp.com). There will be links to other well-developed press centers in the online supplement.

Once you help expand people's personal understanding of where they can go with this technology, it's time to explore with them what wireless tools they are going to need to marry with content to take online PR to its next level.

Get Executives to Lead by Example

As I mentioned earlier, if you want your PR staff and agency to really use the web and wireless technology for all it's worth, senior executives have to roll up their sleeves, get in the trenches, and become an active participant in your online PR activities. Not only is this good for inspiring the troops, you give your PR efforts an extra boost. The most important resources you can offer to journalists are your executives as credible spokespeople who have a grasp of issues within your industry as well as within your organization.

Let's assume your business produces construction materials and one of your PR goals is to become recognized as an industry leader. To reach this goal, build a resource area in your press center and fill it to the brim with construction industry reports, new trends in developing safer building materials, and the like. Also add a form that asks reporters for details such as what type of industry news they cover, what expertise they expect from their contacts, how they like to receive news information, and if they use wireless mobile devices.

Based on the feedback, set up a rapid response system that uses wireless and web technology to link your key executives, PR people, your agency, and a database of press contact data. Get a service such as PR Newswire's *eWatch* (www.prnewswire.com) or *Cyber Alert* (www.cyberalert.com) to send your PR people e-mail and wireless media announcements or news alerts on construction topics that journalists' feedback says is important.

When an important news item hits, your PR people should draft a response that is passed to the appropriate executive (also equipped with a wireless device) to review, edit if necessary, and pass back to PR for distribution to the press. Your PR team also should have a web template in place that allows them to directly post pages with these executive responses to the press center's resource section.

Once you have a final response, turn it around and send it to appropriate reporters wirelessly or by whatever other means they wish. In the meantime, your team should be assembling materials from web searches, calls to customers, or other sources in order to assemble a briefing section in the resource section that supports your response. Then send an alert to the press telling them about the new content, and include a link in this e-mail to the material in the press center.

This entire sequence of events can happen within an hour for routine news items, especially if you work like the daily newspapers and have certain boilerplate content already written, which is possible when you select topics ahead of time for the news alerts. It's also possible to have rapid responses for competitors' announcements (if you already track their news activities) and for ongoing news such as laws working through a city or state legislature that will impact your industry.

The scenario I presented is just the tip of the iceberg of possibilities. You could also incorporate chat rooms for group or individual real-time briefings with executives, or wireless IM technology for interviews when your executives and PR people are scattered across the map. With the increase of bandwidth and multimedia features on mobile devices, one day you should be able to deliver audio and video clips of executives as part of the response.

As you effectively execute one or two of these rapid response activities, your reputation as "the organization to call when you need facts in a hurry" will grow, and should lead to more proactive efforts by reporters to contact you when hot news breaks. At the very least, you should start to see an increase in the number of articles in which your organization is mentioned or quoted. Also, the active participation of executives gives PR people an added measure of motivation to push the technology envelope even further.

Give People the Tools They Need

You will maximum the advantages that wireless technology gives your PR team with two steps: Wireless-enable the people and wireless-enable the environments in which they work. I'm going to wrap up this chapter with examples of the latter. The next chapter is a discussion with various in-house and agency PR professionals who provide examples of how a wireless-enabled PR staff is a more effective staff.

Angelique Faul, general manager of the San Carlos, California office of Evans Partners PR agency (www.evanspartners.com) describes the impact wireless LANs have had on her firm. "Wireless LANs make us more efficient because our entire mobile PR staff can 'office hop' between our two offices (San Carlos and Santa Cruz) and still easily connect to the network."

Before installing the wireless LAN, the previous network could not efficiently support the two offices and 15 employees working as teams. There was also a lot of downtime due to computer problems, modems that had to be constantly configured, and slow dial-up connections between offices, adding up to several hours of lost employee productivity each day. Also, the firm was losing money because they could not bill clients for the time they weren't working.

"Now we can stay on top of client e-mail, share documents, and generally provide the highest level of service since we are never out of touch. For example, we can log onto the network from one office in the morning to work with a journalist on a story, then head to a meeting near our other office. After that we can drop by that office to log on and provide the journalist with the rest of the information they need before a deadline."

The wireless LAN is fast, dependable, and doesn't require go through all of those dial-up procedures. "We are more efficient and bill our clients for a full day of work. Since we lease our wireless LAN, hardware, software, and tech support from a service company called CenterBeam (www.centerbeam.com), we are billed monthly. The bill pretty much pays for itself since we are working almost 100 percent without downtime."

The office isn't the only environment in which you can introduce wireless tools for PR purposes. According to Hugh Scholey, account supervisor at the public relations agency High Road Communications (www.highroad.com), having good web content is important, but so is having wireless access for journalists.

"When I'm at a press conference there are often two journalists I have to think about, the one at the event and one in the newsroom who is helping do research for the story. I can provide materials on a website that benefits the reporters in newsrooms. If wireless access in the conference room can save reporters an extra 10 minutes because they don't have to log in, or the lines are down, they will file their part of the story faster, and this helps your organization.

"Many reporters today, even broadcast journalists, write articles for their websites, which speeds up the once-a-day or weekly deadline to several deadlines per day. They have to file story by 2:00 P.M. to be posted by 4:00 P.M. So as a result, journalists will appreciate PR people who help them make that deadline."

If a press meeting is at your offices where you have wireless LANs or at a meeting room in a facility that has wireless access, the decision to provide access to reporters is a fairly easy one. Stories are more frequent these days about the increase of wireless LANs in public places such as hotels and restaurants, as well as the increasing number of laptops coming standard with wireless modems.

But what if wireless LANs aren't in place? Should you go through the expense of bringing one in just for one meeting or press conference? Maybe not, but if you're in the location of a disaster that will require you meet frequently with the press for several days or weeks, bringing in wireless might be a good idea if the cabling can be put in place without too much trouble. Or you can push materials from the home office to reporters' wireless devices or laptops.

Another environment in which your PR people may be working is at trade shows where you have lots of press meetings, many of which are unscheduled "drop-by's." This is a situation in which a WideRay Jack can help enable you to have the entire collection of press materials available to your staff to facilitate their presentations or beam the materials directly to journalists' mobile devices. The home office can also beam important information to the Jacks that can support PR people, executives, and your press contacts.

After you address the work environmental issues, then you have to look at how you equip your PR staff to meet the wireless challenges. That brings us to Chapter 13.

Public Relations Roundtable: The Impact of Wireless on the Public Relations Profession

Having taken on the role of reporter for this book project, I decided to do as some other journalists have done, and conducted a roundtable interview via e-mail. I asked a combination of in-house and agency PR professionals for their insights and recommendations on the use of wireless technology for media relations, investor relations, and crisis management.

Representing the agency side were Evans Partners' Angelique Faul; Eric Kreller of Eric Mower and Associates (www.mower.com); and Jason Teitler, senior vice president, global interactive practice leader at Porter Novelli (www.porternovelli.com).

In-house public relations executives included Arley Baker, director of corporate communication for the ISP EarthLink; Teresa Moore, director, engineering public affairs at UC Berkeley; Paula Chase-Hyman, public relations manager at Aether Systems; and Associate Professor David W. Guth of the University of Kansas's School of Journalism and Mass Communications (www. ku.edu/~jschool). Professor Guth is co-author of *Public Relations, A Values-Driven Approach,* published by Allan and Bacon.

My first question was to inquire how these organizations are using wireless technology to improve their media relationship building.

BAKER:

Managers on up through the ranks to senior executives use RIM Black-Berries, Motorola T900 Talkabout two-way pagers and Palm Pilots. People are encouraged and expected to not only be accessible, but also really understand how these devices impact or enhance their productivity. I'm getting urgent alerts and news updates from my people no matter where I am, and that convenience really minimizes surprises.

TEITLER:

Public relations professionals at Porter Novelli are beginning to use wireless devices more and more to increase accessibility with clients, media, and each other. It has become critical to provide clients with additional methods for collaboration outside of the 'fixed' workstation world. These tools are invaluable since any delay can have a huge impact in our business and our client's business.

Wireless devices allow us to travel and connect for almost any situation. For instance, I provide my clients, colleagues, and media contacts with my two-way pager e-mail address, which allows them to contact me the moment a question requires answering, if copy or budgets need approval, or calendars need to be checked. I can get back to them while in another meeting, navigating through an airport or after hours.

CHASE-HYMAN:

Members of our PR Department are issued RIM BlackBerries so we can access e-mail, contacts, and scheduling information. We stay in contact with key reporters, key executive spokespersons and they with us as we have 24-hour access to our contact information.

The devices help us to field media inquiries, pass them to the appropriate contacts whether we are in the office, at a trade show, press conference, or wherever. I do just as much work at a trade show as I do back in the office because of the BlackBerry. Using it ensures that we are able to get back to a journalist or at least get the ball rolling on their inquiry immediately. It cuts a great deal of time out of the process.

I have fielded early morning or late evening inquiries from a reporter in London or on the West Coast. There is often a high chance of that opportunity slipping through the cracks due to the time difference, but I'm able to answer such inquiries from home or en route to the office. I can then e-mail the spokesperson and get open slots for potential interviews. By the time I get into the office the next day, an interview is set up and ready to go.

SETTLES:

How do you see wireless technology improving PR professionals' ability to strengthen journalist relationships, increase media coverage, and operate more efficiently?

BAKER:

Many of today's journalists set their own work schedules and it's very assuring to them that we will be responsive to their needs if we respond to an e-mail request within minutes, even if it happens to be from the back of a cab in New York City. Once they have that acknowledgement, they can continue with their outreach to other contacts knowing that we'll circle back with them in due time with the info or the interview they are requesting.

As someone who gets 100 to 200 e-mails a day, I also cannot tell you how nice it is to not spend a couple hours sifting through those e-mails on my office PC or my laptop after a full day of being out of the office. And I haven't held anything up just because I was away from my PC! That's a big perk for PR professionals who are always on call.

TEITLER:

Introducing more opportunities for 'real-time' communications will strengthen relationships between PR professionals and the media over-all, which will help develop even tighter partnerships with clients and a more solid reputation with media. Tighter partnerships with clients re-sult in quicker responses to the media, leading to more inquiries due to the reliability factor. Therefore, less time is invested in communications for a particular activity while overall communications will increase as a result of expanded availability. This will, in most cases, lead to in-creased media coverage.

CHASE-HYMAN:

Journalists require and appreciate prompt response to inquiries—wireless access to PIM functionality ensures you can provide just that. You are much more likely to check your e-mail pager from home or en route to the office than you are voice mail messages.

I can see auto billing solutions for agency pros allowing account execs to bill their time back to the office system immediately after a meeting or event to make sure the time is logged correctly. Wireless access to Bacons, services such as Vocus [www.vocus.com] which maintains press databases, recent contacts with journalists, editorial calendars etc., or other resources would also be ideal. The ability to ac-cess this information while away from the office could enhance produc-tivity of client meetings and brainstorming sessions.

FAUL:

The ability to connect from pretty much anywhere at a fast bps clip is by definition extremely efficient. Everyone knows that being fast to re-spond to journalist inquiries frequently means the difference between getting coverage for your client or company and not, so wireless e-mail is truly a killer application for PR professionals.

MOORE:

[The biggest benefit wireless offers is] speed. Part of the challenge when working in a university environment with media is tracking down the person you want to hook up with a reporter. They are often off campus, out of the country, etc. With wireless they can be easily reached and interviews set up more expeditiously. Obviously, when you make a reporter happy, the relationship improves.

KRELLER:

Creating and maintaining reciprocal relationships with the media and the community is what an effective public relations professional has to do. Wireless technology makes you available. When you're the information provider between the client and the media, you have to be accessible—it can literally make or break a story. Wireless technology can also keep you connected to information through the Internet, e-mail, and text messaging.

Using a wireless device helps the PR person make interviews, photo shoots, press conferences, and events run as smooth as possible. They can add to your credibility and effectiveness in the eyes of the media and community by providing you with the correct information that you can then pass onto everyone else. This all adds up to a wireless device helping you to build a good reputation.

GUTH:

Efficiency is another major bonus of wireless. It extends the reach of the public relations function beyond the office walls. Especially in smaller operations, the practitioner is too often tied to the home office because of technology. In organizations where there are a lot of satellite operations, getting out of the office and "showing the flag" is a good thing. It also allows the practitioner to travel more with the CEO and other executives. That, in turn, makes it easier for practitioners to take on the role of a counselor.

SETTLES:

Do you see wireless playing a role in investor relations?

BAKER:

It's convenient, sure. It makes it easier for our IR team to serve our CFO and senior management. And I think that convenience is going to grow for everyone as applications for opening attachments like Excel spread sheets or Acrobat files from investment institutions become more prevalent on PDAs and other wireless devices.

TEITLER:

Absolutely. Wireless communications allow all sorts of audiences to keep stronger tabs on financial health, act on decisions in a quicker manner, and respond to issues in a more timely fashion. With public relations solutions it has become paramount to be able to communicate quickly and to carry-out research in an instant to counsel clients who may need to react to situations related to earnings announcements, IPO intricacies, and merger propositions.

Wireless technologies allow us to move as quickly as the market does, which permits us to deliver time-sensitive counsel and materials despite geography and time zones.

CHASE-HYMAN:

I see wireless playing a role in a large variety of markets. Eventually there will be specific wireless applications for PR/IR and other marketing roles. For now, e-mail, Internet and PIM [personal information management] functionality serve almost any space immediately.

FAUL:

Yes. The ability to deliver breaking news to investors, no matter where they are, could be a major advantage. Most likely, this would be in the form of an on-demand service in which investors could sign up for anytime, anywhere investment information.

KRELLER:

Because investor relations is all about reaching current and potential shareholders, wireless communication offers a unique opportunity to do so, and it will probably be used a lot more creatively in the future. There are hundreds of existing companies providing Internet investor and public relations services, and the market is so saturated that these days it takes much more to disseminate your message to the masses.

By reversing the approach and targeting a smaller group of people—even one specific potential shareholder—and connecting them all through personal wireless devices, this would allow for a constant flow of information. Using wireless technology, groups of investors can maintain constant contact with each other and the company.

GUTH:

I do, and for many of the same reasons cited previously. Rapid response to changing situations can be the difference between success and failure. In today's "all news all the time" environment, companies must be able to respond to events that could cause a sudden shift in stock prices.

SETTLES:

What type of scenarios do you see for using wireless technology to manage crisis communication?

GUTH:

Organizations are most vulnerable during the period between the onset of the crisis and the time required to put in place the resources necessary to respond. This often involves waiting for people to travel from significant distances. In today's media environment, you can't afford to have key people out of touch for long periods of time. Wireless communications allow these key people to begin managing the crisis while they are still in transit.

At a time when crises strike at the speed of light, wireless communications offer practitioners two things they need most—speed and mobility. Speed is important because there is a limited window of opportunity when the public sits back during crises and reserves judgment. Any time one can save in pulling the elements of a response together is extremely valuable.

Mobility is important because it is often best to direct the crisis response from the point of action. Remember how much grief the CEO of Exxon received for not traveling to Valdez, Alaska? His excuse was that he had all the communications capabilities he needed in New York. While that may have been true, his absence from the scene was, from a public relations standpoint, disastrous.

CHASE-HYMAN:

Crisis communication requires quick and immediate reaction—wireless access to key information facilitates that. I envision press conferences being pulled together using only a wireless device. Accessing press contacts and key company executives via an e-mail blast are all ways to pull the appropriate people together for an emergency press conference.

These tools will not take the place of the PC—but allows PR professionals to get a jump-start on certain initiatives. Using a wireless device means bringing all the key people up to speed without calling a conference and without tipping your hand until everyone is ready to relay the message.

BAKER:

Assume we've had a network outage and I'm on a media tour. My support team can draft the necessary talking points (what happened, where, and for how long) and e-mail them to me so I'm briefed and ready to talk to the media. I don't have to sit on the phone and take notes that I will later have to transcribe into a word processing program.

All the information is in the palm of my hand and can be edited, cut-and-pasted, and forwarded. It's also a great convenience to receive documents on my BlackBerry and then forward them to the most convenient e-mail location around me (say, the Kinko's on the corner or the hotel concierge) where I can have the documents opened and printed.

It's easy to think of similar scenarios when news events happen that need to be conveyed to senior executives as they travel. Five years ago, they'd have to hear it on a phone call or through a fax or e-mail to their laptop. We'd be trying our hardest to get the information to them in writing so they can digest it. Getting the download of key details over the phone takes time and you're unsure of the notes they are taking. It's a distraction, for a senior executive whose mind is operating on many different fronts.

TEITLER:

Standard electronic communication processes and resources such as e-mail and Web monitoring will be supplemented with remote access, thanks to BlackBerry and other wireless tools. This allows public relations professionals to work with clients and media almost at the moment that a crisis or issue presents itself.

In some cases, public relations professionals can pinpoint potential issues and crisis by monitoring online forums and media, clip the statement, and proactively forward it to a client with recommendations on how to handle the situation including collaboration with the media.

In other cases, when reactive tactics require implementation, review processes can be more efficiently expedited. For instance, if a response to a claim that can potentially damage a brand is required for posting onto a Web site or for forwarding to the media, editing can take place while certain parties are in transit. This saves valuable seconds and, perhaps softens the blow or even prevents damage.

Likewise opportunities with extremely tight deadlines can be taken advantage of now that communications are not dependent on being grounded in a specific location for communications access.

MOORE:

A major benefit of wireless is just being able to react quickly to get to the people you have to reach to get the answers you need. It's also beneficial for transmitting critical information or updates to stakeholders, the media, or others. You may be able to assemble groups of people to conference and strategize who may be far apart and not reachable any other way. When dealing with crises, timing is everything.

KRELLER:

I envision a crisis happening with the PR person in complete control; establishing a "home base" for the company and it's spokesperson; and then contacting the media to let them know—and all with a wireless device. E-mails can be answered and constructed, speeches can be written, message points can be constructed, and then sent to all involved by a wireless device.

Web-based teleconferences can be produced; transcripts and press releases can be sent via text messaging and pager; and Palm Pilots can be utilized to access and send important e-mail, as well as beam information from one Pilot to another. Electronic address books make contact information simple to access in emergency situations.

SETTLES:

Have journalists given you any indications how they are using, or might use, wireless technology to do their jobs?

BAKER:

Sure, but keep in mind that a lot of the media we deal with regarding wireless e-mail and Internet access are technology reporters. I do know some tech reporters who now leave their laptops at home and travel to shows and conferences with only a RIM BlackBerry (because they have access to a PC in the media center).

For media people who don't cover technology, wireless adoption depends a lot on the individual's comfort level with technology. I would, however, expect that media will gravitate to wireless devices quicker than consumers at large, since these enabling devices are another way for reporters to communicate on their own terms. It all comes down to a reporter's preference or perception of their necessary level of connectedness.

Keep in mind that PR people and reporters focus on shadowing movers, shakers, and newsmakers. How effective can you be at doing that if your client or the subject of your article cannot reach you because of communication barriers? It's no stretch of the imagination to see how wireless communication could help break a big investigative story by enabling reporters to research and collaborate with each other.

What's especially valuable is a seamless connection to your primary e-mail address. That takes the guesswork out of trying to remember someone's pager number or mobile e-mail address. In the near future, most people will deem their e-mail address more vital than their phone number—and that certainly holds true right now in my PR team's working environment.

TEITLER:

Journalists in high-tech friendly geographies such as the United States, Asia, and Europe, have embraced Net technologies to perform brand and organization research, communicate with a multitude of audiences, and exercise new methods of publishing formats. But wireless devices are conspicuously absent at this time.

As more journalists rely on online news bureaus and news alert systems established by brands and public relations firms, they will have access to news delivered directly to the e-mail address of their two-way pagers and PDAs. As more online tools and resources become available, journalists will adopt more wireless devices and applications to become more efficient.

CHASE-HYMAN:

Currently, many journalists stay in touch with their contact and personal e-mail information via wireless means. For most it is their own PDA linked to their personal e-mail. I've seen no evidence that the actual media outlets are investing in the infrastructure or hardware to equip journalists with corporate e-mail and Internet access via a wireless device.

FAUL:

At a minimum, we see journalists scheduling their interviews, and even downloading information about an interviewee before an interview. This could expand to filing stories more efficiently, collaborating with other writers and editors from anywhere, and so on.

MOORE:

I don't see journalists at this time using wireless devices. But quite frankly, when I surveyed journalists five or six years ago about getting news releases by e-mail most said no. Now look at the situation. E-mail is all they want. So I don't think what's the norm today is really relevant to what we will be doing tomorrow.

GUTH:

They cherish the ability to access and transmit information while on the run. In a business where every minute brings a new deadline, wireless communication is a godsend. We have also seen examples of where journalists get wireless communications just to circumvent attempts to either manipulate or censor stories.

One thing journalists need to worry about is letting the technology get in the way. In their rush to demonstrate a competitive advantage, news organizations have been known to let the technology dictate their coverage. Too often we see live remote reports on subjects not worthy of the treatment. Journalists need to ask themselves whether they are covering something "live" because the event merits it, or because the technology allows them to do it.

Seize the Moment

In early 1994, I took my client Don Campbell on a press tour to show off a new version of his company's OnTime group scheduling program. To demonstrate one of the new product features, we scheduled wireless alerts for each meeting that was sent to us on alphanumeric pagers.

Besides helping to keep Don and me on schedule, this wireless capability allowed us to have a senior tech person available in case an editor needed some detailed technical information, but without bringing him along or keeping him tied up waiting by the phone. By receiving the alerts, he knew when we might need him and he could be easily reached if we actually needed him. It also was a convenient way for our offices to send us updates and answers to questions while we were on the road.

It's likely that the journalists that you work with will be a little slow at adapting wireless technology, but wireless will still play an important role in operational issues that affect your PR efforts. Don and I didn't consider ourselves wireless pioneers in 1994. We weren't even aware of the Net. However, when someone showed us the technology, we seized the opportunity to make the press tour run a little more smoothly.

After speaking with PR professionals and reading about how they are using wireless today, even with some of its rough edges and limitations, I'm more convinced than ever that those who seize the moment will help their clients and agencies prosper. I find it encouraging that some PR people understand the potential of wireless technology more than others understand how to use the Web that's been with us for several years.

Both agency and in-house PR people have demanding bosses, senior executives who are constantly in motion around the office and around the world, and a press audience that feels more under siege as economic and business dynamics change. Meetings, travel, and more meetings are the staple of business life. In this crazed environment, wireless mobile devices give PR staff the ability to better manage your people who meet the press.

Client (and executive) management, particularly in times of crises or important breaking news, is much easier when you have everyone tied in wirelessly. The Web has opened the world to instant communication, which exposes your organization to new and often significant opportunities and potential pitfalls. The line between opportunity and pitfall is a wireless one, and one that your PR people should have well in hand.

It's not good enough to just give your PR people and top executives mobile devices. You must have a plan. Look closely at how the PR executives in this roundtable envisioned wireless being used in investor relations and crisis management. These scenarios are possible only with careful planning, and even rehearsals, for how you will communicate, strategize, and respond to the press with a unified consistent message when executives are in different locations. Good technology poorly applied is bad news.

Another message subtly stated by several people in the roundtable is that close monitoring of news and Internet sources will keep you ahead of the curve so that you do less dodging of the pitfalls, and more exploiting of the opportunities. With the exception of natural and manmade disasters, you can avoid a lot of bad press by having early warning systems in which your PR staff uncovers issues before they become problems and channels them to the right executives for quick resolution.

Of equal importance, this type of wireless implementation positions you to discover fresh opportunities to stay in front of editors with news they can use. A competitor announces a new service, you counter with stories about customers who already receive this service from you. Someone announces a new medical breakthrough, you respond with how this will enhance the services your organization provides to the community. Again, planning is the key, along with an aggressive willingness to use the technology at hand.

Of course, there is the equal obligation that PR professionals have to the press community. It's true that PR people are often in the middle of a tug of war between their company's or clients' needs and journalists' demands. This often uncomfortable position can be converted to a position of strength by using wireless technology to make sure journalists get the information they want in a timely fashion, and also by staying ahead of their needs.

Following the plan I outlined in the previous chapter for an online press center, with the first rule being to walk a mile in the shoes of your journalists contacts, you should know what's important to them. So when the PR staff is monitoring news sources, they can spot items of interest, send the information to clients for their comments, and combine these with other important materials and deliver a useful package of information to journalists as soon as possible.

This process is valuable even if the delivery channel to the press isn't wireless. Journalists don't like to get scooped, so once they see what you're doing with wireless they'll be faster to adopt the technology, which plays in your favor because you will already have mastered this wireless beast.

I'll close this discussion with a story from across the pond (Atlantic Ocean) about how Procter & Gamble seized on wireless technology to tackle one of those bugaboos of the PR profession, getting meaningful face time with journalists at a trade show.

Make Me Beautiful, Baby!

At a cosmetic trade show that lasted several days in Bologna, Italy, Procter & Gamble wanted to draw the attention of journalists and top cosmetic industry figures to several of their products under the Max Factor, Pantene, Oil of Olay, and Noxzema brands. Hiugo hired hostesses to walk through the trade show crowds carrying mobile devices. They picked out journalists and asked them if they wanted to create a profile of their makeup or hair care needs.

Depending on the type of profiles that were created, journalists would get an appointment for a makeover from a beauty consultant at the P&G booth. The booking information was sent to journalists' mobile phones and P&G's PR staff sent wireless reminder alerts about the appointments or about other events at the show.

As a result of this effort, all of the appointment slots were filled for each of the product lines, which equaled 200 appointments per day. This project cost about $10,000, including personnel, set up, etc., and proved to be very useful and cost effective. L'Oreal is P&G's main competitor in the cosmetics arena, but they have a larger product line and were spending more money than P&G's in this space, so there was no interest in trying to match L'Oreal's expenditures.

You may have many a trade show where it is very difficult to catch journalists' attention when competitors have all the big bucks to throw lavish press parties. Develop a promotion to get journalists to opt in wirelessly to some event at the show. Luckily journalists at these shows are tagged so you can spot them in a crowd. Send very targeted messages to foster interaction before and during the show, though you should focus on e-mail and Web-focused contact activities before the show until more journalists have mobile devices with Net access.

I expect that the organizations running trade shows will create wireless access points within the press lounges at these events and on the show floors so journalists with laptops and wireless LAN cards will be able to file stories from anywhere. Keeps tabs on this since you want to be ready to take advantage of this opportunity to communicate with journalists when it presents itself.

You can modify this tactic used by P&G by having your staff use mobile devices to circulate on the show floor to conduct short surveys of attendees. As the results are uploaded and tabulated on the Web, feed news stories to journalists on the trends you are picking up. Yes, I know this is a limited demographic segment, but journalists use these shows as a way to get a snapshot of an industry, not a quantitative survey. You can become a valuable source in this endeavor not only to journalists at the show, but also to those who have to cover the shows from their home offices.

There you have it, some valuable insight from the PR field. Now let's go to the last tactical option that addresses the nuts and bolts of implementing wireless to facilitate internal communication.

Food for Thought

The following questions will help you to define and establish new PR protocols that take advantage of wireless technology.

1. Have you talked to some of the journalists to determine if they use the Net or wireless technology to help them do their jobs, and in what ways?

2. Do you have some friends within the journalism community who can preview your press center to give you candid feedback?

3. Besides the obvious product and company information, do you have additional material posted that will help journalists complete stories without too much additional legwork? Is this information easy to find?

4. Have you made it very easy for the editor on hellish deadlines to find everything he needs, including contact information?

5. Is contact information liberally scattered throughout your press center, and are the contact people prepped to give quick responses to press inquiries?

6. Do you want to create a special section just for your favorite journalists either in the press center, or through a wireless content delivery service such as AvantGo?

7. How do you plan to get press people to your site once you build your press center? What role will wireless communication play in this effort?

8. Can you incorporate information from your press center into wireless presentations so journalists can follow along with a mobile device if they're at a location without desktop PC access to the Net?

9. What's your strategy plan for getting senior executive support and involvement with your online PR activities?

10. Can you get your CEO online for press briefings, particularly in a crisis situation?

11. What approach will you take to enlist your PR agency as an active participant in developing and using your press center and wireless activities?

CHAPTER 14

Inside These Castle Walls: Operational Tactics to Facilitate Successful Wireless Implementation

The goal of the fourth strategic option is to use wireless technology to significantly impact your organization by lowering the costs and enhancing the efficiency of your internal communication. You have the greatest control over this fourth option because, not only do you purchase and manage all of the back-end wireless hardware and software, you also manage the people who use the technology.

However, just because you have direct managerial authority over the entire process doesn't mean that it's an easy one to implement. In fact, I feel this can be such a major undertaking that much tactical thinking has to go into the question, "How do I make all of this wireless stuff work?" What's more, even those strategic options that involve communicating to external audiences such as customers and prospects rely on internal resources in varying degrees, adding even more impetus to tactical planning.

Some organizations may decide to use outside contractors, wireless ASPs, and other vendors to implement their wireless strategies, so the load on their internal resources will be pretty light. However, If you plan to have your internal staff heavily involved in developing and implementing wireless strategies, then you need to pay close attention to the tactical considerations presented in this chapter. You particularly want your tech people to review this chapter because there are some important pointers for the folks whose job it is to turn business objectives into technological reality.

Facilitating the Nuts and Bolts
of Internal Communications

At a tactical level, you need to look at all of the mechanics of using wireless technology in new ways to improve (and maybe dramatically change) the way you do business. I break down the possible tactics you may develop into several subcategories.

First, there are the steps involved with getting executive buy-in and delineating responsibilities for who will actually implement the technology. As I mentioned in earlier chapters, one of the major problems with the Web when it was young was that top executives had no clue about what it could do for them. Sometimes they had no clue what others were doing on the Web in the name of the organization.

Large companies such as Sun had initial websites that were run by rank-and-file employees who put the site up without the knowledge of marketing or management. In some cases, executives in the mid-1990s dismissed the Web as a fad and either squashed any attempts at building a site or washed their hands of any responsibility for the it. Other executives let their enthusiasm get the best of them and they became too involved micromanaging web affairs.

These responses led to lots of wasted resources, damaged brand images, and missed business opportunities. As time progressed, smarter executives started to find the right balance between blissful ignorance and micromanagement, much to the betterment of their web efforts. As you travel down the road to executing effective wireless strategies, you must first determine who's in charge, who's directly involved with implementation, and what the roles of both groups are.

Second, after you resolve the issue of roles and responsibilities, you must tackle the ROI question. I don't have any ironclad rules for how you determine what the ROI from your wireless investment should be. But I do know you must define (or at least estimate) what financial and other benefits to expect, and create benchmarks to measure how well you are progressing as you invest money and time into your wireless efforts.

Being so new on the wireless frontier, many organizations do not have the experience of others to use as guideposts. As I interviewed people, I used their feedback to create general exercises for establishing initial financial benchmark, which I presented in the chapters on the strategic dimensions. In this chapter I will present some additional insights and recommendations on developing ROI from people who are implementing wireless strategies.

Third, you must create the budget for wireless applications. Deciding how much to spend is probably a harder question than determining how much you will gain. In the chapters on strategy I showed how you can do some analysis on available data to determine how much you're spending on various communication activities. But costs for wireless applications are all over the map because of varying hardware prices. These costs also vary depending on whether you decide to use wireless ASPs, hire consultants, buy software, or build your own applications.

How to implement a budgeting process for wireless applications was a question that challenged practically everyone with whom I spoke. I will try to give you some direction in this area, but until you develop a track record from several projects your main budgeting guideline may be to spend less money than you plan to save or earn.

Fourth, vendor selection is an important tactical consideration because the ultimate success of your internal wireless strategy can depend on which external resources you call upon. Some organizations try to go it alone to develop and manage all of their wireless applications, while many others turn to various third parties at least for some aspects of their implementations. Third-party providers are neither inherently good nor bad, but the process by which you go about selecting them will either be a key to your success or an anchor that drags you down.

Fifth, the user interface and operating features of the hardware and software that your employees use is another major factor that will contribute to your success or inhibit your progress. Some executives think that just because they mandate that something be done, it will be implemented posthaste. The reality is, when it comes to technology, employees on the front line have more direct and unintentional ways to neuter the best-laid plans of executives and consultants than you can imagine.

The road to success is paved with the careful attention to the details of designing and buying technology that facilitates how people work and want to work. Spend some hours to develop a good interface that makes it easy for your people to use the technology. You will get great ROI.

Starting at the Top—the Executive Challenge

As I've stated before, a large responsibility for the success of any major wireless implementation that changes the strategic direction of your organization will rest with your senior executives. While I firmly believe micromanaging is a painful cross for employees to bear, I also believe that executives must establish the vision for wireless implementation, and play an active role in the pursuit of that vision. This can be a tricky balancing act to pull off.

You're probably willing to chart a wireless course for your organization, but what if you face resistance from some of the executives who are above you or who share the executive ranks with you? Let's start with looking at some tactics you might take to win the buy-in of the top dogs in the organization. We will then examine how to use that buy-in to begin implementing wireless projects.

Give Executives Hands-On Experience

"You will have the greatest success is getting wireless applications deployed when you discover that the decision makers who control funding also love toys," remarks Michael Pinney, manager of business development for SAR-COM (www.sarcom.com), a national systems integrator. "They are often technology power users and their excitement is contagious, so a project can go from fact finding to implementation in the shortest period of time. Otherwise, you have to wait for the key decision makers who don't like technology to move on, or someone above them to push the issue. Working from the bottom up through management always hits a ceiling."

But what if your top execs aren't gadget freaks? Then you have to focus on showing senior executives how wireless technology will help them personally to make better-informed decisions faster and with greater effectiveness. The way you do this is to put the technology into their hands. Pinney explains how he used this tactic in 1999.

As a systems integrator, SARCOM is responsible for helping organizations implement new technologies that help them run better businesses. Pinney and other colleagues believed that wireless was going to have a major impact on businesses, but SARCOM had to use the technology themselves before they could recommend it to clients.

"What we did to address potential executive roadblocks (some liked PDAs and others didn't) was to initiate a test project by giving everyone in senior management a PDA and training. Some people put it in a drawer and forgot about it. But as they started to meet with their peers who used their devices all the time, those without one started to feel left out.

"If a person didn't have a PDA, they couldn't beam data between Palms to share business cards or exchange schedules, and this moved people over to using the device. There are people who use it more than others, but even the mild users see the benefits of the technology."

This test group at SARCOM expanded until about 100 executives and management staff were using various mobile devices. E-mail and calendar management were the two main applications. SARCOM is developing a wireless field force automation application for their field service people and a CRM application for the sales force. The economic downturn has been a strong motivator to help increase their wireless deployment.

From his observation of clients, Pinney finds that "middle managers who face reluctant executives will find that it is very difficult to jump-start wireless projects. We had a case like this with a prospect and we couldn't find a way to make the project go. Wireless technology seems to be the hardest thing to push through an organization. People's attitude about wireless seems to be 'when there's nothing else to do, then let's focus on wireless.' It seems almost surreal, but until people experience the use of wireless with customer data and see what they can do, you don't get anywhere."

Harrold Mann of Mann Consulting definitely believes that exccutives are key to effective wireless implementations. "If upper management stays clueless and ignores all of the in-fighting between marketing and IT or whomever over wireless, the organization will get burned because they don't have someone to architect the business process of how things are going to work. As a small business owner, I'm passionate about being productive, so I make the decisions about how the technology and the employees will interact to increase productivity. I want people to have convenience of getting something that they need when they need it."

Mann points out one option, outsourcing, as a way to make it easier for executives to buy into wireless. "Outsourcing is a good thing because there are a lot of little things you have to worry about with any wireless implementation. You can build your own infrastructure for wireless applications, but why? If you embrace open standards, use the lowest common denominators, you will have more portability among your vendors."

If you can offload a lot of the implementation and political headaches, it makes it easier to sell management on the technology. After being burned with high-priced Internet projects that wasted money and people, their reluctance is easy to understand. Once you prove success, and if the need merits it, start bringing things in-house.

Some Dissenting Voices

Not everyone, however, believes that executives should be the sole determining factor in the eventual acceptance of wireless applications. Unimobile (www.unimobile.com) markets an application for developing and delivering wireless communication between any mobile device and across various wireless networks.

The VP of Marketing, Vito Salvaggio, thinks that using "the executive 'seeding' approach to introduce wireless applications is a problem because the value of the technology has to be proven on its own merits. Executive enthusiasm is not scaleable across other parts of organization. You are likely to be disappointed. On the other hand, if those at the top don't buy in, the ball won't start rolling.

"People are willing to invest if you can point to a clear ROI. They deploy millions of dollars to train people on technology. You should do a test within a particular department or within a single geographic area. A large bank deployed a wireless application in a small market in Asia. Once they understood how successful user adoption would be, they rolled out the application on a larger scale."

Salvaggio feels that when you're at the point of a company-wide implementation, this is when you need to have senior management involved. "In a Fortune 500-type company, it's hard to say if the top executives will play a key role, but even if they do, these executives may not become the main driver. The line mangers will be the ones to drive recommendations and deployment."

Chief Operating Officer for wireless application vendor Aether Systems, Mike Mancuso, also thinks that this tactic has its shortcomings, but he has a different insight on the issue. "Top executives such as the CEO need to be behind the effort, but this person tends to be an older person who is reluctant to technology, particularly in health care, police, and large corporate organizations. They tend to get involved with new technology decisions when there is a crisis."

Mancuso feels this is analogous to the computer industry in the 1970s when computers were kept in a glass room and operated by techies. Chief information officers were the major driving force behind implementations because senior executives were reluctant to support what they couldn't understand. Part of the problem today is that using wireless technology is difficult, and vendors are not making it easy for people to understand what it does. You almost need a wireless information officer to demystify the technology.

I agree with the thought that executive enthusiasm by itself is going to be difficult to translate into company-wide support in large organizations with various divisions scattered nationally or internationally. However, it's better to have this support than not have it. In midsize and smaller organizations, company politics almost dictate that you have that support. Otherwise you could be in for some bruising political battles.

States Epiphany's Brad Wilson, "When you have large number of choices and limited experiences, everyone's opinion is equal. This was true in the early days of the Web. You need a champion in the executive level who can referee developments and make things happen, a person who has responsibility for budgets and personnel allocations. A committee of 12 people will drift along for a year and get nothing done because things change week to week."

Helping Executives See the Light

Educating senior management can be your best tool to not only get these people on board with the right program, but it also help solidify executives and line managers into a team that can better drive wireless implementations across divisions. There are a couple of ways you can do this—one is through people from within the organization, the other is through outside entities.

Todd Grappone at Sanford Medical School formed a coalition from within the university to educate administrators, move their wireless project forward, and keep it on track. "I think the people who make a lot of decisions don't understand the technology, so they need a guide in layman's terms. When you're meeting with a dean it can be a challenge using the right terms so they understand what you're talking about, but it's something that we (IT) need and they need." By uniting users of the technology with technologists, you can produce a plan in terms upper management understands.

Mr. Grappone sat down with a committee comprised of students, faculty, and staff to map out what they wanted to do, and he put together a budget and a proposal for the dean of the medical school. A larger committee was already in place to discuss computer issues, and that group added input into what became the actual project they launched. The IT group drives wireless implementation, and the committee manages application development projects that are executed by students and faculty.

Cliff Frost at UC Berkeley works with the campus administration in a similar fashion. They focus on the mission and provide the necessary support, but faculty have to show how the applications they are building fit into the mission and define the role that Frost's communication group will play in the implementation.

WideRay's Saul Kato believes the best way for organizations to deal with this lack of executive understanding is to enlist trusted third parties such as value-added resellers (VARs). VARs at least have expertise in a specific industry (i.e., fire and police departments) so they can evaluate options, test technologies, and put together something that solves a need. You can then work with them to educate upper management in terms that make sense for the business.

In my years of doing presentations to large and small organizations, I find that the best approach to educating executives about new technologies is to bring them together with all of the departments that can or will be directly impacted by the technology. If they hear from tech people what the impact will be, plus have these benefits reinforced by managers who add their specific perspectives on how it will help, executives can be educated, motivated, and encouraged to make public commitments to the technology.

One thing to keep in mind though is that even public commitment can fail to produce action if these executives change their minds or get distracted later. Your executive education, besides the hands-on approach that SARCOM used, should include delegating roles and responsibilities while everyone is together. When executives and managers start getting and giving commitments to each other in this environment, it's easier to keep the ball rolling.

Joe Whatley is the systems supervisor at HealthPartners (www.health partners.com), a parent HMO organization. He tells how he used customers as a leverage point to sell top executives on developing wireless applications for communicating with external audiences.

"Pick a task that people high up in the organization will think is the greatest thing since sliced bread, get executive approval, and let the project grow from there. One of the goals for any senior executive in healthcare organizations is to do whatever it takes to make members more health aware, and enable them to give and receive feedback on their care so their condition improves. So we show our executives how they can do this with wireless applications

"We have over 800,000 members. Imagine if our members could get information about their coverage, treatment records, and so forth. Since you can see it on the Web, why can't you provide that in a wireless format? For example, a wireless application at a clinic where members can input information without any wired connections, and where a doctor can also retrieve information. Of course, we had to show that these capabilities are protected with all of the necessary security, and we won't push people to use wireless if they just want to use the Web. We're just giving them an additional option."

Executives have to look at what drives their business and what makes customers feel that the organization is doing something good for them, then do what it takes to implement the necessary systems. Your job sometimes is to bring this point home to them in a way that makes sense.

Now That You're Committed, What About Delegating Responsibility?

Sometimes the problem isn't getting the head honcho to commit, it's getting high levels of commitment and participation without the agony of micromanagement. The equally evil twin of this problem arrives when executives choose the wrong people to handle the execution. You see this play out in companies everywhere and in every industry when the boss says, "I have a [friend, cousin, sister, nephew] who does web design."

Upon hearing these words, people hang their heads in despair because, though they know they have won the battle to get executive support, they are likely going to lose the war to launch an effective web project. So the question is, will this scenario play out repeatedly with wireless implementations, and if so, what do you do to prevent it within your organization? Will senior management be smarter this time around? In the cases where sanity prevails, to whom do you give wireless implementation responsibility?

First, let's look at nipping the "micromanagement/my brother can do it" problem in the bud. Two police departments took slightly different approaches to this vexing issue, and their stories may be good food for thought for those of you who are in a government organization.

Managing Management

Sergeant Ed Koler of the Poughkeepsie Police Department knows from observing other departments that "sometimes a person is given responsibility to deploy some new technology just because they happen to be the one the boss sees tapping on a computer one day. But this person may not know what to do or where to go to find the solutions. Then your problem is compounded when this person who is responsible for implementing the technology is reassigned or promoted.

"Sometimes a boss will use an outsourced application developer and not someone from within their organization, but what's seen as a quick and easy solution can result in other problems. The more outside people you bring, in the worse it can become because of the department bureaucracy, people who have different agendas, and so on. We found someone who we knew was competent, then kept that person on the project until it was finished. If you drop the project midway, then next thing you know you're doing it all over again."

By the way, this doesn't mean that you shouldn't use outsourced resources, but rather than let your top executive make the decision, give the in-house person independent responsibility to delegate any tasks to other employees and outside parties. This person will likely have a better handle on the needs of the project and the organization. The boss should be reviewing results and offering general guidance.

Lieutenant Robert Durko of the Tarrant County, Texas, Sheriff's Department takes the committee approach. "A number of entities need to be involved in the process of selecting and implementing wireless technology—IT people and end users (patrol officers, bike officers, detectives). Include everyone who has to touch the system either through mobile devices, or monitor and manage wireless data and applications back in the home office.

"Executives only see computers in the car, but you need a committee to come in who collectively see the whole picture. IT needs to be involved, but not the driver. You need the communication experts within the organizations defining dispatchers' roles, where communication chains are inside and outside of the organization."

This particular approach seemed to work well for Tarrant County, but don't forget what was said earlier about letting the committee bog down the decision-making process. For smaller organizations I recommend that you give someone high up in the executive food chain veto power, and give the project manager leadership duties that include the power to break up log jams.

Who Carries the Torch

Once you get executives comfortable with delegating responsibilities, someone has to be assigned to carry the operations management torch on a day-to-day basis and keep the project on track. Remember that transition period when the Web went from being a geeky toy that only a handful of people worked on to the "must have" business tool that every organization needed? At that point many organizations' web projects started to resemble a ball in my little cousin's soccer game.

Often, when little kids like my cousin Reid play soccer, the two teams cluster around the ball on the field in this moving huddle that goes wherever the ball goes. So it was with the Web. For a while it seemed everybody in every department was a web expert, had an opinion, wanted a leading role of the web development project, or all three. So many people clustered around the action getting in each other's way that a lot of sites were a mess. To avoid this scenario, you must turn to a few good leaders who can maintain the balance between broad participation and efficient daily management.

"I seriously don't believe that wireless implementation will evolve like it did on the Web," states Unimobile's Salvaggio. "That lack of structure for designing and deploying Web technology won't work out for wireless. One of two groups will be responsible for managing wireless implementations. There is the group that typically develops the business procedures that drive sales. The other is IT if the wireless applications are primarily a part of a cost-saving measure."

While IT is often charged with implementing technology to address cost-reduction objectives, at a minimum they will be the gatekeeper for sales applications, so even when marketing is driving the process IT can veto certain projects. Tom Nogles of ThinAirApps concurs.

"Wireless is too complex as a technology and there are too many vendors that you have to have involved, so grass roots wireless efforts are less likely. Business groups are letting IT lead, or at least asking IT to get involved. As tools improve and standards come into play, department heads might play a bigger role in implementing applications. I expect that business units today will set the objectives, while IT follows these directives and implements the solutions. CIOs are starting to look at themselves as consultants to the business units," says Nogles.

All of this makes sense if we are talking about large organizations. However, roles and responsibilities within smaller organizations vary. Peter Jowaisas is marketing director of Notifact, which manufactures wireless devices for embedding in physical assets. From his experience he's found that "in small organizations, it's the young kid just out of college who can immediately grasp the benefits of technology who will move the company into wireless applications. In larger organizations it's often someone in the engineering department who sees the potential to improve operating efficiency, while other times someone in marketing sees wireless as a way to enhance service and differentiate the company from competitors."

Tom Turner of WhereNet has a similar observation. "In small organizations responsibility for wireless implementations is all over the map. Sometimes it's IT because they feel they can be more responsive to the technology needs. VPs of operations sometimes are the driving force because they have seen wireless work in other companies. Whichever person appears to be best suited to the task for your small organization, the important thing is that this person be recognized by senior management as the driving force behind the implementation, then given the tools and latitude to make things happen.

Rick Goetter, who handles PR for Kyocera Wireless Corp. (makers of the Smartphone) believes that any wireless campaigns that are targeted to external audiences should be directed by marketing and IT working in a cross-functional team. "Marketing should decide what they want to say, then let IT build the site. Internal communication should be more IT's responsibility. They have to work with the departments to help design the content, but IT has to integrate the systems into the bigger technology picture."

Goetter and I discussed the problem of departments such as human resources and PR underutilizing Web sites for external communication and asked if this will carry over to wireless. He said that these departments have to become more proactive to get their pieces of the puzzle developed. This means you need to have either an extended cross-departmental team to bring marketing people in to help, or develop marketing competencies within the departments.

I strongly believe that a lot of this discussion on who's responsible for what should be resolved by answering the following question: Who within your organization is responsible for planning and executing your organization-wide business strategy? When it isn't clear who should be delegated responsibility for managing the implementation of your overall wireless business strategy, or there are a lot of people fighting for the role, this person should decide. In smaller organizations, the chief strategist (who isn't the CEO and overwhelmed with other tasks) should be responsible for managing implementation.

Once you have roles and responsibilities mapped out, you have to consider the financial aspects of wireless implementations.

Show Me the Money—Determining ROI

Few people have clear-cut rules for how to determine ROI, or how much money to set aside for wireless applications. Some of the veterans, people who started working with wireless applications in 1998 or 1999, have some insight based on their experiences that can help you set up some basic guidelines.

Salvaggio states, "During the early days of the Web, the need to justify ROI was not there. There was a mad race to become web-enabled, and executives were more concerned with spending money to become 'webified' rather than to generate ROI. Wireless is being driven now by IT, and their budgets have to have an ROI focus, so any new proposals for wireless spending has to come with clarity in respect to the business needs to be solved. You have to define the goal and define the need of the customer."

There might be one exception, though. Speedware markets software tools and services to help companies develop their wireless applications. Chris Koppe, their director of marketing, believes that companies will still race to be first with wireless applications that are directed to an external audience so they can use this for competitive differentiation, such as the wireless branding tactics discussed in Chapter 7. But where he sees a difference from the early web days is that organizations will implement applications that don't create a financial burden for their bottom line.

"These external applications may be experimental, they could be outsourced, but they definitely will not be critical to the business. The applications for internal communication will be based mainly on a needs analysis and user demand, and they will cost more because you're adding software or hardware to current systems. But eventually people will have to show an ROI, and companies that lead the way will create standard ROI benchmarks."

Koppe does warn that tracking ROI will be tricky. When you're out front leading the charge there it's hard to know what to measure and how to determine success. However, you must set goals of some sort that you hope to achieve. "Don't be too enthusiastic about what the results might be. You should go after momentum—first week results versus fourth week sales, number of leads generated, and so on. How does wireless visibility appear to affect certain business results? Use early trends, measure the results and then extrapolate your ROI," he says.

"Darwin Will Have His Way with Them"

In Chapter 1 I quoted Harrold Mann of Mann Consulting who advises that you go after short-term results that justify your investment, and expand your efforts from there. He's been using wireless applications since 1996.

"The opportunity of failure is in the ego of the people who say 'we can build it ourselves: the VPN [virtual private networks], the extranet, and the application software.' They spend months in development, go over budget, then one of the key people leaves and there's no continuity. Darwin will have his way with them," says Mann. The companies that will be able to gain a competitive edge from wireless are the ones that invest in projects that can be implemented quickly, inexpensively, and show quick ROI.

As an example of focusing on short-term benefits, Mann related a story about a friend of his who is a location scout for ad agencies. For one job Mann's friend took digital pictures of a winding road on which a car advertiser imposed a picture of their vehicle. This saved the ad agency the expense of hauling the car and a platoon of people to the location. While at the location the photographer wirelessly posted these shots to an extranet site for the client, ad agency, and other creative agencies using the Ricochet wireless Internet access service.

"What was he really risking?" asks Mann. "He didn't invent the camera, he didn't invent wireless connectivity, and he outsourced the extranet. He's 'Scotch taping' some off-the-shelf technologies, going to work, and reaping significant benefits. If the digital camera fails, he goes and gets a new one with minimum inconvenience because he knows the source of new ones. If Ricochet goes out of business, he gets a new provider quickly because he has a backup lined up."

While this approach may seem a little simplistic to you (and will strike absolute terror in the hearts of IT people), there are some valuable lessons to be learned. Somewhere between rush to deployment and paralysis by perpetual pondering is the pilot project, especially when you're talking about internal communications. It's easy to define a need. You will have a small expense if you're adding wireless capability to software that's already in place, and you can measure results fairly quickly after launching the pilot.

Practically every company I spoke with didn't start with an organization-wide ROI document that took months to write. They started with some basic financial assumptions, pried loose some dollars, implemented a pilot, and several months later measured the results. In many cases, it didn't even take months. People started seeing a difference from day one. Todd Heintz, director of market development for wireless modem manufacturer Sierra Wireless (www.sierrawireless.com) lays out a good example of how to address the ROI issue.

"In the enterprise, a good portion of the workers have been issued laptops and software, so what you're looking at now is adding the cost of wireless modems. If you look at the value of what the laptops already bring to the organization, then the incremental investment of $600 per year ($50 a month for wireless service) isn't a big leap. Compare the $600 to the $6,000 cost for the laptop, software, and accessories, all of which might not be as productive without the wireless capabilities. And this productivity begins the first time the user takes the laptop on the road."

Heintz believes that smaller companies sometimes have it easier because they don't have to deal with the costs for network and communication security. In real estate for example, the process of calculating the ROI for an independent agent using wireless technology is fundamentally no different than the process for an enterprise operation. If the agent, like the corporate sales rep, closes one more deal because of the wireless capability, the $3,000 or $4,000 they may earn for that sale more than pays for the wireless modem and service. But the small organization doesn't have to deal with the same rollout costs of big enterprise—security, back-end servers, training, and other high-end expenses.

Balancing the Tangibles and Intangibles

Heintz goes on to say that you will eventually need to have an ROI plan for large implementation projects, but ROI in the plan may not be limited to dollars and cents issues. Senior management should look at factors such as how well wireless improves their competitive position by providing better service for customers or providing information faster to people in the field.

He believes every industry will have intangible benefits that justify the investment in wireless. "Wireless data in public safety produces a ton of ROI, but there's also the benefit of officer safety when they stop cars. Some organizations have a real driving need to provide better service, but this produces quantifiable ROI as well. As wireless applications move to blue-collar workers and field staff, they enjoy hard ROI and also produce the intangibles such as improving customer service."

Dr. Richard Fiedotin, Vice President of Business and Product Development for ePocrates (www.epocrates.com), which makes clinical applications for physicians, presented similar scenarios for medical facilities. "If doctors can review lab results at nurses' stations rather than going to the lab itself, you can figure out all the costs of their time, then determine how much you save.

"In hospitals there may be three sources within the same facility that store x-rays and doctors may have to track them down. With imaging systems you can look at these on PCs and save tremendous amounts of time trying to find them and reduce film costs. Add wireless access and you save even more."

In more sophisticated applications such as decision support systems, measuring benefits is harder. A person may come in for treatments, so you evaluate the various options. You can use a care-mapping application and see details associated with your options.

But it is hard to prove in the final analysis that taking any particular approach versus another really saved you specific costs, or made the treatment better for the patient. So have everyone buy into the less-sophisticated benefits, and any of the warm and fuzzy benefits that come are a bonus (i.e., patients appear to have less pain, successful treatment rates increase).

In a university environment such as UC Berkeley, there is very little of the traditional ROI to be measured because the colleges don't make profits. If the goal of a particular department is to make a series of financial investments to improve their research environment so they attract several high-powered professors, how do you quantify this? When you look at using wireless to improve customer service, it gets even harder to measure ROI.

"We can show where we make things less expensive," states Frost. "We can say that we can do more and be more productive, but our efforts aren't going to increase business. This is why having a research partner helps because we don't have to find 'VC' money. If a pilot succeeds in terms of people liking it, the University will find ways to fund it because students and faculty will be able to do their work more effectively. It gives the University a competitive advantage over other campuses."

I think Hans Wynholds of ServiceHub sums up this balance between the tangibles and intangibles pretty well. "When NASA went to moon, they started with some orbits around earth, followed by orbits around the moon, and then they landed on the surface. What you're buying with these pilot projects aren't your first steps of automation, but useful information to make better decisions. So run multiple pilots. Don't be afraid to pay your tuition for your education."

A Structured Approach to Determining ROI

Since there are people who still insist on having some clearly defined path to showing ROI for wireless applications, I spoke at length with a couple of people who have experience with embedded wireless technology in physical assets. There is usually a greater investment of time and money because there is hardware and technology infrastructure that has to be put in place (which isn't a requirement for other wireless applications). But the thinking process for calculating ROI for these embedded applications can be applied to other wireless implementations.

Turner defines three major areas to consider when tackling ROI issues: (1) Can you generate more revenues? (2) Are you using your assets efficiently? (3) Are the workers operating efficiently?

In terms of increasing revenues, you have to ask if there are opportunities to do this by increasing the capacity to deliver products or services to customers. Or, can you produce a higher level of communication between customers and subsequently provide more services to them than differentiate your organization from competitors?

Next you want to examine the physical assets that move around the organization frequently, such as diagnostic equipment in a hospital. How much time do people lose trying to find them, or do you overpurchase to compensate for "lost" items? Auto manufacturers may buy 30 percent more shipping containers than the standard business model says they need because their physical facilities are so vast that workers lose track of them.

Do hospitals have items such as infusion pumps and lab test equipment that are underutilized because people don't know where they are or when equipment has finished the sterilization process? If you have real-time visibility to these assets, there is a quantifiable improvement of their use, and you don't have to buy as many pieces of equipment to support an inefficient organization.

There are many worker productivity issues tied directly to asset management. A lot of nonproductive tasks compromise workers' activities because you can't answer the question "Where is it now?" where "it" is the item you need to go to the next step in the business process. So one ROI equation that estimates a decrease in expenditures to compensate for misplaced assets also produces an ROI equation for increases in worker productivity.

Once you've looked at your operations from these angles, make calculations similar to those proposed in the previous chapters on strategic options. Then you will have financial benchmarks. Next, assemble the vendors who may eventually provide the hardware, software, other technology, and wireless services. Give them the benchmarks, the strategic objectives and tactics you are considering, and ask them to quantify the amount you will need to spend to reach your benchmarks. Also ask them to determine how long it will take in weeks or months to start lowering costs, increasing productivity, and reaping other expected benefits.

What you should get are options for wireless expenditures matched against expected returns. For example, a vendor may say you can create an application to enable your sales force automation software that will cost you $50,000 dollars and you should see sales cycles reduced by 30 percent, which may represent $100,000 in increased annual income. For another $10,000 you can also wireless enable your CRM application and produce an additional 10 percent reduction in the sales cycle. Several vendors can give you PDA or wireless modem costs, while a service provider will lay out your monthly wireless connection costs.

By giving vendors the parameters for what you want to achieve, you can help them define an investment amount to generate a specific return. Of course, only after pilot projects and full-on implementations can you really nail down the specific ROI, but at least you should be able to produce an ROI that justifies the effort.

Turner also notes that there is another component of the ROI evaluation that doesn't take place until after implementation. Within a six to twelve month period, organizations start creating new uses of the same wireless applications, and this adds to the bottom line.

"Sometimes these are simple tasks that have major upside," states Turner. "In an auto plant we have "WhereCall" buttons placed on bins of auto parts that workers push to wirelessly alert the parts replenishment system when the bins need new parts. This customer also has trash containers which three people on forklifts drive around randomly to empty. But it's an inefficient system because drivers never know if the cans need emptying or not until they spend the time to drive by the containers.

"Taking the same WhereCall feature, the customer placed buttons near the trash cans and instructed all the workers to push them when the cans were empty. As a result, they reduced the forklifts used from three to one, redeployed the two drivers to other tasks, and saved several thousand dollars. They didn't have to rebuild the back end, just add a new front-end application that took very little time."

Whether for internal communication, facilitating communication with prospects, or enhancing field service and support operations, once people start using mobile devices and wireless applications, they're going to think of new things to do with these tools. Your job is to track these new uses so you can create new ROI calculations to justify broadening the scope of these activities.

Come Fly with Me and See ROI Analysis at Work

Don Pohly is the business manager for airport information systems at FMC Airport Systems. FMC, a WhereNet customer, sells airports cargo loaders, passenger bridges, and ground support equipment. Pohly has ROI numbers for using embedded wireless technology to reduce equipment requirements, increase employee productivity, reduce aircraft damage incidents, and reduce flight delays at airports. Details on the numbers for these four areas are outlined below.

1. *Reduce equipment requirements.* Airports reduce equipment requirements due to more efficient use achieved by finding the equipment that is not being used and getting it into circulation, plus increasing equipment uptime through better maintenance. At one major hub, this airline has ground support equipment (GSE) with a total value of over $30 million.

The manager of GSE signed up to reduce the total quantity of equipment by 5 percent through use of real-time locating and telemetry (measurement of the performance of mechanical equipment) technologies. Total savings at one airport for this one airline: $1.5 million in capital, about $300,000 in annual depreciation, and about $225,000 more in annual maintenance costs.

2. *Increase employee productivity.* In terms of increased productivity of employees, there is one estimate that 30 minutes is lost at the beginning of each shift as lead employees search out the equipment needed for their crews. Another 30 minutes is lost per day in certain paperwork that could be automated.

Using a wireless location system to track down the equipment and a telemetry system to complete paperwork 'paperlessly,' the savings is about an hour per day for up to 60 lead employees. This is over a half million dollars per year in increased productivity. In addition, numerous employees looking for equipment throughout the day wasted a tremendous amount of time.

The value of reducing searching and expediting is a difficult number to precisely estimate, but conservative analysis put it at over $100,000 annually at one airport. On top of this, a location system can eliminate the need to perform regular physical inventories of equipment—another significant cost savings.

3. *Reduce aircraft damage incidents.* It is relatively rare that GSE damages aircraft due to mechanical failure of equipment. (There are an estimated two events per year at a large hub airport.) But each event is extremely expensive. Relatively minor aircraft repair—such as a damaged fuselage stringer—can easily top $200,000 per occurrence. On top of that is the expense of a cancelled flight, which are both the direct costs and indirect costs of customer dissatisfaction. Preventing even half of the incidents provides significant savings.

4. *Reduce flight delays at airports.* Having the right equipment in the right place at the right time and increasing the probability that it is well-maintained and ready for use can help cut delays in flight departures. The cost of each minute an aircraft is delayed has been valued at fifty-five dollars (different airlines may set this value higher or lower), so saving only forty delay minutes per week nets over $100,000 in annual savings. Given that hub airports run hundreds of flight per day, seven days per week, forty minutes in weekly savings is a very conservative number.

Taken together, the above savings combined with many smaller savings gained elsewhere in the airport's operation have consistently achieved a payback on an embedded wireless system in one year or less. This ROI has been reviewed and estimated with several airlines to date and the payback has been shown to be less than a year each time. Once a wireless infrastructure is installed, people find additional applications for the data gathered and this further enhances ROI.

Budget Management Issues

Whether someone gives you a fixed budget for implementing wireless applications, or you are fortunate enough to establish your own budgets, there are several budget management issues with which you will have to contend. The biggest two issues are the wide-ranging nature of pricing for wireless hardware, software, and services, and the rapid changes that are occurring within the wireless industry. It's difficult to know from one month to the next how much things will cost and if today's popular technology might be obsolete.

Sergeant Ed Koler of the Poughkeepsie Police Department describes his approach to the fixed-budget management challenge. "In 1998 we received grant money for $137,000 to do a wireless implementation. We had to plan carefully and use good judgment because we didn't have a lot of room for error."

He started by reviewing all of their wireless network options, looking at coverage and monthly network charges. These charges are sometimes overlooked when budgeting, but long-term they actually outweigh the costs for mobile devices. "CDPD would have cost thirty to forty dollars per patrol car in monthly charges, plus more if we went over certain usage levels. But with Erickson's EDACS (a trunking system that picks from twenty frequencies of the channel that's available) it costs eighteen dollars a month for unlimited airtime. We also have data that can't go across the Net, so we have to use a closed wireless network."

When Sergeant Koler reviewed his hardware options, he wanted to find the right hardware to withstand the elements, so he went with off-the-shelf Gateway laptops that are still working. While some police departments use PDAs, Koler needed systems that could receive digitized city map files and print them in the cars.

The final issue was the software choice. Koler opted to buy software that would allow his team to integrate their records management and dispatch systems into a wireless application, and also provide a good set of APIs so they can integrate with other software later. Since Koler knew they were going to do their own software integration, he went with Cerlium (now Aether Systems) because the vendor had the right technology and was the most responsive in terms of giving them the customer support they needed.

This brings up a sticky issue—the "build" versus "buy" question—particularly when you're faced with a fixed budget. It may be okay to have your IT people handle software integration or to build one or two wireless applications (if you buy a good set of development tools that have built-in support for various carrier networks, mobile devices, and back-end software).

However, to build all of your own wireless capabilities from the ground up just to save money is asking for trouble if this implementation is beyond the capabilities of your IT staff. Wireless technology is shifting too quickly to keep up. Unless an IT person has been working with these technologies regularly for the past year or two, he'll have a difficult time staying on top of things. Even with good wireless development tools, sometimes it's better to limit the scope of the applications you deploy than limit the amount of budget allocated to buying support from a vendor's professional services group.

I have very little accounting expertise, but I understand that it is easier to draw money from operations budgets rather than capital budgets once they have been established. From this perspective using a wireless ASP option might make sense, especially for pilot projects, by classifying it as an expenditure for services and counting it against your operations budget (rather than your fixed wireless budget). If you show some fast ROI, you'll minimize the hit on your operations budget at the end of the year. Check with you CFO, though, to clarify these points.

Considerations When Establishing Your Budget

When establishing a budget from scratch in an area with few benchmarks, it helps to practice a little restraint. John Reiland, CEO of wireless service provider ServiceIQ, told me about visiting one of the local utility companies in Houston, Texas and learning that they had spent millions of dollars for software and $5,000 laptops for each of their 650 field service staff. For the type of information these people were collecting, PDAs costing a few hundred dollars would have done just as well. This may seem like stating the obvious, but if you're solving a set of simple problems, use economic, off-the-shelf products and save the big technology guns for resolving complex needs.

As a hypothetical budget benchmark, SARCOM's Pinney suggests that you may be able to equip 1,000 people to wirelessly access several company applications such as sales force automation and CRM for $500,000 ($400,000 is for mobile devices and training, $20,000 is for servers, and about $80,000 is for other related infrastructure costs). This doesn't include monthly wireless network airtime.

There may be costs for additional software to enhance these applications. Companies such as Simplylook and VisualGold compress and reformat graphic images and multimedia files so people using different mobile devices can access them with greater ease. Software in these categories can run from $40,000 to $250,000 and above.

Don't forget to factor in the cost of development time for your IT staff to customize applications and provide end-user support. If the vendor does all of the customizing work, sometimes they factor this into the price of the applications while other vendors bill this as a separate cost. If your wireless applications are primarily providing access to existing intranet content and software applications, support costs aren't too high because PDAs and cell phones usually don't cause the kind of headaches that end up with the IT staff.

Todd Grappone at Stanford Medical School reports that "it's been very easy for tech support on PDAs, mainly because devices are mobile so people can get help from each other. It's what we call hallway tech support." When software vendor Avid Technology installed their application for supporting their resellers, their IT people only received a handful of calls and these were from people who didn't read their e-mail with the installation instructions. I fear that, until the end of time, there will be no easy solution for the RTFM gene deficiency.

For some organizations there are additional costs for beefing up the security of the networks and even the devices themselves, particularly in healthcare where one instance of a lawsuit for patient data being lost or stolen can torpedo a wireless application. Joe Whatley of HealthPartners states, "Right now we don't allow data to go out that's not encrypted if it has patient information. This is absolutely mandatory but it will raise the costs of implementing wireless applications. We could provide our own Secure Socket Layer, which costs less, but this is a big pain for both the sender and the receiver."

These costs may make some CFOs a little queasy, but as AvantGo President Richard Owen says, "There's nothing cheap in the enterprise. There's a fixed cost for that is going to be applicable for most types of technologies. If someone says for $10K they'll run your entire wireless business, be suspect. But bear in mind that the amount you've invested in your current technology solutions is high. If you've spent a million dollars, yet people don't use these applications, it's worth it to add some money to add wireless capabilities if this gets people to use them."

I asked Tom Turner to give me an idea about how much you should budget for wireless enabling your physical assets. Plan on a cost of fifty dollars per asset if you plan to track its movements within your physical premises, and anywhere from three hundred to a thousand dollars per asset for items such as vehicles, shipping containers, and other items that leave your premises.

Then budget a cost of about $100,000 for the wireless infrastructure that actually tracks the onsite assets on premises that take up a few dozen acres, such as an average size manufacturing plant or shipping and distribution dock. Infrastructure for a mid-size to large hospital may cost $300,000, and to manage assets on premises the size of a major metropolitan airport you should plan on spending $1 million. If you're tracking assets after they leave your premises, you have monthly wireless and GPS network charges, and this varies according to the amount of traffic you generate.

Just in case you're wondering how long it might take to recapture your investment if you plunk down a cool million bucks, many organizations find this might take a year. But since you're making a capital investment that has a four- or five-year life cycle, your ROI is $3 to $4 million dollars over the life of the technology.

How Small Organizations and Nonprofits Can Approach Budgeting

The previous costs I outlined are for large organizations. Smaller organizations still have the per-person costs of mobile devices and monthly network access charges, but their implementation costs should be much less, particularly if they use a wireless ASP. For example, a simple wireless dispatching system for a small delivery company may cost about 50 to 75 dollars per person each month, including the wireless carrier charges. Set-up charges may cost $1,000 or so depending on the scope of the wireless effort.

It's interesting to note that some corporations that are thinking about implementing wireless applications to communicate with external audiences may opt for the ASP model, according to Federico Aloisi of wireless application vendor neXui in Italy. "If I were trying to reach a mass market, I wouldn't want to divert too many internal resources to this project. My preference would be to find an ASP who can tell you how much it will cost each month per person contacted so that the organization has clear budget parameters and a better way to measure effectiveness."

In Chapter 9, I talked about how UC Berkeley dodged a lot of the budgeting issues by having a corporation to donate a lot of the technology the university is using in its initial wireless rollout. This may be a tactic that many in the nonprofit sector may want to consider, though you do have to be careful how you proceed.

"Many nonprofits have to deal with the perception issues of spending on wireless technology when people think that the money should go to something else," states Anne Riser, president of the Personal Communications Industry Association. "Second Harvest feeds the homeless with reclaimed food. Maybe they should look to industry to donate products by showing that if the delivery people had mobile devices, they could do more to increase food collection. Requesting vendor donations as part of strategy to get technology should be relatively easy. The greater challenge is getting business services donated."

The key to securing these services may be found in the fact that more donors are demanding that nonprofits use better business practices. To comply, nonprofits can seek in-kind donations by executives of wireless product or services companies who join their boards of directors or planning committees. Riser states, "There were a lot of dot-com millionaires who got involved in some high-profile community groups. We hope that this will happen as the wireless market improves."

Even if nonprofits are successful with these tactics, they still have to establish a budget based on the day-to-day operational needs. They have to answer the question, "If it's not integral to the delivery of our main service, is the technology worthwhile?" Riser believes that most of the mid-sized organizations' needs are simple and are probably manageable by ASP-delivered services.

Now that we've looked at the executive leadership and financial elements that influence your ability to implement wireless applications, let's go on to the next chapter to address vendor selection and user interface design.

CHAPTER 15

More Operational Tactics to Facilitate Successful Wireless Implementation

To wrap up the discussion on your tactics for implementing wireless applications within your organization I want to address two main topics: vendor selection and user interface design. Both of these may seem far removed from the executive suite, but these functions are so important to the success of your wireless implementation that you need to keep tabs on the key decisions that are made in these areas.

Vendor Selection Recommendations

One of the issues that organizations struggle with is vendor selection for technology that is as new on the scene as wireless data applications. Fortunately IT is playing a more pivotal role in selecting vendors, and you probably won't have as high an influx of people dropping out of college and into boardrooms to plot wireless content design tactics as you did with Web implementations.

Unfortunate, though, is the volume of hype coming from a number of sources in the wireless industry because this creates confusion among executives as their organizations try to decide which applications are best suited to meet their needs. I expect that market downturns and negative national events have put a damper on some of this marketing noise, so now might be a good time to do a little reasonable reflection on how you can get the best results from you vendor selection process.

Before selecting vendors, assemble an internal group of representatives from different departments or business units who will use the applications, IT staff, and senior management. Define key parameters such as business objectives, budget, technology requirements, and implementation timeline. Include intangible benefits such as increased employee job satisfaction. In the next chapter, which discusses writing your wireless strategy plan, I will cover these topics in more detail.

To help establish the parameters that will guide the selection process, some organizations bring in an outside consultant (not related to any vendor) to help build a request for proposal (RFP) that defines the organization's needs. This document goes out to vendors. Steve Cox of wireless application vendor OpenGrid says, "The consultant needs to be experienced in your industry and also have experience with wireless so they can define the needs in terms that both parties understand. You also should have the consultant involved with the buying process."

Sometimes people just send out a general RFP to several vendors, get their feedback, and then create a formal RFP. This can be dangerous because this feedback may consist of many things that the vendor wants to sell rather than what applications are best suited to your needs, so having an intermediary can reduce that possibility.

Look for the Ideal Partner

SARCOM's Michael Pinney recommends that you find no less than three vendors who can supply what you're looking for, then talk to their customers who are implementing similar applications to get feedback on the pros and cons. A word of caution, though. Don't try to add every feature but the kitchen sink into your application. Wireless is a window back to your data, not a replacement for your business software.

Whether your organization is large or small, there are some benefits of going with smaller vendors to meet your technology requirements, though this tends to run counter to the cautious nature of some IT people. As WideRay president Saul Sato presents it, "Big companies often are motivated by capturing market share, or trying to get entrenched within companies so that they can provide the right solution eventually. With small companies you often get more attention from people who will work closely with you to provide the right solution."

He also recommends that you sift through the marketing materials and vendor presentations to focus on real value. "Look at what customers are really getting from vendors in terms of service, valuable information, and interaction. Then ask for demos that apply specifically for your business and get the application in your hand."

You have to be leery of a lot of forward pitching from large vendors, meaning they tell you "yes, we can do everything you want" but fail to mention that it will be a year later when version 3.0 ships before they can do it. Find out what's usable now and see how it can evolve over the next five years. How will it dovetail into new technology that you might buy later?

FMC Airport Systems' Don Pohly, who has been a buyer and now a supplier of technology applications, believes it's very important to find a known reputable supplier that will partner with you to evolve your application in a long-term relationship. "This type of supplier will sit down and develop a growth plan and help estimate the upfront costs, then proceed with a pilot program so you can run tests to see if the application works as advertised.

"You want to review your existing business procedures to figure out which ones [i.e., expense tracking, research data collection] will work more effectively with the planned wireless application from the beginning. You can start working out new applications to address the other procedures as your experience with the technology increases. The payback to the supplier isn't as fast but this is the only way to go that will work out best for both the supplier and the organization in the long-run."

Pohly suggests that working with an ASP might be a good idea for the short-term, and a company like ServiceHub can be among your long-term vendors since an ASP is good for implementing wireless information distribution applications. But for accessing and manipulating data from assets such as CRM software and mobile workers, you need more complex technology infrastructure that is integrated with their existing hardware and software, which is something an ASP may not be able to do.

For smaller organizations however, where even a modest investment in wireless applications is significant and they often don't have a lot of IT resources, ASPs are a good partner to have. ServiceHub president Hans Wynhold suggests that "if you have the opportunity to run a pilot on an ASP basis, it's like renting a car. You don't have to buy the application but you get the full experience at little risk, and you might get better support because the dynamics of the ASP business are different that that of a regular vendor."

Even though a lot of Internet-related ASPs went out of business with the dot-com bust, wireless ASPs emerging today seem to be made of sturdier stock and should be a potent force in the industry. I expect that in a year or two the large wireless application vendors that sell to the enterprise will also offer an ASP option for small organizations.

This philosophy about forming a partnership with vendors applies to those who help you develop wireless content as well as applications. As Rudi O'Meara of Intraware says, "We were lucky because we found a company that wanted to be a partner. You need someone that will take a vested interest in the nature of your business. All the strategies we developed were in response to very extensive briefings. Lot21 insisted that we go into great detail about our business model, target audience, and other aspects of our business.

"An agency that won't go to that level of detail is the wrong firm for you. A relationship with an agency is ongoing, so if they don't immediately connect with what you've communicated with them about your audience you will have problems."

"To me, the process of selecting a wireless vendor is the same as how people always did in regular world before the Web," says Joe Whatley of Health-Partners who uses ThinAirApps applications. "I stick by my tried and true mantra—service, service, service. If the product does what's advertised and their post-sales support meets their pre-sales advertising, then I'm happy. When I call our vendor I get an immediate answer, and they seem to be progressive with new applications. This level of service is every bit as important as the quality of the products a vendor sells."

Lessons from a Surgical Vendor Selection

Intuitive Surgical (www.intuitivesurgical.com) manufactures the da Vinci Surgical System. This product directly translates the surgeon's natural hand, wrist, and finger movements into corresponding micromovements of surgical instrument tips positioned inside the patient through small puncture incisions, or ports. The company has a team of sales and service reps who cover North America and Europe.

Intuitive Surgical has two teams that are responsible for establishing and growing its worldwide market presence. The sales team must provide products to customers and also serve as the primary liaison for the account, managing long-term objectives with day-to-day needs. The service technicians must conduct proactive maintenance and respond to customers rapidly.

For both teams, real-time, simple access to back-office software with information about customers and equipment is critical. Sales and service reps need up-to-the-minute data, detailed account records. But before the company implemented its wireless application, achieving these goals was difficult for both teams.

Everyone accessed customer information through client/server software and laptops. It was often hard to find a modem connection, the software required more bandwidth than standard modems or wireless connections could handle, remote access calls were expensive, and laptops were cumbersome in certain situations.

Before calling in vendors, Intuitive Surgical mapped out a list of needs. Paramount among these was the ability to work on multiple mobile devices and wireless carriers in the United States and Europe, including locations without available high-bandwidth connections. The application also had to support several back-office programs with different interfaces in addition to the sales and field support, such as e-mail and scheduling.

The wireless application had to be able to send information through e-mail, numeric and alphanumeric pages, voice alerts, and faxes. The company wanted the vendor's application to address the issue of future growth and future wireless or software technology that may impact their business.

It is important to see what factors during the vendor selection process led Intuitive Surgical to choose wireless application vendor Xora (www.xora.com), since some of these might fit into your criteria for whatever vendors you may evaluate.

One factor that caught their attention was that Xora's application didn't require Intuitive's in-house developers to learn how to use a new program because Xora works automatically with the back-office software that Intuitive already has. As you look at other vendors and ASPs, a big consideration is how much training will their applications or services require of your developers, which costs time and money.

You also want to modify as little of your back-end software as possible. Some of the larger software companies such as Siebel and Oracle are building wireless capabilities into their applications so you can more easily add wireless access, and vendors such as Xora are building ready-made software hooks into these applications.

A second factor that Intuitive liked was that Xora has human factors engineers on staff whose expertise is designing software user interfaces (UIs) best suited for users of the wireless applications. UI design is a critical to the success of your wireless applications, as you will see in the last section of this chapter, and either you or the vendor you select have to address this. If neither you nor the vendor have UI experts, then you will need to look at a third-party outfit that can provide this expertise.

Third, Intuitive was insistent that the application be device-independent. Most of the application vendors and ASPs I have written about in the book have made their applications both device and carrier network independent, or have plans to do so. Vendors probably use different technology to enable this capability, but in terms of the final results, they give customers the ability to maximize their hardware investment without the hassles of mandating that everyone use the same device.

Fourth, having an application that automatically formats content for various mobile devices does not mean that all of your work is done for you, so Intuitive was looking for a vendor that could assist with this development work. Brian Salisbury is a director of business development at Motorola who works with their various wireless devices. He states that, "an automated tool can be used to perform the initial format conversions, but field trials with actual users and subsequent 'hand tuning' will be needed before the application is made widely available.

"For an enterprise application to be frequently accessed by mobile workers, you must pay careful attention to the business logic of how data is viewed and manipulated on a mobile device, and this extends beyond what automated tools can provide. The small screen of a mobile device makes it necessary to use multiple screens to represent the same amount of data that users see on a desktop. You have to carefully select which pieces of information to display and which actions users can execute from their devices." So despite what you might read about an application being ready to go "right out of the box," you must insist on a realistic estimate on how much modification of is required on your applications to make them wireless-enabled.

Fifth, Intuitive was sensitive to Xora's ability to facilitate knowledge management. While you are building a wireless application to make it easy to access information, also work with the vendor to make information from mobile workers accessible to others. Every time someone finds a new and faster way to fix a problem, or a new way to overcome a sales objection, this should be fed back into the system for others to access both wirelessly or from their desktops.

The one fly in the ointment of wireless knowledge management for sales force automation (SFA) is the ruthless competitiveness of some salespeople who tend not to share their "secrets to success," especially if you offer incentives to the best sales performers. I don't have a ready solution for this problem, but I do know that you have to factor it into any sales applications designed for sharing expertise.

All Things Being Unequal, No One Vendor Does It All

A factor to consider when selecting vendors is that one vendor, one software platform, one type of mobile hardware device probably won't meet all of the needs within your organization if you have more than a few dozen people. This means that you will have to deal with mixing and matching applications to meet diverse needs. Duncan Bradley, manager of market knowledge for RIM, states, "There is no single device that satisfies everyone. Some people only need a PDA; others only need a phone. Someone else needs e-mail and data base access. You want to minimize vendors, but you will have tradeoffs."

Maybe a department that lives and dies by graphics and color-coded mechanical drawings needs color, but a person doing inventory lookup, and shipping status review doesn't. ROI will be higher if you are delivering a compelling solution to your users, so don't go cheap and try to force devices on people just because they're cheap. Give people what they need to do a good job.

Ray DePaul, RIM's director of product planning, adds, "The key is to make sure you're leveraging the back-end systems you already have in place because you don't want to restructure content and infrastructure any more than you have to. Pick standards that are broadly supported and try not to select proprietary systems because you will limit your options in the future as your needs evolve."

With software, you should try to minimize the number of wireless software applications you bring together. Harrold Mann of Mann Consulting likens integrating too many applications to running a food court. "There are lots of different foods offered that people may like, but none of them are really great in their own right. You should pick products that work well, don't deviate from standards and keep things simple."

It helps if the vendor you connect with has already assembled other vendors' complementary pieces of the application puzzle before you even contact them. Sierra Wireless, for example, is primarily in the wireless modem business. But they created the Wireless Ready Alliances to be able to provide customers with one source for the various technology components that can comprise a complete and effective application. This group of business partners includes wireless carriers, PDA and other hardware manufacturers, software vendors, and system integrators.

Over the years the technology industry has spawned quite a few alliances that were little more than marketing-hype machines, so you can't just take them at face value. But if you research them and find that they have resolved issues such as product quality, service delivery, and interoperability among the respective vendors, they can save you a lot of headaches. If you work with these types of alliances, be sure not to miss one or two of the smaller vendors that are viable businesses with applications that may be ideal for you.

As much as it pains me to say it, you have to assume vendor failure. Watching the Web and wireless vendor casualties drop like flies, I don't think you can't bank on everyone being here in three years, at least not in their present form and ownership. So create a backup plan for every vendor so that you have a quick response and minimal grief and aggravation in case one of them isn't there when you wake up tomorrow. Some vendors don't fail; bigger companies just swallow them up. Then you may have to worry about questions such as: Will the quality of service slip, or will the new owners continue to support the products you have already bought?

The Interface That Launched a Thousand Ships—the Value of Good UI Design

You don't have to be first to be successful, but it definitely helps to have a good interface. The Apple Newton was supposed to be the commercial rocket that would launch the personal computing world into a new era. Instead it sputtered and flamed out, due in no small measure to interface capabilities that were described by the few who used it as overhyped and underdeveloped relative to consumer's needs.

But in 1996, the Palm Pilot 1000 launched and proceeded to take the world by storm. As of this writing about 75 percent of the PDAs in the world are either Palm Pilots or run the Palm operating system. There are thousands of applications available, that support the Palm OS, and this number is steadily rising.

Palm may or may not remain the market leader in two or three years, but there's one important lesson to take from their ascendancy to dominance. The success or failure of your wireless implementations depends as much on the ease with which people can operate the software and hardware UIs, as it does on the value delivered by the applications. When you implement wireless applications, set aside time and resources to make sure that you do this part of the implementation right.

Mariel van Totenhove is currently the director of marketing for Synaptics (www.synaptics.com), which develops touchscreens, input devices, and other interface products that are built into mobile device. She also worked for the Pocket PC group at Phillips and Internet appliances at AT&T, so Totenhove definitely knows about interface design.

She believes there has been one important thing lacking with wireless application design. "People have retained the design of the PC for years when addressing mobility, while focusing on making devices wireless and then on increasing the speed of wireless data transmission. But the problem that people face has little to do with bandwidth. You can access a lot of data as wireless transmission speeds increase, but the difficulty is viewing and manipulating the data.

"People have to think about creating a different UI paradigm, they have to step away from the PC and look at PDAs as the new thing. Right now PDAs have cluttered interfaces, or users have to tap and click through layers of data, and open various windows. Requiring four clicks to get to information is not a good thing."

Totenhove believes that different people have to address this interface issue: wireless hardware and software vendors and the service providers who should know what the needs of their customers are. However, it can't be just the hardware or the wireless software that organizations focus on because everything is interrelated, including how you format the back-end applications that the wireless software accesses.

That being said, it's obvious that your organization may not be able to influence hardware design, but you can control the software and data access features of the applications that you build or buy. You can also control what hardware you buy.

"People are creating simple software forms to access data bases, lists, order forms, etc. from mobile devices," observes Totenhove. "This is definitely a good tact for organizations with applications that focus on verticals markets, or are used internally by your employees for specific functions such as sales force automation." In these applications, there are limited amounts of data that people need to access or input, and you can predetermine what most of this data will be.

However, average consumers need the new device design, which requires that someone build it, then train people on how it works. In the meantime, for applications that you implement to address external audiences, you're going to have to do the best you can to deliver data to devices with interfaces that consumers have now. You have to work within the limitations, and wait for the hardware developers to improve their end of the deal.

Tips and Recommendations on UI Design

UI design is a topic that could be its own book, but I'm going to give you just a few general recommendations to move you in the right direction. It may be that you won't get involved with your wireless application development at the UI design level, but you should understand some of the basic issues so you can better direct those who will be primarily responsible for this task.

This section discusses general business operations issues that will influence UI design, such as deciding how to prioritize what business software data actually gets delivered to a mobile device, and presents tips specifically for UI design.

Operations

First and foremost, you have to focus on simplifying the data that gets delivered to mobile devices. Regardless of the application, people have to be able to easily see the information they need even in bad lighting, have a minimal number of screens to navigate, and a minimal number of screen taps or graffiti writing to input data. By the way, if you haven't done it yet, you really should borrow someone's PDA so you can see what I mean.

If you are creating a new application (as opposed to building a wireless extension to software applications you already use), it is probably an easier task to create a good UI. For one thing, you don't have to modify existing screens, which can be time-consuming. More importantly, right from the start you will be able to structure data specifically for the capabilities and limitations of the various mobile devices.

Making your existing applications wireless-enabled can be a bigger challenge. As Aether System's Mancuso sums it up, "If you're on a desktop accessing a CRM application, you can see everything. Call it 100 points of light. If you're on a mobile device, you go from 100 points of light down to five points. So you have to decide what is the most important information for PDAs to access. Then prioritize the type of data that you will make available as bandwidth increases."

For the organizations that can afford it, he recommends creating a mini-lab for testing devices, interfaces, wireless networks, and so on because the next wave of technology will be wireless. This has potential for a huge amount of positive ROI because the lessons you learn internally can be applied to communicating with external audiences. As economic challenges continue, enhancing the customer relationship wirelessly and maintaining loyalty will be crucial.

Second, you have to consider how people work and the context in which the application will be used. In some cases you may find that some business tasks should not or cannot be wireless-enabled.

I was surprised to learn from Dr. Richard Fiedotin at ePocrates that so many vendors with wireless applications for private medical practices were going broke since there have been many articles published about the potential ways mobile devices will change the medical profession. ePocrates, though, is doing well with over 300,000 healthcare professionals using their software and services. So, what's up, doc?

"Doctors use our products for a very simple task, checking drug and infectious diseases databases that they need to access in a hurry while treating patients. This is something that is vital to their daily practice, and the search procedure is pretty simple. Putting PDA templates on office management applications [which most competitors do] is not popular. If there are few clicks to execute a function, then these applications are too generic. If you offer doctors access to more data details, then the apps will require too many clicks to reach the information."

Patients have so many variables regarding their medical conditions and they talk in such wandering prose that it's hard to capture histories in a PDA that requires linear data input. Writing with graffiti is difficult, so using any software that requires descriptive text is difficult.

The much-hyped use of PDAs to write prescriptions may also be a bust because it requires so much extra time. Doctors have to write the prescription, talk with patients about what pharmacy they use, move to a PC, and wait for data to beam into the PC to be printed for the patient or transmitted to a pharmacist. Wireless transmission of prescriptions is problematic because speeds can be slow and it's difficult for carrier service to reach inside certain buildings.

So what about emergency personnel in ambulances being able to use PDAs to access patients medical records from doctors while they're racing to the ER? "Have you ever seen your patient records at your doctor's office?" Fiedotin asks. "Everything in there is on paper—and will be for quite some time to come."

Your workers may not have the same work practices and idiosyncrasies as doctors, but they most likely have some that are unique to their department, skill levels, age, work environments, or a host of other factors. You have to understand these in great detail to select the right processes to wireless-enable and build the appropriate UIs.

Third, put as much functionality on the mobile device as it can handle. You want to minimize data traffic, maximize data manipulation on mobile devices.

Tom Nogles of ThinAirApps suggest using icons with links to software routines on the mobile devices to speed up data manipulation. "This way, incoming content could be programmed to reference these icons and automatically trigger actions such as popping up menus. Using apps will be easier if you can input voice that becomes a text note when there is a convergence of voice and regular data entry on PDAs. We've talked to unified messaging vendors, so we know that some of the foundation for this is in place today, but I expect to see some actual applications come down the pike by fall of 2002."

Fourth, employee privacy is of maximum importance, and application design must reflect this. One of the biggest dangers for backlash from your workforce is their perception that mobile devices are a means of tracking them every hour of the day. You have to walk a tightrope between helping your employees do their job better and not appearing to be Big Brother.

Lotus recently announced wireless IM features in one of their collaboration tools with an important feature that allows users to manually key their PDAs to tell the organizations that the PDAs are available to receive an IM. If they aren't available for an IM, users can indicate some other means to contact them such as a telephone voice mail.

Competitors, whose applications force users to always be on the network to receive IMs, made a big deal of telling the media that this feature indicates that Lotus doesn't understand the market. What Lotus understands is that there are times of the day when people need to disengage themselves physically and electronically from their workplace for a variety of legitimate reasons. You're dealing with humans being here, and we humans occasionally a need break from being "always on."

Sometimes it's the way that you present features such as tracking or notification to employees, which causes problems. If you tell them you're embedding wireless devices in their trucks to reduce goofing off, you may put the slackers back in line, but the honest workers will resent you. Who knows where that will lead? But if you tell employees that the tracking features in an application help you better manage their trips so you can throw more sales leads and more money their way, everybody will be on your side. They might even show you new ways to make the tracking system more valuable.

Fifth, test today, test tomorrow, test forever to understand not just the UI design, but how people's use of the applications changes. Says Telephia's John Dee Fair, "I can't overemphasize how important getting that feedback is. Our users come back with issues that are 180-degrees different from what vendors think the needs and problems are. Someone using the same device in the same city has different experiences and possibly different expectations depending on the time of day and location from where they're using the device.

"We have conducted surveys and carriers think customers are worried about security, speed and this is why they don't want ads pushed to their devices. But users tell us their number one complaint is screen clutter. You have to talk to real users who are using the devices every day because their answers are more reality-based about the physical devices of today.

Sixth, do yourself a huge favor and buy applications or use service providers that take your content, filter it, and format it automatically for the various mobile devices. You have enough work to do without the workload and headaches of trying to match UIs, content format, and so on, for various devices that are constantly evolving. And while you're at it, see if these vendors do super-compression of data. 3G wireless networks may get here in force this decade, but just in case they don't, hedge your bets. When it comes to wireless content, smaller is better.

Sanjay Shirole, CEO of Xora, offers some additional insights to help you prep for using a new computing platform. "For any application that has been up and running for a while your people have had a certain experience using that software. Make sure that the flow of data entry or how users query data on a mobile device is as similar to what the procedures are on the desktop. The transition can't be jolting or you'll have to spend extra time winning people over and more money retraining them."

Take a Siebel Systems application for example. If you give someone less information on the PDA but they can still drill down the same way they're used to on a PC and find the data they need, then mentally the user feels like very little has changed.

Shirole cautions that your costs do not end at the moment of deployment. There will be ongoing changes because users will always be finding new needs, so once you go wireless the applications become a regularly evolving thing. You need to buy or develop applications and development tools that can make these changes easily.

Another thing is that once everyone starts using these wireless applications, there will be changes in how your employees operate and you have to be ready to capitalize on those changes. For example, when procurement managers leave their offices, purchase order approvals may be held up. But once they're wirelessly connected, this bottleneck disappears, which might give you leeway to streamline other parts of the purchasing and billing process.

An Avid Reminder to Adapt and Perform

Besides integrating wireless applications with your back-end software, also determine if it you should integrate wireless with your website, intranet, and extranet for the purpose of distributing information you create to resellers and other business partners. If so, you have to address many of the same factors as you do with software integration, such as streamlining materials down to the "must have" details. However, be aware that you may require additional UI development time if you can't use the same interface that you develop for your back-end software.

If you work with resellers, this next story about Avid Technology will be helpful. The September 1, 2001 issue of *Internet World* magazine reported that Avid doubled the ROI for this implementation because the application also became popular with the internal salespeople. A similar type of application also can be used with third-party telemarketing, customer service, and support organizations.

Avid Technology (www.avid.com) specializes in tools for creating and editing video, audio, film, animation, special effects, and streaming media. Its technology is used to produce TV shows, news broadcasts, music videos, and CDs.

To market its products, Avid relies on both internal salespeople and outside resellers whom they have to frequently update with new information about promotions and pricing policies. The company moved from printed price books to a secure extranet for resellers to keep their sales forces informed. It was then decided that a wireless application would give Avid more flexibility in delivering time-sensitive data such as new sales messages and competitive analyses.

Avid worked with an AvantGo consultant to help with installing the software to create communication channels, determining how to modify Avid's content for PDAs, and training the staff responsible for managing the software and content. This process took a week. Next, Avid had to actually modify the content for wireless delivery (such as price sheets generated in Microsoft Excel spreadsheets), which took several weeks.

The company discovered that this conversion process was useful because it forced people to decide what is really important to distribute to resellers, and what information can stay on the extranet for people to access through regular desktops. Avid provided Palm IIIe devices to each of its one hundred reseller locations. Many sales reps already had their own Palm V or wireless Palm VII, so about 300 resellers overall now access the extranet through their Palms.

Avid sent resellers e-mail detailing how to install AvantGo and pages on its extranet so users could download the client and documents covering procedures, system requirements, and how to uninstall the software. As resellers got up and running, Avid's in-house salespeople became interested in using the same application because it was an easier way to keep track of a broad product line with many promotions and price changes.

The extranet works well for information distribution because Avid can filter information according to the products that specific resellers or salespeople sell, so they don't waste their time sifting through extraneous information. In the field, sales reps don't waste time going through a lot of printed price books in three-ring binders.

Avid is now looking into how it can distribute information to Internet-ready phones as well. So far, the company isn't enabling resellers to perform transactions with the software, but it may in the future.

Specific UI Design Recommendations

Be aware that even excellent designers and engineers sometimes have a concept of good design that is not compatible with what average people find usable. You don't want a $500,000 wireless application neutered by a bad $10,000 UI design. To articulate forcefully and accurately what you need in interface designs requires that you know some of the basics of this technical process.

A few years ago, Mike Stokowski worked at Geoworks on the team that developed user interfaces for what were to be some of the early PDAs and today's smartphones. He offers some thoughts about UI design for applications that run on mobile devices, and what are some key rules business managers should keep in mind. These are important because someone at the business management level has to be aware of these issues so they can better define the parameters for buying or building wireless applications, and review the end results before deployment.

"UI design, often overlooked in the application design process, is as important as the software coding itself, especially in wireless applications," Stokowski remarks. "The application obviously must solve the problems the user expects it to solve, but the UI must make the solutions easily accessible. For instance, a sales automation tool must make it easy to enter contact information, not just store that information in an elegant database for future use."

In an ideal world, you would design the application's UI before engineers create any code, but often you're lucky if you can even overlap UI design and the coding processes. In either case there are two very important up front tasks: 1) clearly define a UI design process, and 2) hire or contract the right people to do the work. If you hire the right people, they can help define the design process.

Stokowski believes that there are three types of skills to look for in people. You may find one person that has all of these skills, or you may have to "mix and match" a design team, but it is important to have all of the skills covered.

You need a user interface expert who has a background in UI design and human factors engineering. This person should have a passion for good usability design, be experienced interviewing users and testing products with users, and know how to work effectively with engineers and designers.

You also need a designer/artist who has a background in design and illustration. Not all products need this, but having a real designer can make a big difference with applications to be displayed on small screens. It will help if this person has PDA design skills since small-screen design requires slightly different skills than laptop screen design.

Last, you need a standards bearer, someone with engineering or design experience for the mobile devices you plan to use. This person needs to continually check the interfaces during the design process to make sure they meet accepted standards. You want your UIs to be similar to other products on the devices. For instance, when it runs on a Pocket PC, it should look similar to other Pocket PC applications.

Here is a summary of key points in the UI design process and some questions you (or whoever is managing the design process) should ask to be sure that the UI you get is what people will use.

1. Identify the user requirement. (Who is the user? What are real users going to expect to get done with the application?)

2. Define the feature set. (What features do users need to get the job done? What features might get in the way?)

3. Conceptualize the UI. (In general, how will users best navigate and interact with the application?)

4. Design the UI. Lay out the components in a general way with just enough detail to see how they will work together.

5. Layout the UI.

6. Test how well people can operate the UI. You only need a few users for this. The important part here is to clearly identify who the users of the final application will be and find five to ten people who fit the profile. It's not expensive. Make your engineers watch the test.

7. Fix the problems.

8. Code the application.

Is Voice a UI Option?

When I started researching information for this book, I made a general assumption that voice would be a natural way for people to input data into mobile devices, particularly cell phones. I also assumed that voice files would be an important way for receiving data on any mobile device because mobile workers could access information at times when it isn't convenient to read, such as when driving.

One of my first interviews changed my perspective, and subsequent conversations reinforced the idea that voice will have less rather than more importance as a user interface for wireless applications. When I spoke with Rick Goetter of Kyocera about their Smartphone, I was certain he would be a big champion of voice because his product combines the phone with Palm PDA functionality. The Smartphone even allows you to voice activate calls to phone numbers that you enter into the device's phone book application.

Goetter's response? "One of the things we're finding is that the large screen with a nice visual interface makes people more comfortable with wireless devices. I believe the wireless access of the Web will be more visually-driven than voice driven. The applications designed for the screen will drive wireless communication by making it a more compelling experience." Why is that I wondered?

Well, both wireless application vendors and people implementing these applications feel that for data input, speech recognition software isn't bad, but for many it just isn't ready for prime time. Depending on whom you talk to, speech recognition is somewhere between 85 percent and 95 percent accurate at determining what a person says. Some applications can be trained better than others, but if data in your sales force software plays a critical role in your organization even a 5 percent error rate is unacceptable.

In terms of listening to voice files, this is problematic because voice is very linear. You can't scan through it to pick up the highlights of the message or document, and listening to a long file can be tedious. If you miss an important point, it's hard to search back to the item you missed. You're also at a disadvantage if there are sudden noises in the background or if you have trouble understanding the dialect of the voice speaking.

Then there are the software and computing power issues. You have to have extra processing power on the servers (or extra servers) running interactive voice response (IVR) applications and storing voice files. The ability to process voice capabilities will also require extra memory on mobile devices and could significantly shorten the battery life.

Having said that, there are situations in which it makes sense to use a voice. Xora's Shirole concurs. "If you have more than four or five data elements, such as name, purchase date, amount, location, and products bought, people will not be able to absorb the information. They need to see this on the screen. But people will use PDAs to input small amounts of data into an application via voice such as time spent working on a project. You will see PDAs capable of converting voice into data and dropping it into appropriate application files and databases maybe in the next year or two. All of this will depend on the power of future PDAs since battery life, memory, and CPU performance dictate the parameters of these capabilities."

Chris Koppe of Speedware believes you will see voice and data being used. "People will be in a situation where typing and scrolling is a problem, but they still might want to pay a bill or make a bank transaction. Some people are not comfortable listening to a digital voice, or having this voice ask confirming questions. The key is being able to switch from data to voice and back again."

A case can be made for using speech recognition to initiate certain activities from a mobile device. For example, while driving a salesperson can prompt an application to compile all the past sales transactions of a specific customer so it's transmitted to his or her PDA in an easy-to-review format. He or she can then read the information while waiting in the lobby for a meeting to start. When the command options are limited, it's easier for the system to be accurate.

On the flip side, short and focused messages are the best for delivering voice data to mobile devices. I suggest you give people the option to use the stylus to navigate to the information they want, and then have the option to read or listen to the voice document. What drives me (and a lot of other people) crazy is not listening to a digital voice read information, but going through the endless "Press or say 1 if you want this, press or say 2 if you want that" commands.

Companies such as Intuitive implement applications whose back-end systems take simple requests by phone or websites from customers and prospects, then convert them into voice messages and deliver them to cell phones or PDAs that can play audio files. To complete the communication loop, you can record voice messages on some PDAs and pass these back to the home office.

ServiceHub offers customers similar communication features with two voice-based options that complement their wireless services. They create voice interaction as a parallel path to the data that users interact with on their mobile devices. Truck drivers who use ServiceHub's dispatch service can call an 800 number to get their delivery assignments when they're out of wireless coverage.

The application uses text-to-voice technology to deliver the information that the drivers need. A driver can say "accept" to their assignments and the system updates all of the shipping company's necessary files. Everything is received by the mobile devices once they are back in a coverage area. Xora has a similar capability in its application.

The second way ServiceHub uses voice is for their field support service. A technician may check on a drop-down list on his or her mobile device that he or she installed "x" component. But if the person wants to leave a note for the next technician that's too complicated to type on a PDA keypad, he or she can record a voice field note that is saved as a .WAV file. Then he or she links the .WAV file to the job record that's stored on the system so the next technician who gets called out to the site will see an icon for the voice file.

That technician can download and play this voice file back on any mobile device with a speaker, or even on a regular phone if he or she calls in that way to pick up his or her job assignment. The system acknowledges if the person reads or ignores the note. Being a *Star Trek* fan from way back when, I look forward to the ability to have a dynamic intelligent two-way voice conversation with a computer using cool wireless communicators on my lapel. (Beam down Seven of Nine, and let's party!) But alas, I fear that this will be at some star date in the distant future. For the moment, I think your prime directive should be to plan carefully and within the limitations of the technology if you want to incorporate voice UIs into your wireless applications.

So now that we've looked at strategic and tactical options, let's wrap all this together in a written plan for putting wireless technology to work for you at warp speed.

PART **IV**

The Plan

Once you've strategized and brainstormed, and you have the managers whipped up into a frenzy of support for your wireless initiatives, someone has to sit down and commit this vision and these ideas into a written plan for success. Avoid the pitfalls that plagued so many Web projects when executives delegated responsibility for getting the organization online, but didn't demand a plan that would be everyone's guiding light to lead them through the dim maze of possibilities and promises.

CHAPTER 16

Delivering the Written Word—the Wireless Strategy and Tactics Plan

The written wireless strategy and tactics plan pulls together all the pieces of your wireless implementation—strategy, tactics, resource issues, timelines, and other key elements—in a document that is your blueprint for producing the results you want.

The lack of a plan can result in much wireless floundering and resource squandering before you begin to see positive results, if you ever do. Senior executives and line managers alike need to see something on paper that spells out where you're going and why. In this respect, wireless communicating is no different than communicating through conventional media.

People are often too busy trying to get a project out the door, or putting out fires of one sort or another, to devote enough time to planning. Also, wireless communication is changing rapidly, and it's hard to plan when your communication medium is a moving target.

The methodology I gave you in the proceeding chapters will help you to develop a comprehensive plan that is flexible enough so you can adopt new technologies and modify tactics quickly and without losing sight of your strategic objectives. This chapter gives you a guideline for actually writing that plan so you can distribute it to the people who will play a role in implementing your wireless communication campaign.

Before preparing the plan, however, there are two important things that you need to do. The first is to prioritize your strategic objectives, and the second is to conduct a brainstorming session to develop the specific tactics that your organization will use to achieve those objectives.

357

Create a Winning Combination of Strategic Options

Remember our four strategic options? They are:

1. Communicate with existing customers.

2. Provide more effective service and support.

3. Communicate with prospective customers.

4. Reduce costs and improve efficiency of internal business operations.

As you read the chapters about these four strategic options, it probably occurred to you that taking on these tasks simultaneously will probably overwhelm your resources. You're right. For most organizations there won't be the need or the resources to execute all four strategies simultaneously. However, the important thing is to review all four options so you understand the full range of possibilities.

Assemble the Key Players

Now that you have the complete picture of strategic options, bring your executive management team together, along with your department managers, IT staff, and the Web team members who will have a role in the wireless technology selection and implementation. If they haven't read this book yet, I suggest you buy them all copies so everyone has the same strategic points of reference.

Depending on the size of your organization, it may require two or three strategic planning meetings to get all your priorities in order. This is fine as long as you don't let this particular exercise drag out too long. Bringing all of these people together may seem like a lot of work, but if you want wireless to make the biggest possible financial impact on your organization, you need to have the departments well represented.

There is another reason for bringing all of these people together. You want to leverage your wireless efforts across as many departments or business units as possible. For example, an application that helps field sales staff may also be valuable to the field support team. You can save on content development if the different groups participate in this planning process.

It's also good to have these people together at the outset to neutralize that old potential nemesis of forward momentum—office politics. I've sat through a few meetings where it was clear that the client's initial web efforts had been launched without including all of the people who were, or could have been, affected by these efforts. Barely concealed hostilities and active indifference were strong undercurrents. Trying to execute an organization-wide plan is very difficult once this negativity sets in. If your intent is to have wireless communication be a far-reaching force to enhance your financial and competitive positions, you must have all the right players in from the beginning.

Prioritize

When you have everyone together, review each of the four strategic options individually, paying particular attention to the potential financial impact as well as the resource requirements of implementing the respective options. Use the financial exercises I presented, or use your own. It will probably help if the different departments do some preliminary analysis prior to this meeting since some of the calculations could take a while to pull together.

As you start listing the potential ROI for each option, a priority order for which strategy to tackle first, second, and so on should start to become apparent. Be prepared for other factors to enter into the discussion that may not be financial, but will sway which strategy gets a higher priority. For example, enhancing customer service may have low monetary payback in the short term, but it may play such an important role in closing key business partnerships that this is where the primary focus will be.

However impressive the ROI may look, be sure everyone understands what the resource requirements are to make the strategy achieve those numbers. Sometimes organizations may have to settle for a smaller ROI for several months because they don't have the number of people necessary to execute the strategy and their organization has a hiring freeze in place. These factors affect the priority. As you start linking strategic options to resource requirements, be sure the people who are responsible for those resources are part of the discussion.

When you create your priority list based on potential ROI and available resources, be sure to identify what the pilot projects should be if you do not have any that are already underway. The pilots will give you the first indications about what you can realistically expect in terms of financial impact, logistical problems, and additional business opportunities, so you want to be sure these are well thought out.

Balance Is Critical

Before you close the book on your priority list, consider all the ways your wireless activities will impact other aspects of the business. Of course, there are many things you will not be able to predict, but if you define an objective of increasing sales leads by 200 percent you better be ready to process 200 percent more leads from initial call to final shipping of products.

A few years ago a marketing director hired my firm to develop her company's Internet plan. After the first meeting with department managers, where we suggested potential ideas, the highly agitated customer service manager spoke with us about what she saw as marketing's effort to create online programs that would significantly increase service calls.

This type of tension between departments was common with web projects, and I expect the same thing will happen with wireless projects. So make sure parts of your organization don't get blindsided with work overload and resource requirements that they aren't prepared to handle.

I continually tell people about preparing for the Law of Unintended Consequence. For example, a company launches a wireless promotion to increase website sales, but all of a sudden, the phones are ringing off the hook. The promotion is successful, but instead of ordering online, people just do research at the site. They are so impressed that they want to order immediately, but by phone instead of online.

A lot of people tried really hard to make the Web a predictable medium in the same way that they could predict the results of print ads, direct mail, and other marketing activities. In many ways, you won't know until you open the floodgates what indirect effects wireless will have. Subsequently you have to do a continual balancing act between what you want to do on the Web or with wireless. Ideally, you want to have contingency plans in place so in case you have to shift priorities, you don't have to drag everyone into a lengthy debate to sort things out.

Another balancing act you may have to deal with is other business operations that may require the same people or technology resources that you need for wireless deployment. Sometimes everyone leaves the table thinking that their priorities are in order, but they've forgotten about the people in another office who may demand priority for *their* work.

The ultimate balance you have to strike is between people's expectations versus what you can realistically deliver. I remember a few meetings in past years when we'd deliver a final Web project and suddenly there would be dozens of people saying, "I didn't think it was going to look like that. Why don't you . . ." and the list of suggestions and complaints would pour out.

Luckily, wireless applications are not perceived as something simple to develop, so if these don't affect them directly, few people will care one way or the other. But you should get off on the right foot by managing people's expectations, from the rank and file workers all the way up to the executive suite.

Part of the reason for bringing such a diverse team into the strategy-planning sessions is to get their buy-in and participation early in the process. It's easier to manage your CFO's expectations if the CFO contributes establishing to the main objectives. And the reason I advocate having a written plan is that it keeps everyone's expectations in line with what the objectives are.

It is in your best interest to keep tabs on what key people expect from your efforts because they will frequently be reading or hearing about "the latest new thing" in wireless. You don't want their latest fascination to be your latest headache. It's good to be flexible enough to take advantage of new technology, but technology is not the tail that wags the strategic dog.

One last thing on balancing expectations with what you deliver. As you roll out pilot projects, particularly those that involve internal communication, be sure a lot of people get to see the pilots. One, it's easier to make changes if you get feedback early in the project development process. Two, as people put in their feedback, they feel like they are contributing which increases buy-in later, even if you don't adopt their suggestions.

You Must Be Specific

The specific measurable objectives that you set during these strategic-planning sessions collectively are the rock upon which you build your budgets, technology purchase decisions, tactical plans, etc. Don't send people off to launch a pilot or full-blown project with vague or impossible-to-measure directives.

"All our salespeople have to be wireless by the second quarter," is a direct statement, but as an objective it's as clear as a foggy night in London. Better your objective should state, "We will reduce sales costs by $100 per week per salesperson, and reduce sales cycles by 10 percent in the Atlanta region." The tactical plan will address the specific how-tos of achieving these goals, but every person's activity as it pertains to the wireless implementation should be dictated by the specifics of this objective.

For each of the chapters on strategy, I presented in general terms a list of three or four main objectives to help focus your thinking. Your list should be more detailed in description, though you don't necessarily need more objectives. In fact, I recommend you limit your objectives to two or three in the beginning so you maximize your opportunity for success, then maybe develop one or two more objectives later.

When it comes time to dealing with vendors, employees, business partners, and others, it should be crystal clear what you want to accomplish with this technology. And not only should there be objectives with distinct payback, but you also need to have measurable benchmarks along the way so you can regularly check your progress.

Taking the objective above, if the goal is to reduce sales cost by $100, then you should indicate by which point you are saving $25, then $50, and so on. There should be statements in the written plan to the effect of "we will know that we are on target for shortening our sales cycles when leads start coming in two hours after our sponsored content is broadcast."

Include in your list of specifics the names of the people who are responsible for reaching the objectives. You don't want to put people on the spot needlessly, but at the same time, there should be some degree of public ownership if you plan for wireless communication to have organization-wide impact. The people with responsibility need to feel recognized and accountable for their efforts.

Another thing you want to do is communicate these objectives to others in the organization. I remember a conversation with one of my cousins, who is a regional sales director, when I asked him about his previous company's website. His first words were, "I think it's a waste of money."

I asked him what the site was supposed to do for the company. It turns out neither his boss nor anyone else had articulated even one objective for their site. Either the company didn't have any objectives, or no one thought it was important enough to tell the executives and the sales force. You really don't want this happening with your organization and wireless.

When you lay out timelines for your milestones allow for things taking longer and costing more than you expect. Even if you use wireless ASPs that have established fees, something will always come up that affects time and internal costs. Good project management may be more common with wireless than with web development in its early days, but we're still dealing with relatively new technology being used in new ways. Your plan may be one of the few roadmaps to this new frontier, so allow for some unexpected bumps and turns.

Brainstorming for Tactics

The next major task before writing the plan is the brainstorming session to develop ideas for specific tactics that will help you reach your strategic objectives. In this session you will combine what you know about conventional and Internet communication, plus what you've just learned about wireless (and will continue to learn), to stimulate the creative juices. Your brainstorming session should be governed by the philosophy that there is probably nothing that can't be tried, or won't be tried, in the realm of wireless communication before the final chapters are written on the subject.

It is most important that the same group that you assemble for strategy development also participate in the brainstorming, even if they can't stay for the entire session, since your tactics need to be driven by strategic objectives. You want to encourage unbridled creativity during the session, but the final tactical ideas you select need to be grounded in strategic reality.

You can bring in an outside consultant experienced in wireless business applications to facilitate the process since an outsider often brings objectivity and additional insights that will enhance the ideas that you generate. Before the session this person should learn as much as possible about your company, products, or market, as well as your marketing strategy, business operations, and available resources.

When you're ready to start, break out a few six-packs of your favorite beverage, lots of markers and paper, your wireless strategy objectives, mobile devices, and a computer that can access websites you may want to reference to stimulate ideas. If everyone in the room has read the chapters on tactics before arriving at this session, they will be more helpful determining which points apply to your company. This will help inspire some of your brainstorming ideas.

It will also help to have these folks use some mobile devices before the session. If it's hard to find someone within the organization with a PDA, see if people can go to the local CompUSA or Office Depot and play with some of the display units. Everything I've described in the preceding chapters will make more sense once everyone actually experiences the wireless environment.

If your organization has some wireless activities underway, make sure everyone in the group sees them before you begin brainstorming. Encourage them to access some of your business software and visit your website or intranet that may be wireless-enabled. You might be surprised how many people do not know what's going on with their own organization's website.

Once everyone has settled in, give people an overview of what the strategic priorities are. Then, working point by point, turn the session into a creative free-for-all where no idea is criticized, discarded, or immediately accepted. Standard brainstorming rules apply here. To guide you, here are some issues your group may want to consider.

Building Brand Awareness and Loyalty

These are the tactics that will help you build a community of customers who are loyal to your product (brand). Besides customers, these tactics will inform as many people as possible about what your product and organization have to offer. They may not be customers today, but who knows about tomorrow.

Your branding tactics may consist of promotions and creative sponsorships, but they can also include aggressively pushing your wireless content to mobile devices, running joint promotional campaigns with other organizations, or driving people to your website. Don't forget that the experience people have with you wirelessly impacts your image.

Direct Response Communication

Unlike the tactics in the previous section which have the long-term impact of helping to build brand awareness or loyalty, direct response tactics will induce people to take a specific action, and preferably right now (call about a product, download literature).

If you're a new company with immediate cash flow needs, you may be more inclined toward "buy one, get one free" offers, or giveaways to induce swift action. As the number of organizations using wireless increases, even established firms with loyal customers might have a greater need for direct response promotions to help them rise above the increasing communication noise.

Educating Your Various Audiences

Market education goes beyond making people aware of your brand. It includes giving customers and prospects an in-depth understanding of your product or service, your company, or your industry. Many people are more likely to buy a product when they fully understand how it (or the company behind it) works.

Some of these tactics, and much of the content developed to support these tactics, may be useful in other areas such as public relations or service and support. Content, once developed, can easily be sliced, diced, and repackaged for different venues and additional purposes beyond that for which it was originally designed.

Demonstrating Products and Services

Market education is an effective way to build people's comfort levels so they'll be more inclined to do business with you. One of the best ways to educate prospects about your product or service is to demonstrate it. You will derive even greater benefits if prospects are able to demonstrate your product or service themselves.

Because the nature of some companies' products or services will make online demonstrations difficult, such as oilrig manufacturers and relief aid organizations, this portion of the communication plan may cause the greatest brain strain. Be prepared for a good bit of trial and error as you pursue these tactics.

As wireless technologies evolve, especially in the areas of audio and visual capabilities on mobile devices, your options for demonstrating products will increase. For example, for people in real estate, the ability to create 3-D presentations can significantly enhance their capabilities for "demonstrating" their properties. This portion of the plan should address how you intend to keep current with these developments.

Research

Good timely feedback can make the biggest difference in your organization's ability to be profitable. This can be feedback from customers, the market in general, others in your industry, and even your competitors. Wireless communication can deliver more feedback than you know what to do with.

Regardless of the tactics you decide to pursue in this area, you should explore how software tools can help you make the tasks more manageable and less expensive. Having these tools (or the people who can develop them) at your disposal may dictate how aggressively you can pursue particular research activities.

Since things change rapidly in the wireless world, including the demographics as more people get wireless access, your research activities should lean towards ongoing data collection. Plan for a broad range of activities such as testing the effectiveness of new ideas, gauging the market response to particular events in the news, and old-fashioned data collection.

Press Relations

These are the activities that you engage in with the press to produce coverage that shapes how the public views your company and products. PR also includes activities you engage in directly with the public, such as conducting research to identify new trends, which inspire press coverage that also shapes your public image. Push the envelope of creativity to add new dimensions to this age-old business practice.

It is difficult for wireless PR tactics to be effective unless they are integrated with traditional press relationship-building tools such as press tours, press releases, and wire services. For that reason, coordinate this section of your plan with whatever plan that your PR department or agency has been developed.

If you work with an agency, detail in your plan how they will work together with whomever manages your wireless activities to keep content and online projects in sync with the agency's day-to-day activities. It's counterproductive to communicate two different messages to the press or the public.

Tactics for Effective Implementations

The success of your communication plan to reaching internal or external audiences rests heavily on getting your employees to participate in your wireless projects, as well as how you use the technology to increase their productivity. At the very least, your employees should provide the test group for pilot projects. At best, you should see a noticeable change in the way your business operates, a change for the better.

The wireless tactics you create using this point should expand to include wireless-enabling physical assets, as well as your human capital. In the ideal world of wireless communication, within a year or two, you should have an integrated wireless implementation that links your people and machines so that everyone in the organization benefits.

Your efforts should have a positive impact on employee job satisfaction and retention, so be careful how you deploy this new technology. The "P" in PDA stands for personal. Many of your wireless implementations will have personal implications, more so in some cases than personal computers. All of your tactics here should give equal consideration to internal PR as well as internal productivity.

Final Considerations

When you finish working through these tactical points you may need to ask some additional questions.

What constraints are there on people, time, and financial resources? This is good to ask as soon as you realize there are a thousand ideas on the board. If you don't have the resources you need, prepare yourself for the efforts to win over top management to allocate the budget you need, or determine how you will trim and prioritize your list of ideas.

While you're contemplating the issue of winning over the big guns, consider also corporate culture and the way your company conducts business. These factors can facilitate or hinder your ideas. For example, if your management typically waits until new technology is deemed "safe" before they buy it, they may need some hard selling before the execs buy into wireless communication. This is why the financial impact analysis for each of the strategic points discussed earlier is so important, and why you have to develop effective pilot projects.

Once your brainstorming group has asked questions and exhausted the creative possibilities, weed out the obviously bad and absurd ideas. Next, shorten your list to make it manageable relative to your resource constraints.

Refine ideas based on how well they conform to the technical constraints of wireless networks and mobile devices, and general practicality. Some really great ideas hit a stone wall because of the graphical limits of devices and the inability of people in certain locations to get wireless access.

For all of these tactical areas you should determine how traditional communication activities such as direct mail, advertising, and press relations will complement or directly support your wireless tactics. Whenever possible, create synergy between the two, given that you can build market awareness and interest in your company with conventional tactics, and satisfy that interest fully with wireless and Web content.

You will also find that some of these tactical areas can support each other. Direct-response promotions can not only attract interest from potential customers, but also draw editors to special "media" content or increase responses to customer surveys. You can design particular research surveys to gather information that you also use to develop online product demonstrations. As you go through your brainstorming session, you will find other areas where these tactics complement each other.

When you've completed your brainstorming session, and filtered through your ideas to find the best ones to implement, it's time to put it all in writing. Don't be afraid to come back to the brainstorming table from time to time to keep your ideas fresh, and to keep pace with how other organizations are keeping pace with technology developments.

The Written Tactical Plan

Now that you have a list of tactics and the troops are psyched up to move into this new realm of wireless communication, you have to give them a written plan that will guide them once you launch the campaign.

As I mentioned, I'm going to give you a general outline to work with. I don't recommend spending too much time creating a document that looks like a doctoral thesis. If you spend too many days on a dissertation, you might miss some great opportunities. You can supplement my suggestions with as many or as few details as you wish, as long as the final document is complete enough for the people who will work with it.

The Mission Statement

At the beginning of Chapter 3 I told the story about the TV ad in which the guy summed up his Internet strategy as, "For every dollar we put into the Internet we get two dollars back." Your wireless communication mission should be so succinctly summarized—right at the top of your written plan.

You and probably several others are going to be the torchbearers to lead your organization's wireless efforts. It's hard to lead if it takes an hour to describe the main point of your wireless existence. Remember the 30/90 rule from Chapter 7. You have 30 seconds, 90 words, to get people to support your efforts.

You can have a dozen strategic objectives and that's fine. You may only have one. But regardless, your ability to rally people to your side, as well as keep everyone focused and motivated once the wireless plan launches, rests heavily on how clearly the mission is articulated.

You might have to write the plan first before you can condense everything down to one compelling statement, which is fine. I often wait until I assemble all the parts of a plan before the light bulb goes off with an inspired theme or mission statement. Do whatever works best for you.

A good statement should be similar to the one in the commercial. Whether the specific strategies address communicating with customers or prospects, or enhancing service, the statement applies. It doesn't matter if the company wants to save money or generate online sales, the statement should hold true. Even at the tactical level, they could implement PR or market education tactics, and still measure their efforts by the mission statement.

Strategic Objectives

The first section of your plan should address your strategic objectives, listed in priority order as developed through your strategy-planning sessions. For each objective be sure to include the key numbers from your ROI projections and the benchmarks for measuring the progress of your wireless communication efforts. Don't forget to include the intangible benefits you hope to achieve.

It will help if you relate all of the wireless communication to the general business strategies that wireless will complement and enhance. Too many organizations divorced web objectives from business objectives, and it was several years after the Web's launch before they started reaping the benefits of strategies such as integrating the Web with CRM, supply chain, or sales forces automation applications. You don't want to miss the boat with wireless. Committing the alignment of wireless and general business objectives to writing will also make this a valuable document for garnering political support throughout the organization.

Be sure this section summarizes how you intend to balance the needs of the plan with available resources and conflicting agendas. Don't forget one of the biggest balancing acts is that of expectations. You want people to be excited about the prospective impact of wireless on your business, but you want to balance what they expect against what the technology can realistically deliver. You want everything to work out so you under-promise (within reason) and over-deliver.

Of course, within the organization expectations for wireless communications might also be underhyped (oh noooo, Lippy, it will never work!). If this is the situation, address it as well. You don't want to have a lot of naysayers undermining your efforts, so try to chill them out in your plan.

Make it clear who are the audiences of your respective strategic efforts. If it's customers, be sure to define whether it's just the people who buy your products or also resellers and business partners. The same with prospects. The initial plan will have tactics, but your employees will be creating new tactics as you go, so the more clarity about the intended audiences the better.

If necessary, refer back to the strategy discussions in Chapters 3 through 6 to resolve any of the issues I posed here and reaffirm priority, balance, and specifics of your objectives.

Tactics

I think the best approach to this section of the plan is to divide it into categories, one for each of the four strategic dimensions. Under each dimension write the tactics that support it, subcategorized by the appropriate tactical heading ("Building Brand Awareness," "Research," and so on).

Some tactics might support several dimensions, so you need to determine what is the best way to list these. The important thing is for people to be able to see where their actions fit within the bigger picture. You can decide how much detail you want to add for each tactic, but it might make sense to put some of that information into a supplementary document that does to the specific department or person who is responsible for the respective tactics.

When you've presented all of your tactics, place all of the particulars such as content, budget, and so on, into the next sections.

Content

After laying out your tactics, the next section of your plan is "Content." Here, you will describe what documents, graphics, visuals, and so forth you will need for your tactics to be successful.

You need to resolve some questions here. For instance, do you use the same content for customers as for prospects? Will content come from product literature, the website, technical briefing papers, stock information, or brand new material? If you don't use the same content in the different wireless tactics, which content will go to the various sections?

Of course, some of this discussion might be a moot point if you expect people to surf your website wirelessly. Based on the wireless applications I've looked at, you will have to put some effort into reviewing your web content to tag certain parts of it to be streamlined for access by mobile devices.

Since wireless is a new medium, you should consider if there is information that you can provide that will be more valuable to people than typical ads, brochures, and web pages. What information can you give them about your product or company that they can't get in other communication channels? The technical design and limitations of some wireless devices will determine what content you can place there and how your content will look, so be sure you become familiar with these areas.

After jotting down a list of the content you need, outline some general document management procedures that everyone involved with creating and managing content should follow.

Will you use sophisticated wireless development software to design and format content for wireless access, or will you rely on tools provided by wireless vendors whose applications you buy, or services you use? How will you train people to use these programs? If your employees or customers will access data created by interactive databases, will there be development work that you have to do to this back-end software?

Map out the flow of documents from their originators, through a timely approval process and on to whomever actually posts content online. Will you use document management software to automate this flow, or does your web team have other tools that can be used for wireless content as well? How will you monitor documents to make sure outdated content is removed in a timely manner? Where will old content be archived in case it has to be retrieved by customers, your staff, or others?

While you're considering document flow to the outside world, also determine how you'll manage incoming items such as e-mail from your online areas and materials retrieved by software agents. Some people I spoke with recommend Lotus Notes to manage incoming documents that arrive such as e-mail messages, but there are a number of applications available.

When you answer these questions to your satisfaction, move on to describe resources that you will need to carry out this plan.

Resources

After you decide what you want, who will be responsible for creating content and promotions? Will it be marketing, sales, or a web-design agency? Will customer service or human resources develop content? Can they deliver the materials you need to change your content frequently enough to build repeat traffic? If they can't who will?

This is a good time for me to address an issue that I maybe didn't state clearly enough. It's important to get buy-in throughout the company for this wireless communication plan since many of these people may be resources for your content.

If you're the president or executive vice president, you have the power of the righteous mandate. However, similar to Internet communication, wireless can bring together departments that typically don't work with each other, which can be a tough balancing act. Subsequently, you'll probably be more successful if you use tactful salesmanship with a hint of authoritarianism, rather than the executive equivalent of a 2-by-4 upside the head. It doesn't take too much discontent in the ranks to spoil your best-written plans.

If you haven't pulled together the resource commitments you need from some departments by this point, take a draft of this plan door-to-door, starting with marketing and finance since they can be particularly hard nuts to crack. Traditional marketing people may hold out because wireless isn't a traditional marketing medium. Finance could resist because they can't see an immediate sales advantage.

If they give you too much flak, get the rest of the company on your side. Then come back with your allies in tow, and really put the heat on. If they buy into the idea right away, however, you should pretty much consider the battle won. The rest of the company should go along with your wireless plan with little resistance, especially if you assure them that they have a role to play in the wireless effort if they're interested.

Whatever you do, save the lawyers for last (after a company-wide consensus is pretty much a fait accompli). The Internet in general is a place so lax in rules and wrought with peril that it still gives many lawyers hives. Some of them can come up with 100 reasons to kill a wireless project in the time it takes to say "Perry Mason." However, if the bulk of your plan just makes existing applications wireless accessible, then you shouldn't have any resistance from this group.

Looking for a Few Good Project Managers

Once you resolve the issue of getting company buy-in, you have to address the direct care and feeding of your wireless applications. The maintenance or enhancing of websites to accommodate the introduction of wireless communication activities, plus whatever dedicated wireless resources you have to add, requires some resources dedicated specifically to this task.

If you're going to outsource the bulk of your wireless implementation, then you may not have to worry too much about dedicating staff specifically for managing your wireless plan. People in IT, marketing, and a couple of other departments can add wireless tasks to someone's list of responsibilities.

However, if you're planning to make a serious wireless communication effort, you will need at least one person dedicated to managing everything involved with your site from text to technology. On one hand, as I discussed in the last chapter, IT will shoulder a lot of the technology responsibilities. On the other, you still have a lot of business issues and one or two people need to have responsibility for actively managing this side of things.

Then there are the day-to-day tasks such as physically managing content, keeping all the systems up and running, managing document and communication flow between the different departments, the Net, and wherever else your wireless content may be.

Ultimately, your particular circumstances and needs will determine how many staff people you'll need to dedicate to the effort. The key thing is that these resource issues are clearly spelled out in the written plan. If you write the plan before you select any outside vendors, be sure to add them as they are hired by your organization.

As with any business plan, be sure to show who reports to whom and all of those other little details of people-management that ensure everyone knows the order of life as it pertains to implementing the plan.

Timeline

No good plan goes without a timeline. Different people may have different ideas about how detailed these should be.

I recommend you plot specific dates on a calendar as milestones for key elements of your wireless communication efforts. For example, dates for content completion, promotion launches, online seminars, etc. From your list of milestones, you can be as detailed with dates and events as you wish.

Budget

Since many organizations approach budgeting differently, I will leave it to you to decide what's the best form and format to show the numbers. It may be that the budget is only included in copies of the plan that are restricted to senior management or certain department managers, but this, too, is an issue I think is best decided by each organization.

The Wrap-Up

What I've given you in these pages is just a foundation from which you can build your own specific plan. When you access the online component of this book, you'll get another layer of information in the form of real-world examples of the lessons learned in these pages.

Keep this book handy as a reference guide. What you design, the problems you encounter, and the solutions you devise are going to all be new learning experiences. Even if you've been involved with some kind of wireless activity for years, practically every day will bring a new lesson.

I'm happy to do what I can by updating the online component (www. wirelessinconline.com) with new information and examples of how companies are coping with the latest developments in wireless communication. That being said, let me close with some crystal ball gazing by some of the people who are shaping the wireless landscape.

Gazing into the Future

I asked a number of people to share their thoughts about the future of wireless, and how organizations might be impacted by, or at least be better prepared for, future developments. Their parting comments will provide you with some additional food for thought.

Peter Jowaisas, Marketing Director, Notifact

I don't think we've even scratched the surface. Our wireless monitoring products are being used to monitor HVAC (heating, ventilating, air conditioning) systems, but there are future applications for technology such as this in manufacturing, chemical plants, municipal utilities, and energy plants. There may be a need on the residential side, such as notifying homeowners when there is a problem in the house. However, the costs for individual monitoring units have to come down significantly.

This technology's going to get better. Today it enables one-way communication from the equipment being monitored, but we want to move to a point where the data pulled from this equipment can automatically interact with other technology to do things such as make changes to the room temperature. Be sure that the applications you buy today can be easily enhanced to support new technology as it becomes available. You don't want to be stuck with the 8-Track player of the wireless world.

Tom Turner, Senior Vice President, WhereNet

The reality is that this technology is going to change. For example, standards are emerging such as 802.11b and 802.11g wireless LANs, so applications from different vendors should work fairly well together with this technology.

In cases where there are no standards, you want to deal with vendors who will pursue and facilitate standards.

Determine which technology vendors the large organizations are buying products from, and get some sense of their levels of commitment and investment because this funds development in the industry. Vendors that are closing millions of dollars in contracts likely will have the financial staying power to make their technology a standard. Also, if the biggest organizations are buying from a particular vendor, then it's likely this vendor will still be around in a few years to continue to support and enhance the products you buy from them.

Rich Reynolds, IT Manager, Aristasoft

There are two ways to deal with the inevitable changes that will occur with wireless technology. First, initiate relationships with third-party resellers and application developers. These companies are already researching what it takes to make products and technology work, as well as what's needed to do business wirelessly. They often have a broader view of the world, and their goal is to keep you coming back as a customer. Have these guys come in to evaluate your operations and give their opinion on what you should expect to accomplish—or not.

The second thing you have to do is come up with criteria to determine business needs and measure any new technologies against those needs. Hope that, before you spend a whole lot of time and money, you can see which technologies will last. But there's never any guarantees. Go slow initially, buy a couple of systems to distribute on a limited basis, and see if they work.

Sanjay Shirole, Chief Executive Officer, Xora

Because many applications let people use various mobile devices to access the same data and content in the format of their respective devices, battles between hardware vendors will become irrelevant to organizations that deploy wireless applications. Right now, vendors developing wireless access to back-end applications tend to create interfaces that support the lowest common denominator in terms of PDA screen capabilities.

As more devices support color displays, have a sophisticated look and feel, and processing capabilities improve, people might start demanding client side applications so they can do more traditional computing work.

WAP-enabled cell phones will be more suitable for query tasks, such as using the keypad or cursor to scroll through or request specific information, and pick from a list of values or a set of options as you do with sales force automation software. People may also continue to use them to read e-mail. But we're seeing people push phones aside for sending e-mail and doing any type of significant data entry tasks.

We don't see Pocket PC devices dominating the market just because Microsoft dominates in the enterprise. They have an advantage in that one of the main needs of mobile workers is to read e-mail, and to a limited extent, documents. Pocket PCs can easily integrate with Microsoft applications such as Outlook. But other back-end software is also important to wireless applications, such as CRM and sales force automation, which Microsoft doesn't control. These vendors are enabling their software to support any mobile device.

Don Pohly, Business Manager for Airport Information Systems, FMC Technologies

If you are a national or state government agency that is responsible for managing and gathering data from local organizations such as airports or utility companies, you may need to wait until they develop wireless applications before implementing a wireless data-collection strategy. Once these 'islands of coverage' with their wireless infrastructures are in place, you can pull it all together by making your staff responsible for tracking all of this data from organizations across the state or country. The data from the various sites can then be stored in one wireless repository, such as an ASP who will host all of the information and make it accessible.

Lieutenant Robert Durko, Tarrant County, Texas, Sheriff's Department

We're looking at developing wireless applications in public works entities for everyone from safety inspectors to dogcatchers, anyone who has to come back to the office to do reports, find information, or search for the owner of a dog. This also includes reviewing our processes that produce multilayered paper trails.

We government types tend to look only within our own domain and not see what we can learn from what the corporate world is doing, such as barcoding evidence and entering data wirelessly. But this has to change. Eventually we expect to transfer real-time video and even add Voice over IP connection through some wireless device. We have to always try to push the envelope.

Renee Lowe, Ph.D., Laboratory Manager for a National Biotech Services Company

Companies of all types need to look beyond their own industries to unlock the potential benefits wireless offers. Biotechnology and industrial manufacturing are very different businesses. But one day embedded wireless technology that lets you track production processes on the plant floor, and wireless apps that help support staffs to remotely manage inventory on store shelves, can also be used to improve high-throughput laboratory procedures.

Currently, completion of an experimental procedure, such as an enzymatic incubation or DNA sequencing run, can trigger a wireless pager message so the research technicians are alerted to the status of these processes. But it would be great to have the machine alert research assistants on PDAs so they can perform quality-control calculations, input data, and move the process along to the next step, or stop the process if it fails QC requirements. In time-critical and expensive drug development operations, this added efficiency and control can lead to a higher rate of experimental success and lower costs.

Duncan Bradley, Manager of Market Knowledge, RIM

There are interesting things to learn from the teen market, such as what mobile devices should look like over the next couple of years. But teens probably won't influence application design since they don't know what it's like to work with sales force automation or CRM tools. There are concerns within some businesses about what NTT DoCoMo in Japan is trying to do, which is driven in large part by the country's teen wireless behavior. However, there are so many different factors in culture and demographics that you have to be careful when you try to do the same thing in different countries. Until wireless goes fully into consumer market, the needs of teens will have limited impact.

Kate Everett-Thorp, Chief Executive Officer, Lot21

To expand your wireless communication success in the consumer market, you have to convert the behavior of older people. The young generation (under 25-year-olds) is pushing the envelope of the online and wireless user experience. They'll drop a brand if they don't get what they consider appropriate messaging, which includes messages on their wireless devices, because this is consistent with their understanding of the world.

With people who are older you have to shift them from habits and rituals that are embedded in their personality. You have to convince them that using this new technology is better and they have to convince others. With the upcoming generation, all we have to do is make this technology a part of their regular options because they haven't developed as deeply rooted habits.

Denise Stokowski, Regional Vice President, Leading CRM Application Vendor

You will get consumers to use mobile devices for more than scheduling appointments and exchanging cute musical ring tones with each other when there are applications compelling enough to justify the effort to connect to the Net. Many tasks, such as checking flight schedules or stock quotes, can be done more easily and less expensively from a desktop at the office or at home than dialing in with a wireless device.

Compelling applications do not have to be complex. Just make simple but important tasks easy to do. For example, a lot of people carry supermarket shopper loyalty cards, frequent flyer cards, and hotel courtesy cards. It would be nice if your PDA held a universal ID tag that you wirelessly register with the businesses of your choice, which could then wirelessly check you into a hotel or record your store purchases. Each business could maintain records of loyalty points, disburse reward redemptions, and facilitate other transactions that you access with your PDA without compromising privacy.

The key to successfully implementing applications that people will actually find useful is for businesses to learn what consumers really want. It seems many companies spend first and ask questions later.

Brian Korek, Manager of Handheld Products, PocketMail Inc.

Even if your company does not sell directly to consumers, it can be helpful to pay attention to consumer trends. You particularly want to look at which UI designs play a factor in getting people to quickly adopt and use the technology since these techniques can be applied to business applications.

Consumer wireless growth may take place in the home with the introduction of compelling solutions that are otherwise unavailable, easy to use, and affordable. These may be apps that open the front door when you're carrying packages, page you when the washer or dryer is done, turn on heat as you near the house, auto-lock doors and windows as you leave, or monitor the medical condition of family members while you're at work.

Prices must come down before there is widespread adoption, but it's just a matter of time. So far wireless adoption has been slower than anyone expected, so I expect it will take as long as five years before we see big changes. Remember that there are fewer people in the world who are technologically savvy than those in this wireless profession seem to realize.

Roy Martinez, Controller, Borba Farms

Wireless vendors need to talk to smaller companies more, the way we talked to our foremen (see Chapter 6). They need to come out and see if there's a market and how to service that market. I like to go on the Net, but maybe my neighbor doesn't. I belong to several groups of people who use the same software, so we help each other. These are important groups for vendors to reach. The Web gives vendors an opportunity to communicate through e-mail, online discussion groups, etc. to educate the market about the advantages of wireless technology.

Mariel van Totenhove, Director of Marketing, Synaptics

If you are planning to sell products through wireless mobile devices to business or consumer audiences, security will actually be a big issue, maybe more so than the interface. This is why some people won't order products at unknown websites, they have more faith in the sites of organizations that they know and trust. The same will be true of wireless transactions as well. Your challenge, therefore, is to build a high-level of trust with prospective buyers.

Index

academic environments, wireless in, 208–213, 325
ad banners, 166–167, 200–201
Aerie Networks, 24
Aether Systems, 85, 120, 160, 240, 258
agents, search, 256
Aggregate Haulers, 140–141
Aloisi, Federico, on communicating with wireless, 32
Alpha project, 241–242
AltaVista, 254
American Airlines, 158
American Red Cross, 77–78
American Trial Lawyers Association (ATLA), 253
America Online (AOL), 18, 171
Analysts International, 62–63
anticipation, building, 199–200
AOL, see America Online
Apple Computer, 17
Aramira, 38
Aristasoft, 117–118
Asia, 15–16
ASPs, 337
assembly-line staff, 137
assets, physical, see physical assets, managing
ATLA (American Trial Lawyers Association), 253
AT&T, 140, 142, 215, 216
audiences, building relationships with variety of, 115–117; direct response to motivate external, 181–189; educating your, see education; generating responses from, see direct response
automatic bill paying, 215
AvantGo, 38, 39, 104, 163, 183, 240, 348
Avid Technology, 347–348

Baker, Arley, on public relations, 297–300, 303–305
Bank of America, 35
banner ads, 166–167, 200–201
benefits of wireless, 14–15, 33–34
bill paying, automatic, 215
BlackBerry, 23, 27, 36, 160, 298, 303, 304
Blackstock, Gordon, 122
Blue Mountain Greeting Cards, 198
Bluetooth, 25
BMW, 155

Borba Farms, 14, 141–142
Bradley, Duncan, 36, 340, 376
brainstorming, 362–364
brand awareness, 156, 363–364
brand building, 156
brand experience, 155
branding, 10, 153–179; and communication of brand message, 162–171; definitions related to, 154–156; ensuring consistency in, 176–178; and first impressions, 171–173; and logo in wireless milieu, 156–157; and wireless branding campaign, 173–176; and wireless medium as brand message, 157–162
brand loyalty, 10, 156
brand message, 155
Brandow, Peter, on retailing, 120–121
Brandow Group, 120
British Motor Car Distributors, 122
budgeting for wireless implementation, 329–334, 372
Burger King, 217–218
business processes, monitoring, 133–134

California, 254
Cambridge University, 204–205
Campbell, Don, 306
Caner, John, on fleet tracking applications, 131
Carolina Hurricanes, 116, 191, 200–203
Carpenter, Shawn, on WallStreetView, 257, 258
Carter, James, 202
CAS, see Centre Auto Sécurité
CDNow, 234
cell phones, 32; in foreign countries, 15–16; future U.S. use of, 16–18
cellular networks, 22
Centre Auto Sécurité (CAS), 266–267
CEO Express, 254
Chase-Hyman, Paula, on public relations, 298, 299, 301, 302, 305
Cisco, 177
click-through rate, 153
clothing, 246
CMP Media LLC, 161–162
CNN, 262–263
CNN Mobile, 166
communication, 7, 30–34; benefits of wireless technology for improved,

33–34; of brand message, 162–171; with existing customers, 9; internal, see internal communication; need for restraint in, 190–191, with prospective customers, 9, 101–103
Compaq, 27, 241
CompUSA, 183, 184
Computer Select, 242
computer-telephony integration (CTI), 69, 215–216
construction product companies, 51
consulting services, direct-experience demonstrations of, 239–241
contests, 169–170, 203–204, 247
Cox, Steve, on meeting customers' expectations, 40; on simple implementations, 35–36
CRM, see customer relationship management
CTI, see computer-telephony integration
customer relationship management (CRM), 57–58, 68–72, 113
customers, see existing customers; prospective customers
customer service and support, see service and support
CyberAlert, 294
cyberspace, 6

data, automated collection of, 256–257, 264–265; automated tabulation of, 264
databases, research, 252–254
demonstrations, 11, 232–250, 364–365; direct experience, 237–241; guidelines for creating effective online, 248–249; limited experience, 241–244; as part of marketing mix, 247–248; simulated, 244–247; and type of organization, 233–235; types of online, 236–237
department-specific communications, calculating costs of, 135–136
DePaul, Ray, on choosing wireless systems, 341; on KISS approach to wireless, 37
desktop thinking, avoiding, 39–41
dial-up remote access, 126–127
Digital Equipment Corp., 241–242
direct-experience demonstrations, 236; of consulting services, 239–241; of information services, 238–239; of software, 237–238

directories, Internet, 253–254
direct response, 10–11, 169, 180–206; creating a mystery/contest with, 203–204; creating a sense of urgency with, 198–203; indirect, 197–198; for motivation of external audiences, 181–189; within the organization, 193–197; for prospective customers, 189–192; and service/support, 191–193; tactics for, 364–367
DocCheck, 254
Durko, Robert, 85, 86, 319–320, 375

"early warning systems," wireless, 89–92
EarthLink, 145
Edsel (automobile), 174–175
education, 11, 207–231, 364; internal, 225–231; market, 213–214; of outside audiences, 213–225; and role of wireless in academic environments, 208–213
802.11a/802/11b networks, 24
e-mail (to journalists), 279
employee communication, calculating costs of, 135
employees, prospective, 108–109; support of, for public relations, 290–296
entertainment industry, 243–244
Environmental Protection Agency (EPA), 214
Epiphany, 69, 71
ERI, see Event Risk Indicator
Erlanger Medical Center Emergency Heart and Stroke Center (Chattanooga, TN), 270
Europe, 15
Event Risk Indicator (ERI), 239–240
Everett-Thorp, Kate, on clickthroughs, 153; on focusing on mindset of customers, 40–41; on future of wireless, 376; on marketing objectives, 167–168; on selling via wireless, 33; on web advertising, 176
eWatch, 256–257, 294
executives, and direct response, 196; participation by, 42–43; and public relations, 290–296; responsibility of, 8; support of, for implementation, 313–322
existing customers, 49–72; communicating with, 9; determining need to focus on, 49–53; financial impact of communicating with, 53–57; increasing referrals from, 59–61; increasing revenue from, 57–59; knowing your, 52–53; selling to, 33; strategic objectives with, 61–68
ExpertSeller, 119
Extensity, 113–114
Exxon, 302

Fair, John Dee, 14; on banner ads, 166–167; on future of selling, 19; on getting feedback, 346
Famous Footwear, 94–95, 121
Faul, Angelique, on public relations,

299, 301, 305; on wireless LANs, 295
Federal Communication Commission (FCC), 23
Federal Express (FedEx), 13, 20, 79
feedback, gathering, 93–94, 294, 346
Fidelity Investments, 67
Fiedotin, Richard, 325, 344–345
financial impact, of communicating with existing customers, 53–59; of communicating with prospective customers, 104–110; of improved internal communication, 135–138; of providing improved service and support, 79–82
financial services companies, 51, 76
first impression, making a good, 171–173
FitSync, 220–222
fleet tracking applications, 131
FMC Airport Systems, 328
FMC Technologies, 19
focus, 4, 5; on communication, 7, 30–34; on executive participation, 42–43; on implementation, 34–41; on selection/deployment of wireless applications, 7–8
Ford, Henry, on Model Ts, 245
foreign countries, wireless in, 15–16
Fort Worth (Texas), 85–86
Frost, Cliff, 211–212, 317, 325
FTD.com, 198
Fujitsu PenCentra, 96
future of wireless, 373–378

General Packet Radio Systems (GRPS) networks, 25, 28
giveaways, 247
Global Positioning System (GPS), 26–27, 195
Goetter, Rick, 321–322, 350–351
Gomez, Hans, 218
Google, 254
government organizations, benefits of wireless for, 14–15; as customers, 51; relationship building by, 114; service demonstrations by, 234–235; as service providers, 77
GPS, see Global Positioning System
Grant, Gale, on designing surveys, 261–262
Grappone, Todd, 210–211, 317, 331–332
GRPS networks, see General Packet Radio Systems networks
Guth, David W., on public relations, 300–302, 306

Handango, 237
Handspring, 28
Handspring Visor, 27
HealthPartners, 318
Heintz, Todd, on ROI, 324–325
Hiugo, 168–169, 202, 203
Home Finishes, Inc., 86–88
HP Jornada, 27
human resources (HR) department, 129, 136–137, 196, 261
Hyatt Hotels, 244–245

IBM, 45

i-loft, 69–70
implementation of wireless, xiv–xv, 7–8, 34–41, 311–353; avoiding desktop thinking in, 39–41; and big technology picture, 41; budgeting for, 329–334; executive support for, 313–322; and mechanics of wireless technology, 312–313; and minimizing connection times, 37–38; misconceptions about, 12–13; operational tactics for successful, 12; and ROI, 322–329; simplicity in, 35–37; tactics for, 366; and user interface, 342–353; and vendor selection recommendations, 335–342; see also strategy and tactics plan
indirect direct response, 197–198
information services, limited-experience demonstrations of, 238–239
Information Superhighway, 6
infrared technology, 26
"in-line" upgrades, 192–193
in-person data tracking, 264–271
inquiries, responding quickly to, 172–173
instant messaging, 235
interactive voice response (IVR), 351
internal communication, 10, 124–147; determining need to focus on, 124–135; financial impact of improved, 135–138; strategic objects for improving, 138–146
internal education, 225–231
Internet directories, 253–254
Internet technology, 3
Intraware, 163–165
Intuitive Surgical, 338–340
investor relations, 195
iPAQ, 27, 166
IPOs, 67–68
i-pot, 65–66
IT department, 128, 136, 165, 186–187, 196, 320–321
IVR (interactive voice response), 351

The Jack, 121–122, 205, 224
Japan, 15–16
journalists, creating resources for, 287–288; as customers, 51–52, 57, 108, 116; relationships with, 274–282, 289–290
Jowaisas, Peter, 321, 373
J.P. Morgan, 239–240, 255

Kato, Saul, on banner ads, 167; on getting executive support, 317; on wireless in academic environments, 209
Kellar, Kyle, 140, 141
King, Martin, 91
KnowledgePoint, 293
Koehn, David, on wireless-enabled training, 226–228
Koler, Ed, 40, 319, 329–330
Koppe, Chris, 322–323, 351
Korek, Brian, on future of wireless, 377
Kreller, Eric, on public relations, 300, 301, 304
Kyocera Smartphone, 28, 93

learning, mobile, 226
Legacy Chiller Systems, 14, 91–92
LexisNexis, 252, 253
LGC Wireless, 78, 158
limited-experience demonstrations, 236, 241–244
Lincoln (Nebraska), 84–85
location-based services, 6
logos, 154, 156–157
Lot21, 40–41, 163, 165, 240
Lotus Development, 216–217
Lowe, Renee, on future of wireless, 375–376
Lowe, Todd, on wireless in academic environments, 209
loyalty, brand, 10, 156

Madonna, 262–263
Mancuso, Mike, 316, 344
Mann, Harold, on achieving ROI, 20; on danger of focusing on short-term benefits, 323; on getting executive support, 315; on laptops, 89
Mann Consulting, 14, 88–89
manufacturers, service and support provided by, 81
market education, 213–214
marketing department, 128–129, 136, 255
Martinez, Roy, 141, 377–378
Maryland, 160
Maynard, Kirsten, 159, 160, 205
McBride, Christian, 243
McDonald's, 111–112
McGinnis Lockridge & Kilgoe LLP, 88
m-commerce, 6, 19, 32–33
meetings, with employees, 131–132; with existing customers, 62–63
Metreon entertainment center (San Francisco), 158–160
Metricom, 60
Microsoft PocketPC OS, 27
Middleberg, Don, on Internet research by journalists, 280–282
Miller, Jerry, 253
mission statement, 367–368
m-learning, 227, 229–231
mobile devices, demographics of users of, 28–29; wireless, 27–29
mobile learning, 226
mobilePlanIt, 36, 78
The Mobile Technology Question and Answer Book (Ron Schneiderman), 21
monitoring software, 34
Moore, Teresa, on public relations, 300, 304–306
Motorola, 23–24
Motorola Accompli, 28
Motorola Personal Communicators, 23
Murphy's Law, 193
mystery, creating a, 203–204

National Institute of Standards and Technology (NIST), 253
NetReturn, LLC, 119
networks, wireless, 22–27
new economy, 6
news reports, 193

neXui, 32
Nissan Motors, 70–71
NIST (National Institute of Standards and Technology), 253
Nogles, Tom, on government use of wireless, 14; on role of IT department, 321; on use of icons, 345; on value of embedded wireless, 125
nonprofit organizations, benefits of wireless for, 14–15; as customers, 51; relationship building by, 114; service demonstrations by, 234–235; as service providers, 77–78
Notifact, 91, 321
nTeras, 132
NTT DoCoMo, 15

Oakland Public Library (California), 234
O'Meara, Rudi, 163, 165, 337–338
on-going relationships, building, 114–117
online press centers, 282–290; core information in, 284–285; supporting information in, 285–286; value-added information in, 286–287
online surveys, 260–264
OpenGrid, 36, 40, 78, 161–162
operating efficiency, improving, 145–146
operational tactics, 12
outsourcing, 315
Owen, Richard, 39

pager networks, 23
Palm, 18, 27, 240
Palm OS, 27
Palm Pilot, 27, 342
panic website development, 4
PassageWay, 215–216
Pave, Sasha, on generating quick responses, 182–183; on sending messages in waves, 191
pay-as-you-go software, 238
PCIA (Personal Communications Industry Association), 188
PDAs, see personal digital assistants
Perseus Software, 259–260
Personal Communications Industry Association (PCIA), 188
personal digital assistants (PDAs), 17–18, 27–29, 32, 351; for customer service and support, 83–85, 88, 95; for data collection, 268; and direct response, 183–186, 193–194, 198; for educating your audiences, 214–217, 220–222; efficiency gains from use of, 126; and existing customers, 54, 56, 65, 67; for financial services companies, 51; and personal productivity, 143–145; for product/service demonstrations, 235, 237, 240, 242, 246; and prospective customers, 112, 113, 115, 119–121
personal productivity, increasing, 143–145
PHT Corporation, 268
physical assets, managing, 125, 132–133, 138, 196–197
pilot projects, 19–20

Pinney, Michael, on getting executive support, 314–315; on vendor selection, 336
Placeware, 290
plan for implementation, see strategy and tactics plan
Pohly, Don, on finding suppliers, 337; on future of wireless, 375; on ROI, 328; on wireless technology, 19
Port Discovery (Baltimore), 78, 160–161, 235
Porter Novelli, 298
Portland CitySearch, 114–115
PR, see public relations
press relations, see public relations
press releases, 279
primary research, 259–264
Pringles, 169, 170
printed materials, 81–82
PR Newswire, 256
Procter & Gamble, 169, 308, 309
product demonstrations, see demonstrations
productivity, personal, 143–145
prospective customers, 99–123; assessing current level of communication with, 101–103; barriers when selling to, 31–33; communicating with, 9; determining need to focus on, 99–104; direct response for, 189–192; financial impact of effective communication with, 104–110; removing barriers to, 103–104; strategic objectives with, 110–122
PR Works, 235
Prion Workahout, 266, 267
public relations (PR), 11–12, 273–310, 365; creating an online press center for, 282–290; and direct response, 195; executive and employee support for, 290–296; and interacting with journalists, 274–282; roundtable discussion on, 297–309
"puppy dog sales," 232, 233
Purser, Billy, 201

Qualcomm pdQ smartphones, 271

radio frequency (RF) networks, 23–24
RealNetworks, 290
referrals, increasing customer, 59–61, 64–65
Reiland, John, on ASPs, 96; on budgeting restraint, 331
relationships, on-going, 114–117
remote access, dial-up, 126–127
requests for proposal (RFPs), 336
research, 251–272, 365; primary, 259–264; secondary, 252–258; via in-person data tracking, 264–271
research databases, 252–254
Research in Motion (RIM), 23, 36, 125
resellers, 107–108, 116, 195–196
responses, generating immediate, see direct response
retailers, as customers, 56
retailers, as customers, 51
retention, customer, increasing, 65–68; tracking, 175

return on investment (ROI), 20, 70–71, 125, 322–329, 359

Reynolds, Rich, on future of wireless, 374; on Richochet, 118; on security, 118–119

RF networks, see radio frequency networks

RFPs (requests for proposal), 336

Ricochet, 60, 118, 127–128, 237

Ricochet Networks, 23–24

RIM, see Research in Motion

Riser, Anne, on member mobilization, 188; on spending on wireless implementations, 333–334

ROI, see return on investment

Ross, Steven, on Internet research by journalists, 280–281

Ross, Ted, on customer relations at Nissan, 69–71

Sadel, Howard, 191, 200, 201

SAFECO Field (Seattle, WA), 158

Safeway supermarkets, 67

sales, service contracts and potential for, 92–97

sales cycles, reducing length of, 106–109, 112–117

sales force, 109–110, 117–119

sales force automation (SFA) software, 37, 117, 340

Salisbury, Brian, 340

Salvaggio, Vito, on getting executive support, 315–316; on needing to justify ROI, 322; on wireless implementation, 320

SARCOM, 19–20, 314–315

Sato, Saul, 336

Saturn, 246

Schneiderman, Ron, 21

Scholey, Hugh, 295–296

ScorePad software, 267, 268

search agents, 256

secondary research, 252–258

security, 118–119

Security and Exchange Commission, 67

senior management, see executives

service and support, 9, 73–98; creating sales opportunities from, 92–97; creating wireless early warning systems for improved, 89–92; determining need to focus on, 74–79; and direct response, 191–193; distinction between, 73–74; financial impact of improved, 79–82; increasing efficiency of, 83–89, 129–130; strategic objectives for, 82–83

ServiceHub, 14, 140–142, 352

ServiceIQ, 95–97

SFA software, see sales force automation software

shipping department, 138

Shirole, Sanjay, on future of wireless, 374–375; on PDAs, 351; on transitioning to new computer platform, 346–347

Siemens, 216

Sigma-Tau Pharmaceuticals, Inc., 144

Simplylook, 331

simulated-experience demonstrations, 236, 244–247

SkyTel, 35

small companies, benefits of wireless for, 14

smartphones, 28, 93

software, direct-experience demonstrations of, 237–238

Sony, 158–159

spamming, 175–176

sponsored content, 166–171

SportsPilot, 267–268

SportsWriter, 267–268

Stanford University, 78, 209–212

Starbucks Coffee, 158

Stetz, Michelle, 160–161

Stokowski, Denise, on future of wireless, 376–377

Stokowski, Mike, on UI design, 349

strategic objectives, 368–369; with existing customers, 61–68; for improving internal communication, 138–146; with prospective customers, 110–122; for service and support, 82–83

strategic options, 45–48

strategic thinking, 4–5

strategies, need for effective, 8–10

Strategis Group, 29

strategy and tactics plan, 357–373; assembling key players for, 358–359; balance in, 359–361; brainstorming for, 362–364; direct response communication in, 364–367; mission statement in, 367–368; prioritizing in, 359; specificity in, 361–362; writing, 367–372

Stuyt, Sharka, 222–223

Sun Microsystems, 312

support, see service and support

support calls, 79

surveys, 52, 260–264

Sweden, 15

Symantec, 275, 288–289

Synaptics, 342

tactics, 5, 149–151; brainstorming for, 362–364; need for effective, 10–12

technology, 3, 41

Technology Marketing Magazine, 292

Teitler, Jason, on public relations, 298, 299, 301, 303, 305

Telecom Italia Mobile (TIM), 204

Telephia, 14

Televoke, 131

ThinAirApps, 127

30/90 rule, 162–163

3G networks, 25

Ticketmaster, 114

TIM (Telecom Italia Mobile), 204

Tonner, Simon, 162

Totenhove, Mariel van, on future of wireless, 378; on wireless application design, 342–343

training, costs of, 82; wireless-enabled, 226–228

Transparent Language, 175

TREO, 28

Trojan Room coffee machine, 204–205

Turner, Tom, on future of wireless, 373–374; on growth of wireless, 13; on improving efficiency, 134; on responsibility for implementation, 321; on ROI, 327–328

UI, see user interface

Unimobile, 315

United States Postal Service, 265–266

University of California (Berkeley), 78, 209–212

University of Toronto, 270

upgrades, "in-line," 192–193

urgency, creating a sense of, 198–203

U.S. Surgical, 119

user interface (UI), 36–37, 339, 342–353

vehicles, 130–131

vendors, selection of, 335–342

Venetian Hotel (Las Vegas), 158

Villa, Denise, 204

VisualGold, 245, 331

WallStreetView, 257–258

warehouse staff, 137–138

Wayport, 23–24, 158

WCA (Wireless Communications Alliance), 254

WEB2001 and Internet + Mobile Conference and Exposition, 161–162

website development, panic, 4

Weiss, Tony, 183

Whatley, Joe, 318, 338

WhereNet, 13, 134

Whirlpool, 66

WideRay, 121–122, 167, 205, 224

Wilson, Brad, on customer relations, 71; on getting executive support, 316–317

WindWire, 201, 202

wireless (as term), 21–22

wireless business plan, developing a, 4–5

Wireless Communications Alliance (WCA), 254

wireless local area networks (wireless LANs), 24–25, 127–128, 295–296

"wireless mobile net," myth of, 18–19

wireless surveys, 260–264

wireless technology, as business communication tool, *xiii*

Wittrock, Paul, 220, 221

W.K. Kellogg Foundation, 160

World Trade Center, 127

Wynholds, Hans, on government and nonprofit organizations, 14–15; in tangibles vs. intangibles, 325–326

Xora, 87–88, 339, 340

Yahoo, 253, 254

Yastrow, Steve, 244

Ziff-Davis, 242

Zojirushi Corp., 65